D1692289

Claude E. Barfield · Günter Heiduk
Paul J. J. Welfens (Editors)

Internet, Economic Growth and Globalization

Perspectives on the New Economy
in Europe, Japan and the USA

With 34 Figures and 67 Tables

 Springer

Dr. Claude E. Barfield
The American Enterprise
Institute
1150 17th Street NW
Washington, D.C. 20036
USA
cbarfield@aei.org

Professor Dr. Günter Heiduk
University of Duisburg-Essen
Institute for International and
Regional Economic Relations
Lotharstraße 65
47057 Duisburg
Germany
iwbheiduk@uni-duisburg.de

Professor Dr. Paul J. J. Welfens
Jean Monnet Professor for
European Economic Integration,
President of EIIW
at the University of Potsdam
August-Bebel-Straße 89
14482 Potsdam
Germany
welfens@rz.uni-potsdam.de
http://www.euroeiiw.de
and
http://www.interneteconomics.net

ISBN 3-540-00286-3 Springer-Verlag Berlin Heidelberg New York

Cataloging-in-Publication Data applied for
A catalog record for this book is available from the Library of Congress.
Bibliographic information published by Die Deutsche Bibliothek
Die Deutsche Bibliothek lists this publication in the Deutsche Nationalbibliografie; detailed bibliographic data is available in the Internet at <http://dnb.ddb.de>.

Springer-Verlag Berlin Heidelberg New York
a member of BertelsmannSpringer Science+Business Media GmbH

http://www.springer.de

© Springer-Verlag Berlin · Heidelberg 2003
Printed in Germany

Hardcover-Design: Erich Kirchner, Heidelberg

SPIN 10905487   43/3130-5 4 3 2 1 0 – Printed on acid-free paper

Internet, Economic Growth and Globalization

Springer

Berlin
Heidelberg
New York
Hong Kong
London
Milan
Paris
Tokyo

Table of Contents

Introduction

In the wake of the stock market boom, the internet hype of the 1990s is over. However, the digital economy – the information and communication technology (ICT) sector – is well alive in OECD countries; once the sector has become so important for overall investment, it is only natural that ICT dynamics become more cyclical. Moreover, the well-known imperfections of information markets present some specific obstacles for strong positive growth-enhancing effects of the internet business. There are also some hard facts which should not be overlooked when discussing the New Economy. In 2000, the number of software engineers in the US exceeded the number of all engineers in traditional fields for the first time. At the same time, it is true that there is considerable uncertainty about the scope and nature of productivity growth acceleration in the US, Europe and to a lesser extent in Japan within the period after 1985; the renewal of global US economic leadership is strongly linked to the long economic boom of the 1990s to which ICT dynamics have contributed considerably. With the share of ICT value-added in overall GDP in the US almost doubling in the 1990s and coming close to 10% at the beginning of the 21st century and with quality improvements playing an enormous role in the chip and computer industry, respectively, the topic of hedonic price measurement has been emphasized in the US and, more recently, in Europe. All the EU countries will adopt hedonic price indices in 2003. Beyond methodological issues, there are important economic aspects to be analyzed. These range from productivity and growth issues to issues of capital market financing, regulation of telecommunications and the internet at the national and international level to questions of labor market deregulation and workplace organization in large and small firms. While the New Economy has economic significance in itself, one must also raise the question to which extent it will stimulate sectors in the Old Economy.

The introductory chapter by Paul J.J. Welfens and Andre Jungmittag gives an overview about some key issues, recent findings in the literature and new research results from the authors. The starting point is, of course, the transatlantic growth differential and changes in innovation dynamics in the 1990s. Moreover, the authors take a closer look at selected theoretical issues, including the productivity debate over the relative role of the ICT-producing sector and the ICT-using sector, respectively – briefly, the Gordon-Van Ark debate, where the evidence is in favor of both sectors playing a key role for raising productivity. Finally, Welfens and Jungmittag present some new research results on the link between the use of telecommunications and growth as well as their new empirical findings for the links between telecommunications and foreign trade – the latter in the context of a modified gravity equation which clearly shows a positive significant impact of the use of international telecommunications. The authors also point out considerable differences of ICT dynamics within the EU and argue that improving economic policy in Europe could help to fully exploit the benefits from the digital ICT sector.

Yukio Noguchi's contribution has its focus on obstacles to the IT revolution in Japan. He takes stock of IT utilization in Japan and government IT policy which clearly wants to encourage the use of the internet and digital communication. Social factors seem to inhibit the diffusion of the internet to some extent; while private use of internet applications, including mobile internet services, is growing rapidly in Japan it still is unclear whether Japanese companies will translate new digital opportunities into productivity growth and rising competitiveness.

With respect to the stock market and other structural characteristics, traditional companies – the Old Economy – is still dominating Japan's economy; comparing the US and Japan, one can clearly see a lag in Japan's New Economy. Existing and new firms from the New Economy obviously face specific problems. Noguchi argues that Japan will have to embrace reforms of the economic system – in particular strengthening stock markets and reducing the role of bank lending - if the opportunities of the digital revolution are to be fully exploited.

Caroline Freund and Diana Weinhold analyze the impact of the internet on international trade within a cross-country study. The authors use a gravity equation of trade among 56 countries where they find weak evidence of the internet on total trade flows in 1995 and only weak evidence of an effect in 1996. However, they find an increasing and significant impact from 1997 to 1999. Specifically, the results imply that a 10 percent increase in the relative number of web hosts in one country would have led to about one percent greater trade in 1998 and 1999. Surprisingly, they find that the effect of the Internet on trade has been stronger for poor countries than for rich countries, and that there is little evidence that the internet has reduced the impact of distance on trade. The evidence is consistent with a model in which the internet creates a global exchange for goods, thereby reducing market-specific sunk costs of exporting.

The focus of Marieke de Mooij is on the link between the internet and culture. She points out that while there might be technological convergence, there is no international convergence in consumer behavior. The analytical background is Hofestede's model with the five dimensions of national culture: power distance, individualism/collectivism, masculinity/femininity, uncertainty avoidance and long-term orientation. The author highlights various fields relevant for communication and culture, finding areas of convergence and also some of non-convergence. Finally, she discusses specific traits of the internet relevant for culture, e.g. the egalitarian impact of the internet; moreover, the internet is undermining centralization, although this does not automatically imply a stimulus for more democracy. Hence, acceptance and usage of the internet differ internationally, and per capita income is not the only significant variable for explaining such differences.

The internet is affecting the economy in many ways where reduction of transaction costs and network effects are most obvious. Nicole Pohl takes a look at another important dimension, namely the spatial organization of the financial sector. There is no doubt that the internet is already playing an important role in many niches of the financial sector and that the mode of transactions in the financial sector will be affected by the internet. However, thick externalities are known to stimulate the role of financial centers, and the author indeed raises the issue of whether the status of traditional financial centers will be affected by the internet. Pohl emphasizes that financial market radius will grow while the role of financial centers will largely be maintained. Information aspects and certain traits of skilled labor markets seem to support the role of financial centers in the digital age – at least in Europe and the US.

Mariko Fujii discusses how the internet will change the Japanese financial perspective. In the beginning, Japan gradually embraced the internet. It remains to be seen how the interplay of market opening-up in fixed network telecommunications, the computer revolution and the rapid diffusion of powerful mobile telecommunications will affect the Japanese economy and the Japanese society; the crowded island could experience rapid diffusion once digital innovations in certain fields are introduced; indeed, the author takes a closer look at the Japanese financial system and at first gives descriptive statistics which show a rapid growth of online trading; but despite a rapid growth of online accounts, the majority of securities firms have no plans to roll out an internet trading channel. Financial markets are characterized by rather gradual changes and increasing diversification in the context of internet applications. E-banking is rather wide-spread in Japan, but its economic significance still seems to be modest. Moreover, it seems that the internet is effectively reducing barriers to entry and improving profit perspectives – at least if one judges by the fact, emphasized by the author, that Japan Net Bank was the first newcomer in the Japanese banking industry to acquire a new license in decades. With respect to medium-term challenges, Mariko Fujii points out the increasing role of broadband access for digital financial transactions and that government is promoting the use of broadband networks. Finally, the author evaluates the impact of electronic financial transactions on market structure. There are signs of falling transactions costs and increasing competition, but it is too early to determine whether there will be sustained intensification of competition. Government has plans to support the digital financial sector but the supply-side perspective is only one element of the market, and it remains to be seen whether firms and private households will broadly accept the new opportunities in digital financial markets.

Matthias Bank takes a closer look at European financial markets in the context of growing internet applications. Having presented basic statistics on selected fields of the digital economy, the author turns to the importance of risk capital in Europe; digital firms active in the New Economy have stimulated the growth of EU risk capital markets in the late 1990s – however, Europe still lags behind the US in this field. It is not surprising that the end of the bubble in stock markets in 2001 brought heavy losses for digital newcomers and problems for risk financing in Europe; it remains to be seen whether there will be a sustained wave of newcomers in the digital economy. While it is clear that a period of low growth rates in Europe inhibits growth of newcomers in the digital economy, it is also obvious that falling barriers to entry in certain market niches should create positive growth perspectives for internet-based firms which offer innovative value-added for digital markets; however, the author critically points out that fast growth in internet business does not necessarily translate into relatively high valuations of internet firms. There is solid skepticism in financial markets whether internet firms can really deliver outstanding profit rates over the long-term. Finally, the author takes a look at selected problems of firm valuation and discusses from crucial points of the recent internet bubble the perspective of behavioral finance.

Günter Knieps raises some key issues of regulation of telecommunications and internet services. A crucial starting point in his analysis is digital convergence, which will shape the IT sectors. While network business will continue to play an important role in the modern economy of the 21st century, marginal growth could be most rapid with respect to internet service provision. Access to the internet is, of course, crucial for the dynamics of the internet business; in this respect there are many differences in terms of pricing and leading technologies across OECD countries. However, there are also theoretical issues that have to be addressed – only on the basis of sound theoretical analysis will policy makers be able to adopt a consistent policy for promoting an efficient use of the internet. Knieps points out many important issues related to internet backbones which play a crucial role for the global internet business.

The economic opening-up of telecommunications markets in continental EU countries in 1998 is the background for Friedhelm Dommermuth and Christoph Mertens who discuss – with a focus mainly on Germany - regulatory economics and the internet. The German regulatory authority RegTP, newly established after opening up the German market, has been quite important and influential in promoting sustained competition in the EU's largest telecommunications market. The authors at first describe major market trends and the importance of the internet in Germany. Their analysis then turns to the key areas of RegTP policy to the extent that this is relevant for the internet. Wholesale rates for metered and unmetered access, DSL, line sharing and internet telephony are relevant fields. The authors also discuss the impact of the internet on the publicly-switched telecommunications network and ISDN.

Finally, they discuss medium-term regulatory perspectives whereby a balanced view is presented on several issues. It is obvious that RegTP is a leading player among European regulators and is likely to adopt a liberal approach in the internet field while maintaining broad regulations in the telecommunications sector until sustained competition can be expected.

Donald Stockdale presents a US view on regulation, deregulation and non-regulation of telecommunications and the internet in the United States. The US has embraced liberalization of telecommunications almost 15 years earlier than continental EU countries, and the FCC has been a competent regulator in the thorny field of fixed network telecommunications. With regard to computer networks and data communication, respectively, the FCC for many years has emphasized the need to avoid regulation for the sake of encouraging innovation and efficiency; this translates into a liberal internet regime in the US. In the fields of telecommunications, however, the FCC has developed certain doctrines and approaches which clearly reflect a rather strict regulatory framework. Certainly it develops over time as laws change (e.g. the 1996 US Telecommunications Law); court cases bring adjustment needs, and the growth of mobile telephony changes the dynamics of markets. Stockdale first highlights the two-pronged approach for enhancing competition, namely antitrust and regulation. His paper gives an outline of the basic FCC approach to the regulation of telecommunications, where recent developments in long distance markets and local telephony are discussed. The US developments have partly been shaped by both regulatory authorities and court decisions. The FCC made a landmark decision in 1969, granting MCI's request to provide voice service and other telecommunications services in competition with AT&T. The author describes some of the most important initiatives and proceedings taken by FCC in order to enhance competition. Moreover, it provides interesting insights into the interplay between the US Department of Justice and the FCC, including important issues relating to competitive and other safeguards. With regard to the introduction into local telephony, the regulatory process has been relatively complex and competition is only gradually unfolding. Quite interesting and important is the non-regulation of enhanced services. Here the FCC anticipated early on the convergence of computers and telecommunications technology. Donald Stockdale gives an interesting overview of how the non-regulation of computer networks naturally leads to non-regulation of the internet.

Koichiro Agata analyses the deregulations of the telecommunications and the non-regulation of the internet in Japan. The regulation of telecommunications started in 1985 and gradually increased in the following years. The author gives an overview about the actors in the internet and telecommunications market and describes the various stages of telecommunications deregulation. Interestingly, private organizations from the manufacturing industry have played an increasing role in 1990s. Agata also discusses crucial pending issues and the main problems concerning internet regulation. While technological standards seem to be industry driven – partly on the international scale – policy makers have increasingly focused on content problems in the internet. A very digital and global nature of the internet apparently makes effective regulation difficult.

Claude Barfield describes and analyzes the major challenges presented by electronic commerce in the GATS (General Agreement on Trade in Services) negotiations in the current WTO Doha Round. The paper discusses six issues in particular: classification (whether E-commerce is a good or a service); taxation; scope or modes of supply that are distinguished on the basis of the territorial presence of the supplier and consumer of the service (viz., cross-border, consumption abroad, commercial presence; presence of natural persons); regulation; privacy issues; and intellectual property. The paper points out that in every issue area large unresolved substantive questions remain unresolved and present potentially insurmountable obstacles to the achievement of meaningful WTO rules for electronic commerce. At the end of the Doha Round, WTO members may be forced to go outside of the existing GATS regime, and create a wholly new set of rules for E-commerce—a result that has been fiercely opposed by many in the private sector and virtually all trade negotiators.

William H. Dutton provides a contribution on the internet and society. His analysis brings up many new issues and perspectives from a politological point-of-view, emphasizing social aspects of the New Economy. The author argues that the information age thesis is too narrow to fully cover the various impacts of digital communication. Moreover, he shows that there is a crucial role of tele-access and that policies can make a distinct impact with respect to the speed and breadth of such access. The author argues that tele-access might be more important for enhancing modern communication than the internet. Policymakers who wish to influence the modernization of society have to take into account social factors shaping choices. Finally, there are new dimensions of influence and the mass media in the internet age; there will be political conflicts over how to achieve some control over the enormous digital technological dynamics.

Elena Arnal, Wooseok Ok and Raymond Torres present an OECD study on knowledge, work organization and economic growth. Productivity effects of the internet and of the increasing role of digital services have often been discussed in technological terms in the literature, but the important issue of how changes in work organizations contribute to higher productivity and economic growth has been neglected. The authors' analytical point is that the use of ICT will allow faster diffusion and accumulation of knowledge and therefore requires organizational adjustments in all firms which wish to exploit the new technologies and information as an input for value-added in industry and the service sector. The authors discuss the changing nature of work, including the telework. They also focus on skill shortages and give new data about the importance of knowledge-intensive employment. Moreover, many additional statistics related to ICT and work are presented. It becomes fairly clear that the great bonus of ICT can be fully realized only if firms and society are able to change work practices. Hence there are several policy issues including training, education and migration in the digital economy. Finally there is the issue of how collective bargaining will be affected by the gradual shifts to the knowledge economy.

Comments on the papers presented were given by Torsten J. Gerpott, Günter Heiduk, Thomas Gries, Christiane Jäcker, Thomas P. Gehrig, Christian Thygesen, and Harald Sander. We gratefully appreciate the important comments by all discussants. Moreover, we are grateful for the speech by Sigmar Mosdorf, the Undersecretary of State in the Ministry of Economics. He points out Germany's policy approach to the internet, as well as EU dimensions of digital policy; the rapid diffusion of the internet, equal digital opportunities and intra-European network building are some key dimensions in these policy fields.

This book is partly the outcome of a twin conference that took place in Duisburg and Potsdam in August 2001, but it also contains analytical papers from the broader Digital Economics Triad Group (DECTRIG). The European Institute for International Economic Relations (EIIW) at the University of Potsdam and the International Institute for Pacific Studies have teamed up to host a conference which brought together leading economists from Europe, Japan and the US. The idea was to bring forward common trends as well as different dynamics in the triad as well as to identify alternative policy approaches relevant in major OECD countries. Both institute are grateful to the Volkswagen Foundation and the Duisburger Universitätsgesellschaft for financial support; in addition we are grateful for support by AOL. We also appreciate editorial support from Tim Yarling, Indianapolis, as well as Michael Agner and – in particular – Jaroslaw Ponder, Potsdam. Finally, we appreciate the intellectual support of Kozo Yamamura, University of Seattle, who has encouraged the organizers in Duisburg and Potsdam. We hope to continue our triad research in the future; one may anticipate digital cycles to accelerate, and there certainly is need to conduct more long-term research into the global digital economy. The internet certainly poses many analytical challenges, but it also facilitates cooperation of researchers worldwide. While the changes in industrial firms and the services sector are increasingly understood there is many unsolved issues related to the functioning of digital markets and the changing relative speed of adjustment in markets in the real and financial sphere. Moreover, there are new topics and issues for organizing democratic open societies.

Washington DC, Duisburg and Potsdam, September 2002

Claude E. Barfield, Günter Heiduk and Paul J.J. Welfens

A. Telecommunications, Internet, Innovation and Growth in Europe

Paul J.J. Welfens and Andre Jungmittag

1. Telecommunications, Internet and Transatlantic Growth Differentials

1.1 Telecommunications and the Internet

Technological progress and deregulation plus privatization have stimulated the growth of the internet which can be used in many ways, including for international and national telephony based on the internet protocol (IP); voice-over-IP is most interesting for cable TV firms which thereby could become powerful telecommunications firms, too. About $ 1 billion was spent in 2000 on voice-over-IP services with some $ 6 billion expected for 2005 worldwide; an upgraded cable TV network is the basis for AT&T´s roughly 0.7 million local telephony users which still is less than 1/200 of circuit-switched lines in the US. However, in the long term IP calls running over a private data network – instead of low quality public internet networks – could become a fast growing business in the United States (US) and elsewhere.

The internet in both the US and Europe is rather unregulated at the beginning of the 21st century, but telecommunications is regulated on both sides of the Atlantic – an indirect incentive for internet services to expand. To the extent that Internet Service Providers (ISPs) and end users need access to the fixed-line network, telecommunications regulations will affect the internet business (WELFENS, 2001a).

Technically, the internet differs from telecommunications; the latter establishes a dedicated line between two partners, whereas internet traffic consists of data packages which are split over several lines and recombined at the end so that the recipient will get the data from the sender. Internet business is largely based on computer networks. From this perspective the growth of the internet is crucial for the hardware and software industry. Given the dominance of the US in the hardware and software market, the developments in the huge US markets are of particular relevance.

Deregulation in the US and Europe

Following the divesture of AT&T in 1984 the US has had competition in long distance telephony, while the local loop remained in the hand of the newly created

"Baby Bells" which were hived-off the old AT&T (SCHWARTZ, 1997; SPINDLER, 1999). Until the Telecommunications Act of 1996 cable TV firms and telecommunication operators were not allowed to compete, but with the digitization of telecommunications and TV this restriction became obsolete in technical terms. The Telecommunications Act therefore removed the legal market demarcations; moreover, it allowed long distance companies to enter the local loop, while regional Bell companies were allowed to enter the long distance market provided that they had opened the market for local telephony. AT&T has entered the local market via its newly acquired cable TV subsidiary. Cable TV companies offer local telephony, broadband internet services and TV programs.

In the UK competition in long distance and international telephony was introduced in the form of a duopoly in 1984, followed by broader competition after 1990 in this field (local telephony is becoming open for competition only as of 2001). US cable operators – facing restrictions at home – entered the British market in the early 1990s and offered new service packages including internet services. In order to create competition the dominant telecommunications operator BT was not allowed to enter the cable TV market; in the Netherlands the government forced the ex-monopoly operator KPN in 1998 to reduce its share to one of over 300 regional cable franchises; and to a minority position.

1998 was the starting date for EU liberalization in telecommunications network operation and telecommunication services. Several smaller EU countries obtained an extended grace period. The number of ISPs in Europe has strongly increased in the 1990s, but at the turn of the century the ISP business has internationalized and consolidated. While many leading ISPs in Europe are subsidiaries of the formerly dominant telecommunications operator, the leading players in the US were newcomers to the telecommunications sector, namely AOL, YAHOO and MSN (Microsoft); Excite@home is the only major ISP in the US which is a subsidiary of a major telecommunications operator, namely AT&T. US telecommunications companies were slow to understand the economic significance of the internet. However, US computer and chip producers have strongly pushed for the growth of the internet and the information society, respectively (BRESNAHAN, 1999; MACHER / MOWERY / HODGES, 1999).

1.2 Telecommunications and Technological Dynamics

The 1990s have witnessed an enormous increase in patent applications and patents granted in telecommunications, both in the US and Europe. There has been a clear acceleration of patent dynamics at the U.S. Patent and Trademark Office, largely in the context of mobile telecommunications and internet-related technologies (Figure 1).

Figure A1:   Telecommunications-Relevant Patents Granted at the U.S. Patent and Trademark Office

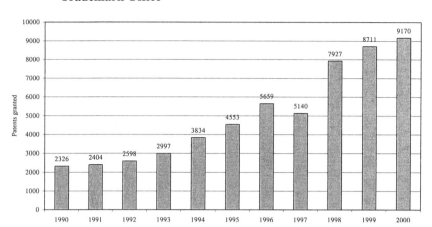

Note: Telecommunications relevant patent classes: 370,375, 379 and 455; all patent documents including utility, plant, and reissue patents as well as statutory invention registrations and defensive publications
Source: U.S. Patent and Trademark Office, Patent Counts by Class and Year; own calculations.

Table A1:   Specialization (Relative Patent Share in Interval -100, +100) in 1995-97 in Technology-intensive Fields with High Growth Rates in Patents*

	Growth	USA	Japan	Germany	France	UK	Switzerland	Canada	Sweden	Italy	Netherlands
Telekommunication	13,6	10	-3	-34	-7	17	-75	50	70	-67	18
Turbines	10,6	-8	-74	-40	87	8	83	-84	-7	-96	-52
Railway Systems	8,5	-74	-41	67	9	-67	58	-22	-19	0	-26
Paper-Making Equipment	7,6	-4	-88	28	-71	-43	-54	30	85	-41	-62
Automobiles	6,7	-47	-14	57	35	-31	-84	-71	-12	10	-56
Medi. Sector, Instruments	6,6	46	-80	-38	-36	-7	38	-64	32	-20	-29
Advanced Electronics	6,4	-18	46	1	-21	-18	-52	42	-52	-44	48
Power Distribution	6,4	-20	8	16	34	-23	-27	-53	13	-7	-36
Agrochemicals	6,1	35	-59	0	-3	5	22	52	-53	-13	-69
Medi. Sector, Electronics	5,8	42	-31	-47	-64	-9	-48	-19	10	-65	35

* Average Annual Growth of Patent Applications at the European Patent Agency in 1989-1997
Source: FhG-ISI, Karlsruhe

The growth rate of telecommunication patents was the highest among the top ten fields of patent applications at the European Patent Office (see Table 1). Advanced electronics, which has links to telecommunication and computer networks, is also among the top ten in Europe. The figures on technological specialization show that the US and a few European countries (Sweden, the Netherlands and Finland) have a positive patent specialization in telecommunications; Germany is negatively specialized in this field.

While telecommunications has been a traditional part of the Old Economy, it became a major part of the New Economy in the 1990s. The main reason is that the dismemberment of AT&T in 1984 and pro-competitive laws (in the US in 1996 and in the EU related to the deregulation date 1998) have stimulated competition and technological dynamics in this field; moreover, privatization of incumbent operators has further contributed to innovation dynamics since telecom operators which face declining telecommunication prices in a more competitive environment naturally try to raise revenue by product innovations and new services. Part of the high-technology dynamics in telecommunications is, however, not covered by patents. Advanced software plays a key role in both fixed and mobile telecommunications.

The innovation race has been stimulated in European fixed line telephony and in mobile telecommunications by many US operators investing in joint ventures. By contrast, only a few European network operators have invested in the US. The British Vodafone has been a successful investor. Deutsche Telekom´s acquisition of Voicestream - one of the three US cellular companies using GSM - is an important case since it shows that GSM technology, which has been the hallmark of EU mobile telecommunications can be rolled out successfully in the US. However, Voicestream is only No. 6 in the large US mobile telephony market; if Congress should block moves of Deutsche Telekom to acquire other mobile operators Germany`s leading network operator might have to pull out of North America which would be to the disadvantage both of Deutsche Telekom and to customers in the US and Canada. While US operators can easily acquire EU telecommunications operators EU firms face broad restrictions in the US and Canada; since part of the digital information market is a global marketplace such asymmetries do not reflect a level playing field and impair global market integration and industry consolidation. With share prices in Worldcom falling strongly in 2002 – after announcing of improper accounting which had overstated profits – the US telecommunication sector might face strong pressure for further consolidation. In Europe former monopoly operators also are facing problems as a consequence of falling profit rates and declining ratings which have forced many privatized operators to scale back earlier investment plans.

The growth of the internet could create a virtuous circle between the telecommunications sector and the technologically highly dynamic computer industry, governed by Moore´s law that the power of chips can be doubled every two years without significant cost increase. The internet plays a crucial role here not only as a novel service, but the internet protocol also has an important role in that it is now increasingly used by fixed network operators to build new digital networks.

1.3 Taking Stock: Transatlantic Growth Differential

In the period 1991-2000 the United States (US) recorded a formidable growth rate of about 3% p.a. where a considerable impulse for high and sustained growth stems from high investment in information and communication technology (ICT). Between 1993 and 2000 the US even recorded 4% growth where the acceleration in labor productivity growth in the second half of the decade was quite remarkable. Roughly one-half of investment growth in the second half of the 1990s can be attributed to ICT which mainly is comprised of telecommunications and computers/PCs plus software. Euroland by contrast has grown only by about 2% in the period 1991-2000 where the large core countries of Germany, Italy and France have not even achieved 2%; Germany's growth rate in 1992-2001 was 1.5% while that in partner countries in the euro zone was 2.3% - hence reunited Germany recorded relatively low growth (with no improvement in the late 1990s compared to the first half of the decade).

Given the long and strong economic upswing in the US in the 1990s, it was rather surprising that the inflation rate has remained very low in the US. Obviously, the nonaccelerating inflation rate of unemployment has reduced in the US, but it is rather unclear why this should be the case.

The economic upswing in the euro zone in 1999/2000 was rather modest, and already in 2001 the growth rate of Euroland fell below 2%. The EU has had lower investment growth than the US and also has failed to position itself adequately in the changing global innovation race (WELFENS ET AL., 1998; WELFENS ET AL., 1999). However, one should not overlook remarkable intra-EU differences in economic growth; the UK, Ireland, Spain, Portugal, the Netherlands, Finland and Sweden recorded higher growth than the three EU core countries Germany, Italy and France.

With the US – after the end of the Cold War – no longer devoting roughly 55% of its R&D budget to the military, the international innovation race has accelerated and increasing specialization should have been realized in EU countries. Empirical studies point, however, to technological despecialization in OECD countries in the 1990s (JUNGMITTAG ET AL., 1998). Given intensified technological competition Schumpeterian rents in medium-technology-intensive sectors can be expected to have reduced so that rates of return for the respective German firms might have fallen. At the same time the R&D conversion process in the US, France and the UK after 1990 has stimulated technological upgrading in the civilian tradables sector which lets one expect that profitability and stock market performance in those countries should improve relative to Germany – and to Japan which is the other G-5 country which had a tradition of devoting more than 90% of R&D funds to civilian markets. Focusing on Euroland´s performance relative to the US the negative German developments together with the positive French civilian R&D dynamics might cancel out; at the bottom line the structural R&D effect of the end of the Cold War seems to have worked in favor of the US.

There is no doubt that the Maastricht convergence process has reduced economic growth since prior to the start of the euro and the ECB in 1999 many countries, including Italy, Germany, France and Spain had to reduce government-GDP ratios in order to reduce deficit-GDP ratios and subsequently excessive debt-GDP ratios. Germany, Spain and France were close to the 60% maximum for the debt-GDP requirement in 2000; among the large EU countries only Italy still had an excessive debt with 110.7% of GDP – but well below the peak ratio of 123.9% in 1994. While the Maastricht convergence process required fiscal retrenchment in some countries it also is true that downward interest rate convergence brought a reduction of the interest payments relative to GDP.

The euro has continuously lost value vis-à-vis the dollar since the start of the new currency in January 1999; the overall loss was close to one-fourth in the period 1999-2000. This is not so critical in the staggered introductory phase of the euro which is being completed with the introduction of coins and notes in early 2002. While the euro zone has witnessed a modest acceleration of growth in the late 1990s, the US recorded a sustained upward shift in the expansion path of the production potential, whereas Japan recorded a downward kink in the growth rate of the production potential (COUNCIL OF ECONOMIC ADVISORS, 2001). Thus the question arises why there are such strong differences in the triad. Subsequently we will only focus on transatlantic differences where a major aspect concerns employment growth. Average annual employment growth reached 1.5 % in the US in 1991-2000 but only 0.5% p.a. in the euro zone (the same growth rate for EU-15 as well). Employment dynamics and labor markets, respectively, thus have played a major role for transatlantic growth differences. Another aspect concerns the investment-output ratio which fell in Euroland from a peak of 21.7% in 1991 to about 20% in all years from 1995-98 (20.8% and 21.4% in 1999 and 2000, respectively) while the US investment-GDP ratio increased from 16.3% in 1991 to 21.1% in 2000 – with a year on year increase in each year of the period from 1991-2000 (EUROPEAN COMMISSION, 2000).

The considerable depreciation of the euro raises the question whether this is a transitory development or a more long-term phenomenon. We will argue that it is likely to be a sustained problem unless policymakers in Euroland take adequate measures and revise their current policy stance.

The main effects of a strong real devaluation of the euro are the following:

- Stimulating Euroland´s exports towards the dollar area automatically makes Euroland more dependent on the US business cycle.
- The inflow of foreign direct investment from the US and other non-EU countries could increase since, following FROOT / STEIN (1991), foreign investors can – in a world of imperfect capital markets – acquire firms more cheaply than before.
- A risk premium emerges as reflected in the interest rate; as of 2001 there was not yet a euro risk premium visible, but with a sustained devaluation of the euro such a premium might gradually emerge. A risk premium would raise the real interest rate and reduce the investment-GDP ratio.
- The inflation pressure in Euroland is increasing since the import of more expensive imported intermediate products and final products will translate into a rise of tradables prices.

The critical question indeed concerns the medium and long-term development of the euro. Based on transatlantic interest rate differentials and relative stock market prices WELFENS (2000) presented a robust out-of-sample forecast. In the following sections we want to shed further light on the devaluation issue.

Taking a closer look at the transatlantic growth differential we find several remarkable points in the 1990s (RÖGER, 2001; WELFENS, 2001a):

- The USA has grown continuously faster than Euroland in the 1990s.
- The growth rate of labor productivity in high technology clearly outpaced that of the EU after 1993. Germany – representing one-third of Euroland´s GDP – faces not only a considerable gap vis-à-vis the US; worse yet is that the labor productivity in technology-intensive fields was lower than the average for the overall economy in the mid-1990s.
- The US has exploited the economic potential of the internet revolution much faster than the EU; both the user density (demand side) and the host density (supply side) have increased much faster in the US than in France, Italy and Germany. The US has a firm lead in computer density, being one-fifth ahead of Germany and one-fourth ahead of France; Italy has just half the US computer density and was matched in 2000 by the Republic of Korea.
- The fall in prices of ICT goods – relative to the GNP deflator – reached about 8% in 1981-94, but after 1995 it increased to 15% p.a which has considerably stimulated innovations, both process innovations and product innovations, including novel digital services. Falling relative prices clearly stimulate diffusion. This should benefit the US even more as the world´s leading computer producers and software firms are located in the US. With the US facing tightening labor markets in the mid-1990s the incentives for firms to invest in labor-saving ICT increased – leading to a sustainable ICT investment growth in the late 1990s.
- A study by the OECD (2000) shows clearly that countries with a high R&D intensity in the ICT field also have a high R&D intensity for the overall economy. While Sweden, Finland, Korea, the US and Japan are leading economies from this perspective, Germany is only in a medium position. This OECD study, based on ICT dynamics with respect to employment, value-added, trade and R&D, suggests that Germany is among the lower third of the 29 countries.
- High investment in ICT has considerably contributed to high US growth. While the share of ICT investment in national output has remained constant in the EU (see the following table), the figure for the US has roughly doubled. It reached 4.5% of GDP in 1999 which was almost twice as high as the figure for the EU. The UK, Sweden and the Netherlands recorded figures in the range of 3-4%. Denmark, Belgium, Finland and Ireland were in the range of 2.3 to 3%. Germany and France were close to 2%, with Italy even at 1.8%. In the US almost 2/3 of the increase in the overall investment-GDP ratio is due to the rise in the IT investment-GDP ratio.

With the investment-GDP ratio strongly increasing in the US in the late 1990s there was a considerable increase in labor productivity. Labor productivity growth and overall output growth accelerated in the US in the second half of the 1990s as is shown in the following table. Germany's labor productivity growth reduced in the period 1995-2000 in comparison to 1977-95. The same is true for Japan. Only

France and the UK achieved an improvement over time, and both countries did so on the basis of accelerated output growth (by contrast, in Germany output growth reduced). In the 1990s Japan – having launched a successful economic and technological catching-up process in the 1970s and 1980s – faced the problem of having reached the technological frontier and for various reasons found it very difficult to switch from a strategy emphasizing catching-up to one of global Schumpeterian leadership.

Table A2:   Investment in Information Technologies and Total Investment in the 1990s

	(1)	(2)	(3)	(4)	(5)	(6)
	IT investment/GDP			Total fixed investment/GDP		
	1992	1999	(2)-(1)	1992	1999	(5)-(4)
Austria	1.61	1.89	0.28	23.50	23.65	+0.15
Belgium	2.12	2.59	0.47	21.29	20.99	-0.30
Denmark	2.04	2.72	0.68	18.14	20.97	+2.83
Finland	1.61	2.48	0.87	19.61	19.28	-0.32
France	1.70	2.05	0.35	20.93	18.86	-2.07
Germany	1.74	2.17	0.43	24.04	21.29	-2.76
Greece	0.75	1.80	1.05	21.32	23.00	+1.69
Ireland	1.82	2.32	0.50	16.59	24.13	+7.53
Italy	1.49	1.77	0.28	20.47	18.43	-2.04
Netherlands	2.23	3.09	0.86	21.32	21.47	+0.15
Portugal	0.96	1.81	0.85	25.01	27.48	+2.46
Spain	1.52	1.58	0.06	23.09	23.69	+0.60
Sweden	2.49	3.64	1.15	18.26	16.47	-1.79
UK	2.43	3.76	1.33	16.53	17.97	+1.44
EU*	1.81	2.42	0.61	20.72	21.26	+0.54
USA	2.60	4.54	1.94	17.01	20.33	+3.32

Notes: Nominal shares of GDP. Percentage points. 'Belgium' also includes Luxembourg data; * unweighted.
Source: DAVERI, F. (2001), Information Technology and Growth in Europe, p. 5.

Table A3:   Labor Productivity Growth in Selected OECD Countries

	1995-2000*	1977-95
US	2.2	1.4
Japan	2.0	2.6
Germany	1.8	1.9
France	1.8	1.6
UK	1.5	1.9

* estimate
Source: OECD (2000)

Table A4:   GDP Growth in Selected OECD Countries

	1995-2000*	1977-95
US	4.00	3.00
Japan	1.25	3.50
Germany	1.75	2.25
France	2.50	2.25
UK	2.75	2.25

* estimate
Source: OECD (2000)

A modest trend output growth rate of Germany – much lower than that of the USA, France or the UK in the second half of the 1990s – points to a specific weakness of the German economy. Part of the slow growth puzzle might be related to German unification and low economic growth in eastern Germany, respetively (WELFENS, 1999). Since 1997 the growth rate of eastern Germany has been lower than in West Germany. East Germany´s labor productivity rate achieved about 1/3 of the West German figure in the late 1990s, but economic catching-up with western Germany, so strongly visible in the 1990s, seems to have achieved a critical threshold. However, the West German economy also has achieved only rather modest growth – except for the regions Baden-Wuerttemberg, Bavaria and Hessia.

2. Theoretical Analysis

2.1 ICT Dynamics and Growth

It was not fully clear until 2001 whether high US growth in the 1990s was significantly related to high productivity growth in information and communication technologies. GORDON (1999) claimed that the acceleration of US productivity growth in the 1990s was mainly due to cyclical factors on the one hand, and to high productivity growth in the production of information technology goods (which would account for the remainder of accelerated productivity growth) on the other. A skeptical view also comes from KILEY (2000) who points to high adjustment costs associated with information technology (IT) investment implying a reduction of productivity growth in a period of high IT investment. The contrasting view that both production of IT goods and use of IT contributed considerably to aggregate productivity growth in the 1990s has been particularly emphasized by JORGENSEN / STIROH (2000), OLINER / SICHEL (2000), WHELAN (2000a,b), and the COUNCIL OF ECONOMIC ADVISORS (2000, 2001), all of which provide some empirical evidence for their view.

With different researchers holding opposite views on an important empirical phenomenon, here the acceleration of productivity growth, the most straightforward way to clarify the issue is theoretical research on the one hand and more detailed empirical research on the other hand. As regards theoretical aspects we will subsequently present some reflections where we will argue that differences in productivity growth in the US and Euroland / Germany in the 1990s can partly be explained by differentials in ICT dynamics and the associated direct and indirect growth effects. As regards the empirical side it seems that three papers have brought clear evidence that both the production of IT goods and the use of IT were important for the acceleration of productivity growth in the 1990s. STIROH (2001) has presented an empirical study with industry-level data for the US. He shows that most IT-intensive sectors recorded significantly larger productivity gains than other industries. Using a battery of econometric tests he shows a strong correlation between IT capital accumulation and labor productivity where a novel decomposition of aggregate labor productivity is presented. The crucial conclusion is that virtually all of the aggregate productivity acceleration can be traced to the industries that either produce IT or use IT rather intensively with hardly any contribution coming from sectors that are less involved in the IT revolution. STIROH writes (2001, p.2-3):

"Industry-level data show that the recent U.S. acceleration in productivity is a broad-based phenomenon that reflects gains in a majority of industries through the late 1990s....For example, the mean productivity acceleration for 61 industries from 1987-95 to 1995-99 is 1.09 percentage points and the median is 0.67 percentage points. Nearly two-thirds of these industries show a productivity acceleration. Even when the particularly strong productivity industries that produce IT (or even durable goods manufacturing as a whole) are excluded, the data show a significant acceleration in productivity for the remaining industries. This suggests that U.S. productivity revival is not narrowly based in only a few IT-producing industries....The productivity acceleration in the late 1990s for IT-intensive industries, for example, is about 1 percentage point larger than for other industries. Moreover, rapid IT capital deepening in the early 1990s is associated with faster productivity growth in the late 1990s, even after controlling for other input accumulation and productivity growth in the early 1990s. Production function estimates also show a significant and relatively large output elasticity of IT capital.... If cyclical forces were driving the productivity gains, one might expect these gains to be equal across industries or at least to be independent of IT-intensity....The data show a contribution to aggregate productivity in the 1990s from all three groups, although the vast majority comes from IT-related industries. For example, the 26 IT-using industries contributed 0.66 percentage points to the aggregate productivity acceleration and the two IT-producing industries 0.16. The 33 remaining industries contributed only 0.08. Once one accounts for reallocation of intermediate materials, the industries that either produce or use IT account for all of the aggregate productivity acceleration, with the other industries making a negative contribution to the acceleration of aggregate productivity growth in the late 1990s."

This finding is quite important since it points to a shift in Schumpeterian dynamics in the US and possibly in other OECD countries as well. In Europe only Sweden, Finland, Ireland, the UK, and the Netherlands show a high share of ICT dynamics, and it is unclear whether major EU countries such as Germany, France, and Italy can catch up. DAVERI (2001) shows in his empirical analysis for Europe that the UK, the Netherlands, Sweden, and Ireland are not much behind the US, but other EU countries have a considerable lag. Cross-country differences in IT investment and accumulation rates are closely linked to growth effects from information technologies except for Ireland. CREPON / HECKEL (2001) also find for France that productivity growth is strongly associated with a small number of industries that make an intensive use of computers; all in all they estimate the contribution of computerization in France to have reached 0.7 percentage points in annual growth in the period 1987-1998.

Aggregation Problems and Sectoral Aspects: ICT-Producing Versus ICT-Using Sectors

When labor productivity growth is measured at the aggregate there is considerable scope for misleading conclusions; e.g. if in a three sector economy with three input factors labor, capital (non-ICT) and ICT-capital there is high labor productivity growth in sector I (say ICT-producing sector), average labor productivity growth in sector II (ICT-using sector) and negative labor productivity growth in the third sector. Simple aggregate growth accounting might find that the economy under consideration has not experienced any productivity acceleration in the context of ICT growth. An aggregate view without accompanying disaggregated analysis is totally inadequate to the analytical challenge of the ICT problem.

In a three-sector perspective one has to take into account three sectors where both the ICT-producing sector and the ICT-using sector can have spillover effects – both within the broadly defined ICT sector (A+B) and with respect to the overall ICT sector vis-à-vis the non-ICT sector. Some of the ICT-internal spillover effects could be magnified via network effects (see Figure 2). While technological dynamics will influence the ICT sector economic policy and the NGOs – including employer organizations and trade unions – also can have an impact on the productivity growth in each sector and the overall economy, respectively.

The usefulness of disaggregate analysis is fully discussed in the STIROH (2001) paper in which it is shown that virtually all of the aggregate productivity acceleration in the US during the 1990s can be traced to the industries either producing ICT or using ICT intensively – with no or negative contribution from the remaining industries that are less involved in the IT revolution. It is worth noting that the gross output growth rate for agriculture, forestry and fishing in the US fell from 0.58% p.a. in the period 1987-95 to -0.67% in 1995-99 and in construction remained negative (at around –0.8%) in both periods whereas durable goods manufacturing had a growth rate which increased from 3.97% to 6.47% and retail trade increased from 0.97% to 3.03% p.a.

Figure A2:   ICT and Productivity Growth

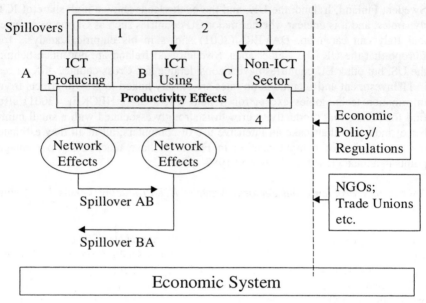

Another important contribution to growth accounting is by VAN ARK (2001) who makes a distinction between ICT-producing manufacturing and service industries, intensive ICT-using manufacturing and service industries and the non-ICT sector (the rest of the economy). VAN ARK presents measures of the contribution of each sector to growth and acceleration of growth in output, employment and labor productivity for ten OECD countries during the 1990s: Productivity growth differentials between the US and most EU countries are partly explained by a larger and more productive ICT-producing sector in the US, but also by bigger productivity contributions from ICT-using industries and services in the US. The annual percentage point contribution of the ICT-using sector in the US increased from 0.3 in the period 1990-95 to 1.37 in 1995-99 while the overall increase in labor productivity was 1.15% in the first period and 2.54 in the second period; the ICT-producing sector contributed 0.31 points in the first period and 0.65 points in the second period. By contrast, labor productivity growth in Japan was only about 0.8 percent p.a. in both periods, and the role of the ICT-using sector contributed only about 0.35 points with a slight decline over time. In Germany, the annual labor productivity growth fell from 2.10 percent in the first period to 1.66 percent in the second period. The ICT-producing sector accounted for 0.1 points in the first period and for 0.4 points in the second period; a similar result is found for the Netherlands. However, while the contribution to labor productivity growth in Germany's ICT-using sector fell from 0.53 percentage points in the first period of 0.52 points in the second period, the contribution of the Dutch ICT-using sector increased from 0.32 percentage points to 0.61 points in the 1990s. In Denmark,

Finland and the Netherlands (and the US) the contribution of the ICT-using sector slightly exceeded that of Germany's respective sector in the second half of the 1990s; it is also worthy mentioning that France and Italy had a rather low contribution of the ICT-using sector in both subperiods of the 1990s. Finally, it was remarkable that the non-ICT sector in the US accounted for a stable contribution to overall labor productivity growth while it fell in Canada, Denmark, Finland, France, Germany, Italy and the Netherlands in the 1990s.

Against such a background the analysis of the ECB (2001) – not taking into account relevant theoretical and empirical analysis – is partly doubtful. The ECB is suggesting that there is no New Economy effect in the euro area in the 1990s, but the ECB does not look into any disaggregated analysis nor does it try to decompose cyclical and trend effects. Furthermore, it limits the analysis (due to data problems) to Germany, France, Italy and Finland; in the case of aggregate growth accounting the Netherlands is also included which means that three-fourths of Euroland is covered. Comparing Euroland with the US on the basis of this limited sample is also inadequate since the comparable basis would be roughly California plus Washington, New York, Michigan, Illinois, Massachusetts and Florida.

The ECB's first statement, namely that in the period 1990-2000 GDP per hour worked in the euro area and the US was roughly equal, namely 1.8% and 1.7%, is misleading since the US unemployment rate has reduced whereas it has increased in the euro area; a methodologically correct analysis would calculate a hypothetical "comparable employment labor productivity growth" (CELPG) – that is with a lower unemployment rate / a higher employment rate in the euro zone whose development would match that of the US; the CELPG rate would on theoretical grounds certainly be lower than 1.8% for Euroland. The ECB's second main statement is based on the comparison of the US with Germany plus France, Italy, and Finland which is doubtful per se and even more so when the main conclusion is derived: "This suggests that also in the United States there is little evidence of positive spillover effects from ICT-producing sectors to the rest of the economy in the period from 1991 to 1998" (ECB, 2001, p.43); however, the empirical analysis of STIROH (2001) and VAN ARK (2001) suggests the opposite. The third statement of the ECB also is rather doubtful and is based on an aggregate growth accounting exercise with France, Germany, Italy and the Netherlands representing Euroland. The ECB shows with respect to explaining labor productivity growth – which declined from 2.4% in 1991-95 to 1.3% in 1996-99 – that ICT capital deepening has gained in relevance for labor productivity over time: 0.39 percentage points in 1996-99 compared to 0.26 in 1991-95. The role of other capital deepening has declined from 0.73 percentage points to 0.28; that of total factor productivity growth has fallen from 1.41 points to 0.61 percentage points – the latter might however simply reflect a complex overlap of procyclical effects with unclear labor market effects on the one hand and ICT spillover effects on the other hand. The conclusion drawn by the ECB is not well founded as it states (ECB, 2001, p. 48): "The analysis of output and productivity developments in the euro area undertaken in this article suggests that in the period up to 2000 there were only very limited, if any, positive spillover effects from the use of ICT." It is unclear why the ECB is not also taking a look at non-euro member countries such as the UK and Sweden.

For the ECB in its certainly difficult challenge to conduct monetary policy in a way which is both noninflationary and supporting growth and employment – the latter to the extent that this causes minor inflation risks.

ICT Analysis Versus ICT Potential Dynamics

It is not only important to understand the actual ICT dynamics in the EU which may or may not be characterized by spillover effects in ICT use; it also is important to analyze the potential of ICT dynamics by taking a closer look at advanced US states and advanced EU countries (e.g. Sweden, Finland, the UK, Ireland, Germany, France, and the Netherlands). A serious problem in the context of such benchmarking analysis could be that Euroland´s ICT dynamics are rather weak for reasons related to problems in telecommunications competition (with international intra-Euroland calls being several times more expensive than in the US – taking a look at long distance rates) or in labor markets where a declining wage drift in several EU countries reduces the ability of expanding firms to attract skilled labor away from declining sectors – and this in a period in which the full exploitation of the New Economy growth effects would require accelerated intersectoral relocation of labor. In Germany effective wage rates increased in the period 1991-2000 by 28% while the negotiated wage rate increased by 40.9%. These figures – based on Deutsche Bundesbank – indicate that labor market rigidity and lack of wage drift (and wage dispersion) could be part of the relatively low ICT dynamics in Germany and possibly in some other countries in the euro zone as well.

Recent Analysis

According to DAVERI (2001) the growth contribution differs considerably across OECD countries (see subsequent table). Daveri also finds that in terms of the share of IT capital (augmented by the software component), the EU faced considerable differences. In 1999 IT capital accounted for roughly 6% of overall value-added in Sweden and the UK, 5% in Ireland and the Netherlands, but only about 3% in Germany, Italy, France, and Spain, with Portugal and Greece being only 2.5%. In the US the share of IT capital in overall value-added was 8% (0.029 for hardware, 0.034 for software, and 0.016 for communications equipment) which is 1/5 of the value-added share for total capital. In Greece, Italy, Spain, and Ireland communications equipment absorbed about 2/5 of the IT capital share of value-added. In most other EU countries the distribution of value-added to the various IT categories was more similar to that found in the US.

The growth contribution of IT capital reached almost 1% in the US in 1991-99 – actually increasing over time in the 1990s. Ireland, Denmark, the Netherlands and the UK also were rather strong performers. IT capital contributed between one-half and roughly one percentage point to overall growth in Ireland, Sweden, Finland and Ireland in 1996-99; in the US and the UK IT capital contributed as much as 1.45 and 1.17, respectively. As regards the US and the UK the software component seems to have been almost as important as the hardware component. One may state the hypothesis that the financial services sector – being relatively large in the US and the UK – plays a crucial role for the Anglo-American lead. The US economy has shown a very high growth rate of nominal software expenditure which rose by about 15% p.a. in the period 1992-99; the figure for Germany was only a meager 7% p.a.; the ratio of software expenditures to hardware expenditures was 1.44 for the US in 1995 while Germany had a ratio of 1.08; however, by 1999 the ratio in the US had reached 220:100 while expenditures on hardware and software in Germany were roughly 100 dollars of software expenditures for every 100 dollars spent on hardware (DEUTSCHE BUNDESBANK, 2001). As regards the statistical bias emerging from different methods of price measurement and real output measurement the DEUTSCHE BUNDESBANK (2001, p.43) argues that the German growth gap vis-à-vis the US was reduced by about 0.4 percentage points in the second half of the 1990s; however, the transatlantic growth differential of roughly 2 percentage points in the period 1996-99 remains high. For both the European Central Bank and national policymakers in EU countries it would be important to fully understand the phenomenon of the New Economy.

Table A5:   The Growth Contributions of IT Capital and its Components

	(1)	(2)	(3)	(4)	(5)	(6)
	1991-99	**1991-95**	**1996-99**	**1991-99**	**1991-99**	**1991-99**
	IT	**IT**	**IT**	**HW**	**SW**	**TLC**
USA	0.94	0.53	1.45	0.50	0.36	0.08
Ireland	0.64	0.38	0.96	0.30	0.12	0.22
Denmark	0.52	0.42	0.65	0.29	0.14	0.09
Netherlands	0.68	0.65	0.72	0.33	0.22	0.13
UK	0.76	0.43	1.17	0.39	0.26	0.11
Portugal	0.43	0.39	0.49	0.18	0.05	0.19
Austria	0.45	0.47	0.43	0.23	0.12	0.11
Spain	0.36	0.38	0.34	0.17	0.06	0.14
Greece	0.34	0.25	0.46	0.12	0.04	0.18
Finland	0.45	0.21	0.74	0.27	0.10	0.08
Belgium	0.48	0.48	0.49	0.23	0.14	0.11
Sweden	0.59	0.38	0.85	0.38	0.13	0.08
Germany*	0.49	0.54	0.45	0.24	0.12	0.13
France	0.41	0.40	0.44	0.20	0.11	0.11
Italy	0.31	0.28	0.35	0.15	0.05	0.11

Notes: IT = HW+SW+TLC = Hardware+Software+Communications equipment. Data in percentage points.
* Germany = 1992-1999
Sources: DAVERI, F. (2001), Information Technology and Growth in Europe, p. 6.

Table A6:   The Growth Contributions of IT and Non-IT Capital, Labor and Total Factor Productivity, 1991-99

	(1) GDP	(2) IT CAPITAL	(3) NON-IT CAPITAL	(4) Labour	(5) TFP
USA	3.34	0.94	0.42	0.90	1.08
Ireland	6.91	0.64	0.63	1.93	3.72
Denmark	2.87	0.52	0.60	0.34	1.40
Netherlands	2.83	0.68	0.31	1.09	0.75
UK	2.68	0.76	0.37	0.51	1.04
Portugal	2.47	0.43	1.05	-0.35	1.34
Austria	2.33	0.45	1.29	-0.46	1.04
Spain	2.32	0.36	1.10	0.36	0.51
Greece	2.25	0.34	0.65	0.46	0.78
Finland	2.13	0.45	-0.13	-1.05	2.86
Belgium	1.88	0.48	0.68	0.00	0.72
Sweden	1.86	0.59	0.32	-0.28	1.23
Germany*	1.65	0.49	0.56	-0.23	0.83
France	1.64	0.41	0.49	-0.19	0.92
Italy	1.41	0.31	0.82	-0.30	0.58

Notes: data in percentage points. Column (1) presents GDP (business sector, measured at factor costs) growth rates in 1991-99. Column (2)-(5) present the contributions of employment (hours worked), IT and non-IT capital and total factor productivity to GDP growth.
* Germany = 1992-1999
Sources: DAVERI, F. (2001): Information Technology and Growth in Europe, p. 7.

While the US recorded an acceleration in growth contribution from IT capital, namely from 0.53 in 1991-95 to 1.45 in 1996-99, Germany had a rather flat contribution from IT capital, namely 0.5. Insufficient structural change, the monopoly of telecommunications until 1998, and lack of cheap internet rates (including the refusal of Deutsche Telekom AG (except for the second half of 2000) to offer a flat rate for standard telecommunications users could be main elements in explaining the modest IT contribution in Germany (WELFENS, 2001b, 2001c; WELFENS/JUNGMITTAG, 2001). Comparing the US and the EU it is quite obvious that computer density in the Community is much lower than in the US. Germany reached three-fourths of the US computer density; France was slightly weaker, and Italy, with about one-half of US computer density, was just at the level of Korea in 1999. In the EU only the Scandinavian countries had a computer density comparable to the US. It is noteworthy that Sweden's tax policy contributed actively to raising computer density by giving firms tax incentives to sell used PCs at discount prices to employees.

In the digital economy the inventory-output ratio is lower than in the traditional economy since computerization allows improved production planning and logistics. At the same time the digital economy consists to a considerable extent of digital services where the supply elasticity is obviously very high. In the case of services provided via the internet [e.g. software (application sharing services) or music] the supply elasticity is extremely high. This could contribute not only to higher growth in fields where demand follows a logistical expansion path over time but also could reduce the inflationary pressure for any given money supply growth; that is, in economic upswings the inflation rate will increase less than in the traditional economy. This seems to indeed have been the case in the 1990s. CREPON / HECKEL (2001) find that computer use and total factor productivity gains in the ICT sector have reduced the inflation rate by 0.3 and 0.4 percentage points in the period 1987-1998, a considerable impact with respect to the average inflation rate of 1.4% in this period in France.

JORGENSEN/STIROH (2000) have argued that US growth resurgence is partly related to an increasing use and production of ICT. OLINER / SICHEL (2000) have also concluded that the revival in US productivity growth is strongly related to information technology dynamics. About two-thirds of the rise in US labor productivity in 1996-99 can be explained by an increasing use and production of information technology. This two-thirds can in turn be partly assigned to capital deepening and partly to higher total factor productivity growth. DAVERI (2001) argues that growth in EU countries is also partly an information technology story. The following table shows that IT capital accumulation can explain a considerable part of cross-country growth gaps. The shares of the growth gaps explained by IT capital is roughly 25-30% of the total for six EU countries (Germany, France, Italy, UK, Sweden, and Belgium), but this fraction is larger for Denmark (90%), and Greece, Spain, Portugal, the Netherlands, Austria and Finland (50-60%). As regards capital input, differences in the overall contributions of capital cannot explain much of the EU growth gap vis-à-vis the US. It is noteworthy that the growth gap observed in Italy, Germany, France, and Sweden vis-à-vis the US is largely explained by gaps in the contribution of labor. Following similar experiences in the 1960s, 1970s, and 1980s (DOUGHERTY / JORGENSEN, 1996), the growth contribution of labor was negative in many EU countries in the 1990s. As regards total factor productivity growth, several EU countries show higher TFP growth rates than the US. DAVERI (2001) emphasizes that while it is difficult to draw clear conclusions with respect to TFP given the residual character of this variable, the time variations of the TFP growth rates are interesting. The five largest countries in the EU had smaller TFP growth in 1996-99 than in the 1980s and the first part of the 1990s. However, TFP growth has increased in Portugal, Greece, Finland, and Ireland over time. This intra-EU difference is not fully understood, although BASSANINI / SCARPETTA / VISCO (2000) argues that the increase in TFP was relatively high in countries with flexible labor markets and less regulated product markets. However, Spain, the UK, and the Netherlands were indeed countries with considerable labor market deregulation in the 1980s and 1990s. One cannot simply rule out that labor market deregulation is important, as a combination of high ICT investment with accelerated structural changes develops towards a dynamic service society. In the services sector we have, however, well-known problems in measuring productivity (ARK / MONNIKHOF / MULDER, 1999; BOSWORTH / TRIPLETT, 2000). With respect to the impact of labor one cannot rule out that rising unemployment rates in the 1980s and early 1990s contributed to growth positively via a positive effort effect of those having a job, but the combined effect of labor quantity and labor effort obviously was negative in many EU countries.

Table A7:   ICT Investment Effects; Contribution to Potential Growth in the 1990's (% Points)

	ICT Price Decline in the EU identical to that in the US		ICT Price Decline in the EU = 50% of that of the US	
	1992-1994	1995-1999	1992-1994	1995-1999
Belgium	0.35	0.60	0.35	0.51
Denmark	0.22	0.38	0.22	0.32
Germany	0.25	0.41	0.25	0.35
Greece	0.12	0.21	0.12	0.18
Spain	0.19	0.39	0.19	0.33
France	0.24	0.42	0.24	0.35
Ireland	0.84	1.91	0.84	1.64
Italy	0.25	0.42	0.25	0.36
Netherlands	0.41	0.67	0.41	0.56
Austria	0.24	0.41	0.24	0.34
Portugal	0.25	0.55	0.25	0.47
Finland	0.31	0.63	0.31	0.53
Sweden	0.30	0.68	0.30	0.57
UK	0.35	0.64	0.35	0.54
EU15	0.27	0.49	0.27	0.41
US	0.40	0.87	0.40	0.87

Source: Mc MORROW, K., ROEGER, W. (2001), Potential Output: Measurement Methods, "New" Economy Influences and Scenarios for 2001-2010 – A Comparison of the EU15 and the US; Economic Papers Nr. 150, April 2001, p. 71.

According to McMORROW / RÖGER (2000) there has been some acceleration in the growth contribution of ICT in EU countries where the authors distinguish between two cases, namely EU computer price reductions equal to the US and (ii) the case of only a 50% price reduction, which might reflect various impediments to low prices in Europe, including government regulations in Germany forbidding high rebates on products (this law is being abolished in late 2001). At the bottom line the contribution of ICT to potential output growth in the US has been about twice as high as in the EU-15. Among EU countries only Ireland, itself strongly shaped by US multinational investment in ICT, showed a growth contribution of ICT exceeding that in the US in the 1990s. Disregarding Ireland only Sweden, Finland, the UK, the Netherlands, and Belgium came within a range of about two-thirds of US figures in 1995-99. With a direct ICT investment effect of almost 1 percentage point in the late 1990s, the US clearly benefited from high nominal investment growth in ICT when prices were falling in relative terms.

ICT dynamics are certainly not the full story behind the different growth per-formance of various OECD countries. However, ICT is one crucial element.

Moreover, rapid accumulation of ICT capital might facilitate the exploitation of new knowledge and stimulate innovation as well as diffusion. This is particularly interesting when we take a closer look at the development of R&D-GDP ratios in general and at the development of high technology labor productivity. As regards the latter RÖGER (2001) shows that the US has established a clear lead vis-à-vis the EU since 1993; with a lag of about two years the US world market share of high technology exports has increased strongly while that of Germany and Japan has fallen since 1993. Both Germany and Japan no longer benefit from the exceptional position they had in the Cold War era, namely that they were special among the largest five OECD countries in devoting almost their entire R&D resources to civilian projects.

As the following graph shows, there is a general tendency of R&D-GDP ratios to rise in the late 1990s. Sweden is the leader in the OECD with an increase of slightly more than 1 percentage point in the 1990s, bringing the country to a top figure of roughly 4%. Finland also shows a strong increase and reached 3.2% in 1999. Germany's R&D ratio decreased for more than a decade after 1987, and it has increased only modestly from a bottom figure of about 2% in 1996. The US had a slight reduction of the R&D ratio in the early 1990s but increased in the second half of the decade and was close to 2.3% in 2000. The temporary reduction of the US R&D ratio is, however, mainly due to the falling expenditures on military R&D. This also holds for France and the UK which, however, stabilized R&D ratios in the late 1990s. While Canada and Italy were close together in 1989 with slightly less than 1%, Canada has increased its R&D-GDP ratio, while that of Italy has fallen to a very low level of roughly 0.6% in the mid-1990s. Interestingly, both Japan and Korea reached R&D-GDP ratios slightly above that of Germany in the 1990s.

Given the fact that most EU countries are high wage economies, it is obvious that these countries must achieve high labor productivity if full employment is to be reestablished or maintained. High capital intensity (referring here to non-ICT-capital), high ICT intensity, and high knowledge intensity are the three pillars upon which a high wage economy can be built. Facing EU eastern enlargement, one may anticipate that many plants in capital-intensive sectors, e.g. automotive or steel, will be relocated to eastern Europe. Hence it will be all the more important that high wage EU countries generate sufficient increases in R&D capital, human capital, and ICT capital.

If the expenditures on R&D and software were to systematically increase in OECD countries in the early 21st century this would mean that the share of sunk costs in most products would increase. From a theoretical point of view this reduces price flexibility in the sense that innovative products are typically less exposed to price competition than standardized goods. However, high sunk costs imply that incumbent firms have considerable room to maneuver with respect to temporary price cutting when a newcomer wants to enter the market. They could disregard all sunk costs to fend off the intrusion of newcomers. If newcomers were to try to enter new markets particularly in phases of an economic upswing, this could imply that price increases in the economic upswing will be less pronounced in the future.

Figure A3:   R&D GDP Ratios in Selected OECD Countries, 1981-2000

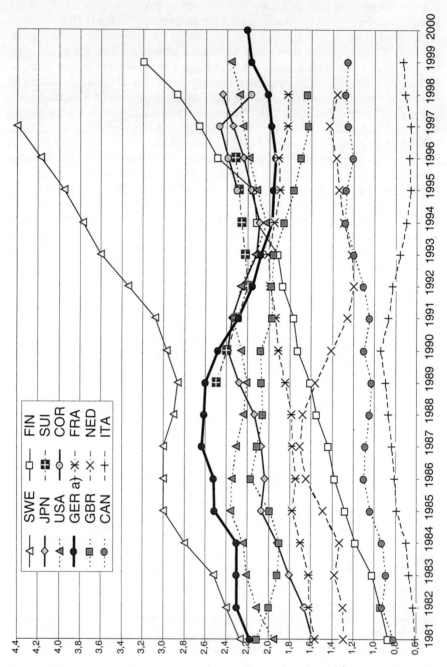

Source: ZEW

2.2 Perspectives on Inflation and Growth

US inflation rates were low throughout the 1990s. This is surprising given the considerable boom in the second half of the 1990s. High economic growth could in itself be an explanation of low inflation to the extent that high growth rates were anticipated in stock markets – we will show a formal model below. Moreover, the strong appreciation of the dollar – in the late 1990s especially vis-à-vis Asian countries – has helped to maintain low inflation rates; this holds at least until 1999/2000 when international oil and gas prices increased strongly. While the previous period of a strong dollar in the mid-1980s was accompanied by a high current account deficit and a high budget deficit, the strong dollar of the late 1990s developed only in combination with a high current account deficit. This current account deficit is not necessarily pointing to competitiveness problems of US industry; rather it seems to be the mirror of high capital inflows in a system of fixed exchange rates. A relatively high marginal product of capital in the US generates high capital inflows; at the same time the low growth rate of Euroland´s three core countries, namely Germany, France and Italy, points to a rather low marginal product of capital in Euroland which is part a broader analysis explaining the weak euro in 1999/2000 (WELFENS, 2000).

When US stock market indices started to fall in 2000/2001 the euro could not improve its position. Anticipation of changing US long-term interest rates might explain the coincidence of falling stock market prices in the US and a stable dollar; portfolio investors would not switch from the US stock market towards the stock markets in Euroland; rather US investors would move from the US stock market to the US bond market. In both the US and EU-15 a shift in the Phillips curve was observed; that is, unemployment rates could fall without causing inflation rates to rise as steeply as in previous decades; the NAIRU has reduced (RICHARDSON ET AL., 2000). It is unclear whether the shift in the Phillips curve is mainly reflecting changes in goods markets or in labor markets. Part of the explanation might be that the elasticity of the supply side in goods markets has increased in the context of an expanding New Economy; with more and more digital services being developed and sold within the business community and directly to consumers the fact that digital services hardly face any capacity constraint suggests that at least in the services sector the supply elasticity has increased. To the extent that international outsourcing of labor-intensive services is facilitated by the internet, there is another argument why tightening labor markets would not lead to wage increases as fast as in the past.

The strong depreciation of the euro in 1999/2000 raises the issue of links between the exchange rate and the price level. A strong depreciation will raise the price of tradables with a certain time lag unless there is a high rate of process innovations which would bring about reductions in unit labor costs (or in capital costs). Even with a depreciation of the currency it remains to be seen how monetary policy will behave on the one hand and how stock markets will develop on the other hand. For the inflation analysis we will focus on a modified quantity equation (WELFENS, 2000):

(I) $MV'(i,Y) = PY + \phi(i,....)P'Q,$

where M is the nominal stock of money, V′ velocity of money, Y real output, P
the price level (with $P=(P^T)^\beta(P^N)^{1-\beta}$; where ß is the share of tradables in overall
demand), ϕ the velocity of the representative portfolio – indicating how often the
stock of bonds and equities invested have been sold – P′ the price of stocks, and Q
the number of stocks. With the assumption $V= v(i)Y^\chi$ – with the absolute value of
$0<\chi<1$ – dividing by PY results in the following equation where ϕ is assumed to
negatively depend on i and other variables.

(II) $[M/P]\, v(i)Y^{\chi-1} = 1+ \phi(i,...)$ [h],

The symbol h denotes the value of stocks relative to GDP. Assuming that ϕ[h] is
relatively small so that we can use the approximation ln $(1+x)\approx x$ then – assuming
ϕ is constant and denoting growth rates by g – we obtain after taking logarithms:

(III) $g_P=g_M - (1-\chi)g_Y - \phi dh/dt.$

If purchasing power parity holds for tradables (T) in the form of e $P^{T*} = P^T$ and if
we define $P=(P^T)^\beta(P^N)^{1-\beta}$, then $g_e + g_{PT*} = g_{PT}$ and therefore $g_P = g_{PN} + ß(g_e + g_{PT*} -
g_{PN})$ so that we obtain the growth rate of tradables prices as the difference between
the inflation rate and the change of the relative price ratio $(g_e + g_{PT*} - g_{PN})$
weighted by ß.

   According to (III) for a constant nominal interest rate and a given growth rate
of the money supply it holds that the inflation rate is the smaller the higher the
growth rate of real output and the stronger the increase in the ratio of stock market
capitalization relative to output. The coincidence of high growth and exceptionally
growing stock market capitalization – relative to output – could indeed explain the
inflation puzzle in the US in the 1990s.

Growth Analysis in a Two-Sector Model

Why was growth so high in the US in the 1990s? We consider a two-sector economy so that overall output Y is composed of the ICT sector (sector 1) which accounted for about 10% in the US in 2000 while the US recorded only about 6%.
Denoting the relative price P_1/P_2 as q" we have

(IV) $Y = q"Y_1+ Y_2,$

Assuming that sector 2 is the consumption sector, then output in terms of consumption units is given by

(IV.I) $g_Y = (Y_1/Y)\,[g_{q"} + g_{Y1}] + (1-(Y_1/Y))\, g_{Y2}$

From this equation it is clear that the relative fall of computer prices reduces overall growth as measured in units of the consumption good. For statistical purposes the real output growth rate is measured in a different way, namely on the basis of constant historical prices:

(IV.I′) $g_Y = (Y_1/Y) [g_{Y1}] + (1-(Y_1/Y)) g_{Y2}$

Here we can directly see that the high growth rate of the US is partly related to the higher share of the ICT sector in overall output and partly due to the high output growth rate of the ICT sector. The US statistical system has made two changes in the 1990s which go beyond the above formula but which almost have no net effect. Introducing a chain-weighted index – reducing the well-known problem of substitution in the presence of relative price changes – for real GDP measurement showed that real GDP growth had to be slightly revised downwards. At the same time the introduction of hedonic pricing which takes into account quality improvement – highly significant in the ICT sector (especially in the case of computers) – brought an upwards revision of real GDP. One can only wonder why Eurostat is not making similar adjustments in its SNA procedures.

We now turn to the analysis of output growth on the basis of factor inputs and total factor productivity (TFP) growth. The US recorded in some years two-digit growth rates of total factor productivity growth in the 1990s. Overall TFP is the weighted sum of sectoral TFPs, that in our case is of two sectors; here α_i (i=1,2) is the share of nominal sector 1 output relative to overall nominal output.

(V) $TFP = \alpha_1 TFP_1 + \alpha_2 TFP_2$

In a simple growth model based on a production function VF(K,L,Z,Q) with inputs capital K (without computers), labor L and computers Z we can decompose output growth as follows where we use $E_{Y,X}$ to denote partial output elasticities:

(V.I) $g_Y = E_{Y,K} g_K + E_{Y,L} g_L + E_{Y,Z} g_Z + g_V$; here $g_V = TFP$

(V.II) $g_Y = E_{Y,K} g_K + E_{Y,L} g_L + E_{Y,Z} g_Z + \alpha_1 TFP_1 + \alpha_2 TFP_2$

The input factor computer is a proxy for ICT goods used as inputs in firms. Total factor productivity growth in the ICT sector has been enormous in the 1990s in the US and is expected to remain high; while the EU also has had an increase in productivity growth in ICT it is unlikely that West European countries will be on par with the US. It is true that Sweden, Finland, Ireland and some regions in Germany and France have a dynamic ICT industry, but global industry leaders clearly are firms from the US which also spend more than twice as much as the Europeans on software (OECD, 1998). While it is unlikely that the US lead in ICT will continue forever, it might well maintain a considerable lead over several decades.

Next we turn to the issue of heterogeneous labor; that is, we will distinguish between unskilled labor L and skilled labor H. The substitution elasticity of L and H with respect to computers is crucial, and here again we might find differences in the US and Europe. However, even if the substitution elasticity in the US would be higher than in the EU high investment in ICT would not necessarily mean a rise of unskilled unemployed in the US. The crucial question is whether the labor market is flexible enough to transitorily allow wage rates of unskilled labor to fall – with employment growth and output growth continuing, finally the demand for unskilled labor will grow strongly; this holds in part because well-paid skilled labor will increasingly demand all kinds of services which are often not very skill-intensive.

Next we will slightly modify the production function and assume that infra-structure capital Q enters the production function, too. Assuming a linear-homogeneous function F(...) and a production function Y= QVF(K,L,H,Z), we can write output per unit of skilled labor as follows – with $Y/H := y^h$, $k' := K/H$, $l' := L/H$, $Z/H := z'$ and w, w´ as real wage rate for unskilled and skilled labor and r and p´ denoting the real interest rate and the price of computers, respectively:

(VI) $y^h = f(k'(r/w, w'/w, p'/w), l'(r/w, w'/w, p'/w), z'(r/w, w'/w, p'/w), Q, V)$

(VII) $dlny^h/dt = E_{K/H,r/w}\, g_{r/w} + E_{K/H,w'/w}\, g_{w'/w} + E_{K/H,p'/w}\, g_{p'/w} +$
$+ E_{L/H,r/w}\, g_{r/w} + E_{L/H,w'/w}\, g_{w'/w} + E_{L/H,p'/w}g_{p'/w} + E_{Z/H,r/w}\, g_{r/w} +$
$+ E_{Z/H,w'/w}\, g_{w'/w} + E_{Z/H,p'/w}\, g_{p'/w} + E_{Y,q'}\, g_Q + E_{Y',V}(\alpha_1\, TFP_1 + \alpha_2\, TFP_2)$

Assuming for simplicity that r/w is constant, then the growth rate of output per unit of skilled labor is given by

(VII´) $dlny^h/dt = (E_{K/H,w'/w} + E_{L/H,w'/w} + E_{Z/H,\, w'/w})\, g_{w'/w}$
$+ \{[E_{K/H,p'/w} + E_{L/H,p'/w} + E_{Z/H,\, p'/w}]g_{p'/w}\} + E_{y',v}(\alpha_1\, TFP_1 + \alpha_2\, TFP_2)$

Note that the elasticities $E_{y',q'}$, $E_{y',v}$ stand for the elasticity of output per unit of skilled labor with respect to infrastructure capital Q and the level of technology V, respectively. In the US the growth rate of $g_{w'/w}$ was positive in the early and mid-1990s; in Euroland it was close to zero. As the three partial elasticities in the first bracket are positive, it is obvious that the skill premium in the US has contributed to growth while for Germany and Euroland, respectively, there was no such growth impact as trade unions managed to maintain or even transitorily reduce vertical wage dispersion. This indeed would have reduced the growth impact of ICT to the extent that expansion of ICT would have required a rising vertical wage dispersion. The direct growth contribution of computers is indicated by the last bracket term{...}. The first two elasticities are positive, and the last one $E_{Z/H,p'/w}$ is negative since the ratio of using computers per unit of skilled labor will fall if computer prices should increase. If the absolute value for this elasticity exceeds $E_{K/H,p'/w} + E_{L/H,p'/w}$ – and this is a realistic case – then the fall of computer prices will go along with a positive value of the term {...}. While government expenditures relative to GDP were 3% p.a. in the US in the 1990s, they were close to 2 % in Germany and only slightly higher in Euroland. If the supply elasticity of infra-structure capital were of equal size in the US and Euroland, the slower growth rate of g_Q in the latter – mainly caused by low infrastructure expenditures in Germany, Belgium and Austria – would explain part of the transatlantic growth differential. Germany together with Belgium indeed recorded the lowest ratio of public investment to GDP in 2000; this might be understandable in Belgium where government is facing the challenge to reduce a debt-GDP ratio of more than 100% in 2000, but for reunited Germany that is a real puzzle since its debt-GDP ratio stood at an uncritical 60%; additionally since economic catching-up of eastern Germany requires relatively high public investment one would expect Germany to have one of the highest public investment-GDP ratios among the members of Euroland.

If we assume for the medium term that the number of skilled labor is exogenous – not a realistic presumption for the long run taking into account long-term opportunities for training and education – then the growth rate Y/H in the above equation is identical with the overall growth rate of output.

3. Innovation, ICT Dynamics and Growth: Theoretical and Empirical Aspects

3.1 Basic Theoretical Issues

The positive impact of technological change and innovation on fostering economic growth is generally acknowledged. Although the growth enhancing effects of new products and processes had been known for some time, it took some decades to attract the interest of researchers to study technical change. This lack of interest may be explained in part by complex procedures ruling science and technology (S&T) and the unknown mechanisms translating innovations into broad-based economic effects. However, it is a matter of fact that technological change is a driving force behind economic growth.

Thus, it is not surprising that recent approaches in growth theory pay much attention to technological change or its "mate": human capital or knowledge. The basic models of the new growth theory which are in the meantime standard in modern textbooks are presented in ROMER (1986), LUCAS (1988) and ROMER (1990). A large part of new growth theory assumes a beneficial know-how "transfer" from a knowledge-generating sector which performs R&D to the sector of the economy in which companies simply adopt it. Part of this knowledge as a result of R&D efforts is paid for by the receiving firms while some part diffuses without appropriate compensation. Thus, external effects of knowledge creation (so called spillover effects) are followed by increasing returns in production of the remaining sectors and cause all-over economic growth. One essential difference between neo-classical and new growth theory may be found in these growth-creating effects. This recent line of research regards national growth to be independent of stocks of knowledge and human capital elsewhere. Thus, economies with their own knowledge-creating or human capital-creating sectors are growing faster in the long run than those without.

New growth theory is no exception to other economic modeling, as it does not pay much attention to the details either of what generates external effects in innovation or of the channels which link knowledge generation and adaptation (see e.g. JAFFE / TRAJTENBERG / HENDERSON (1992)). Moreover, to switch from the inward perspective of new growth theory to a more outward "global" perspective seems to be useful because it would be highly unrealistic (particularly for developed countries) – for the economies of the European Union, it would be simply wrong – to assume that knowledge flows will not leak out of the area delimited by national borders. In view of the increasing share of trade in worldwide production and the recent surge in the exchange and mobility of production factors, technological as well as economic developments are influenced to a nonnegligible degree by other economies via world markets. In this respect think, for example, of those channels where scientific and technological knowledge accompanies exports of goods and services, the mobility of human capital within global firms or the policy of the European Commission to support preferentially transborder R&D in the community. An extensive discussion of the trend, motives and consequences of the globalization of R&D and technology markets can be found in JUNGMITTAG / MEYER-KRAHMER / REGER (1999). Here, taking into account new trade theory and some strands of evolutionary economics following the Schumpeterian tradition, which have in common a certain overlap with traditional theory but stress the importance of technology and innovation as complementary determinants, can provide additional insights (see JUNGMITTAG / GRUPP / HULLMANN (1998) and GRUPP / JUNGMITTAG (1999)).

As far as new trade theory is concerned, a model that has been developed as part of a comprehensive analysis by GROSSMAN / HELPMAN (1991, chapter 9) is particularly instructive. It deals with the situation most common in high technology trade among OECD countries. The focus is on the long-term growth prospects of countries opening up – step by step – to different degrees of market integration. Basically, the model is built according to the following principles: countries are "endowed" with labor, human capital and technological knowledge. To keep the analysis of the model's main properties simple, Grossman and Helpman restricted complexity in that the economy consists of one sector only. The focus is set on the working of integration – not on structural change within any one country. Technological knowledge generates external effects and increasing returns for the production of traded goods. In the long run, adding some further – more technical – assumptions, growth rates depend on innovation rates – that is, on the speed with which new technological knowledge is built up.

Integrating two economies similar (or even identical) in terms of traditional endowments would lead to either unchanged trade patterns and growth rates or to increased specialization and higher growth rates in both countries. The dynamic properties of this model heavily depend on the characteristics of the stock of accumulated knowledge before integration. Because of similar endowments with traditional factors the only difference before globalization lies in the degree of knowledge specialization in different areas. Given that both economies are completely specialized on complementary fields of knowledge, integration will have no effects, neither on technological, production and trade patterns nor on long-run

growth. Instead, if the stocks of knowledge have a certain overlap in both economies (e.g. knowledge accumulated in the same fields of science and technology)
integration will weed out these "inefficiencies". Each country specializes on one
part of this knowledge available to both economies via full integration of markets.
In this situation growth is higher in both countries compared with those in closed
economies. To the extent that the Internet facilitates accumulation of knowledge
and reduces international integration costs one may expect a growth bonus due to
faster technological progress within a larger radius of integration. At the same
time the rising adjustment speed in digital financial markets might contribute to
more market volatility and hence transitorily or permanently reduced growth rates.

Apart from new growth and new trade theory, evolutionary economics in a
Schumpeterian tradition is concerned with the relationship between technology,
trade and growth. Although it lacks a consistent body of formal modeling tools,
evolutionary economics has provided a lot of interesting insights into the details of
the working of economic systems. Evolutionary thinking is fundamentally based
on the variation-selection principle which allows one to look at the dynamic properties of systems and, thus, it is based on economic development. Basically, evolution is thought of as being generated by creating a variety of different products and
processes. Selection processes (e.g. markets) then work on reducing this variety to
a certain number of viable products. The diversity of evolutionary theorizing cannot be dealt with here (on this see DOSI / PAVITT / SOETE (1990), WITT (1993)
or HODGSON (1993)). One of the main forces that generate new products or
processes (and, thereby, increase variety) is innovation and technological change.

Concentrating first on variation, empirical studies have found that higher rates
of innovation lead to higher rates of economic growth (e.g. FAGERBERG
(1988)). The larger the number of different products and the higher the rate of new
product generation the higher the rate of long-run growth. Saviotti has worked out
a conceptual and semi-formal tool to show that we are observing a constantly
increasing number of different products. Higher degrees of product variety cause
higher consumer utility. This is a main reason for economic growth (SAVIOTTI
(1991)). This mechanism mainly works through better adaptation to specific consumer needs (higher utility) as well as through higher efficiency of production
processes. The Internet allows a very broad variety of digital products and services
to be sold in enlarged markets.

When we turn to the selection environment, most studies have found tighter selection mechanisms to favor higher growth. Here the transparency enhancing
effects of the Internet could be important.

From a theoretical point of view, tighter selection does not necessarily prove
more efficient because in this case a large number of product variants, which have
incurred development costs, are selected out. However, this waste of resources
may be compensated by long-run efficiency of fewer but superior products (see
e.g. COHENDET / LLERENA / SORGE (1992) for a discussion of this fundamental problem in evolutionary economics). Market competition as one of several
possible selection environments in an ideal sense weeds out all inefficient types of
products in order to ensure the survival of the best-fitting alternatives. Then, in
face of selection, generation of new products adapts to the characteristics of the

successful variants. Therefore, it is essential for economic agents to learn quickly from the fate of successful as well as unsuccessful products on the markets and, then, to develop better variants which sell at higher prices or larger quantities. Thus, the particular strength of companies comes from learning adaptation. However, learning and adaptation are fundamentally path-dependent processes. That means, the probability to learn something useful will be much higher in areas where knowledge has already been accumulated in former times. This path-dependency of technological change and learning may be observed at the level of single companies, industries, regions and countries. It does not only explain a great deal of innovation but also the dynamics of division of labor and economic development. DOSI (1982) used this basic principle for a "theory" of technological change. Scientific and technological change is following "trajectories" until a "breakpoint" (radical change) disrupts the smooth and gradual development.

The stock of accumulated knowledge does not only consist of scientific or otherwise codified and easily accessible findings but also of acquired "tacit" practical skills. Knowledge therefore has a "public" and a "private" part. Apart from a few really globalized and highly science-based technologies the main part of worldwide knowledge has a local character in that its geographical diffusion is limited in scope because of mobility barriers to human capital or skilled labor. Accordingly, empirical studies have found a lot of evidence that the ability to learn and to innovate greatly differs between sectors, regions and countries. See e.g. PAVITT (1984), PAVITT ET AL. (1987), DOSI / PAVITT / SOETE (1990) and GEHRKE / GRUPP (1994). Thus, stocks of technological knowledge differ in scope and character between economic entities over long periods of time. The Internet seems to be ambiguous since a high rate of ICT change implies relevance of private tacit knowledge; at the same time the global Internet facilitates development of public international knowledge within the triad.

3.2 Empirical Links Between Innovations and Output

The empirical investigation of the effects of technological change or more generally innovation on economic growth has produced a voluminous and diverse literature. Roughly, there are three types of studies: historical case studies, analyses of invention counts and patent statistics, and econometric studies relating output or productivity to R&D or similar variables (GRILICHES, 1995). Here, we will confine ourselves to econometric studies, which use some indicator variables to approximate the impact of technological change and innovations.

First, one important input factor for technological change and innovation can serve as a proxy variable: R&D. Most research in this vein uses an augmented Cobb-Douglas production function which includes some kind of a R&D stock besides the usual production factors. The coefficient belonging to this R&D stock can then be interpreted as production or output elasticity of R&D. Alternatively, this kind of production function is transformed into growth rates, and the R&D intensity (R&D/Y) is included. The parameter belonging to this R&D intensity yields the rate of return to knowledge. Similar to these approaches is another procedure where total factor productivity is calculated first. Then again, either the logs of levels of total factor productivity are linked to some kind of log R&D stock or the first differences of log total factor productivity are regressed on the R&D intensity. The interpretation of the estimated coefficients is the same as before: the regression of the levels of log total factor productivity on a log R&D stock yields a measure of the elasticity of output to knowledge, while the regression of total factor productivity growth yields a measure of the social gross (excess) rate of return to knowledge (GRILICHES / LICHTENBERG, 1984 and GRILICHES, 1995).

A general problem for the measurement of the effects of R&D on output is that a number of externalities arise in the innovation process. Summarizing the relevant literature on this topic, CAMERON (1998) distinguishes between four kinds of externalities. First, a *standing on shoulders effect* which reduces the costs of rival firms because of knowledge leaks, imperfect patenting, and movement of skilled labor to other firms. In a wider sense international technological spillovers due to foreign trade can also be considered as within the standing on shoulders effect. Secondly, there exists a *surplus appropriability problem* because even if there are no technological spillovers, the innovator does not appropriate all the social gains from his innovation unless he can price discriminate perfectly to rival firms and/or to downstream users. Thirdly, new ideas make old production processes and products obsolescent: the so-called *creative destruction effect*. Fourthly, congestion or network externalities occur when the payoffs to the adoption of innovations are substitutes or complements. This is sometimes called the *stepping on toes effect*. The adequate consideration of these effects in empirical investigations offers a wide field for further research. Up to now, these effects are only taken rather roughly and partially into account in most empirical studies.

Generally, studies which are based on time series data on levels of output and R&D stocks for individual US, French and Japanese companies found output elasticities lying between 0.06 and 0.1 (GRILICHES, 1995). Considering results of this kind of studies for Germany and France at different levels of aggregation, the estimated output elasticities turned out to be somewhat higher. For the total economy of West Germany PATEL / SOETE (1988) estimated 0.21 as the output elasticity of R&D. However, in a recent study BÖNTE (1998) estimated only output elasticities between 0.03 and 0.04 for the R&D stock of selected sectors of West German manufacturing. At the firm level CUNEO / MAIRESSE (1984) estimated for the R&D stock output elasticities between 0.22 and 0.33 for France; MAIRESSE / CUNEO (1985) estimated values between 0.09 and 0.26, and MAIRESSE / HALL (1996) values between 0.00 and 0.17. At the level of the total economy PATEL / SOETE (1988) estimated a value of 0.13 for the output elasticity of R&D for France. COE / MOGHADAM (1993) estimated with their preferred specification an output elasticity of 0.17 for the R&D stock of France.

When growth rates are used as dependent variables and R&D intensities as independent variables, the estimated rate of return lies – summarizing the bulk of empirical results for different countries and different levels of aggregation – mainly between 0.2 and 0.5, with most of the recent estimates falling in the lower part of this range (GRILICHES, 1995). However, the results for West Germany are a little bit puzzling. At a firm level, BARDY (1974) estimated direct rates of return to R&D between 0.92 and 0.97. However, at an industry level MÖHNEN / NADIRI / PRUCHA (1986) estimated a direct rate of return to R&D of 0.13, and O'MAHONY / WAGNER (1996) found at the same level a direct rate of return of 0.00. With a different approach BÖNTE (1998) calculated net rates of return for selected sectors of West German manufacturing between 0.23 and 0.3. This is quite in accordance with the general results and with the results for France at the firm level where GRILICHES / MAIRESSE (1983) estimated a rate of return to R&D of 0.31, and HALL / MAIRESSE (1995) found values between 0.22 and 0.34.

However, most of the studies considered here simply treat R&D as another form of investment and do not allow for the effects of the externalities mentioned above. Therefore, it is unclear whether such studies underestimate or overestimate the effects of R&D. JONES / WILLIAMS (1997) derived an endogenous growth model, which takes these externalities into account, and calibrated it to a range of plausible parameter values. They find that in most cases the excess returns to R&D (calculated as the social return minus the private return) are positive, but less than 20 per cent. We may add that due to the globalization power of the Internet the divergence between private and social returns to R&D might increase – not least if the Internet reinforces international knowledge spillovers. This raises problems for R&D cooperation.

If the large degree of risk and uncertainty in the innovation process as well as information asymmetries between capital markets and R&D spenders are taken into account, it is not surprising that large social returns to R&D can coincide with relatively low rates of R&D investment. JONES / WILLIAMS (1997) conclude for the USA that the optimal amount of R&D investment is about four times the amount actually invested. However, other studies found less overwhelming empirical evidence. BARTELSMAN ET AL.(1996) applied the Jones / Williams model to Dutch manufacturing firm-level data and found that the private rate of return probably underestimates social returns by only a few percentage points. Examining the effects of R&D on productivity in a panel of French and US manufacturing firms, MAIRESSE / HALL (1996) found that R&D earned a normal private rate of return in the USA during the 1980s. For selected sectors of German manufacturing, BÖNTE (1998) concluded that his results provide no evidence for "above-normal" rates of returns due to intra-industrial spillovers.

Another important source for externalities is international R&D spillovers, i.e. the impact of foreign R&D on domestic productivity and output. COE / HELPMAN (1995) captured these effects by augmenting the above mentioned total factor productivity equation with import-weighted foreign R&D stocks. For West Germany they calculated elasticities of total factor productivity with respect to foreign R&D of 0.056 (1971), 0.072 (1980) and 0.077 (1990). The elasiticities for France were a little bit lower: 0.045 (1971), 0.061 (1980) and 0.067 (1990), whereas the elasticities for Sweden were higher: 0.067 (1971), 0.087 (1980) and 0.093 (1990). BAYOUMI / COE / HELPMAN (1999) applied the same approach to a larger sample of countries and found important differences between the values of the coefficients for domestic and import-weighted foreign R&D for different groups of countries. Comparing the G-7 countries and small industrial countries, the coefficient of import-weighted R&D stocks has the same value, but the coefficient for domestic R&D turned out to be much smaller for small industrial countries. For developing countries they assume that R&D capital is constant, and the coefficient of import-weighted foreign R&D turned out to be clearly higher. To the extent that the Internet stimulates business-related services trade in particular and trade in general, the Internet might have trade-related growth effects.

Next one has to consider different possibilities of financing R&D. R&D can either be financed by companies or by government, and there is a lively controversy about the effects of government-financed R&D on output and productivity. In his summarizing overview GRILICHES (1995) concluded that most elasticity estimates are not sensitive to whether one uses total or only company-financed R&D stocks, but that there are other indications in the data that government-financed R&D produces less benefit than privately-financed R&D. Concretely, he presents estimations where the privately versus government-financed R&D mix variable has a significant positive coefficient, indicating that the premium on government-financed R&D is smaller, but still quite large. GRILICHES / LICHTENBERG (1984) found that spillovers between academic research and some types of government R&D and the private sector exist, but they are smaller than those between firms themselves. ACS / AUDRETSCH / FELDMAN (1994) concluded that small firms (particularly high-tech start-ups) might benefit more from such spillovers. Furthermore, ADAMS (1990) found the output of the academic science base is a major contributor to productivity growth, but the time lag is approximately twenty years. The Internet creates new options for finding venture capital, and it creates enormous opportunities in international R&D cooperation.

Connected to the controversy about privately or government-financed R&D are other empirical findings concerning basic research. GRILICHES (1995) presents estimation results where the basic research coefficient is highly significant and shows a rather large size. He concluded that firms which spend a larger fraction of their R&D on basic research are more productive and have a higher level of output relative to the other measured inputs, including R&D capital, and that this effect is relatively constant over time. Based on other estimation results and additional computations he concluded that the premium for basic research over the rest of R&D is 3 to 1 as far as its impact on productivity growth is concerned.

Secondly, one output of the innovation process can be used as a proxy variable for technological change and innovation: patent applications or the stock of patents. Such a proceeding has several advantages. On the one hand, this indicator variable avoids a lot of technical data problems; e.g. unlike R&D stock measures, no artificial depreciation rate must be assumed; on the other hand, it also includes the results of other knowledge sources apart from explicit R&D activities. BUDD / HOBBIS (1989a) estimated for UK manufacturing long-term output elasticities with respect to a constructed stock of patents between 0.21 and 0.23. In a second paper, they estimated with a slightly different approach long-term elasticities of patenting of 0.114 for France, Germany and the United Kingdom, whereas the elasticity for Japan was 0.135 (BUDD / HOBBIS 1989b). For the West German business sector in the period from 1960 to 1990, JUNGMITTAG / WELFENS

(1998) estimated an output elasticity of the real patent stock of 0.23. For a longer time period from 1960 to 1996 and with a slightly different approach, JUNGMITTAG / BLIND / GRUPP (1999) found output elasticities of the patent stock lying between 0.16 and 0.19. Altogether, these results suggest that the estimates of the output elasticities of the R&D stock and the patent stock are in most cases very similar and that they contribute substantially to economic growth. The Internet will stimulate growth in OECD countries to the extent it facilitates storage and dissemination of knowledge on the one hand; on the other hand Internet technology facilitates R&D specialization at the international level.

3.3 ICT as a General Purpose Technology?

For assessing the impact of ICT on economic growth, we have to differentiate between two kinds of innovations. Many innovations concern the generation of new products or changes of production processes within specific sectors. Some innovations, however, result in the development of new, general purpose technologies, i.e. broad technologies with wide applications (BRESNAHAN / TRAJTENBERG, 1995; HELPMAN, 1998). These general purpose technologies give rise to changes in a wide range of industries and probably affect production processes, interindustry relations, work organization and skill requirements (OECD, 2000). Two often cited historical examples for such epoch-making technologies are the steam engine and electricity (the electric motor), which caused the first and second industrial revolution. On the other hand, there were very important innovations in the past which affected only one sector but which had a great impact on overall economic growth. For example, mechanical spinning-machines developed in the second half of the eighteenth century in the UK (the spinning jenny by Hargraves (1767) and the water frame by Arkwright (1769) as well as the following incremental innovations) affected only textile production, but due to the fact that at that time a large share of economic activity in the UK was textile production, the productivity gains associated with this new technology had a significant impact on the UK's total economic performance.

Various scholars argue that ICT is such a general purpose technology with broad impact on many sectors of the economy. Furthermore, the advocates of the "New Economy" assert that ICT products create spillovers which are not appropriated by the investor or the consumer. Hence, ICT products might increase total output and income beyond what is indicated by the actual prices paid for it (ARK, 2000). Against this optimism some other scholars assign ICT the role of the modern "mechanical spinning-machine" because in their view the growth acceleration at the end of 20th century was mainly due to improved productivity growth in the ICT-producing sector (JORGENSEN / STIROH, 2000). Ultimately, it is a question of empirical research to assess the role of ICT in growth and structural change. However, it is a common feature of new general purpose technologies that it takes a long time before they are implemented (including organizational changes) and used in such a way that they could develop their abilities to the fullest (DAVID, 1991). In this case, the productivity gains of ICT will only be reflected in increased overall productivity with a rather large delay (ARK, 2000).

4. The Role of Telecommunications and the Internet for Trade and Growth

Jungmittag and Welfens presented three studies to assess the impact of telecommunications and the Internet on economic growth (JUNGMITTAG / WELFENS, 1998; WELFENS / JUNG-MITTAG, 2000; WELFENS / JUNGMITTAG, 2001b). In the following section we will summarize some of the major findings and highlight additional issues.

4.1 Telecommunications, Innovation and Economic Growth in Germany 1960 - 1990

In the first study alternative sources of technical progress were identified and approximated by means of indicator variables, which were then considered when estimating long-term production functions for the business sector of the Federal Republic of Germany, without agriculture, forestry, and fishing and without housing sector from 1960 until 1990 (JUNGMITTAG / WELFENS, 1998). They distinguished between technical progress which is the result of one's own research and development activities, and the import of technological know-how through licensing agreements. The first source of technical progress was approximated through the time lagged stock of patents at the German Patent Office (Deutsches Patentamt); the second was approximated by the real fees for licenses captured in the balance of payments of the Federal Republic of Germany. In addition, the use of telecommunications was integrated in the long-term production function in that it is approximated by the indicator variables – the number of annual telephone calls.

With the technological innovations and the role of information and communication explicitly taken into consideration, the extended Cobb-Douglas production function now is in logarithmic form:

$$(1) \qquad y_t = a + \alpha \cdot k_t + \beta \cdot l_t + \gamma \cdot pat_{t-2} + \delta \cdot lex_t + \varepsilon \cdot tc_t + u_t,$$

where y represents the output, k the capital employed and l the amount of labor (lower cases denote logarithms). The parameters α and β represent the partial production elasticities of the factors capital and labor. Furthermore, *pat* represents the stock of patents, *lex* the actual expenditure on licenses and *tc* the number of telephone calls.

For estimating the long-term production functions, the concept of the cointegration of time series introduced by Engle and Granger (cf. ENGLE / GRANGER, 1987) was used. This concept allows the differentiation between actual long-term relations and merely spurious regressions if time series are trending. Since in this study only the long-term relations and not the short-term dynamics between the output, the usual production factors and the indicator variables for technical progress, as well as for the role of information and communication were considered, first of all the first step of Engle and Granger's two-step procedure was applied, in which existing long-term relations were identified and estimated without specifying the short-term dynamics. However, the distribution of the estimators of the cointegrating vector provided by such a static regression is generally non-normal, and so inference cannot be drawn about the significance of the individual parameters by using the standard 't' tests. For this reason the three-step procedure, proposed by Engle and Yoo (cf. ENGLE / YOO, 1991) was subsequently used to remedy this shortcoming. Their third step, added to the Engle-Granger two-step procedure, provided a correction to the parameter estimates of the first stage static regression which made them asymptotically equivalent to FIML and provided a set of standard errors which allows the valid calculation of standard 't' tests. The superior long-term production function was then used to at least roughly assess the effects of the technical progress approximated by the indicator variables and of the need for information and communication, approximated by the number of telephone calls, as well as the impact of the usual production factors on economic growth from 1961 until 1990.

The estimation results for the unrestricted and restricted version of this long-term production function are reported in Table 8. A view of the *t*-values calculated for the estimates of the third step of the Engle / Yoo procedure shows that all coefficients of the unrestricted as well as the restricted estimation are unequal to zero at a significance level of 1 %. Therefore, all three indicator variables have a highly significant power of explanation. Furthermore, the magnitudes of their coefficients verify that the factors approximated by the indicator variables make contributions to real gross value-added that cannot be neglected. The estimates of the coefficients of the factors capital and labor also seem to be very reliable. They are rather similar to the estimates in SCHRÖER / STAHLECKER (1996) where a long-term Cobb-Douglas production function is estimated using quarterly data from 1970 until 1989. SCHRÖER / STAHLECKER (1996) introduced after a data mining process a dummy variable which changes the slope of the time trend to approximate a change of technical progress. The R^2s of 0.9977 and 0.9974 for the first step of the Engle / Granger procedure and 0.9976 and 0.9966 for the third step of the Engle / Yoo procedure indicate a very good fitting of the models to the observed data. The DW test statistics suggest that the presence of first order autocorrelation can be excluded. Turning to the EG test statistics it can be seen that the unrestricted as well as the restricted production function forms a cointegration relation at significance levels of 8.59 % and 2.61 %. Therefore the sum of the partial production elasticities is now permitted beyond all usual significance levels as the F-test shows. Based on these estimation and testing results, the restricted product function containing all three indicator variables is superior to other augmented production functions with only one or two indicator variables which had been considered during the empirical investigation, but are not reported here due to the limitation of space.

Table A8:   Estimation Results for the Augmented Production Function

Variable	First step of Engle/Granger		Third step of Engle/Yoo	
	unrestricted	$\hat{\alpha}+\hat{\beta}=1$	unrestricted	$\hat{\alpha}+\hat{\beta}=1$
Constant	-3.1574	-2.7882	-3.4344	-3.1174
	(-4.8813)[a]	(-5.5155)	(-12.8774)	(-8.4231)
k_t	0.4073	0.3634	0.4372	0.3448
	(4.9118)	(5.3738)	(11.2103)	(5.9142)
l_t	0.7460	0.6366	0.7893	0.6552
	(5.4446)	--	(15.9455)	--
pat_{t-2}	0.1611	0.1833	0.1738	0.2315
	(1.6913)	(1.9955)	(6.2744)	(3.4501)
lex_t	0.0494	0.0631	0.0498	0.0833
	(1.5696)	(2.2805)	(4.4865)	(3.5447)
tc_t	0.1580	0.1803	0.1390	0.1795
	(2.7992)	(3.5497)	(5.7917)	(4.2943)
D80	-0.0168	-0.0165	-0.0169	-0.0161
	(-2.1905)	(-2.1551)	(-7.6818)	(-2.9815)
D81	-0.0202	-0.0223	-0.0202	-0.0239
	(-2.6738)	(-3.0828)	(-8.7826)	(-4.3455)
R^2	0.9977	0.9974	0.9976	0.9973
R^2_{adj}	0.9970	0.9967	0.9969	0.9966
DW-test	2.0108	2.1136	--	--
EG-test	(28, 6)[b]	(28, 5)	--	--
	-5.3968	-5,6735	--	--
	(0.0859)[c]	(0.0261)	--	--
F-test of the restriction			1.4396 (0.2345)[c]	

[a] empirical *t*-values in brackets but statistical conclusions on the base of usual t-tests are only permitted if the third of the Engle/Yoo procedure has been applied; [b] Number of observations available after forming lags and first differences and number of I(0) variables in brackets; [c] Significance levels in brackets.

Table A9:   Sources of Growth in the Business Sector, Germany 1961 - 1990

Source	Average annual percentage changes						
	61 - 90	61 - 65	66 - 70	71 - 75	76 - 80	81 - 85	86 – 90
k_t	1.5	2.5	1.9	1.8	1.1	0.8	1.0
l_t	0.2	0.7	0.1	-0.6	0.5	-0.6	1.1
pat_{t-2}	0.1	0.3	0.2	-0.3	0.2	0.1	0.3
lex_t	0.3	0.4	0.3	0.3	0.0	0.0	0.8
tc_t	1.1	1.2	1.7	1.2	1.3	0.7	0.7
Total : fitted	3.3	5.2	4.3	2.3	3.2	0.9	4.0
realized	3.3	5.2	4.4	1.7	3.6	1.1	3.8

Note: Differences between the sums of the individual components of the growth rates and the fitted total growth rates are caused by rounding up and down and by joint effects.

Due to the approximation of different sources or causes of technical progress and of information and communication by means of appropriate indicator variables, it was then possible to assess, at least roughly, the effects of these variables as well as of the usual production factors on the growth of real gross value-added. The results of the ex-post forecasts of average annual growth rates for the whole observation period as well as for different subperiods are reported in Table 9. The comparison of the realized total and the forecasted total growth rates of real gross value-added in the business sector without agriculture, forestry, and fishing and without housing rental shows a good fitting of the model to the observed data. Only in the first half of the seventies when the first oil price crisis takes place does the model overestimate the growth rate by 0.6 percentage points. Partly to even things out, the model underestimates growth by 0.4 percentage points in the second half of the seventies.

Turning to the individual factors, it can be seen that the development of the capital stock has the greatest impact on the growth rates of gross value-added in most cases, accounting for 0.8 to 2.5 percentage points. This result is in accord with the results for other countries (cf. BUDD / HOBBIS, 1989a, BUDD / HOBBIS, 1989b and COE / MOGHADAM, 1993). The influence of telephone calls (as an indicator for information and communication) is in second position, accounting for 0.7 to 1.7 percentage points of the average annual growth rates. Here, it must be stressed, that even in phases of low growth rates this influence was a substantial engine of the remaining economic growth. The impact of the factor labor on economic growth is strongly influenced by fluctuations of the number of employees due to business cycles. Especially the reductions of the number of employees after the first and second oil price crises had negative impacts on economic growth. On the other hand, the strong increase of the number of employees in the second half of the eighties fostered economic growth. The lagged stock of patents and the real license expenditures had in most cases a moderate influence on growth. Nevertheless, these two sources of technical progress account for slightly more than 12 % of the total increase of gross value-added. Their share increases even to 27.5 % in the second half of the eighties, mainly due to the strong increase of real license expenditures.

Altogether, the results suggest that the considered sources of technical progress as well as the increasing requirement for information and communication contribute substantially to economic growth in West Germany.

4.2 Growth and Employment Effects of an Internet Flat Rate in Germany

The second study was concerned with the impact of an Internet flat rate on growth and employment in Germany (WELFENS / JUNGMITTAG, 2000). The starting point of this study was the fact that the dissemination of knowledge and the efficient information sharing that results from it are of central importance to economic growth. Assuming that (given a liberal regulatory environment) Internet use will become a means of knowledge dissemination in the middle and long term – at low rates determined by common sense or by competition – and will contribute to growth on a similar scale as telecommunications, then – going back to the elastic-ities assessment in JUNGMITTAG / WELFENS (1998) – a one percent increase in knowledge dissemination via the Internet would drive economic growth in the corporate sector (excluding the atypical sectors of agriculture and forestry, fishing and residential rentals) up by a good 0.18 percent. The accelerated information sharing associated with increasingly intensive telecommunications network use in the latter half of the 20th century has had positive diffusion effects on product and process innovation. At times, there has been accelerated demand for telecommuni-cations based on network effects. For existing telecom users in the corporate sec-tor, the user value of telecommunications rose as other companies increasingly availed themselves of modern telecommunications services such as fax and ISDN. In the case of Internet use, which is still at an early expansion stage in Germany, there are most likely considerable positive network effects to be realized. More-over, the Internet is a novel way to link creative potential in the household, corpo-rate and science sectors, thus promoting innovation.

Table A10: Persons Employed in the Information Industry 1997-1999

Sector	Persons Employed			Change (%)	
	1997	1998	1999*	97/98	98/99
Hardware, Software & Serviceı	**973,500**	**1,001,500**	**1,037,420**	**3**	**4**
Information Technologyı	379,000	396,000	433,160	4	9
- Manufacture of Office Machines and DV Devices	*147,000*	*128,000*	*135,680*	*-13*	*6*
- Software and IT services	*232,000*	*268,000*	*297,480*	*16*	*11*
Telecommunications	322,000	338,000	338,000	5	0
- Manufacture of Optical Telecom-munications Devices	*101,000*	*101,000*	*101,000*	*0*	*0*
- Telephone/telecommunication services	*221,000*	*237,000*	*237,000*	*7*	*0*
Electronic Components	83,500	83,500	81,500	0	-2
Entertainment Electronics	41,000	36,000	35,280	-12	-2
Specialised Dealers and Distribution*	148,000	148,000	149,480	0	1
Media	**692,000**	**691,020**	**698,690**	**0**	**1**
Publishing Industry	222,000	217,000	219,170	-2	1
Print Industry	285,000	284,000	284,000	0	0
Film & Video Production, Rental, & Distribution; Movie theatres	24,000	32,000	32,640	33	2
Radio & TV, Program Production	72,000	62,000	65,100	-14	6
Correspondence & News Offices, Free-lance Journalists	38,000	44,000	45,760	16	4
Book, Magazine & Music Trade*	51,000	52,020,	52,020	2	0
Total	**1,665,500**	**1,692,520**	**1,736,110**	**2**	**3**

* estimated

Source: Professional Association for Information Technology in the VDMA and ZVEI; Federal Statistics Office, (1) FV Communications Technology; (2) FV Construction Ele-ments

If flat rate pricing brought about a 20 % price reduction, the share of the population having Internet access at home – at a conservative estimate – would rise from 16 % to 17 % (greater reductions in usage costs are conceivable in the long term). Assuming a proportionality between Internet access and knowledge dissemination, the latter would be increased by roughly 6.5 %, which would in turn generate a percentage point of added economic growth in the corporate sector. A similar scenario results if one uses the broad definition of Internet use. Here, a 20 % price reduction would cause Germany´s 33 % share to rise to approximately 38 %, implying corporate sector growth effects of just over 2 %. Meanwhile, the broader indicator naturally is fraught with more uncertainty. If this assessment is applied to the economy as a whole (including the housing industry, agriculture and forestry, fishery), a realistic growth surplus of a good one-half percentage point emerges for Germany as a consequence of flat rate pricing – with an implied price reduction of 20%.

Even today, the employment growth in the information industry contributes greatly to overall employment growth. In all, the number of employed persons rose by 128,000 between 1997 and 1998. This is equivalent to an increase of approximately 0.4 %. Alone in the Hardware, Software and Services subsector, the number of employed persons grew by 27,900, an increase of approximately 2.9 % (see Table 10). This sector, with a 2.7 % share of the total labor force in 1997 and a 2.8 % share in 1998, supplied 21.8 % of Germany's total employment growth. Its contribution to employment becomes even more pronounced when we take a look at its Software and IT Services subsector. Here, the number of employed persons rose by 36,000 from 1997 to 1998. At shares of 0.65 % and 0.75 % of the total labor force for the years 1997 and 1998, respectively, this subsector was responsible for 28.1 % of the total growth in employment. It also contributed significantly to the rise in employed persons from 1998 to 1999. While Hardware, Software and Services together register a growth of employed persons of "only" approximately 4 %, the figure is approximately 11 % for just the Software and IT Services subsector.

Again assuming a proportionality – between Internet use and employment – a 20% reduction in Internet use costs (using the "At-Home Internet Access" indicator) would mean an increase in employed persons in the Software and IT Services subsector of roughly 18,500 beyond the expected growth. If one uses the broader indicator for Internet access, which is probably the more relevant one in this case, the number of employed persons added in this subsector would be roughly 45,000. Assuming this proportionality for the information industry as a whole, there would be 108,000 newly employed persons using the "At-Home Internet Access" indicator, and 263,000 additional employed persons using the broader Internet access indicator – all in addition to the expected trend-driven growth. In a more drastic scenario assuming a 50 % reduction in Internet use costs – which is, however, subject to a considerably higher uncertainty, as it entails shifting to the edge of the available sample of observations – then the consequences of the narrow and wide indicator definitions switch. While the broader indicator for Internet access now shows additional employment of 360,000 persons, the "At-Home Internet Access" indicator would lead to roughly 430,000 additional employed persons in the information industry. This result also implies that a drastic price reduction would decrease the validity of the broader indicator for private Internet use and increase the importance of "At-Home Internet Access". Thus, the present conclusion is absolutely in agreement with intuitive expectations. In the face of unemployment figures near four million at the turn of the year 1999/2000, the possibility of creating 100,000 to 400,000 additional jobs through more liberal price-setting policies in the Internet sector should be seen as momentous for Germany in any case.

A number of more indirect effects could not be quantified in greater detail within the scope of this middle-term analysis. For example, the Internet has other demand-side growth effects due to its increasing utilization of realizable transaction cost reductions. The commodities in question can thus afford a rise in demand, which translates to a positive real income effect. Meanwhile, it cannot be ruled out that the Internet-based growth of some sectors will be connected with shrinking effects in other sectors. Based on US experiences, a positive net effect can be assumed with a high degree of certainty. Moreover, higher Internet use - rates and more favorable conditions for Internet use in households and businesses are crucial for Germany in its international competition for location. Germany could attract more direct investments, especially in the sector of communications-intensive industries, and thus reduce its international weakness in per capita direct investment influx in the OECD sector, which has been in evidence for years (naturally, this would also involve developments in the corporate tax reform and other measures).

Figure A4: Actual and Desired Levels of Teleworking in Europe

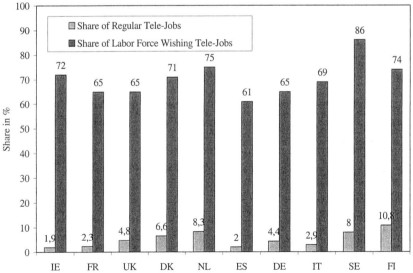

Source: EcaTT (1999)

Finally, a powerful and ubiquitous Internet facilitates the start-up of new businesses and the creation of virtual businesses and considerably increases their chances for growth. Thus, the American City Business Journal writes that small businesses that use the Internet grow 46 % faster than those that don't use it (INTERNET ECONOMY INDICATORS, 1999). In Germany's Business-to-Business sector – especially in small and medium-sized businesses – there is considerable room for expansion. The same applies to teleworking, where Germany has only remained in the European center field to date (ECaTT, 1999 and INSTITUT DER DEUTSCHEN WIRTSCHAFT, 1999) – even though employed persons in all European countries have shown a marked interest in this mode of working (see Figure 4).

So flat rate pricing will lead to a steep rise in demand for private and corporate Internet use. This will likely result in increased investment in transmission capacities, due to time-related bottlenecks. The resulting employment effects will likely represent a rising share of the predicted increase in total employed persons (using the broader Internet use indicator) in the total information industry. Flat rate pricing at the retail level demands the introduction of similar models in the wholesale sector or rather in relations between dominant network operators and service providers (CAVE / CROWTHER, 1999).

Meanwhile, there are indeed ways for Internet providers to influence the times at which users access the system. One conceivable option is that of bonus points for users who go on the Internet at off-peak times, where the bonus points could be used as "admission fees" for buying information stored in user clubs or for free access to certain services. Other user incentives are also conceivable in the interest of optimizing Internet use.

According to a number of current studies, the cost of data traffic based on Internet protocol are significantly lower than in conventional telephone traffic; orders of magnitude of 1:10 and more are quoted. This creates interesting growth perspectives for Internet telephony services and other Internet-based services. Still, the Internet expansion potential hinted at here can only be realized if new types– albeit cost-oriented by all means – of flat rate models are applied at the wholesale and retail level.

4.3 Telecommunications and Foreign Trade

International trade among OECD countries and worldwide has strongly increased after World War II. Explaining trade traditionally rests upon differences in factors supplies and relative prices on the one hand (survey CAVES / FRANKEL / JONES, 1990); on the other hand Schumpeterian influences associated with product cycle trade or trade with differentiated products plays a major role; the latter has stimulated models with monopolistic competition (e.g. DIXIT / NORMAN, 1980; KRUGMAN, 1979; LANCASTER, 1980; HELPMAN / KRUGMAN, 1990). Technological aspects also are important for goods characterized by static and dynamic scale effects. A very important link exists between per capita income and trade: on the one hand rising per capita income will raise the demand for differentiated products; on the other hand an increase in national output will raise the demand for intermediate and final products. Thus the impact of a rising aggregate output can – with population given – reflect two different links between trade and income.

From a theoretical point of view, transaction costs and information costs play an important role for international trade, but little empirical research has been made about this. Transaction and information costs basically are like tariffs so that exports and imports are affected negatively. At the same time such costs add to overall costs which reduces overall profitable output.

Establishing and expanding international business always involves the use, storage and processing of relevant information – information about suppliers, markets, prices, technology trends and export or import markets. Precise and adequate information is required for choosing optimum market penetration strategies. With reduced international communication costs expanding into international markets becomes more easy, and therefore modern and more efficient telephone systems can be expected to have a positive impact on trade. From a theoretical perspective – taking into account that foreign direct investment can be an alternative for serving foreign markets which depends on the size of firm-internal transaction costs relative to the costs of market transactions – technological progress in telecommunications might create a bias in favor of more firm-internal transactions. Indeed, in a dynamic perspective there might be both more foreign direct investment and more trade, the latter reflecting creation of a larger market radius as a consequence of falling international information and transaction costs while a rise of FDI could reflect the interplay of the enlargement of market radius and of reduced firm-internal transaction costs.

Given the gradual EU liberalization of telecommunications services – beginning in 1984 already and culminating in the 1998 deadline for the liberalization of network operation and telecommunications services – one may anticipate that international information and communication costs will fall; it would indeed be interesting to assess the potential impact of telecommunication systems on trade in Europe and elsewhere. In this paper we focused on the link between the telecommunication system and trade within the gravity approach (WELFENS / JUNGMITTAG, 2001b).

EU integration created a customs union by 1968 and thereafter the single market by end-1992 so that trade barriers have been reduced over time. Among the important elements of the single market program the opening-up of public procurement is rather important; moreover, the elimination of customs controls has reduced international transaction costs. This could mean that the role of information costs for trade has increased over time.

International trade relations can be modeled in various ways. Particularly prominent is the gravity equation which is based on market size in the importing and the exporting country on the one hand; on the other hand distance plays a crucial role. Certainly, there are also other important variables, including the role of telecommunications which will be analyzed here.

The natural point of departure is that international telephone calls are an important element for finding out about and arranging sales abroad or profitable imports. The number of telecommunication minutes is one potential proxy variable for measuring international telecommunications. From an economic perspective increasing international telecommunication links amount to a reduction of information and trading costs. While it is true that the internet has increasingly become an important source of information at the beginning of the 21st century it is realistic to assume that traditional telephony has been the dominant source of international information in the 1990s – and international telephony indeed will continue to play an important role in the future. From a data perspective it is important in principle that data on international telecommunications are available in a distinct way: we know how many international telephone calls went from country i to j (there is, however, depending on national competition conditions and prices, respectively, a potential bias with respect to originating calls coming relatively more often from i or j). With internet data traffic the direction of information diffusion is more difficult to assess. This holds particularly since preferred routings often use the US; even intra-Asian internet traffic is partly routed via the US which offers a cheap hub function due to low prices in leased lines and IP services (FCC, 2000).

By taking into account the role of telecommunications in a gravity model – as a new element in research – we can offer a better explanation of international trade than in previous approaches. Moreover, we also have the opportunity to come up with, based on refined empirical analysis, more adequate forecast analysis which could be particularly relevant for eastern Europe and other areas in the world economy. Assuming that telecom density and the use of telecommunications are proportionate we can furthermore provide an estimate of the trade potential for the case that telecom densities should increase in the future in eastern Europe and Asian (and other) NICs. With respect to eastern Europe EU accession can be expected to stimulate the growth of telecommunication penetration rates.

The main result of our analysis – summarized in Table 11 – is that we can for the first time provide empirical evidence of the positive impact of telecommunications on trade. Moreover, we find that the elasticities of GDP in both the exporting and the importing country are smaller in the augmented model than traditionally. This implies that trade generation effects of output growth in eastern Europe and NICs will be smaller than assumed traditionally. At the same time this points to the enormous relevance of adequate telecommunication liberalization and investment-enhancing regulation in the telecommunications sector; in particular this could be relevant for the Stability Pact and the economic reconstruction of the western Balkans, respectively (WELFENS, 2001d).

Table A11:   Results for the Restricted Estimations of the Augmented Gravity Model

	(1) 1995	(2) 1996	(3) 1997	(4) 1995	(5) 1996	(6) 1997
Const.	3.676	3.830	3.892	3.407	3.562	3.665
	(8.113)	(8.404)	(8.213)	(7.463)	(7.720)	(7.644)
$\log(GDP_i)$	0.619	0.603	0.595	0.638	0.624	0.609
	(8.127)	(7.926)	(7.412)	(8.356)	(8.102)	(7.540)
$\log(GDP_j)$	0.481	0.447	0.439	0.500	0.467	0.452
	(7.031)	(6.433)	(6.024)	(7.215)	(6.569)	(6.150)
$\log(DIST_{ij})$	-0.600	-0.602	-0.600	-0.622	-0.628	-0.625
	(-7.089)	(-7.098)	(-6.810)	(-7.347)	(-7.307)	(-7.110)
Language	-0.040	-0.104	-0.110	0.000	-0.061	-0.073
	(-0.260)	(-0.679)	(-0.728)	(0.003)	(-0.385)	(-0.472)
EU	0.293	0.241	0.264	0.307	0.257	0.277
	(2.716)	(2.285)	(2.259)	(2.843)	(2.426)	(2.378)
$\log(TM_{ij} * TM_{ji})$	0.218	0.237	0.241			
	(5.413)	(5.866)	(5.758)			
$\log(TM_{ij} + TM_{ji})$				0.408	0.442	0.456
				(5.042)	(5.377)	(5.456)
Adj. R^2	0.908	0.905	0.893	0.906	0.902	0.891

1) t-statistics in brackets. White's heteroskedasticity-consistent estimators of the variance matrix of the regression coefficients are used to calculate t statistics..

5. Some Long-Term Aspects

In the US productivity growth in the 1980s and 1990s has benefited from growing trade – indeed mainly from rising import penetration as is shown in the empirical analysis of MANN (1998); she also shows that Germany had no significant productivity-enhancing effect from trade. This might reflect lack of flexibility of firms in Germany´s tradable sector, but it also could indicate the different regional trade orientation of the US and Germany over time. While the US has strongly increased imports from Asian NICs which increasingly have realized high R&D-GDP ratios and thus can be expected to export more technology-intensive products over time, Germany´s imports from Asia have been rather modest.

A strange finding for Germany also concerns the fact that labor productivity in the high technology sector was lower than average in the 1990s (WELFENS 2002; GRIES/ JUNGMITTAG/WELFENS, 2001a). This might point both to weaknesses of Germany´s high technology firms and to inefficient R&D subsidization. From this perspective Germany seems to be rather poorly positioned to exploit growing high technology dynamics in the OECD. One may also point out that the R&D expenditure-GDP ratio reached a historical peak of 2.9% in 1989 but then fell – when Theo Waigel was Minister of Finance – to 2.3% in 1998; this ratio has not improved in 1999/2000; and the new Minister of Finance, Hans Eichel (a teacher!), seems to be determined to pursue the benign neglect attitude for R&D

promotion. By contrast, the OECD´s leading country in terms of R&D-GDP ratio, Sweden, recorded a ratio of 4% in 2000. Germany´s expenditure on education also is meager: 4.7% in 1998 is slightly more than half the top figures of roughly 8% in Scandinavian countries and also much worse than the US with about 6%. Add to this the fact that Germany ranks – according to OECD analysis focusing on employment, output, exports and R&D in ICT – among the lower third in ICT among the 29 OECD countries. Finally, Germany´ labor markets are rather inflexible and tax reform has been biased in favor of large multinational companies which undermines the growth perspectives of new firms in the digital sector.

Germany also is facing problems in the telecommunications sector where the former monopoly operator – under the supervision of the Ministry of Finance – has not been fully privatized. This is much in contrast to the UK, Spain, Italy and several other OECD countries. In addition the internet subsidiary of Deutsche Telekom has dropped its offer of a flat rate for normal telephone users (narrow band and ISDN) as of January 2001. This is much to the disadvantage of a full exploitation of digital growth opportunities; to make matters worse, Deutsche Telekom has offered as a "substitute" DSL which not only is not available at short notice but cannot be used in most parts of eastern Germany where modern glass fiber networks imply the impossibility of benefiting from DSL. The DSL technology is a kind of turbo for fixed networks based on standard twisted copper lines. Thereby Deutsche Telekom is directly undermining the growth potential of eastern Germany which is facing problems in keeping up with west German growth figures.

At the bottom line we find that the ICT sector is a crucial element for productivity growth and long term structural change in the US, Japan and Europe. We support the basic conclusion of VAN ARK (2001, p.20):" ...part of the U.S. advantage during the late 1990s can also be ascribed to greater productivity gains from the ICT-using sector. Indeed European countries have not succeeded to extend their increase in employment sufficiently to ICT-using industries. Various reasons may explain these differences, but lack of structural reforms in product and labor markets may be one reason for Europe's lack of employment and productivity growth in the ICT-using sector." Since the role of the ICT-using sectors is so important for labor productivity growth in OECD countries the renewal of the old economy partly is associated with digital dynamics. Comparing the US and the EU the European lead in mobile telecommunications could become a crucial EU advantage if UMTS networks are combined with innovative digital products and broad regional market integration. While the European Commission has proposed expansion of broadband networks in the Community there are not enough incentives for digital innovations. Both national and supranational economic policies – including innovation policies - have not paid much attention to the imperfections of information markets; since digital information stands for experience goods or confidence goods so that the quality of the respective product is difficult to assess and thus the marginal willingness to pay is rather low it is quite important to promote approaches which combine digital products with reputation building and market segmentation. Only with strong market segmentation will average revenues in digital markets be rather high (WELFENS, 2002) so that investors in the digital information market will be able to generated sustained high revenues necessary to finance high costs of investment and innovation.

In highly competitive international telecommunications markets only a few dynamic competitors will achieve high profit rates; revenue from mobile date traffic may well offset the falling per customer revenue from mobile voice telephony – here both Japan and the EU offer encouraging developments at the beginning of the 21st century. Moreover, provision of quality information and customer-taylored knowledge could be quite important for a profitable new economy. The tendencies observed in Germany and other EU countries are worrying: In most EU countries leading internet providers are forming alliances with tabloid papers and not with top publishers from the scientific community, but fishing for digital mass markets with almost zero willingness to pay could be a favorite dead end of internet portals. There might be no sustainable knowledge economy if segmented profitable information markets cannot be established. Since information markets are known to be rather imperfect markets government support for selected innovative projects and for quality certification agencies should be considered. More structural reforms in Europe and revised budget priorities also are needed in the Old World.

Appendix: Methodological Issues in Growth Statistics

Comparing Germany / Euroland and the US there are considerable differences in statistical procedures concerning the measurement of inflation and growth, respectively. Since 1995 the US BEA has been using a chained Fisher quantity index for determining real GDP. While the US approach uses current price structures – taking into account substitution effects which tends to generate rates of growth in the year following the base period which are smaller than those generated with traditional approaches – Germany and most other EU countries use a Laspeyres price index. US hedonic pricing approaches for measuring inflation reduces the US inflation rate and a fortiori raises the real growth rate. Since Germany and most other EU countries were not using hedonic pricing there is a bias in transatlantic growth comparisons. The overall bias from the US use of the Fisher chain index and from hedonic pricing is in the range of 0.3-0.4 percentage points (DEUTSCHE BUNDESBANK, 2001).

Table A12:   The Tax Burden on Low and Middle Wages

(Income tax plus social security contributions in 1999 as % of labour costs)

	(1)	(2)	(3)	(4)
B	34.9	41.3	51.2	52.4
DK	14.6	31.0	40.9	40.9
D	31.1	34.5	47.0	47.0
EL	34.3	36.8	35.2	36.5
E	28.4	30.3	332.6	36.2
F	31.5	38.8	40.4	43.5
IRL	-5.2	19.9	21.5	24.7
I	28.2	37.4	44.2	44.7
L	4.7	11.4	30.0	27.9
NL	21.8	34.2	40.3	41.1
A	19.0	31.8	41.7	43.7
P	22.0	26.0	30.3	32.1
FIN	27.6	40.3	43.3	45.4
S	40.9	44.5	48.8	49.7
UK	14.2	23.8	26.2	25.5
US	12.6	24.5	29.3	29.8
JP	14.7	14.7	18.3	18.4

(1) single individual with two children, earning 67 % of the APW (Average wage of production workers).
(2) married couple with two children and a singel earner at the APW.
(3) single individual with no child, earning 67% of the APW.
(4) married couple with two children and two earners, with earnings split between the two partners at 100% and 67% of the APW.
Source: European Commission (2001), European Economy, Supplement A, No 1

Table A13: Public Expenditure on Education (% of GDP)

	1995	1996	1997				
	Total	Total	Pre-primary + Not Allo-cated	Primary	Secon-dary	Terti-ary	Total
B (1)	n.a.	n.a.	0.7	1.2	2.7	1.2	5.7
DK	8.0	8.8	1.2	1.8	3.2	1.8	8.0
D(2)	4.8	4.7	0.6	:	3.0	1.1	4.7
EL(3)	2.9	3.1	:	1.1	1.3	0.8	3.2
E	4.9	4.8	0.3	1.2	2.2	0.9	4.6
F	6.0	6.0	0.7	1.2	3.0	1.1	6.0
IRL	5.2	5.0	0.1	1.6	2.0	1.3	4.9
I	4.7	4.9	0.5	1.1	2.2	0.7	4.5
L	4.4	4.3	0.0	1.9	2.1	0.2	4.1
NL	5.2	5.3	0.4	1.2	1.9	1.4	4.8
A	5.6	6.5	0.6	1.3	2.9	1.7	6.4
P	5.8	5.7	0.6	1.7	2.4	1.0	5.7
FIN	7.3	7.4	0.8	1.6	2.3	2.0	6.7
S	7.8	8.0	0.5	2.1	3.2	2.1	7.9
UK	5.2	5.1	0.4	1.1	2.1	1.1	4.7
EU-15	5.2	5.3	0.5	0.9	2.5	1.1	5.0

Includes public institutions and government-dependent private institutions
(1) The data for B are for 1994
(2) The data for D include primary and secondary combined
(3) The data for EL include pre-primary and primary combined
Sources: European Commission (2001), European Economy, Supplement A, No 1

Table A14:   ICT Sectors in Europe and the US, Value Added (% of GDP)

	1992	1995	1996	1997	1998	1999	95/99 annual change
B		3.3	3.5	3.5	3.8	4.1	8.6
D	3.5	3.4	3.3	3.6	3.7	3.9	5.1
E		2.8	3.0	3.2	3.4	3.6	12.6
F	3.9	3.8	3.9	4.0	4.1	4.3	6.2
IRL		6.5	6.7	7.5	7.3	7.6	17.8
I	3.4	3.3	3.3	3.3	3.5	3.7	10.3
NL		4.3	4.4	4.5	4.7	5.0	7.9
A		4.7	4.4	4.2	4.4	4.8	1.0
P		3.4	3.5	3.7	4.0	4.3	12.5
FIN		4.3	4.6	5.5	5.5	5.8	21.4
S		4.3	4.8	5.4	5.9	6.5	16.3
UK	5.0	5.2	5.2	5.2	5.4	5.6	7.3
EU11	3.8	3.6	3.7	3.8	4.0	4.2	7.7
US	5.0	5.3	5.5	6.1	6.4	6.8	12.9

Source: CSFB

Table A15:   Spending on Information and Communication Technology (% of GDP)

	1992	1993	1994	1995	1996	1997	1998	1999	2000
B	5.4	5.5	5.4	5.4	5.7	6.2	6.1	6.7	7.1
Dk	6.1	6.4	6.1	6.2	6.4	6.7	6.6	7.0	7.3
D	5.3	5.5	5.2	5.1	5.2	5.6	6.2	6.6	7.0
EL	2.4	2.3	3.7	3.8	3.9	4.1	4.8	5.5	5.9
E	3.8	3.8	3.7	3.7	3.9	4.1	4.5	5.0	5.3
F	5.7	6.0	5.7	5.8	6.0	6.5	7.0	7.6	8.0
IRL	5.4	5.2	5.8	5.7	5.8	5.5	5.3	5.3	5.2
I	3.6	3.8	4.1	4.1	4.1	4.3	4.9	5.5	5.9
NL	6.4	6.4	6.3	6.3	6.6	7.0	7.3	7.8	8.1
A	4.9	5.1	4.5	4.6	4.7	5.2	5.7	6.2	6.5
P	2.7	2.9	4.4	4.8	4.9	5.1	5.8	6.1	8.3
FIN	4.6	5.1	5.5	5.5	5.9	6.0	6.3	6.8	7.0
S	7.4	8.3	7.6	7.5	7.4	8.1	9.0	9.6	10.1
UK	7.1	7.4	7.2	7.8	7.8	7.8	7.5	8.0	8.4
EUR-12	4.9	5.1	5.0	5.1	5.2	5.5	6.0	6.5	6.9
EU-15	5.3	5.5	5.4	5.5	5.6	6.0	6.4	6.9	7.2
US	7.1	7.3	7.4	7.5	7.7	7.7	8.0	8.1	8.3

Source: EITO OBSERVATORY (2000); D = Germany

Table A16: **ICT Production Effects, Contribution to TFP Growth over the 1990's (% Points)**

| | TFP Growth Increase in the EU's ICT Sector identical to that in the US | | Two Scenarios for 1995-1998 | |
| | | | No TFP Growth Increase in the EU's ICT Sector | TFP Growth Increase in EU ICT Sector = 50% of that in the US |
	1990-1995	1995-1998		
Belgium	0.16	0.22	0.14	0.18
Denmark	0.04	0.06	0.04	0.05
Germany	0.13	0.19	0.12	0.16
Greece	0.02	0.04	0.03	0.03
Spain	0.09	0.14	0.09	0.12
France	0.14	0.25	0.15	0.20
Ireland	1.09	2.17	1.41	1.79
Italy	0.13	0.19	0.12	0.15
Netherlands	0.18	0.27	0.18	0.22
Austria	0.10	0.18	0.11	0.14
Portugal	0.11	0.22	0.13	0.17
Finland	0.16	0.38	0.25	0.31
Sweden	0.15	0.27	0.17	0.22
UK	0.17	0.33	0.21	0.27
EU15	0.14	0.24	0.15	0.19
US	0.23	0.50		

Source: Mc Morrow, K./ Roeger, W.: Potential Output: Measurement Methods, "New" Economy Influences and Scenarios for 2001-2010 – A Comparison of the EU15 and the US; Economic Papers Nr. 150, April 2001, p. 69.

Table A17:   Sectoral Developments in the Euro Area[1] and the USA

		Share in nominal value added		Growth in real value added		Growth in employment		Growth in labour pro-ductivity	
		1991	1998	1991-98	1995-98	1991-98	1995-98	1991-98	1995-98
		%	%	%	%	%	%	%	%
ICT producing sectors, manu-facturing	EU	0.9	0.7	6.5	11.5	-5.6	-2.3	12.9	14.2
	USA	1.5	1.8	20.9	25.6	1.4	3.5	19.2	21.3
ICT producing sectors, servi-ces	EU	3.6	4.2	5.5	8.1	-0.5	0.1	6.1	7.9
	USA	4	4.8	6.3	7.8	3.9	5.3	2.3	2.4
ICT using sectors, manu-facturing	EU	4.5	3.9	0.8	1.6	-3	-1.1	3.9	2.7
	USA	3.4	3	2.4	2.9	-0.9	0.1	3.3	2.7
ICT using sectors, ser-vices	EU	11.3	12	2.4	3.2	2.2	2.9	0.2	0.3
	USA	10.4	13.1	4.7	7.4	3.4	4.5	1.2	2.7
Manufacturing	EU	21	18.6	0.7	1.5	-2.5	-0.6	3.3	2.1
	USA	17.4	16.4	4.5	4.1	0.3	0.6	4.2	3.5
Business servi-ces	EU	47.9	51.8	2.2	2.7	1	1.8	1.2	0.9
	USA	48.3	52.7	4.8	6.6	2.6	2.9	2.2	3.7
Total economy	EU	100	100	1.5	1.9	-0.3	0.4	1.8	1.4
	USA	100	100	3.5	4	1.8	2	1.7	2

1) Euro area estimate based on Germany, France, Italy and Finland, which together account for around 73 % of euro area nominal gross value added.

Note for EA: Owing to the rapid decline of measured prices in the ICT producing manufacturing sector, its share in nominal value added decreased, despite high rates of growth in real value added. Manufacturing and business services include the ICT

Note for USA: Owing to the rapid decline of measured prices in the ICT producing manufacturing sector, its share in nominal value added hardly increased, despite high rates of growth in real value added. Manufacturing and business services include the ICT sectors sectors.

Source: ECB, Monthly Bulletin, July 2001

References

ACS, Z., AUDRETSCH, D., FELDMAN, M. (1994), R&D Spillovers and Recipient Firm Size, in: The Review of Economics and Statistics, 76, pp. 336–340.

ADAMS, J. (1990), Fundamental Stocks of Knowledge and Productivity Growth, in: Journal of Political Economy, 98, pp. 673 – 702.

ARK, B. van (2001), The Renewal of the Old Economy: An International Comparative Perspective, STI Working Papers 2001/5, Paris: OECD.

ARK, B. van (2000), Measuring Productivity in the "New Economy": Towards a European Perspective, in: De Economist, 148, 87 – 105.

ARK, B. van, MONNIKHOF, E., MULDER, N. (1999), Productivity in Services: An International Comparative Perspective, Canadian Journal of Economics, Vol. 32, 471-499.

BARDY, R. (1974), Die Produktivität von Forschung und Entwicklung, Meisenheim am Glan.

BARTELSMAN, E., LEEUWEN, G., van, NIEUWENHUIJSEN, H., ZEELENBERG, K. (1996), R&D and Productivity Growth: Evidence from Firm-Level Data in the Netherlands, Paper presented at the Conference of the European Economic Association, Istanbul.

BASSANINI, A., SCARPETTA, VISCO, I. (2000), Knowledge, Technology and Economic Growth: Recent Evidence from OECD Countries, mimeo, Paris: OECD.

BAYOUMI, T., COE, D.T., HELPMAN, E. (1999), R&D Spillovers and Global Growth, in: Journal of International Economics, 47, pp. 399 – 428.

BÖNTE, W. (1998), Wie produktiv sind Investitionen in Forschung und Entwicklung, Diskussionspapier, Institut für Allokation und Wettbewerb, Universität Hamburg.

BOSWORTH, B.P., TRIPLETT, J.E. (2000), What´s New About the New Economy? IT Economic Growth and Productivity, Brookings Institution, mimeo.

BRESNAHAN, T.F. (1999), Computing, in: MOWERY, D.C., ed. (1999), U.S. Industry in 2000: Studies in Competitive Performance, Washington, D.C.: National Academy Press, 215-244.

BRESNAHAN, T., TRAJTENBERG, M. (1995), General Purpose Technologies: "Engines of Growth"?, in: Journal of Econometrics, 65, 83 – 108.

BUDD, A., HOBBIS, S. (1989a), Cointegration, Technology and the Long-Run Production Function, Discussion Paper, London Business School Centre for Economic Forecasting.

BUDD, A., HOBBIS, S. (1989b), Output Growth and Measure of Technology, Discussion Paper, London Business School Centre for Economic Forecasting.

CAMERON, C. (1998), Innovation and Growth: A Survey of the Empirical Evidence, Working Paper, Nuffield College, Oxford.

CAVE, M., CROWTHER, P. (1999), Call Origination and Termination Charges for Accessing the Internet, in: International Journal of Communications Law and Policy.

CAVES, R.E., FRANKEL, J.A., JONES, R.W. (1990), World Trade and Payments: An Introduction, 5th ed., Harper Collins.

COE, D.T., HELPMAN, E. (1995), International R&D Spillovers, in: European Economic Review, 39, pp.859-887.

COE, D.T., MOGHADAM, R. (1993), Capital and Trade as Engines of Growth in France, in: IMF Staff Papers, 40, pp. 542–566.

COHENDET, P., LLERENA, P., SORGE, A. (1992), Technological Diversity and Coherence in Europe: An Analytical Overview, Revue d'Economie Industrielle, 59, pp. 9-26.

CUNEO, P., MAIRESSE, J. (1984), Productivity and R&D at the Firm Level in French Manufacturing, in: GRILICHES, Z. (ed.), R&D, Patents and Productivity, Chicago.

COUNCIL OF ECONOMIC ADVISORS (2001), Economic Report of the President, Washington, D.C.

COUNCIL OF ECONOMIC ADVISORS (2000), Economic Report of the President, Washington, D.C.

CREPON, B., HECKEL, T. (2001), Computerisation in France: An Evaluation Based on Individual Company Data, INSEE, Timbre.

DAVID, P.A. (1991), Computer and Dynamo: The Modern Productivity Paradox in a Not Distant Mirror, in: OECD (1991), Technology and Productivity: The Challenge for Economic Policy, Paris, pp. 315-48

DAVERI, F. (2001), Information Technology and Growth in Europe, University of Parma, May 2001, mimeo.

DEUTSCHE BUNDESBANK (2001), Problems of International Comparisons of Growth – A Supplementary Analysis, Monthly Report, May, Frankfurt/M.

DIXIT, A. K., NORMAN, V. (1980), Theory of International Trade, Cambridge, MA.

DOSI, G. (1982), Technological Paradigms and Technological Trajectories: A Suggested Interpretation of the Determinants and Directions of Technical Change, in: Research Policy, 11, pp. 147-162.

DOSI, G., PAVITT, K., SOETE, L. (1990), The Economics of Technical Change and International Trade, New York.

DOUGHERTY, C., JORGENSEN, D.W. (1996), International Comparisons of the Sources of Economic Growth, American Economic Review, Vol. 86, 25-29.

ECaTT (1999), Electronic Commerce and Telework Trends: Benchmarking Progress on New Ways of Working and New Forms of Business across Europe, http://www.ecatt.com/ecatt/.

ECB (2001), New Technologies and Productivity in the Euro Area, ECB Monthly Bulletin, July 2001, 37-48.

EITO (2000), European Information Technology Observatory 2000; Frankfurt/Main

ENGLE, R. F., GRANGER, C. W. J. (1987), Co-integration and Error Correction: Representation, Estimation, and Testing, in: Econometrica, 55, pp. 251 – 276.

ENGLE, R. F., YOO, B. S. (1991), Cointegrated Economic Time Series: An Overview with New Results, in: Engle, R. F. and Granger, C. W. J. (Eds.),

Long-Run Economic Relationships – Readings in Cointegration, Oxford et al.

EUROPEAN COMMISSION (2000), The European Economy: 2000 Survey, Brussels.

EUROPEAN COMMISSION (2001), The European Economy, Supplement A, No. 1.

FAGERBERG, J. (1988), International Competitiveness, in: Economic Journal, 98, pp. 355 – 374.

FCC (2000), Trends in Telephone Service, Washington, D.C.

FROOT, K.A., STEIN, J.C. (1991), Exchange Rates and Foreign Direct Investment: An Imperfect Capital Markets Approach, Quarterly Journal of Economics, November, 1191-1217.

GORDON (1999), Has the New Economy Rendered the Productivity Slowdown Obsolete?, Mimeo.

GEHRKE, B., GRUPP, H. (1994), Hochtechnologie und Innovationspotential, Heidelberg.

GRIES, T., JUNGMITTAG, A., WELFENS, P.J.J., eds. (2001), Wachstumsdynamik und Wachstumspolitik in den USA und Europa, Heidelberg: Springer.

GRILICHES, Z. (1995), R&D and Productivity: Econometric Results and Measurement Issues, in: STONEMAN, P. (ed.), Handbook of the Economics of Innovation and Technological Change, Oxford, UK / Cambridge, MA, pp. 52–89.

GRILICHES, Z., LICHTENBERG, F. (1984), R&D and Productivity Growth at the Industry Level: Is There still a Relationship, in: GRILICHES, Z. (ed.), R&D, Patents and Productivity, Chicago, pp. 465-496.

GRILICHES, Z., MAIRESSE, J. (1983), Comparing Productivity Growth: An Exploration of French and US Industrial and Firm Data, European Economic Review, 21, pp. 89–119.

GROSSMAN, G., HELPMAN, E. (1991), Innovation and Growth in a Global Economy, Cambridge, Mass.

GRUPP, H., JUNGMITTAG, A. (1999), Convergence in Global High Technology? A Decomposition and Specialisation Analysis for Advanced Countries, in: Jahrbücher für Nationalökonomie und Statistik, 218, pp. 552–573.

HALL, B., MAIRESSE, J. (1995), Exploring the Relationship between R&D and Productivity in French Manufacturing Firms, in: Journal of Econometrics, 65, pp. 263 – 294.

HELPMAN, E. (ed.) (1998), General Purpose Technologies and Economic Growth, Cambridge, MA / London.

HELPMAN, E., KRUGMAN, P. R. (1990), Market Structure and Foreign Trade, Cambridge, MA / London.

HODGSON, G.M. (1993), Economics and Evolution: Bringing Life Back to Economics, Cambridge.

INSTITUT DER DEUTSCHEN WIRTSCHAFT (1999), Telearbeit in Deutschland und Europa – Neue Chancen, Neue Arbeitsstrukturen (Tele-jobs in Germany – New Opportunities, New Job Structures), Köln.

INTERNET ECONOMY INDICATORS (1999), Facts & Figures, http://www.In ternetindicators.com/facts.html.

JAFFE, A.B., TRAJTENBERG, M., and HENDERSON, R. (1992), Geographic Localization of Knowledge Spillovers as Evidence by Patent Citations, NBER Working Paper, 3993, Cambridge, Mass.

JORGENSEN, D.W., STIROH, K.J. (2000), Raising the Speed Limit: U.S. Economic Growth in the Information Age, Brookings Papers on Economic Activity, 125-235.

JONES, C.I., WILLIAMS, J.C. (1997), Measuring the Social Return to R&D, Working Paper, Stanford University.

JUNGMITTAG, A., BLIND, K., GRUPP, H. (1999), Innovation, Standardisation and the Long-term Production Function, in: Zeitschrift für Wirtschafts- und Sozialwissenschaften, 119, pp. 209–226.

JUNGMITTAG, A., GRUPP, H., HULLMANN, A. (1998), Changing Patterns of Specialisation in Global High Technology Markets: An Empirical Investigation of Advanced Countries, in: Vierteljahreshefte zur Wirtschaftsforschung, 67, 1, pp 86 – 98.

JUNGMITTAG, A., MEYER-KRAHMER, F., REGER, G. (1999), Globalisation of R&D and Technology Markets – Trends, Motives, Consequences, in: MEYER-KRAHMER, F., ed., Globalisation of R&D and Technology Markets – Consequences for National Innovation Policies, Heidelberg / New York, pp. 37 – 77.

JUNGMITTAG, A., WELFENS, P.J.J. (1998), Telecommunications, Innovation and the Long-Term Production Function: Theoretical Analysis and a Cointegration Analysis for West Germany 1960-1990, Discussion Paper No. 52 of the EIIW at the University of Potsdam.

KILEY, M.T. (2000), Computers and Growth with Frictions: Aggregate and Disaggregate Evidence, Federal Reserve Board, Mimeo.

KRUGMAN, P. R. (1979), A Model of Innovation, Technology Transfer, and the World Distribution of Income, in: Journal of Political Economy 87, p. 253-266.

LANCASTER, K. (1980), Intra-Industry Trade under Perfect Monopolistic Competition, in: Journal of International Economics 10, p. 151-176.

LUCAS Jr., R.E. (1988), On the Mechanics of Economic Development, in: Journal for Monetary Economics, 22, pp. 3-42.

MACHER, J.T., MOWERY, D.C., HODGES, D.A. (1999), Semiconductors, in: MOWERY, D.C., ed. (1999), U.S. Industry in 2000: Studies in Competitive Performance, Washington, D.C.: National Academy Press, 245-285.

MAIRESSE, J., CUNEO, P. (1985), Recherche-développement et performances des entreprises: Une étude économétrique sur des données individuelles, in: Revue Économique, 36, pp. 1001 – 1042.

MAIRESSE, J., HALL, B. (1996), Estimating the Productivity of Research and Development in French and United States Manufacturing Firms: An Exploration of Simultaneity Issues with GMM Methods, in: WAGNER, K. and van ARK, B., eds., International Productivity Differences: Measurement and Explanations, Amsterdam.

MANN, C.L. (1998), Globalization and Productivity in the United States and Germany, in: BLACK, S., ed., Globalization, Technological Change, and Labor Markets, Dordrecht: Kluwer, 17-44.

McMORROW, K., RÖGER, W. (2000), Time – Varying Nairu / Nawaru Estimates for the EU´s Member States, Economic Papers No. 145, European Commission, Brussels.

MÖHNEN, P., NADIRI, M., PRUCHA, I. (1986), R&D, Production Structure and Rates of Return in the US, Japanese and German Manufacturing Sectors, in: European Economic Review, 30, pp. 749–771.

OECD (1998), The Software Sector: A Statistical Profile for Selected OECD Countries, Paris.

OECD (2000), Measuring the ICT Sector, Paris, mimeo.

OLINER, S.D., SICHEL, D.E. (2000), The Resurgence of Growth in the Late 1990s: Is Information Technology the Story?, Journal of Economic Perspectives, Vol. 14, 3-22.

O'MAHONY, M., WAGNER, K. (1996), Changing Fortune: An Industry Study of British and German Productivity Growth over Three Decades, in: MAYES, D. (ed.), Sources of Productivity Growth in the 1980s, Cambridge.

PATEL, P., SOETE, L. (1988), L'Évaluation des effets économiques de la technologie, in: STI Review, 4, pp. 133–183.

PAVITT, K. (1984), Sectoral Patterns of Technical Change: Towards a Taxonomy and a Theory, in: Research Policy 13, pp. 343 – 373.

PAVITT, K., ROBSON, M., TOWNSEND, J. (1987), The Size Distribution of Innovating Firms in the UK: 1945-1983, in: Journal of Industrial Economics 35, pp. 297 – 316.

RICHARDSON, P. et al. (2000), The Concept, Policy Use and Measurement of Structural Unemployment: Estimating a Time Varying NAIRU across 21 OECD Countries, OECD Economics Department Working Paper No. 250, Paris.

RÖGER, W. (2001), Structural Changes and the New Economy in the EU and the US, in AUDRETSCH, D., WELFENS, P.J.J., eds., (2002), The New Economy and Economic Growth in Europe and the US, Heidelberg, New York: Springer.

ROMER, P.M. (1986), Increasing Returns and Long-Run Growth, in: Journal of Political Economy, 94, pp. 1002–1037.

ROMER, P.M. (1990), Endogenous Technological Change, in: Journal of Political Economy, 98, pp. 71-102.

SAVIOTTI, P.P. (1991), The Role of Variety in Economic and Technological Development, in: SAVIOTTI, P.P. and METCALFE, J.S. (eds.), Evolutionary Theories of Economic and Technological Change: Present Status and Future Prospects, Reading.

SCHRÖER, G., STAHLECKER, P. (1996), Ist die gesamtwirtschaftliche Produktionsfunktion eine Kointegrationsbeziehung? Empirische Analyse vor und nach der Wiedervereinigung, in: Jahrbücher für Nationalökonomie und Statistik, 215, pp. 513 - 525.

SCHWARTZ, M. (1997), Telecommunications Reform in the United States: Promises and Pitfalls, in: WELFENS, P.J.J. and YARROW, eds. (1997), Telecommunications and Energy in Systematic Transformation, Heidelberg and New York: Springer, 213-270.

SPINDLER, J. (1999), Full Competition in Telecommunications: The US Perspective, in: WELFENS, P.J.J., YARROW, G., GRINBERG, R., and GRAACK, C., eds. (1999), Towards Competition in Network Industries, Heidelberg and New York: Springer, 123-130.

STIROH (2001), Information Technology and the U.S. Productivity Revival: What Do the Industry Data Say?, Federal Reserve Bank of New York, mimeo.

WELFENS, P.J.J., ed. (1999), Economic Aspects of German Unification, 2nd revised and enlarged edition, Heidelberg and New York.

WELFENS, P.J.J. (2000), European Monetary Union and Exchange Rate Dynamics: New Approaches and Application to the Euro, Heidelberg and New York: Springer.

WELFENS, P.J.J. (2001a), Wachstum, Produktivität und Innovationsdynamik in den USA, Europa und Japan, in: GRIES, T., JUNGMITTAG, A., and WELFENS, P.J.J., eds., Wachstumsdynamik und neue Wachstumspolitik in Europa und USA, Heidelberg: Springer (forthcoming).

WELFENS, P.J.J. (2001b), www.interneteconomics.net

WELFENS, P.J.J. (2001c), Macroeconomics of the Internet, in: Interneteconomics.net, download from www.euroeiiw.de and www.interneteconomics.net.

WELFENS, P.J.J. (2001d), Stabilizing and Integrating the Balkans: Economic Analysis of the Stability Pact, EU Reforms and International Organizations, Berlin / Heidelberg / New York.

WELFENS, P.J:J. (2002), Interneteconomics.net, Heidelberg and New York: Springer.

WELFENS, P.J.J., AUDRETSCH, D., ADDISON, J., GRUPP, H. (1998), Technological Competition, Employment and Innovation Policies in OECD Countries, Heidelberg and New York: Springer.

WELFENS, P.J.J., AUDRETSCH, D., ADDISON, J., GRIES, T., GRUPP, H. (1999), Globalization, Economic Growth and Innovation Dynamics, Heidelberg and New York: Springer.

WELFENS, P.J.J., JUNGMITTAG, A. (2000), Effects of an Internet Flat Rate on Growth and Employment in Germany, Discussion Paper No. 81 of the EIIW at the University of Potsdam.

WELFENS, P.J.J., JUNGMITTAG, A. (2001a), Internetdynamik, Telekomliberalisierung und Wirtschaftswachstum, Heidelberg and New York: Springer.

WELFENS, P.J.J., JUNGMITTAG, A. (2001b), Europäische Telekomliberalisierung und Außenhandel: Theorie, Gravitationsansatz und Implikationen, in: Jahrbücher für Nationalökonomie und Statistik.

WHELAN, K. (2000a), Computers, Obsolescence, and Productivity, Federal Reserve Board, Finance and Economics Discussion Series, No. 6.

WHELAN, K. (2000b), A Guide to the Use of Chain-Aggregated NIPA Data, Federal Reserve Board, Finance and Economics Discussion Series, No. 35.

WITT, U., ed. (1993), Evolutionary Economics, The International Library of Critical Writings in Economics, 25, Aldershot.

B. Is the IT Revolution Possible in Japan?

Yukio Noguchi

1. Introduction

"The IT Revolution" has become one of the most popular key words in the recent economic discussions in Japan. The Mori Administration (1999 to 2001) raised "the revitalization of the Japanese economy through the IT Revolution" as one of the main objectives of its economic policy. Japan put the "IT Revolution" in the main agenda of the 2000 Economic Summit held in Okinawa in July 2000. Keizai Hakusho (the Government Economic White Paper) published in July 2000 pointed out that the IT Revolution would bring about huge impacts and a fundamental transformation of the Japanese society. The present Koizumi Administration adopts the same policy directions arguing that the IT Revolution is the key to revitalizing the Japanese economy.

Although heated enthusiasm has somewhat faded due to the fall in the stock prices of IT-related companies in the U.S., strong expectations for IT still remain. This is because many people believe that the Japanese industrial structure needs a fundamental reform and that the IT-related activities will become the leading sector in the future economy.

The necessity to change the Japanese industrial structure is indeed urgent because Japan faces a fundamental change in the economic environments. In particular, the rapid growth of the export-oriented manufacturing industries in Asian countries is having profound impacts on the Japanese economy. Industries in these countries are catching up, and in some aspects surpassing their Japanese counterparts. In fact, the productivity figures for the iron and steel industry and the shipbuilding industry in Korea are now higher than those in Japan. Similar changes will occur in such key industries as automobiles and electric machinery in the near future. The improvements in the quality of goods produced in China have brought about competition with Japanese producers, especially in the textile industry. Imports from China are causing the price of consumer goods in Japan to fall significantly.

Faced with this situation, it is obvious that something must be done to reconstruct Japanese industry. It seems that the IT Revolution provides us with a very promising opportunity.

Problems exist, however, and some of them are quite serious and fundamental. Is it possible to utilize IT within the existing framework of Japanese society? If reforms are necessary, are they possible? Does the introduction of the technology really increase productivity or does it have nothing but destructive effects? The purpose of this paper is to consider these questions.

I first review in Section 1 the present state of IT utilization in Japan. In Section 2, I will review the government IT policy and point out that an excessive emphasis is given to the hardware side, especially the improvements of the communication facilities. I will argue that this is nothing but a continuation of the long-lasting Japanese public policy bias which primarily aims at providing job opportunities for the workers in the related industries.

In Sections 3 and 4, I will point out that since the utilization of IT is not a purely technological matter, the social factors are extremely important. I will raise several examples in which regulations prevent wide use of new technology. I will also point out that Japanese industry is still dominated by traditional big companies even in the IT-related area. I will then argue that this is the fundamental cause of the present difficulty in Japan and the most serious cause of the delay in the utilization of IT. I conclude by saying that the most important objective of economic policy must be the reform of the old system.

2. The Present State of IT Utilization in Japan

It is widely recognized that Japan has been left behind in the IT Revolution. According to a recent survey by the Nikkei BP, 90 percent of those answering replied that Japan is behind other countries. The reasons they raised are the high cost and low speed of communication networks and the government's poor services on the Internet[1].

In 1999, the number of Internet users per one hundred members of the population in Japan was twentieth in the world ranking. This position was lower than such Asian countries as Singapore, Hong Kong, Korea and Taiwan.

The most recent figures shown in Table 1 indicate some improvements. Although still lower than Singapore and Hong Kong, Japan has succeeded in getting a higher position than Korea and Taiwan. (Needless to say, if we look at the absolute numbers, Japan's figure is quite large, as shown in Table 2). The growth of Internet users is also seen in the figures in Table 3[2].

The communication environment is also improving. In December 2000, NTT (The Japan Telephone and Telegraph Company) began to provide the ADSL service (downward maximum speed 1.5 Mbps and upward maximum speed 512 kbps) in the Tokyo and Osaka areas at a monthly cost of 4.6 thousand yen (initial installment cost is 16.5 thousand yen). Other communication providers have begun to provide similar services, some of them at costs lower than that of NTT.

---

[1] The survey also shows that 46 percent of users use ISDN; 36 percent use traditional telephones; and 13 percent use CATV. As for the monthly Internet expenditure including fees for providers, 38 percent of users paid 5 to 10 thousand yen; 29 percent paid 3 to 5 thousand yen; and 21 percent paid 1 to 3 thousand yen. Source: http://npc.nikkeibp.co.jp.

[2] There are some contradictions between Tables due to differences in definitions and other factors.

Table B1: **Internet Penetration Ratios (The Ratio of Households Connected to the Internet)**

	1996	1997	1998	1999	2000
Numbers of users		11 550	16 940	27 060	47 080
Penetration ratio for firms with more than 300 employees	50,4	68,2	80,0	88,6	95,8
Penetration ratio for households	3,3	6,4	11,0	19,1	34,0

Source: White Paper on Information and Communication, 2001

Table B2: **Percentage of Households Connected to the Internet**

	Country	Percent		Country	Percent
1	Sweden	56.4	12	Bermuda	39.7
2	U.S.A.	55.8	13	New Zealand	39.0
3	Norway	52.6	14	Japan	37.1
4	Iceland	52.1	15	Austria	36.9
5	Hong Kong	48.7	16	Korea	34.6
6	Denmark	48.4	17	U.K.	33.6
7	The Netherland	45.8	18	Switzerland	33.1
8	Singapore	44.6	19	Taiwan	28.8
9	Australia	43.9	20	Ireland	27.5
10	finland	43.9	21	Belgium	26.4
11	Canada	42.8			

Source: White Paper on Information and Communication, 2001

Table B3: **Number of Internet Users in Japan (in Thousands)**

Year	Number of Users
Aug.1988	12 228
Feb.1999	15 085
Feb.2000	19 377 (30)
Feb.2001	32 636 (6,535)
Dec.2001	36 280 (8,200)

Note: The numbers in parenthesis are those using only mobile phones. The number for Dec. 2001 is an estimate.
Source: The Internet White Paper

The figures of e-commerce trading volumes shown in Table 4 show that the volume of e-trading in Japan is not so small in comparison with the U.S. if the difference in the total economic size is taken into account. In particular, the figures of B to B trading can be regarded as being a similar level to that of the U.S. Also, the future figures of B to C trading in Japan show a remarkable catching up trend. From these observations, it may be concluded that the present state of Japan is not so problematic.

Table B4:   E-commerce Trading Volumes (in Trillion yen)

	Japan				U.S.	
	1999	2000	2003	2005	1998	2003
B to C	0,34	0,82	5,62	A	2,25	21,30
B to B	n.a.	21,60	67,00	111,00	19,50	165,30

Source: The Ministry of Economy and Industry

The Internet trading of stocks is also becoming popular. The number of securities companies providing Internet trading of stocks was 67 as of May 2001. The number of accounts is 2.3 million as of the end of June 2001. This is about eight times the number in October 1999 when Internet trading was first introduced in Japan. The volume of trading in March 2001 was 1.8 trillion yen, which was 5.8 percent of total trading. As for trading by individual investors, Internet trading was 33.9 percent of the total during the period from October 2000 through March 2001.

If we look closer, however, it can be pointed out that problems still remain. First, a significant portion of the recent increase in Internet users is due to the increase in mobile phone (cellular phone) users as verified in Table 3. The most popular mobile phone service is provided by NTT Docomo and is called "i-mode". This enables the users to send and receive e-mail through their mobile phones. This service has brought about an explosion of enthusiasm among the youngsters, especially girls.

It is doubtful, however, whether this can be regarded as full fledged Internet use. In fact, most e-mail messages are nothing but "Hello! How are you?" and so forth, and are in no way related to data processing activities or other business uses. In contrast, more than 60 percent of Internet users in Korea are connected to high speed networks so that they use the Internet for such services as ticketing and stock trading.

Second, most of the B to B transactions in Japan are carried out through the traditional EDI (Electronic Date Interchange), which uses limited-access private networks rather than the Internet. This means that most of B to B in Japan is carried out among a closed circle, i.e. among the limited members of the already established trading partners or their subsidiary companies, and that the system does not contribute to finding new trading partners.

It is said that the introduction of B to B trading realizes dramatic cost reductions, especially in the procurement of materials and parts. It must be noted, however, that such significant cost reduction becomes possible because Internet transactions help firms to find new trading partners. If trading partners do not change, as would be the case for most Japanese firms, it would be difficult to expect significant changes in economic efficiency. This point will be discussed again in Section 3.

3. The Government IT Policy

Some people argue that the inactive use of the Internet in Japan has been brought about by the slow commitment of the Japanese government in this area. It is pointed out that other Asian countries moved much earlier: Singapore launched the "IT 2000 Plan" as early as 1992; Taiwan's "National Plan for Communication Networks" was formulated in 1994; Malaysia launched the "Multimedia Super Corridor Plan" in 1995; Korea made the "Super High Speed Networks Plan" as well as "Cyber Korea 21" in 1995; and Hong Kong launched "The Digital 21" in 1998.

The Japanese government recently formulated its IT policy package. The present policy package is called the "E-Japan Strategy"(hereafter EJS), which first appeared in Prime Minister Mori's address in the Diet in November 2000 and was formally decided by the cabinet in January 2001.

The EJS maintains that the IT Revolution will bring to society a major historical transformation comparable to the Industrial Revolution. It raises several objectives as follows:

1. The volume of e-commerce in 2003 should be increased to ten times the 1998 level. B to B transactions should increase to 70 trillion yen and B to C transactions to 3 trillion yen.
2. The world's most advanced communication networks should be made available by 2005. At least 30 million households (about eighty percent of total households) should be connected to the high speed network, and 10 million households should be connected to the super-high speed network.
3. The number of MA and Ph.D. holders in the IT-related fields should be increased to a level comparable to the U.S.
4. The invitation of 30 thousand highly skilled foreign workers.

Many people believe that now that the government has realized the importance of IT, Japan will catch up to front runner countries and will become one of the most advanced IT countries in the world. They also believe that it is the government's initiative to make the IT Revolution possible, and that the objective will be achieved if sufficient government money is spent.

I cast doubt on this view. The basic reason is that whether IT can be highly utilized or not in actual business activities or in the daily life of individuals is not a purely technological matter. As I will argue in the latter sections, it depends heavily upon social and economic factors, so that the basic situation will not change unless substantial changes in the economic structure take place. This means that improvements in such indices as the number of Internet users, the communication speed, or the communication costs alone would not change the basic situation.

The problem with the EJS is its heavy bias towards improvements in communication facilities. It has long been pointed out that Japanese public policies put too much emphasis on the construction of facilities. As a result, too many facilities such as highways, bridges and public buildings have been constructed especially in the rural areas, without contributing much to the improvement of the quality of life. Such bias arises because the decisions regarding public works are influenced by the consideration of job creation for the construction industry. It is very probable that the same bias will be repeated in the IT area.

On the other hand, public policy is quite weak on the software side. In particular, the supply of government data on the Internet is quite insufficient. For instance, the Government Economic White Paper in 2000 was not available on the Internet, in spite of the fact that its main theme was the "IT Revolution". Although it is true that more and more government data is becoming available on government websites, the present situation is far from satisfactory, especially in comparison with the U.S. federal government. The government has launched such new programs as the "The Prime Minister's Net-Magazine" and the "Internet Banpaku (The Internet International Exposition)", but their usefulness is quite doubtful.

It is said that most Japanese regional cities and local towns have magnificent "culture center buildings" equipped with the most modern theaters, concert halls and international conference rooms, thanks to huge government spending and subsidies. The only problem is that there are no programs to be played or performed there. Namely, we have the "empty box syndrome". It is very probable that in the IT era we will suffer from the "empty line syndrome".

It must also be noted that competition among private companies is important. The story behind the introduction of ADSL in Japan is quite suggestive.

In the U.S. this service has been provided since 1997. The formal introduction in Japan was as late as December 2000 (Test services were provided by NTT and private providers in 1999). This delay was not due to technological difficulties.

NTT, which is the biggest network provider and the monopolistic holder of the cables in the urban area, was reluctant to introduce ADSL because it has heavily invested in ISDN, and the use of the ADSL in the same cable will bring about mutual interference. For this reason, NTT did not allow its cables to be used for ADSL by other providers. It was the pressure of private providers that finally pushed NTT to allow the cables to be used for ADSL.

In September 2001, Yahoo introduced a high speed ADSL service (downward 8 Mbps) at a cost of 2280 yen per month. This triggered a heated competition among providers, and the use of ADSL is growing rapidly.

According to a government survey the number of ADSL users has increased from 1605 in July 2000 to as many as 1.2 million at the end of November 2001[3].

The cost is also falling. The average monthly cost of ADSL use has fallen from 6760 yen in August 2000 to 5429 yen in July 2001. This cost is lower than that in the U.S.[4].

The above story strongly suggests that competition among private companies rather than governmental initiative is essential for the growth of Internet use.

---

[3] Asahi Newspaper, Dec. 13, 2001.
[4] Asahi Newspaper, June 14, 2001.

4. Social Factors Prevent the IT Revolution

Some people argue that the IT-related activities do not grow in Japan because most Japanese are reluctant to use PCs or the Internet. Others argue that such barriers as the high cost of communication or the low speed in the communication networks prevent efficient and comfortable usage. Some also argue that the fundamental cause can be found in poor creative ability of Japanese people. It is pointed out that although Japanese are very good in imitating technologies developed elsewhere, they are unable to develop new technologies.

Although these arguments cannot be totally neglected, they cannot be regarded as the fundamental cause of the problem. For example, although it is true that older generations are reluctant to use PCs or the Internet, the same trends can be observed in other countries. Even in Japan, younger generations have no problems in using the new technology. Also, although it is true that the communication costs in Japan are higher than those in other countries, the present costs are not prohibitively high, and the situation is improving as mentioned in Section 1.

As for the ability of Japanese to create new technologies, it must be noted that some of the basic breakthroughs in IT were done by Japanese. The problem is that such technological efforts have not materialized as an actual business or the creation of a new industry.

The essential reasons can be found in the social and economic factors such as the regulations or the behavior of the traditional companies. In fact, there are many social and economic factors that make Japan lag behind other countries in the IT-related activities.

First, various regulations and restrictions restrict the wide use of the Internet. An evident example is the fixed price regulation of books (Books must be sold at the price printed on the book, so that no discount sales are allowed. This regulation applies to newspapers and magazines as well). Because of this regulation, book prices cannot be reduced even if costs are dramatically reduced by the use of Internet technology. On the contrary, the total cost becomes higher than the ordinary cost if bought through the Internet because the delivery costs are added.

This clearly works as an obstacle for widespread use of Internet book shopping in Japan. This can be verified by statistics: The total amount of Internet book sales in Japan is only about three percent of that of Amazon.com alone. It must be noted that the figure has fallen from five percent in the previous year.

One might argue that fixed price regulation should be abolished in order to make Internet book shopping grow. This is far from being an easy task, however, because the newspapers and the publishing companies are the beneficiaries of this regulation. This means that the voices demanding the abolishment of the regulation hardly appear in the mass media.

There are other examples in which regulations and restrictions prevent wide use of Internet technology. The regulation that hospitals may not make detailed advertisements, the regulation that the insurance contracts must be made in a face-to-face situation with the customer, and strict restrictions on employment agencies are just a few examples.

The importance of deregulation is evident if we look at Internet stock trading. The stock trading business in Japan was strictly regulated until recently. It required government licensing so that new entry was almost impossible. The commission fees were also strictly regulated, and no discounts were allowed.

The "Big Bang" policy in the late 1990s has changed the situation dramatically. Thanks to the abolishment of the license requirement, new entrance has become quite easy because a firm can start a securities business simply by sending a notice to the government. The commission fees were completely deregulated in October 1999. As a result, freedom in the securities business has been substantially enlarged.

Reflecting this, the number of stock companies which provide Internet trading services has increased. Also, the number of users has increased as mentioned in Section 1. (Some people regard the competition in Internet trading as excessive. Even big traditional securities companies like Nikko have recently introduced "zero commission" trading.)

The second factor that prevents the growth of IT-related businesses in Japan can be found in the rigid relationships between firms. This is particularly problematic for B to B transactions. Even if Internet technology enables a firm to find a new supplier of parts, for example, it would be difficult for a Japanese company to discontinue the relationship with the present part suppliers because in most cases they are subsidiaries of the company; the relationship is quite strong and has lasted for many years. As a result, as mentioned in Section 1, most B to B transactions are carried out through the limited access private networks rather than through Internet networks.

It may be worthwhile here to recall the so-called "leap frog" effect. This means that when the technological paradigm goes through a big and discontinuous change, latecomers are in the same position as the predecessors because existing facilities, existing human skills and other economic factors, which are geared to the traditional technology, do not matter. For this reason, the latecomers may leap like a frog and may be able to get a more advanced position than the predecessors in the new field.

In the case of IT, the advantage of latecomers may be greater. As I argued above, one of the reasons why Japan cannot fully enjoy the benefits of IT is the resistance from the old sector of the economy. If such resistance did not exist in the latecomers' society, they could easily adopt the new technology. It is widely recognized that constructing a new building is much easier than renovating an old one. The same thing can be said about the IT Revolution.

I have pointed out in Section 1 that most B to B transactions in Japan are carried out between long lasting trade partners. This is a typical example of the old economy preventing change.

If we look at the figures in Table 1, it may be said that most of the continental European countries including Germany are in a similar situation as Japan in the sense that they are not catching up in the worldwide trend of the "IT Revolution". Not only Japan but also continental European countries are suffering from the "predecessors' syndrome".

If this trend continues, it may be possible that Japan and the continental European countries are left behind Asian countries including mainland China in the coming IT age.

There are many historical examples in which a newcomer takes the front runner's position when a radical technological change occurs. For example, when the leading industrial technology changed from that of a light-industry-oriented one to that of a heavy-industry-oriented one, Germany took the front-runner position which used to be held by Great Britain. We may observe similar phenomena in the coming decades.

However, we must at the same time note that the United States and Nordic countries which no doubt are the predecessors in traditional industrial society are doing very well in IT, at least as judged from the figures in Table 1. This might mean that whether a country can adapt to IT depends upon much more deeply rooted factors of the economic structure.

In the following sections, I will analyze the basic elements of the Japanese economy and discuss their relationships with IT.

5. The Traditional Companies Still Dominate the Economy

In this section, I will point out that the industrial structure in Japan is quite different from that in other countries, especially the U.S.

The most remarkable difference can be found in the PC industry. In Japan, all major PC producers are big companies in the electric or electronics industry. NEC and Fujitsu used to be, and still are, producers of telecommunication equipment. Toshiba and Hitachi are long-time giants in the heavy electric machinery industry. Sony and Matsushita are producers of consumer-related electric appliances. All these companies have existed for many years.

This structure of the PC industry is remarkably different from that in the United States and in Taiwan, where most PC manufacturers are newly established companies. For example, Dell computer was established in the 1980s and has become the top PC manufacturer by its successful introduction of a new PC production procedure, the Direct Model. Other PC manufacturing companies such as Compaq, Sun-Micro, Apple and Gateway are also relatively young companies and were established for the purpose of producing PCs. IBM is the sole company in the American PC industry which already existed in the pre-PC era.

A similar difference can be observed in the Internet stock trading business. In the United States, such newcomers as E-trade and Charles Schwab introduced the new method of stock trading and had strong impacts on the traditional companies such as Merrill-Lynch. In Japan, on the other hand, Internet trading was introduced by such traditional big securities companies as Nomura, Daiwa and Nikko. Although it is true that some previously small companies such as Matsui have become major players in the new business, their impacts are far smaller than those of E-trade or Schwab in the United States. The securities trading business in Japan is still dominated by the traditional giant securities houses. The same trend can be observed in the insurance industry, book sales and car sales.

In the consumer oriented e-business in Japan, there is virtually no growth of companies similar to the "dot com companies" that we observe in the United States. In Japan, there are no counterparts of Amazon.com. Such traditional booksellers like Maruzen and Kinokuniya provide Internet book sales. To summarize, while the U.S. economy is led by new companies, the Japanese industry is still dominated by traditional big companies.

This can be verified by looking at the list of market values of companies (Table 8). In the United States, the top position of the recent list is occupied by such new companies as Microsoft, Intel, Cisco Systems, and AOL. These companies were only negligibly small or did not even exist until the early 1980s.

Some symbolic facts can also be observed in the Table. For example, Intel is now above IBM which used to be the leader of the information industry until the 1980s. AOL which is a new company in the Internet industry is now above AT&T which was the giant in the traditional communication industry.

In Japan, on the other hand, no new companies comparable to Microsoft or Intel have emerged. The top position on the list is still occupied by traditional companies such as NTT and Toyota.

It may be necessary here to take a brief look at the collapse of the IT Bubble in Japan, which occurred around April 2000. Some companies' stock prices fell to more than one twentieth of their highest level. A more serious problem was that most of these companies were nothing but fakes because they had no solid business models. For example, Hikari-Tsusin (The Light Communication) was said to be the hero of the Japanese venture business in IT. Despite this charming name and the enthusiastic appraisal by stockbrokers, their actual business was no more than the sale of mobile phones by a rather dubious manner.

Why are new start-ups so difficult in Japan? The first reason can be found in the labor market structure and the corporate structure. The Japanese employment system is characterized by the practice of lifetime employment and the seniority wage system. Although changes are taking place in recent years, especially in small and medium sized companies, the traditional practices are still dominant in large corporations.

Under this employment system, it would be very risky for a person to leave a corporation, especially a large corporation, and to start a new business. The reason is that if the new business fails, he or she can find no places to return. Thus, most people are reluctant to leave a corporation even in a case when there is a chance to start a new business. The lack of mobility in the labor market is thus a basic reason why able persons do not undertake new businesses and why healthy venture businesses do not flourish in Japan.

This means that able young workers are "trapped" in large organizations, and that the supply of able persons to a new industry becomes insufficient. Also, students from good universities try to find jobs in large organizations rather than to begin their own venture businesses.

The second reason can be found in the Japanese financial structure, which is usually called the "indirect financial system". This is a system in which banks play the major role, and fundraising from the capital market plays only a marginal role. The problem with this structure is the difficulty in supplying the risk money for venture businesses.

The third reason is the closed environment of business activities, namely, that most of the business-to-business transactions are carried out among related companies. The old "Zaibatsu" ties are still strong among Mitsubishi, Mitsui and Sumitomo family companies. Most big companies have subsidiary companies. This means that it is difficult for a newcomer to establish a business relationship with them. This is particularly problematic in IT-related activities because small venture companies can best provide many new services.

On the other hand, there are several reasons why traditional large companies cannot do well in the new field of IT.

First, decision making in large organizations tends to be slow, and this poses a serious problem in the IT-related business where the "speed" is the most important requirement.

Second, traditional companies are reluctant to undertake radical changes. This is because new economic activities are usually contradictory to their established basic business models. This can be best understood by looking at Internet trading of securities which makes the stocks salesmen obsolete or even useless. The most important objective of the traditional large Japanese corporations is to secure the welfare of employees rather than to increase profits for the benefit of the shareholders. Therefore, if the introduction of a new technology is harmful to the existing jobs, it is almost impossible to introduce it on a large scale[5]. In other words, the Japanese corporations are cooperative associations of employees rather than profit maximizing organizations.

6. The Reform of the 1940 System

The factors mentioned in the previous section (lifetime employment, the seniority wage system, the lack of mobility in the labor market, and the indirect financial system) are the basic characteristics of the Japanese economy. They are usually regarded as the basic components of the so-called "Japanese Economic System".

---

[5] It may be argued that this statement contradicts the fact that the Japanese corporations were eager to introduce new technologies for the purpose of increasing productivity during the rapid growth era.

It must be noted that during the rapid growth era, the total size of the economy grew at a tremendous speed, so that it was possible to provide the workers with alternative jobs. For instance, when automatic elevators were introduced, young ladies who were operating the elevators could find clerical work in the offices. Such reallocations of workers were done in most cases within the same organization. It was therefore possible to introduce new technologies without arousing serious social conflicts. The problem mentioned in the text arises because the Japanese economy is suffering from zero growth situations.

It would therefore be difficult to expect the IT Revolution to occur in Japan as long as the present system remains.

It is important to note, however, that the "Japanese Economic System" is not necessarily "intrinsically Japanese" in the sense that it has a long root in the Japanese history. Rather, it is an artificially introduced system for the purpose of World War Two. Because the major reforms were undertaken during the period around the year 1940, I will call this the "1940 System".

Before the reforms were introduced, the market was an essential element of the Japanese economy. In this sense, the Japanese economy was very similar to the Anglo-Saxon type economies.

This can be best seen in the financial sector. Until the 1930s, most Japanese corporations raised funds directly from the capital market by issuing stocks and bonds; namely, the Japanese financial system was the "direct financial system". Because of this financial structure, large stockholders had strong influences on corporate decisions; namely, the corporate governance structure was also the Anglo-Saxon type.

It was government initiative that changed the whole picture. In order to control the flow of funds and to concentrate economic resources for the war-related industries, the government strengthened the banking sector and discouraged fundraising from the stock market.

The lifetime employment and seniority wage system were also introduced during this period for the purpose of raising labor productivity. In pre-war Japan, workers moved from one company to another rather frequently.

I argued in the previous section that since large Japanese companies are like cooperative associations of employees, it would be difficult to introduce changes that work against the benefit of the present employees. This characteristic of Japanese corporations is a direct result of the above-mentioned reforms in the corporate structure.

The government-business relationship, the relations between the central and the local governments and the tax system also changed drastically and fundamentally during the period around the year 1940. By these changes, the Japanese economy which used to be a market-oriented economy was transformed to a more organization-oriented one.

This system, which was originally introduced for the purpose of war, remained in the post-war period. (In this respect, there is a huge difference between Japan and Germany which experienced a total dismantlement of the pre-war system.) Moreover, the system functioned as a basic framework to realize the rapid economic growth during the 1960s. The indirect financing system was the basic financial structure which supported the growth of the heavy industries. The system also worked very well in fighting the oil crisis during the 1970s.

The basic reason why the 1940 system functioned so well is that the group-oriented nature of the system matched the economic environment well. Cooperation was possible because the objective was singular and well defined and accepted by all members of the group. Whether the objective was fighting a war or realizing economic growth or increasing energy efficiency was not essential.

Needless to say, changes are taking place recently due to the changes in the economic environment. The lifetime employment and the seniority wage system are disappearing even in large organizations. Mobility in the labor market is increasing although at a very slow speed. There are also changes in the financial system.

In recent years, several attempts have been made to increase the direct finance channel. Establishment of a new OTC market called "Mothers" in the Tokyo Stock Exchange is an example. Its major objective is to provide funds to newly established venture firms especially in the IT industry.

Because IT requires individual innovative initiatives rather than group-oriented cooperation, reform of the economic system is urgent. We must bear in mind that the 1940 system is by no means a reflection of the long historical developments of Japanese society; nor is it related to the cultural elements of Japanese. This means that reform of the system is in principle possible, and this will be the basic condition to make the IT Revolution possible in Japan.

Annex: Tables

Table B5:   Internet Use in Asian Countries

	Thailand	Malaysia	Indonesia	The Philippines	China	World
The Number of Internet Users (in Thousands):						
- 1995	40	40	20	20	60	34,000
- 1999	800	1500	900	500	8,900	257,000
- 99/95	20	37,5	45	25	148,3	7,6
Internet Users	1,3	6,9	0,4	0,7	0,7	
Number of Phone Lines	8,6	20,3	0,9	4	8,6	
Number of Mobile Phones	3,8	13,7	1,1	3,7	3,4	
Number of PCs	2,3	6,9	0,9	1,7	1,2	
Percentage of Digital Lines (% in 1998)	100	100	99,2	92	99,8	
Percentage of Digital Mobile Phones (% in 1999)	44,1	84,9	95,6	48,1	88,4	

Source: ITU Yearbook of Statistics, February 2000 (http://www.itu.int/home/index.html, http://www.itu.int/journal/200008/E/html/indlcat.htm, http://www.itu.int/ti/industryoverview/)

Table B6:   Internet Use in ASEAN Countries and China

Country	Population (million)	GNP ($ billion)	Number of Internet Users (million)	Number of Highspeed Network Users (million)	Number of Mobile Phones (million)
Japan	126,85	4460,7	37,19	0,468	6,219
Korea	47,28	406,7	16,40	3,040	26,480
Taiwan	22,07	323,7	5,94	0,166	11,540
Hong Kong	6,78	168,7	2,68	0,326	4,040
Singapore	3,87	91,2	1,88	0,060	2,248

Source: Nikkei BP

Table B7:   Number of PCs (in 1995)

Country	In Thousand	Per 1000 People
Singapore	550	189,7
Malaysia	810	41,1
Indonesia	980	5,1
Thailand	1 100	19,0
The Philippines	660	9,9
Brunei	8	28,7
Vietnam	50	0,7
Myanmar	25	0,5
Cambodia	10	1,0
Laos	3	0,6
Japan	18 300	145,4
India	1 600	1,8

Source: The 8th Annual Computer Industry Almanac

Table B8:   Total Market Values of the Top U.S. Corporations (July 22, 2001)

Rank	Corporation	Total Market Value (billion US dollars)
1	General Electric	461,6
2	Microsoft	390,5
3	Exxon Mobil	297,2
4	Pfizer	259,6
5	Citigroup	252,1
6	Intel	201,4
7	AOL Time Warner	190,1
8	IBM	180,6
9	GlaxoSmithKline	178,3
10	BP OLC	177,3
11	Johnson & Johnson	164,2
12	Verion	154,6
13	Merck	154,3
14	SBC Communications	147,6
15	Cisco Systems	129,9

Source: Yahoo! Finance Stock Screener Search (http://screen.yahoo.com/)

Table B9:   Total Market Values of the Top Japanese Corporations (July 19, 2001)

Rank	Corporation	Total Market Value (ten billion Yen)
1	NTT Docomo	1 816,5
2	Toyota	1 544,0
3	NTT	1 060,0
4	Sony	660,6
5	Sumitomo Mitsui	593,8
6	Mitsubishi Tokyo FG	572,8
7	Honda	511,6
8	Takeda Chemical	497,1
9	Mizuho HD	468,6
10	The Tokyo Electric Power	401,1
11	The Nomura Securities	393,6
12	Matsushita Electric	380,6
13	Canon	369,7
14	Seven-Eleven Japan	358,1
15	Hitachi	350,5

Source: Nikkei Net (http://rank.nikkei.co.jp)

References

ECONOMIC PLANNING AGENCY (2000), Keizai Hakusyo (Economic White Paper), July, (in Japanese) (http://www5.cao.go.jp/j-j/wp/wp-je00/wp-je00-00201.html#sb2_1_1) .

NOGUCHI, YUKIO (1995), 1940 Taisei (The 1940 System), Toyo Keizai Shimposha, (in Japanese).

NOGUCHI, YUKIO (1996), Leaving The "1940" System and Moving into a New System, Japanese Economic Studies, Vol.24, No.3, May-June, pp.83-94.

NOGUCHI, YUKIO (1998), The 1940 System: Japan Still under the Wartime Economy, American Economic Review, May.

POSTAL SERVICES AGENCY (2001), Joho Tsushin Hakusyo (White Paper on Information and Communication), (in Japanese) (http://www.home.soumu.go.jp/hakusyo/tsushin/index.html).

C. The Internet and Evolving Patterns of International Trade

Caroline L. Freund and Diana Weinhold[1]

1. Introduction

News about the Internet and trade absolutely permeates the popular press these days. Web statistics of staggering proportions and every variety constantly make their way into reports and political speeches, and the phenomenon is not limited to the industrialized world. Anecdotal accounts of South American village women selling baskets to Swiss bankers, virtual medical advice being offered in Sub-Saharan Africa and other internet success stories have caught the imagination of more than one development agency. Both the UN and the IADB have special sections devoted to internet-related development initiatives, and at the Japanese meetings of the G-8 last year, the development agenda was dominated by talk not only of debt relief, but also of increased "wiring" up of the developing world

There can be no doubt that very fundamental innovations are underway and that the internet is close to the heart of matter. Nevertheless, so far most of the international evidence of systematic change has been primarily anecdotal in nature, and much of the statistical data available on the use of the web seems strangely disembodied. There are numerous "snapshot" figures of web use, growth of web use, and bandwidth usage etc. Academic studies of particular industries in certain countries carefully delineate the advantages and problems that firms have had to face in developing e-commerce opportunities. Innumerable policy documents talk about and emphasize the huge potential benefits of e-commerce for developing countries in international trade. However there has been a dearth of systematic, international statistical evidence of the effects of internet usage on trade patterns.

This paper attempts to quantify the effect that the Internet has had on international trade patterns across countries in recent years. We base our empirical work on a theoretical model of trade presented in Freund and Weinhold (henceforth FW) (2000 and 2002a) that illuminates the possible effects of the Internet in a world with imperfect competition and sunk costs. Evidence suggests that market-specific sunk costs have historically been very important for a large share of trade in goods and thus the Internet has the potential to reduce these costs because sup-

---

[1] The authors would like to thank Bruce Blonigen, Simeon Djankov, Andrew Levin, James Rauch, John Rogers, Andrew Rose, Phillip Swagel, David Weinstein, Kei-Mu Yi and seminar participants at Columbia University, the Federal Reserve Board, the University of Virginia, and the Empirical Investigations in International Trade Conference for helpful comments, and Kathryn Zweig for research assistance. All errors and omissions are our own.

pliers can advertise to numerous buyers at once. This has important implications for trade volumes and for bilateral trade patterns. In particular, it implies that the Internet will reduce the importance of past linkages on current trade and is likely to have the greatest impact on exports of countries that have not historically had strong trade ties. FW 2000 also show that the effect of distance on trade will be reduced if distance impacts trade mainly through sunk costs, for example, by improving access to information about distant markets. Alternatively, if distance impacts trade primarily because of transport costs then it is unclear if the development of the Internet will change the way in which distance affects trade.

We use a gravity model of trade among 56 countries over the years 1995 to 1999 and test whether Internet usage can help explain the observed trade patterns. In brief, we do not find evidence of an effect of web access on international trade in 1995, and only very weak evidence in 1996. However from 1997 to 1999, we find a significant and increasing impact of the Internet on trade flows. Specifically, we find that a relative increase of 10 percent in web hosts in 1999 would have led to about 1 percent greater trade. We find that the Internet has had the strongest impact on trade flows among developing countries, which is consistent with the model's prediction that countries *without* established trade links have the most to gain from Internet technology. Surprisingly, we find little evidence that the Internet has reduced the impact of distance on trade, suggesting that distance influences trade patterns mainly as a result of transport costs. We also find evidence that the Internet has reduced the importance of past linkages on trade flows.

It should be noted that while the Internet is likely to impact trade in both goods and services, the effects on the two are likely to be very different. Trade in goods will be affected because Internet technology makes the development of global markets for goods possible. Trade in services will be impacted because new services can now be traded almost costlessly, irrespective of location. In this paper, we focus on goods trade; readers interested in the effect of the Internet on services trade are referred to FW (2002b).

The paper proceeds as follows: Section 2 reviews related literature and briefly reviews the theoretical framework developed in FW (2000) describing the effect of the Internet on trade. Section 3 briefly reviews the gravity model of trade, Section 4 discusses data and measurement issues, Section 5 presents the results, Section 6 offers a sensitivity analysis of the results and discusses alternative interpretations. Section 7 concludes.

2. Brief Review of a Theoretical Framework for Empirical Tests

In order to explore the possible effects of the introduction of the Internet on international trade patterns, FW 2000 and 2002a develop a theoretical model of trade with imperfect competition, segmented markets and sunk costs. They show that the internet has the potential to reduce market-specific sunk costs that have historically been very important for a large share of trade in goods.

This view of trade patterns is well documented in the literature as a number of recent papers have emphasized the importance of sunk costs in explaining trade flows (see, for example, BALDWIN (1989), EICHENGREEN and IRWIN (1998), TYBOUT and ROBERTS (1997), and FREUND (2000)). Other models have emphasized the importance of local networks to overcome costs associated with imperfect information (see, for example, RAUCH (1996, 1999, and 2000). Both types of models imply that trade patterns will be persistent, and indeed empirical work has shown that past trade flows have large and statistically significant explanatory power in predicting current patterns of trade, even after controlling for all the standard variables.

In the FW 2000 model the Internet aggregates world demand and world supply into a single market and lowers search costs and informational asymmetries; implying that access to the Web has the potential to have the greatest impact on exports of countries that have not historically had strong trade ties by compensating for a lack of strong historical trade linkages. In particular the FW model yields four predictions about how the internet will affect trade flows.

*   Overall, trade will expand as the number of firms with access to the internet increases.
*   Access to the internet reduces dependence on historical patterns of trade.
*   Countries that exported to a small number of countries before the internet will have the greatest increase in trade.
*   The effect of distance on trade flows will be reduced if distance mainly influences trade because of information and hence sunk costs. If distance affects trade because of transport costs then the effect of the internet on this relationship is ambiguous.

Perhaps the most striking prediction of the model is that, contrary to popular belief, the importance of distance in international trade patterns is not necessarily destined to decline. For a more indepth discussion of this and other theoretical points of the model interested readers are refereed to FW (2000 and 2002a).

3. Specification of the Gravity Equation of Trade

We test the predictions of the theoretical model using cross sectional "gravity" models of trade. Gravity equations have been used extensively in the literature (see, for example, DEARDORFF (1995), McCALLUM (1995), FRANKEL, STEIN and WEI (1995), HELLIWELL (1996), and WEI (1996)) as a means of empirically describing a "natural" pattern of trade based on the economic sizes (i.e. "mass") and geographic distances between countries. In addition, DEARDORFF (1998) has shown that a basic gravity specification can be derived from a number of theoretical trade models. The model in the previous section is also consistent with a gravity equation for trade—trade increases with the size of the foreign market and the size of the domestic economy (as measured by the number of firms in the model), and decreases with distance. The empirical fit of the gravity specification tends to be quite good, generally explaining between 60-70 percent of the cross section variance of trade volumes.

The gravity equation is fundamentally based on the underlying "gravitational" relationship

(I) $TOT_{ij} = \omega(GDP_i GDP_j / DIST_{ij})$, $TOT_{ij} = \omega(GDP_i GDP_j / DIST_{ij})$,

where *TOT* is the total bilateral trading volume between countries i and j. Taking logs on both sides produces the specification

(II) $tot_{ij} = \beta_0 + \beta_1(gdp_i gdp_j) + \beta_2 dist_{ij} + \varphi_{ij}$,

where $gdp_i gdp_j$ is the log of the product of the GNP's of country i and j.

Slightly embellishing the basic specification as is common in the literature, we start by estimating the following equation:

(III) $tot_{ij} = \beta_0 + \beta_1 (gdp_i gdp_j) + \beta_2(pop_i pop_j) + \beta_3 dist_{ij} + \beta_4 ADJ_{ij} + \beta_5 LANG + \beta_6 LINK + \beta_7 FTA + \varepsilon_{ij}$,

where $pop_i pop_j$ is the log of the product of the populations of country *i* and *j*, and ADJ, LANG, LINK, and FTA are dummy variables which take the value 1 for adjacent countries, country pairs which share a common language, countries which share some colonial linkages, and country pairs which are both members of a free trade area, respectively.

Finally, including a measure of the "cybermass" of the two countries, the appropriate specification of the gravity equation becomes

(IV) $tot_{ij} = \beta_0 + \beta_1 (gdp_i gdp_j) + \beta_2(pop_i pop_j) + \beta_3 dist_{ij} + \beta_4 ADJ_{ij} + \beta_5 LANG + \beta_6 LINK + \beta_7 FTA + \beta_8(cmass_i cmass_j) + \varepsilon_{ij}$,

where $(cmass_i cmass_j)$ denotes the log of the product of the cybermasses of countries *i* and *j*. If the Internet has a positive effect on trade then the coefficient on cybermass should be positive.

4. Data

To measure cybermass, we use data from the Internet Software Consortium (ISC) to count how many web hosts are attributed to each country by counting top-level host domain names. A top-level domain name is either an ISO country code or one of the generic domains (com/org/net/etc). However, this is certainly not an ideal measure. ISC notes that, "There is not necessarily any correlation between a host's domain name and where it is actually located. A host with a .NL domain name could easily be located in the U.S. or any other country. In addition, hosts under domains EDU/ORG/NET/COM/INT could be located anywhere. There is no way to determine where a host is without asking its administrator. ... In summary, it is not possible to determine the exact size of the Internet, where hosts are located, or how many users there are" (www.isc.org).

Thus the best we can hope for is that our measure of cybermass, which we call *HOST*, is at least somewhat correlated with the relative quantity of host sites in each country. However, even if a host site with, say, a Swedish top-level domain name is located in the USA, it is likely that the content of the web site is aimed Swedes. Thus the number of "Swedish" sites, regardless of physical location of the computers, should to a large extent reflect the "wiredness," or cybermass, of the country. In all of the specification reported in the paper, we do not attribute hosts under the domains *.org*, *.edu*, *.net*, *.com* or *.int* to any particular country.[2]

Because of the possible problems with the data noted above, we also use estimates of the number of Internet users in each country (as provided in the World Bank, World Development Indicators), as an alternative measure of cybermass. These data are available for 34 of the 56 countries in our sample.

Data on bilateral merchandise trade flows, GDP, and population are from the IMF. Data on geographic distances between countries was generously provided by SHANG-JIN WEI who compiled them from Direct-Line Distances (1986). Data on common linguistic heritage and colonial links were compiled from RAND McNALLY and Co. Historical Atlas of the World (1994) and are available from the author. Data on free trade areas come from the World Trade Organization web site (www.wto.org).[3] All data were collected for 56 countries for the years 1995-1999.

Table 1 lists all of the countries included in the study. Summary statistics on the number of host sites by top-level domain name, for the 56 countries in the sample, are presented in the top panel of Table 2. Between 1995 and 1997 the number of such host sites approximately doubles each year. In 1998 and 1999 this exponential rate slows slightly, but is still quite high. The lower panel of Table 2 presents the same statistics for developing countries, defined as countries with 1995 per-capita income below $2,000.

---

[2] As the vast majority of sites with *.org*, *.edu*, *.net*, *.com* or *.int* domain names could be expected to reside in the United States, we expect the cybermass measure for this country to be biased downward. To check whether this particular bias could have an effect on the results, the analysis was repeated including a dummy variable for any country pair that included the US, interacted with our cybermass measure, *HOST_12*. While this interaction term was statistically significant (and negative) for 1996 and 1997 (but not for 1995), its inclusion in the regression did not significantly change any of the other results. We also redo the regressions assuming that 85 percent of these sites are in the United States (not reported). The results were very similar to the base case.

[3] The FTAs included are the EU, NAFTA, Mercosur, ECO, Sparteca, Bangkok, ASEAN, EFTA, CEFTA, and the Tripartite agreement.

Table C1:   List of Countries

Algeria	Finland	Kenya	Saudi Arabia
Argentina	France	Kuwait	Singapore
Australia	Germany	Malaysia	South Africa
Austria	Greece	Mexico	South Korea
Belgium	Hong Kong	Morocco	Spain
Bolivia	Hungary	Netherlands	Sweden
Brazil	Iceland	New Zealand	Switzerland
Canada	India	Norway	Thailand
Chile	Indonesia	Pakistan	Tunisia
China	Iran	Paraguay	Turkey
Colombia	Ireland	Peru	United Kingdom
Denmark	Israel	Philippines	United States
Ecuador	Italy	Poland	Uruguay
Egypt	Japan	Portugal	Venezuela

Table C2:   Summary Statistics for Host Sites by Country Top-Level Domain Names

All Countries					
Year	N	Mean	Std Dev	Minimum	Maximum
1995	56	29770.64	54367.70	0	241191
1996	56	63456.91	112886.26	0	452997
1997	56	114035.04	193965.52	0	734406
1998	56	191086.11	329857.61	17	1226568
1999	56	266346.20	460465.73	25	1718935

Less Developed Countries					
Year	N	Mean	Std Dev	Minimum	Maximum
1995	13	150.23	190.20	0	569
1996	13	674.77	851.84	0	2351
1997	13	3114.77	5644.49	28	19739
1998	13	4637.46	6233.80	17	16930
1999	13	6501.62	7505.33	25	18538

Source: Internet Software Consortium (http://www.isc.org/)

5. Discussion of the Results

As illustrated in section 3, the advent of the Internet is likely to influence trade patterns. First, access to the web is likely to increase exports as countries have more information about foreign markets and costs of accessing these markets are reduced. Second, access to the web should reduce the importance of past linkages in trade. Third, as has been incessantly heralded in both the popular and scholarly presses, the web could significantly decrease the significance of physical distance as an impediment to trade. Note, however, that theory is agnostic on this point, if distance primarily feeds into information costs then distance is likely to become less important for trade. However, if distance affects trade because of transport costs it is not clear whether the effect of distance on trade should increase or decrease.

Results from the baseline gravity equation, for 1995 to 1999, are reported in Columns (1) through (5) of Table 3. Columns (6) through (10) include the Internet variable, HOST. In 1995 HOST is not significant and in 1996 it is only weakly significant, but from 1997 to 1999 HOST is positive and statistically significant and appears to be increasing in importance as the Internet develops, with a slight drop-off in magnitude in 1999. The coefficient of 0.14 in 1999 suggests that a 10 percent increase in the number of hosts in one country would have led to about 1.4 percent greater trade.

Table C3:   Gravity Model of Trade

Dependent Variable: Log (Total Trade Volume)					
	1995	1996	1997	1998	1999
	(1)	(2)	(3)	(4)	(5)
Constant	5.157**	5.511**	3.948**	4.395**	4.497**
	(5.90)	(5.84)	(3.72)	(5.58)	(5.55)
GDP_{ij}	1.194**	1.217**	1.196**	1.165**	1.191**
	(36.21)	(35.59)	(35.56)	(36.00)	(37.22)
POP_{ij}	-0.125**	-0.157**	-0.124**	-0.123**	-0.125**
	(-4.40)	(-5.24)	(-4.13)	(-4.77)	(-4.53)
DIST	-0.892**	-0.850**	-0.768**	-0.771**	-0.818**
	(-17.36)	(-13.47)	(-10.46)	(-14.73)	(-14.54)
ADJ	0.550**	0.507*	0.383	0.542**	0.547**
	(2.73)	(2.42)	(1.16)	(2.84)	(2.83)
LANG	1.008**	1.135**	1.053**	0.959**	0.995**
	(7.78)	(8.41)	(7.22)	(7.48)	(7.24)
LINK	0.530*	0.552*	0.561**	0.511*	0.456*
	(2.34)	(2.44)	(2.56)	(2.37)	(2.01)
FTA	0.076	0.161	0.385*	0.273*	0.303*
	(0.60)	(1.14)	(2.26)	(1.99)	(2.18)
$HOST_{ij}$					
No. Obs.	1515	1507	1507	1535	1537
R-square	0.6756	0.6506	0.6320	0.6956	0.7025

Please note: heteroskedasticity-consistent t-statistics in parentheses.
** indicates statistical significance at 1%, and * at 5%

Table C3:   Continued

Dependent Variable: Log (Total Trade Volume)					
	1995	**1996**	**1997**	**1998**	**1999**
	(6)	**(7)**	**(8)**	**(9)**	**(10)**
Constant	4.772**	3.257*	0.713	-0.688	-0.047
	(3.70)	(2.22)	(0.45)	(-0.59)	(-0.04)
GDP_{ij}	1.173**	1.090**	1.003**	0.863**	0.925**
	(21.85)	(17.42)	(16.38)	(15.45)	(17.12)
POP_{ij}	-0.111**	-0.081	-0.018	0.041	0.019
	(-2.61)	(-1.75)	(-0.40)	(1.16)	(0.52)
DIST	-0.893**	-0.861**	-0.814**	-0.856**	-0.900**
	(-17.34)	(-13.57)	(-11.32)	(-16.12)	(-16.24)
ADJ	0.560**	0.536*	0.371	0.540**	0.504**
	(2.75)	(2.55)	(1.17)	(2.82)	(2.61)
LANG	1.000**	1.110**	0.984**	0.870**	0.894**
	(7.73)	(8.26)	(7.13)	(6.86)	(6.59)
LINK	0.533*	0.565**	0.576**	0.517*	0.484*
	(2.35)	(2.56)	(2.65)	(2.34)	(2.08)
FTA	0.070	0.131	0.261	0.068	0.124
	(0.55)	(0.93)	(1.64)	(0.52)	(0.93)
$HOST_{ij}$	0.009	0.059*	0.103**	0.161**	0.144**
	(0.43)	(2.12)	(3.28)	(5.82)	(5.33)
No. Obs.	1515	1507	1507	1535	1537
R-square	0.6757	0.6520	0.6381	0.7090	0.7110

Please note: heteroskedasticity-consistent t-statistics in parentheses.
** indicates statistical significance at 1%, and * at 5%

Including the host variable in the Internet regression has a notable impact on the coefficients on GDP and population. This suggests that there is significant multicollinearity between the host variable and these variables, most likely because the number of Internet sites in a country is positively correlated with per-capita income, and GDP and population together capture per-capita income in the baseline gravity equation (log(GDP/POP)=logGDP-logPOP). This implies that our estimate of the coefficient on the Internet variable in Table 3 overestimates its true value, and should be interpreted as an upper bound of the effect of the Internet on trade.

To account for this possible upward bias, we include initial trade patterns from 1995 in the regression equation. Including past trade is important because the model shows that historical exports will be important in determining current exports if sunk costs are important. In addition, this lagged dependent variable will capture all of the country- and pair-specific unobservable characteristics that are time invariant (and a good deal of the time varying characteristics as long as these are changing relatively slowly). Including this variable therefore ensures that our HOST variable is not just picking up the effects of some inherent country traits, such as relative wealth.

Table 4 reports the results when 1995 trade is included in the regression equation for other years. As expected, the statistical significance of population, distance and some other control variables are not longer robust across all time periods. However the HOST variable remains positive and robustly statistically significant from 1996 to 1999.[4] Not surprisingly, the coefficient falls somewhat when past trade is included. The coefficient of 0.043 in 1999, in combination with the coefficient on past trade of 0.515, implies that a 10 percent increase in hosts in one country would have led to about 0.9 percent $(0.043/(1-0.515)=0.09)$ higher trade. This is our preferred estimate of the effect of the Internet on international trade.

Table C4:   Gravity Model Including Initial Conditions

Dependent variable: Log (Total Trade Volume)				
	1996	**1997**	**1998**	**1999**
	(1)	**(2)**	**(3)**	**(4)**
Constant	-0.448	-2.689*	-0.050	1.162
	(-0.58)	(-2.27)	(-0.08)	(1.58)
GDP_{ij}	0.097*	0.127*	0.331**	0.446**
	(2.11)	(2.15)	(5.65)	(8.04)
POP_{ij}	0.010	0.064*	0.025	-0.008
	(0.43)	(2.17)	(1.16)	(-0.32)
DIST	-0.082	-0.081	-0.349**	-0.423**
	(-1.61)	(-1.23)	(-8.39)	(-9.27)
ADJ	0.049	-0.021	0.185*	0.116
	(0.62)	(-0.08)	(2.06)	(1.22)
LANG	0.241**	0.331**	0.401**	0.438**
	(5.01)	(4.14)	(5.83)	(5.51)
LINK	0.099*	0.128	0.222*	0.187
	(2.05)	(1.56)	(2.05)	(1.61)
FTA	0.094	0.228*	0.072	0.125
	(1.35)	(2.04)	(1.11)	(1.71)
$HOST_{ij}$	0.032**	0.063**	0.071**	0.043**
	(2.82)	(3.20)	(4.02)	(2.56)
$TRADE_{ij}\_95$	0.860**	0.766**	0.542**	0.515**
	(23.03)	(16.52)	(13.14)	(12.00)
No. Obs.	1507	1507	1512	1514
R-squared	0.8854	0.8299	0.8522	0.8376

Please note: heteroskedasticity-consistent t-statistics in parentheses.
** indicates statistical significance at 1%, and * at 5%.

---

[4]   The model also suggests that the Internet should reduce hysteresis in trade. To test this we include an interaction term of the host variable and past trade. The coefficient has the expected negative sign, indicating that in countries with more Internet hosts, past trade does not have as much explanatory power. While these results (not reported) always had the expected sign, they were not always significant at a standard level.

In contrast to the coefficients on population and GDP, the effect of distance on trade changes only slightly when HOST is included in the regression equation. In the baseline gravity equation, as shown in the first five columns of Table 3, the coefficient on distance falls slightly over time. When the host variable is included in the regression equation, as shown in the next five columns, the coefficient on distance becomes more stable, providing some evidence that the Internet has reduced the way in which distance impacts trade. This marginal effect could be because it is too early to find more substantial evidence of a decline in the importance of distance.[5] Alternatively, as the model suggests, it could be that distance affects trade primarily through transport costs, not information.[6]

There could be a legitimate concern about the direction of causality between *HOST* and trade flows. Rather than increased Internet usage spurring more trade, it is possible that countries that trade a lot have greater incentive to launch web initiatives to facilitate that trade. Although we cannot completely control for this possibility, in Table 5 we use two- and four- year lagged values of *HOST* instead of the contemporaneous variable.[7] The results show that the lagged HOST variable is not statistically significant in 1996 in the regression, indicating that the Internet had no or very little systematic effect on trade flows during this time period. The lagged values are significant from 1997 onward. The coefficient in 1999, of 0.09 suggests that a 10 percent increase in the number of hosts in one country would have led to about 0.9 percent more trade in 1999.

The results suggest that during 1995 the Internet had no significant effect on international trade patterns. In 1996 there is some weak evidence of a small effect, but this result disappears with the use of lagged values of HOST. However, by 1997 there is increasing evidence that the Internet is indeed having an impact. The positive and statistically significant effect of the Internet on trade continues through 1998 and 1999. In addition, the fact that these effects remain statistically significant for lagged values of HOST is a strong indication that the direction of causality runs from Internet host sites to trade, rather than the reverse.

---

[5] We also try interacting distance with the host variable (not reported) and the sign and significance were not robust across time and across different specifications.

[6] However our results are not conclusive in this regard. In particular, Portes and Rey (1999) find that distance still has an important (negative) impact on international equity flows despite the fact that they are "weightless" and thus do not entail transport costs in the traditional sense. Using telephone call traffic and international bank branches to proxy for information transmission, their results suggest that distance could be proxying for informational asymmetries.

[7] We use two-year lag because the data on hosts is less likely to persistent on a two year horizon than a one year horizon. We also try various different lag lengths, and the results were qualitatively similar.

Table C5: Gravity Model of Trade, Lagged Host

Dependent Variable: Log(Total Trade Volume)					
	1996[a]	1997	1998	1999	1999
	(1)	(2)	(3)	(4)	(5)
Constant	4.007**	-0.008	-1.464	1.939	0.481
	(2.90)	(-0.00)	(-1.23)	(1.83)	(0.40)
GDP_{ij}	1.133**	0.978**	0.821**	1.031**	0.959**
	(20.51)	(15.49)	(14.32)	(22.24)	(19.98)
POP_{ij}	-0.102*	0.019	0.079*	-0.038	0.026
	(-2.28)	(0.37)	(2.04)	(-1.13)	(0.65)
DIST	-0.854**	-0.773**	-0.812**	-0.867**	-0.839**
	(-13.53)	(-10.68)	(-15.32)	(-15.49)	(-14.96)
ADJ	0.546**	0.485	0.602**	0.512**	0.620**
	(2.56)	(1.53)	(3.16)	(2.68)	(3.14)
LANG	1.101**	0.990**	0.943**	0.936**	0.928**
	(8.19)	(7.03)	(7.30)	(6.96)	(6.81)
LINK	0.564*	0.585**	0.545**	0.473*	0.489*
	(2.52)	(2.66)	(2.58)	(2.10)	(2.14)
FTA	0.138	0.319*	0.165	0.193	0.223
	(0.98)	(1.97)	(1.25)	(1.43)	(1.64)
$HOST_{ij}(-2)$	0.034	0.087**	0.159**	0.086**	
	(1.62)	(3.46)	(6.23)	(4.21)	
$HOST_{ij}(-4)$					0.093**
					(4.99)
No. Obs.	1507	1507	1535	1537	1537
R-squared	0.6513	0.6369	0.7085	0.7071	0.7087

Please note: heteroskedasticity-consistent t-statistics in parentheses.
** indicates statistical significance at 1%, and * at 5%
a. HOST is lagged only one year in this regression.

In Table 6 we examine whether the impact of the Internet on trade is similar for both industrialized and developing countries. We disaggregate the effect of *HOST* into country pairs of two rich countries (*HOST*_RR), of one rich and one poor (*HOST*_RP), and of two poor countries (*HOST*_PP), where "rich" is defined as a country with per-capita GDP above $2000 in 1995. We do not find a statistically significant effect for any of the groups in 1995, a result consistent with the previous analysis. In 1996, however, we find small but statistically significant effects for pairs of rich countries (although this is significant only at 5 percent level) and rich-poor country pairs, but none for poor-poor country pairs. In 1997 the coefficients for the rich-rich and rich-poor country pairs grows in magnitude and statistical significance. Significantly, the coefficient on the poor-poor country pairs is also now significant and its magnitude is not statistically different from the latter two groups. In 1998 the number of host sites in poor-poor country pairs has an even greater impact, both in magnitude and in statistical significance, than either the rich-poor or even the rich-rich country pairs. By 1999 this pattern has further solidified: we see the smallest effect for rich-rich pairs, and intermediate effect for rich-poor pairs and the largest impact on poor-poor country trading partners.

Table C6:   Gravity Model of Trade, the Net's Effect on Rich and Poor Countries

Dependent Variable: Log (Total Trade Volume)					
	1995	1996	1997	1998	1999
	(1)	(2)	(3)	(4)	(4)
Constant	5.702**	3.266*	1.207	0.913	2.688
	(3.94)	(2.07)	(0.70)	(0.65)	(1.77)
GDP_{ij}	1.207**	1.091**	1.024**	0.927**	1.029**
	(20.97)	(17.23)	(15.48)	(13.98)	(16.87)
POP_{ij}	-0.152**	-0.083	-0.040	-0.030	-0.104*
	(-2.98)	(-1.61)	(-0.76)	(-0.61)	(-2.03)
DIST	-0.887**	-0.858**	-0.811**	-0.840**	-0.875**
	(-17.13)	(-13.61)	(-11.27)	(-15.75)	(-15.88)
ADJ	0.596**	0.564**	0.390	0.586**	0.593**
	(2.87)	(2.68)	(1.23)	(3.04)	(2.99)
LANG	1.020**	1.109**	0.992**	0.919**	0.985**
	(7.76)	(8.21)	(7.15)	(7.07)	(7.03)
LINK	0.506*	0.540*	0.558**	0.490*	0.442
	(2.25)	(2.48)	(2.60)	(2.25)	(1.93)
FTA	0.080	0.162	0.270	0.084	0.126
	(0.61)	(1.13)	(1.67)	(0.64)	(0.95)
$HOST_{ij}$ _RR	0.007	0.058*	0.101**	0.155**	0.141**
	(0.35)	(2.10)	(3.23)	(5.54)	(5.22)
$HOST_{ij}$ _RP	0.025	0.067*	0.109**	0.172**	0.169**
	(1.05)	(2.21)	(3.37)	(6.21)	(6.05)
$HOST_{ij}$ _PP	0.033	0.031	0.104**	0.178**	0.189**
	(0.65)	(0.62)	(2.57)	(5.52)	(5.78)
No. Obs.	1515	1507	1507	1535	1537
R-squared	0.6764	0.6528	0.6383	0.7104	0.7150

Please note: heteroskedasticity-consistent t-statistics in parentheses.
** indicates statistical significance at 1%, and * at 5%.

Theory suggests that the Internet should diminish the importance of past link-ages on trade flows. In Table 7 we explore this hypothesis by including two inter-action terms, HOST with language and HOST with our colonial links variable. If the Internet is making old linkages less important then the interaction terms should be negative. However, the Internet could make the effect of language on trade flows more important if countries with the same language are more likely to ac-cess each others web sites. Alternatively, if most businesses are using a single language in web products (eg. English), the Internet should tend to reduce the importance of this bilateral linkage. In 1997-1999 the interaction with LINK takes the expected negative sign but is not statistically significant (note however that LINK also becomes statistically insignificant). Our interaction variable with LANGUAGE is also negative, and is consistently statistically significant in all the years. These results suggest that the Internet is indeed starting to break down old ties (i.e. favoring partners who share one's language), although the overall results also suggest that it is still very early in this process.

Table C7: Gravity Model with LINK Interaction Terms

Dependent Variable: Log(Total Trade Volume)					
	1995	1996	1997	1998	1999
	(1)	(2)	(3)	(4)	(4)
Constant	4.403**	2.684	0.510	-1.014	-0.266
	(3.36)	(1.78)	(0.32)	(-0.86)	(-0.21)
GDP_{ij}	1.181**	1.095**	1.028**	0.884**	0.956**
	(22.00)	(17.53)	(16.81)	(15.71)	(17.50)
POP_{ij}	-0.111**	-0.078	-0.028	0.033	0.007
	(-2.61)	(-1.69)	(-0.63)	(0.94)	(0.19)
DIST	-0.872**	-0.835**	-0.787**	-0.823**	-0.865**
	(-16.81)	(-13.05)	(-10.78)	(-15.33)	(-15.49)
ADJ	0.559**	0.547**	0.382	0.539**	0.501**
	(2.90)	(2.77)	(1.24)	(2.97)	(2.77)
LANG	2.494**	3.478**	4.108**	4.080**	4.783**
	(6.40)	(6.77)	(6.26)	(6.12)	(6.27)
LINK	-0.100	-0.720	0.967	2.209	1.806
	(-0.08)	(-0.44)	(0.50)	(1.25)	(0.86)
FTA	0.078	0.134	0.275	0.097	0.156
	(0.62)	(0.97)	(1.74)	(0.74)	(1.18)
$HOST_{ij}$	0.015	0.071*	0.106**	0.165**	0.145**
	(0.71)	(2.47)	(3.35)	(5.93)	(5.35)
$HOST_{ij}$*LANG	-0.096**	-0.135**	-0.159**	-0.156**	-0.180**
	(-4.01)	(-4.94)	(-5.09)	(-5.06)	(-5.39)
$HOST_{ij}$*LINK	0.042	0.072	-0.017	-0.075	-0.056
	(0.53)	(0.84)	(-0.18)	(-0.91)	(-0.60)
No. Obs.	1515	1507	1507	1535	1537
R-squared	0.6773	0.6546	0.6404	0.7117	0.7140

Please note: heteroskedasticity-consistent t-statistics in parentheses.
** indicates statistical significance at 1%, and * at 5%.

The results presented in Tables 3-7 show a clear pattern of increasing importance of the Internet in determining general trade patterns, especially among poorer countries. However, theory focuses on the effect of access to the Internet on the exporters. If exporters pay sunk costs to enter a new market and the Internet removes these costs, then number of firms with Internet access—measured as the number of hosts – should have a greater impact on exports than on imports. In Table 8 we re-do the analysis using exports only, rather than total trade. For these regressions we distinguish between the country of origin (country i) and the country of destination (country j) in the analysis. Table 8 presents the exports-only gravity equation for 1995 to 1999.

Table C8:   Exports Gravity Model of Trade
              i = country of origin, *j* = destination country

Dependent Variable: Log (Exports from i to j)					
	1995	1996	1997	1998	1999
	(1)	(2)	(3)	(4)	(5)
Constant	3.557**	2.934*	-0.367	-3.757**	-1.837
	(3.22)	(2.14)	(-0.31)	(-3.38)	(-1.65)
GDP[i]	1.209**	1.143**	1.066**	0.831**	0.904**
	(17.95)	(12.97)	(14.16)	(11.64)	(13.72)
GDP[j]	1.211**	1.159**	1.007**	0.934**	1.006**
	(19.94)	(16.13)	(16.17)	(14.97)	(16.01)
POP[i]	-0.070	-0.096	-0.004	0.125**	0.110*
	(-1.33)	(-1.50)	(-0.07)	(2.73)	(2.36)
POP[j]	-0.110*	-0.058	-0.004	0.032	-0.036
	(-2.32)	(-1.06)	(-0.10)	(0.73)	(-0.82)
DIST	-1.037**	-1.074**	-0.943**	-0.915**	-1.003**
	(-21.59)	(-20.48)	(-17.60)	(-15.66)	(-18.13)
ADJ	0.497**	0.325	0.306	0.489	0.530**
	(2.94)	(1.58)	(1.38)	(1.58)	(3.19)
LANG	1.230**	1.390**	1.138**	1.122**	1.105**
	(11.12)	(11.87)	(10.44)	(7.65)	(9.82)
LINK	0.669**	0.688**	0.671**	0.591**	0.583**
	(3.58)	(3.63)	(3.90)	(2.96)	(2.97)
FTA	0.075	0.004	0.188	-0.493*	0.087
	(0.68)	(0.03)	(1.56)	(-2.29)	(0.65)
HOST[i]	0.084**	0.154**	0.164**	0.319**	0.259**
	(3.15)	(4.05)	(4.31)	(8.82)	(7.55)
HOST[j]	-0.029	0.002	0.084**	0.099**	0.096**
	(-1.23)	(0.06)	(2.92)	(3.42)	(3.23)
No. Obs.	3035	3023	3023	3073	3075
R-squared	0.6003	0.5807	0.6078	0.5756	0.6307

Please note: heteroskedasticity-consistent t-statistics in parentheses.
** indicates statistical significance at 1%, and * at 5%.

The results show a pattern broadly consistent with those from the more general analysis[8]. In particular, in each year we find the impact of the Internet on the exporting country to be significantly greater than for the importing country, and the coefficients for the importing country are not statistically significant until 1997. For both the exporter and importer the impact of the Internet is increasing over

---

[8] We have also estimated the export-only gravity estimation with the HOST variable interacted with the rich and poor country dummies in order to investigate whether the Internet is having a differential effect on developing countries. Again the pattern is broadly consistent with previous results, with HOST playing a more important role in determining exports and having a greater effect in poor countries, for imports as well as for exports. The statistical significance of the results for exports in poor countries in not particularly robust in 1995 and 1996, but from 1997 onwards HOST has a significant effect at the 1 percent level of confidence.

time. As in the general total trade results from Table 3, the coefficient estimates fall slightly in 1999 but are still highly statistically significant. The coefficients from 1999 can be interpreted as implying that a relative increase of 10 percent in domestic hosts would lead to about a 2.6 percent increase in exports, and about a 1 percent increase in imports.

6. Sensitivity Analysis and Alternative Explanations

In order to examine the robustness of our results we re-estimate the basic gravity equation using an alternative measure of cybermass—the number of Internet users. This data (from the World Bank, World Development Indicators) is available for 34 countries of our 56 countries, so the data set is somewhat smaller. The results are reported in Table 9. They show a similar pattern to the one noted above. There is little evidence of an impact of the Internet on trade in 1995 and 1996, with a greater impact in the next three years.

Table C9: Total Trade Regressions with User Data

Dependent Variable: Log (Total Trade Volume)					
	1995	1996	1997	1998	1999
	(1)	(2)	(3)	(4)	(5)
Constant	8.55**	10.20**	8.49**	3.56*	4.55*
	(4.41)	(4.90)	(4.75)	(1.96)	(2.24)
GDP_{ij}	1.00**	1.05**	0.88**	0.43**	0.61**
	(10.09)	(8.68)	(8.13)	(3.45)	(4.19)
POP_{ij}	-0.14*	-0.20**	-0.14*	-0.01	-0.06
	(-2.38)	(-2.88)	(-2.35)	(-0.24)	(-1.02)
DIST	-1.07**	-1.13**	-1.09**	-0.96**	-1.00**
	(-10.43)	(-10.93)	(-11.44)	(-10.38)	(-10.93)
ADJ	0.51	0.28	0.31	0.45	0.40
	(1.90)	(1.00)	(1.14)	(1.72)	(1.47)
LANG	0.98**	1.07**	0.77**	1.01**	0.94**
	(5.03)	(5.47)	(4.28)	(5.07)	(4.58)
LINK	0.96*	0.85*	0.77*	0.37	0.47
	(2.33)	(2.13)	(2.20)	(1.01)	(1.22)
FTA	0.40	0.39	0.39	0.61*	0.61
	(0.39)	(1.34)	(1.39)	(2.07)	(1.95)
$USER_{ij}$	0.14*	0.12	0.22**	0.52**	0.42**
	(2.18)	(1.54)	(2.86)	(5.58)	(3.99)
No. Obs.	555	551	551	559	559
R-squared	0.68	0.69	0.73	0.75	0.77

Please note: heteroskedasticity-consistent t-statistics in parentheses.
** indicates statistical significance at 1%, and * at 5%

Tables 3-9 have shown that there is significant empirical evidence of a correlation between increased Internet usage and trade, especially in 1998 and 1999. These results show that the effect is particularly strong for poor countries, and that Internet usage and has reduced the importance of past linkages in explaining trade patterns. We have interpreted this as consistent with our theoretical model from FW (2000) discussed in section 2, but there could be alternative explanations of the observed correlation. We have directly addressed the question of endogeneity by including lagged Internet measures in the analysis. In particular, we find that the variation in host sites in 1995 is not significant in explaining trade in that year, however, the 1995 host variable is significant in explaining some of the observed trade patterns in later years. This suggests that the internet has affected trade flows.

A second possible objection to our interpretation could be that countries with more Internet hosts trade more because a growing amount of trade is in high-tech products like telecommunications equipment and other technology related products. In this case, countries with relatively more hosts would trade more, simply because they produce and consume a lot of high-tech products. As our data is not disaggregated by commodity we cannot directly rule out this possibility. Nevertheless, the results are not consistent with this particular interpretation. It is reasonable to assume that the countries leading the trade in higher technology goods would be the more developed nations. If our Internet data were simply a proxy for high-technology trading countries, then we would expect to find the strongest results for the richer countries and less or none for the developing countries, the opposite of our actual results. In addition, by 1995 and 1996 countries had already been producing high-tech products for many years, so it would seem unlikely that the Internet variable would be insignificant in those years if the variable is only picking up high-tech trade.

A third possibility could be that our Internet HOST measure is proxying some other unknown factor that is associated with trade as well as with the Internet, but that the Internet itself does not affect trade. For example, countries with more hosts may also have similar tastes and therefore these countries trade more, or the Internet may be proxying for the effect of developed infrastructure on trade. Again, while it is impossible to completely rule out some possible omitted variable bias, our results are not consistent with this latter hypothesis. In particular, if the presence of Internet sites were in fact just a proxy for similar tastes or better infrastructure then we would expect to see statistically significant and relatively similar results across the sample period. We find no evidence of an effect of the Internet on trade in 1995, only very weak evidence in 1996, and much larger impacts in subsequent years, indicating that we are capturing an effect which has strengthened over time and is not a proxy for some country time-invariant (at least over a 5 year period) characteristics.

7. Conclusions

This paper has presented a series of gravity equations to test some empirical implications of a theoretical model of the impact of the Internet on international trade. In particular theory produces a number of specific implications; first, it suggests that trade should expand because sunk costs associated with trade are reduced. Second, the development of global markets via the Internet implies that historical linkages should be less important. Third, countries with the fewest past trade linkages (most likely the poor countries) have the most to gain from the Internet. Finally, while public rhetoric has emphasized the "death of distance", the theory does not offer such a definite prediction with respect to its fate.

Using recent trade and Internet data we estimate a series of gravity equations which strongly support the predictions of the model. We find no robust relationship between the Internet and total trade in 1995 and 1996; from 1997 onwards, the Internet shows a positive, increasing and statistically significant impact on the global pattern of trade flows. As predicted by the model, the effect of the Internet is felt primarily through exports, and those countries with relatively more Internet presence also display less dependence on historical determinants of trade such as a common language. Perhaps more importantly, the results suggest that the benefits of the Internet may accrue disproportionately to poorer countries.

Our results reinforce the importance of policies aimed at reducing the "digital divide" between industrialized and developing countries. We have shown systematic and statistically significant evidence that increased Internet access can have positive effects on the exports of poorer countries, and our theoretical model strongly suggests that these movements should be welfare enhancing. If developing countries are limited in their access to the World Wide Web they will not be able to take advantage of the benefits accruing to wealthier countries, and the rise of Net will therefore be associated in increased global inequality. On the other hand, we have argued that given sufficient access to the Internet, the overall effect of the web should be to lessen historically determined inequalities in trading patterns and to increase export opportunities for developing countries, thus reducing global inequality.

References

BALDWIN, R. (1988), Hysteresis in Import Prices: the Beachhead Effect, American Economic Review, 78/1988.
BRANDER, J., KRUGMAN, P. (1983), A 'Reciprocal Dumping' Model of International Trade, Journal of International Economics 15/1983.
DEARDORFF, A.V. (1998), Determinants of Bilateral Trade: Does Gravity Work in a Neoclassical World? in: FRANKEL, J., ed. (1998), The Regionalization of the World Economy, Chicago: University of Chicago Press.
INTERNET SOFTWARE CONSORTIUM (http://www.isc.org/)
EICHENGREEN, B., IRWIN, D. (1998), The Role of History in Bilateral Trade flows, in: FRANKEL, J., ed. (1998), The Regionalization of the World Economy, Chicago: University of Chicago Press.
FITZPATRICK, G.L., MODLIN, M.J. (1986), Direct-Line Distances, International Edition, The Scarecow Press, Inc. Metuchen, N.J., and London.
FRANKEL, J., STEIN, E., WEI, J.S. (1995), Trade blocks and the Americas: the natural, the Unnatural and the super-natural, Journal of Development Economics, no. 47/1995.
FREUND, C. (2000), Different Paths to Free Trade: The Gains from Regionalism, Quarterly Journal of Economics.
FREUND, C., WEINHOLD, D. (2000), The Effect of the Internet on International Trade, Federal Reserve Board of Governors International Finance Working paper no. 693.
FREUND, C., WEINHOLD, D. (2002a), The Effect of the Internet on International Trade, Revised version.
FREUND, C., WEINHOLD, D. (2002b), The Internet and International Trade in Services, American Economic Review.
HELLIWELL, J.F. (1996), Do national borders matter for Quebec's trade? Canadian Journal of Economics, vol. 29 no. 3.
McCALLUM, J. (1995), National Borders Matter: Canada-US regional trade patterns, American Economic Review, vol. 85 no. 3.
PORTES, R., REY, H. (1999), The determinants of cross-border equity flows, NBER Working Paper no. 7336.
QUAH, D. (1999), The weightless economy in economic development, CEP Discussion Paper no. 417.
RAND McNALLY AND CO. (1994), Historical Atlas of the World, Rand McNally and Company, Chicago.
RAUCH, J.E. (1996), Trade and Search: Social Capital, Sogo Shosha, and Spillovers, NBER Working Paper no. 5618.
RAUCH, J.E. (1999), Networks Versus Markets in International Trade, Journal of International Economics 48/1999, 7-35.
RAUCH, J.E., TRINDADE, V. (2000), Information and Globalization: Wage Co-movements, Labor Demand Elasticity and Conventional Trade Liberalization, NBER Working Paper no. 7671, April 2000.

ROBERTS, M., TYBOUT, J. (1997), The Decision to Export in Columbia: An Empirical Model of Entry with Sunk Costs, American Economic Review, 87/ 1997.

SANDERS, M. (2000), Sizing Global Online Exports, The Forrester Report, November 2000, www.forrester.com

WEI, S.J. (1996), Intra-National versus International Trade: How stubborn are Nation States in Globalization? NBER Working Paper 5331.

D. Internet Dynamics, Trade and Globalization
(Some Comments on the paper by Caroline L. Freund and Diana Weinhold)

Thomas Gries

1. General Comments

The Internet is one of the driving forces for the resent third wave of globalization. At least in the public debate the importance of the Internet seams to bee a sort of common wisdom. Even if plenty of anecdotes seem to back this postulate there is almost no empirical study analysing this proposition extensively. Therefore, this contribution is an important benchmark for getting a better insight into the real effects of the Internet on global market integration.

The present contribution is a carefully developed paper. The authors started by choosing a suitable theoretic model. The motivation why this model can be applied to the defined problem is discussed extensively. From the model the relevant testable implications are extracted and summarized. The testable implications are transformed into appropriate estimation equations. The data set and the chosen variables and indicators of the estimation equations are carefully discussed. The estimations methods are evaluated and a sensitivity analysis has been done after a check if the results match the derived predictions from the theoretical model. Looking at the methodology applied there is little to complain.

From the analysis of the authors we obtain the following major results:

- The Internet increased trade after 97: A 10% increase in hosts goes along with an increase in trade by about 1%.
- The Internet has not affected the relation of distance and trade: Distance, as an important determinant of trade has not been affected. Distance still matters.
- The Internet has reduced importance of past linkages: The history of trade becomes less important as a predictor for future trade.
- The Internet has strongest impact on trade among developing countries.
- All results are consistent with the theory introduced.

With these findings the debate of globalization and trade effects of the Internet has the first reliable results. Even if I believe that these results are robust, there are two areas in which I would like to make some more comments.

2. Comments on "Internet Increased Trade"

The result "Internet increased trade and international integration" leads to the expectation of an increasing trade share of GDP during the time of Internet. If these effects are strong they should be visible in simple export share graphics. Therefore, export shares of the US; the Eurozone (and Germany) and Japan are examined. If the Internet use has strongly contributed to trade expansion the naive expectation is, that the US as the mother country of the Internet with a large and strong increasing diffusion in the last 15 years should show a clear and larger positive trend towards growth in trade shares than e.g. the less expanding and less dynamic Internet region Eurozone or Japan. The results are presented in Figure 1.

Looking at the facts concerning the change in trade shares gives a little surprise. While generally trade shares increased in the 90s, i.e. during the time of Internet expansion, trade shares increased more rapidly in Europe than in the US, the major country of Internet use. Therefore, the question remains, if something might have affected trade positively especially outside the US? The answer is: may be yes. The 90s were not only the decade of Internet expansion, the 90s were also a decade of an extraordinary decrease in trade barriers. Trade liberalization in many Eastern European countries might have fostered trade shares especially in Western Europe. Trade liberalization gives a second explanation for increasing trade. Therefore, the Internet might be a considerable but not the only driving force for increasing trade shares.

3. Comments on "Internet Distance Trade"

The finding distance influences trade pattern via transportation costs and not via information costs is a consistent interpretation within a model of homogeneous goods. The story becomes different if innovation competition with heterogeneous goods or a full supply chain management is taken into account. In these cases market access and information become more important and information cost should matter. Since trade between developed countries basically is an exchange of non homogeneous goods within innovation competition, it seems at least unexpected that in transportation costs play the major role and information costs are of minor importance.

Figure D1:   Trade Shares of GDP

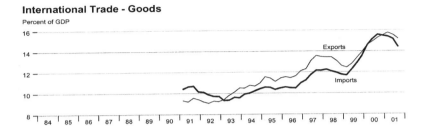

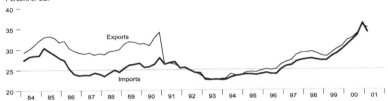

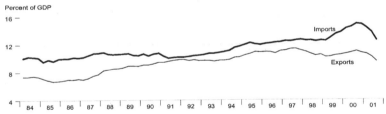

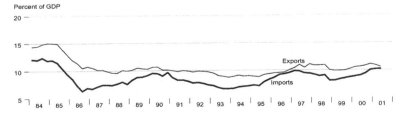

E. Internet and Culture

Marieke de Mooij

1. The Convergence Thesis

The spread of technology across the world, part of the globalisation process, is often linked with the convergence hypothesis: countries and their inhabitants are assumed to become similar in their systems and behaviour. In the developed world, nations are indeed converging with respect to income and demographics, worldwide they are not. There is increasing evidence that at the macro-economic level the convergence hypothesis must be questioned (CRAIG, DOUGLAS and GRAIN, 1992; HOLLANDERS, SOETE and TER WEEL, 1999; SARKAR, 1999). This article provides evidence that also at the micro-level, much of consumer behaviour does not converge.

In business journals and books however, convergence of income, media and technology is assumed to lead to converging needs, habits and tastes of consumers. The following quotations reflecting this assumption are representative of many others:

"In many vital ways, the trend [in Europe] is towards convergence, not divergence" [...] "A single youth culture is forming across Europe, even if it often mimics a kind of American model. Europe's teenagers listen to the same music [...] on their MP3 players, talk to each other on their Nokia GSM phones, and surf and chat on the Net. Many Europeans are now more alike each other than they are distinct" (ROSSANT, p. 2000).

"In many ways, consumers are growing more alike, and we all know why. Mass communications, travel, multinational companies, the whole apparatus of the global village" (BULLMORE, 2000, p. 48).

Also in academia the general assumption is that convergence of technology, global media, increased communication between people, increased trade and travel act to bring people together. In textbooks of international marketing there are plenty of statements on convergence of lifestyles and values but they are not based on empirical evidence. Examples of such statements are "The development in communications will bring convergence in consumer markets" (BRADLEY, 1991, p. 384) and "With technological advancement also comes cultural convergence" (CZINKOTA and RONKAINEN, 1993, p. 167).

MCLUHAN's (1964) concept of the 'Global Village' made many authors believe that in particular the new global media and increased travel will lead to convergence of values, lifestyles and consumption. ASSAEL (1998), author of one of the leading textbooks on consumer behaviour, states:

"Because of the advent of worldwide cable networks, television has become a global medium. Propelling this phenomenon is the global influence of MTV, the rock video channel, and CNN, the worldwide news channel. [...] Heavy viewers of TV will develop similar perceptions of reality because they are exposed to similar stimuli. [...] This implies that global TV networks such as MTV and CNN are promoting similar norms and values on a global basis" (ASSAEL, 1998, p. 499).

Reality is different. Few people watch international (English language) television programs regularly. Understanding the English language still varies widely and few Europeans, apart from the British and the Irish, regularly watch English language television without translation or subtitles (EMS 1996/1997). The English language cross-border channel CNN had to introduce Spanish and German language versions. MTV increasingly localizes its content across Europe.

In his famous article "The Globalization of Markets", TED LEVITT's (1983) argument was that new technology would lead to homogenisation of consumer wants and needs. Consumers were expected to prefer standard products of high quality and low price to more expensive diversity. This is based on the concept of a rational consumer who wants to maximize profit. This may be true in some cases for some individual consumers, but it cannot be generalized. There are more drivers of consumer behaviour than available money.

A few scholars have pointed out that globalisation remains mainly a belief since no empirical evidence has been brought to show homogenisation of tastes or the appearance of universal price-minded consumer segments (USUNIER, 1997). There is indeed little evidence of convergence of consumer behaviour across countries. The scarce empirical evidence available is based on macro-developmental data, such as the numbers of telephones, television sets, personal computers and passenger cars per 1,000 population. Such macro-level data often mask diversity at micro-level (INKELES, 1998). Convergence at macro-level (e.g. convergence of GNP/capita) does not necessarily imply convergence of micro level elements. "Countries similar economically are not necessarily similar in their consumption behaviour, media usage and availability patterns" (SRIRAM and GOPALAKRISHNA, 1991, p. 140). Infrastructural and economic integration usually occur at a higher speed than the cultural and mental integration of consumers. Although there certainly is evidence of globalisation of markets, there are also clear signs that differences in local consumer behaviour are persistent. Customs and traditions tend to persist and therefore concepts such as a "European consumer" are misnomers. As people around the globe become better educated and more affluent, their tastes actually diverge. With increased wealth, people increasingly accord greater relevance to their civilizational identity (SAVITT, 1998; USUNIER, 1996).

At the national level, national wealth is no more the best predictor for variance of consumption across nations. When markets become economically more homogeneous, GNP/capita loses its predictive power. Predictions for future sales are, however, often based on economic development of countries or related factors. In the publication of the Economist "The World in 2001", John Chambers, CEO of

Cisco Systems refers to the link between prosperity and E-readiness of countries. He measures this E-readiness by the bandwidth per capita (BPC) and says, "In Europe, for example, the Scandinavian countries lead in BPC. It is no coincidence that Denmark, Sweden and Norway, are also the leaders in e-commerce spending per capita. The implications are clear: the ability to create a prosperous economy is linked to the quality of its networking infrastructure". There is indeed a strong link between GNP/capita and infrastructure. It is more interesting to understand the fundamental drivers behind BPC, beyond economic development. The question is: What are the characteristics of countries that drive the development of a good infrastructure? Why are some countries leaders in Internet development while others lag and how do we explain the differences in usage of the Internet and other means of the new economy?

This article offers answers to these questions, presents findings of convergence, divergence or continuing diversity and patterns that can help predict the future.

2. Meta-Analysis of Consumption and Consumer Behaviour

The findings presented in this paper are based on meta-analysis of time-series data of a large number of product categories at national level. Coefficients of variation (CV) and means of convergence[1] are used. In order to demonstrate the varying influence of national wealth, three groups of countries are compared: an economically heterogeneous group of 44 countries worldwide[2], an economically more

---

[1] For measuring convergence or divergence, the coefficients of variation (the ratio of the standard deviation to the mean) were computed and compared over time. The coefficient of variation (CV) is explained in WILLIAMSON and FLEMING (1996, p. 349-350), who prefer the coefficient of variation rather than "the more common alternatives such as the standard deviation or variance because the coefficient of variation is adjusted for shifts in the mean. The greater the decrease in the coefficient of variation over a specified period of time, the greater the convergence".

WILLIAMSON and FLEMING (1996, p. 354) express the mean convergence per year symbolically as follows:

$$MC/year = \frac{(CV_{t1} - CV_{t2})}{CV_{t1}} \times 100 / (t_2 - t_1)$$

where MC/year = mean convergence per year, CV_{t1} = coefficient of variation at the earlier date, CV_{t2} = coefficient of variation at the later date, t_1 = the earlier date, and t_2 = the later date.

[2] The 44 countries of this group are: Argentina, Australia, Austria, Belgium, Brazil, Canada, Chile, Colombia, Costa Rica, Denmark, Ecuador, El Salvador, Finland, France, Germany, Great Britain, Greece, Indonesia, India, Ireland, Israel, Italy, Japan, South-Korea, Malaysia, Mexico, Netherlands, Norway, New Zealand, Pakistan, Panama, Peru, Philippines, Portugal, South Africa, Singapore, Spain, Sweden, Switzerland, Thailand, Turkey, Urugay, U.S.A., Venezuela.

homogeneous group of 26 countries worldwide (GNP/capita > \$8,000)[3] and an economically homogeneous group of 15 countries in Europe[4].

To analyse patterns of convergence-divergence we distinguish between macro- and micro level data. Generally the distinction macro-micro refers to the level of aggregation. This distinction is not useful for comparative research across nations, as data at national level are all aggregate. We follow the distinction of HUNT (1976) and PETERSON and MALHOTRA (2000) who describe micro-level data as being more concerned with buying behaviour of consumers, as opposed to macro-level data being indicators of the macro-economic environment of countries.

Next to convergence or divergence we demonstrate the diminishing effect of income and persistence of culture's influence by correlation and step-wise regression analysis[5] using income (GNP/capita) and Hofstede's cultural variables as independent variables against data on product consumption or ownership and media usage as dependent variables. We discuss how cultural differences explain variance in consumer behaviour and focus on the old and the new media including the means of the new economy such as the Internet and mobile phones.

"Culture" is for many a fuzzy concept. Only recently, scholars have made the concept more concrete. Countries can now be compared via dimensional scales and values of national culture can be quantified and correlated with various aspects of consumer behaviour. In particular HOFSTEDE's (1980, 1991, 2001) dimensions of national culture are useful because of availability of country scores for a large number of countries. Hofstede's five dimensions relate for example to country differences in motives for buying products and services, dependence on brands, adoption of new technology and media use. Many consumption differences can be explained and predicted by correlation and regression analysis between consumption data and country scores of Hofstede's dimensions.

---

[3] The 26 countries of this group are: Argentina, Australia, Austria, Belgium, Canada, Denmark, Finland, France, Germany, Greece, Ireland, Israel, Italy, Japan, Korea, the Netherlands, New Zealand, Norway, Portugal, Singapore, Spain, Sweden, Switzerland, United Kingdom, USA, Venezuela. Currently, Venezuela's GNP/capita is below US\$8,000, but Venezuela used to be part of the "top 25 income countries" until 1988 when South Korea took its place. For continuity in our time-series calculations we kept including both Venezuela and South Korea in all our calculations.

[4] In this article, when we refer to calculations for Europe, these are for 15 countries: Austria, Belgium, Denmark, Finland, France, Germany, Ireland, Italy, Netherlands, Norway, Portugal, Spain, Sweden, Switzerland, United Kingdom. When Eurostat data (available only for EU countries) are used, calculation is only for 13 countries (Norway and Switzerland excluded).

[5] Correlation analysis: significance was established with the Pearson product moment correlation coefficient. Significance levels are indicated by $*p < .05$; $**p < .01$; and $***p < .005$, one-tailed. Linear regression analysis: significant contributions in stepwise regression, R^2 = share of variance explained.

3. Hofstede's Dimensions of National Culture

Hofstede distinguishes five dimensions of national culture: power distance (PDI), individualism/collectivism (IDV), masculinity/femininity (MAS), uncertainty avoidance (UAI) and long-term orientation (LTO). For those who are unfamiliar with the model, a short description follows.

Power Distance is the extent to which less powerful members of a society accept that power is distributed unequally. In large power-distance cultures (e.g. France, Belgium, Portugal, all of Asia) everybody has a rightful place in society and ownership of status objects to demonstrate this position is important. In small power distance cultures people try to look younger and powerful people try to look less powerful (e.g. Great Britain, Germany, the Netherlands and Scandinavia).

Individualism versus *Collectivism*. In individualist cultures people look after themselves and their immediate family only; in collectivist cultures people belong to in-groups who look after them in exchange for loyalty. In individualist cultures people want to differentiate themselves from others. In collectivist cultures the need for harmony makes people want to conform to others. North-Americans and Northern Europeans are individualists, in the South of Europe people are moderately collectivist. Asians, Latin Americans and Africans are collectivists.

Masculinity versus *Femininity*. In masculine cultures the dominant values are achievement and success. The dominant values in feminine cultures are caring for others and quality of life. In masculine cultures performance and achievement are dominant values. Status products and brands are important to show success. Feminine cultures have a people orientation, small is beautiful and status is not so important. In masculine cultures there is large role differentiation while in feminine cultures male and female roles overlap. Examples of masculine cultures are the US, Great Britain, Germany, Italy and Japan. Examples of feminine cultures are the Netherlands, the Scandinavian countries, Portugal, Spain and Thailand.

Uncertainty Avoidance is the extent to which people feel threatened by uncertainty and ambiguity and try to avoid these situations. In cultures of strong uncertainty avoidance, there is a need for rules and formality to structure life. Competence is a strong value resulting in belief in experts as opposed to weak uncertainty avoidance cultures with belief in the generalist. In weak uncertainty avoidance cultures people tend to be more innovative and entrepreneurial. The countries of South and East-Europe as well as Japan score high on uncertainty avoidance, England, Scandinavia and Singapore low.

Long Term Orientation versus *Short Term Orientation*. This fifth dimension distinguishes between long-term thinking and short-term thinking. Other elements are pragmatism, perseverance and thrift. This dimension distinguishes mainly between Western and East Asian cultures. Variance in degrees of thrift has implications for the use of credit cards: low in long-term oriented cultures and high in short-term oriented cultures. In Europe the differences are small, but in some cases significant. The Netherlands score relatively high as compared with the UK and France.

The dimensions are measured on a scale from 0 to 100 (index), although some countries may have a score below zero or above 100, because they were measured after the original scale was defined. HOFSTEDE (2001) provides scores for 66 countries and three regions. The combined scores for each country explain variations in behaviour of people and organisations. The scores indicate the relative differences between cultures.

4. With Increased Wealth Cultural Values Become Manifest

Most of the differences in product usage and buying motives are correlated with Hofstede's dimensions (DE MOOIJ, 1998, 2000, 2001). These differences are stable or become stronger over time. This is because people's attitudes and behaviour, related to consumption, are based on their values. Values and attitudes of people are surprisingly stable over time. The new economy does not produce "new values". In what we call "post scarcity" societies "old" values become manifest in consumption and consumer behaviour. If people have enough of everything to live a comfortable life, they will spend their incremental income on the things that fit their value pattern best. The ultimate American ideal is a five-car garage, the Dutch buy even more luxurious holiday caravans and the Spanish will go out eating with larger groups of people. Additional income gives people greater freedom of expression and their choices follow their distinct value patterns. This phenomenon also applies to the means of the new economy. People use the new media for the same purposes as they used the old media.

An example of how value differences can increasingly be explained by cultural variables can be found in the Reader's Digest (2001) report "European Trusted Brands". In the survey a few questions were asked that were also asked in an earlier survey by Reader's Digest (1991). These were questions about the degree of trust in institutions such as the police and the legal system. Differences in trust in the police and the legal system correlate significantly with Hofstede's cultural dimension power distance: in cultures of large power distance there is less trust than in cultures of small power distance. Regression analysis shows that for the thirteen countries involved in both surveys[6], in 1991 the percent of variance explained by power distance was 52 for trust in the police and 41 for trust in the legal system. In 2001 the percents are 72 and 69.

5. Culture and Consumption

How people spend their private income is related to culture. As an example of how culture explains variance of consumption categories we use the structure of private consumption in Europe. The examples are of 1996, but they are representa-

---

[6] Belgium, Denmark, Finland, France, Germany, Italy, Netherlands, Norway, Portugal, Spain, Sweden, Switzerland, United Kingdom

tive for a longer time span: between 1986 and 1996 the differences have remained stable. Consistently, the collectivist cultures of Europe spend a higher percent of private consumption on food than the individualist cultures, also in the economically homogeneous Europe. In collectivist cultures food has a much more important role in social life than in individualist cultures. The explaining variable for differences in expenditures on clothing, footwear and furniture is uncertainty avoidance. In two of the four categories, GNP/capita plays only a secondary role in explaining variance.

Often mentioned examples of assumed convergence in Europe are 'greying populations' and increased spending on services such as leisure activities (LEEFLANG and VAN RAAIJ, 1995). Leisure expenditures, however, do not converge. Between 1986 and 1996 in Europe, the percents of private income spent on leisure have diverged with a mean divergence per year of 1.35 percent. The differences are related to culture. Table 1 presents the correlation coefficients for four consumption categories and the Hofstede dimensions.

Table E1:   Structure of Private Consumption

Structure of private consumption in Europe (13 countries) 1996: Correlation Coefficients					
Percent private expenditures	PDI	IDV	MAS	UAI	GNP/capita
Food and beverages	.43	-.79***	-.15	.49*	-.69***
Clothing and footwear	.31	-.56*	.41	.59*	-.55*
Leisure, entertainment, recreation	-.75**	.05	-.15	-.50	.33
Furniture and household equipment	.42	-.11	.48*	.67**	.11

Sources: Eurostat Yearbook 1998/1999 and Hofstede 1991

6. Convergence-Divergence: A Pattern

Time-series data demonstrate that at macro level and at micro level, both convergence and divergence take place, but to varying degrees in different regions. If convergence takes place, it is weakest in economically heterogeneous regions and strongest in economically homogeneous regions. But even in economically homogeneous regions, such as Europe, only a few cases of true convergence can be demonstrated. There are many large differences between countries that are stable over time, or countries diverge.

Most examples of convergence are at the macro level. Penetration of the communication means of the "new economy" converges and convergence is strongest in the developed world. More interesting than macro-level penetration of the means of the new economy is how they are used, what people do with them, so what happens at the micro-level. We find that convergence of ownership of products does not mean convergence of usage. People may own modern technology, but they do not use it the same way across countries. So, even if convergence takes place at macro-level, substantial differences exist at micro-level. For example, countries have convérged for the total number of cars per 1,000 population, but the distribution across the population, numbers owned per household, or type of car diverge. Also behaviour of the group of business people, part of the top 20 percent incomes of Europe, as measured by the European Media and Marketing Surveys (EMS), by theorists thought to be a homogeneous target group for certain luxury articles, varies considerably across countries.

In Europe, in 1997, for 20 product categories reviewed[7], the CVs varied from .66 (sales of real jewellery) to .11 (TV sets per 1,000 population). If we take as criterion for convergence a threshold of convergence at .20, there are only a few categories that have truly converged. In Europe, only a few categories have reached a CV below that level: television sets per 1,000 (.11), telephone main lines per 1,000 (.17), and passenger cars per 1,000 (.18). These are all examples of convergence of durable products at macro-level: the average numbers of a product category per 1,000 population. Of the non-durable categories examined (e.g. food, drink, personal care products), the only categories that had more or less converged were household cleaning products (CV is .34) and soft drinks (CV is .29). These are the two product categories that have been dominated by American multinationals during the past half-century. They are not representative of the total package of consumption.

Even in the durable product category, there are only a few examples of true convergence: passenger cars per 1,000 population and TV sets per 1,000 population. These are relatively recent high investment products. While in Europe in 1998 the number of television sets per 1,000 people of countries had converged, countries had diverged with respect to penetration of ownership of an older medium: radio.

Generally speaking, ownership of the investment type of durable products such as cars and television sets converges, while the differences between countries with respect to lower investment durable products and media such as radios and newspapers are stable or increase.

In Europe, the CV for TV sets/1,000 population decreased from 1.00 in 1960 to .11 in 1998. The CV for radios was only .33 in 1960 and it decreased to .24 in the next ten years. After 1970 it increased again, to .36. In the time-span 1970-1998, the mean *convergence* per year of television sets/1,000 was 2.26 percent, while the mean *divergence* per year of radios/1,000 was 0.37 percent. The differences between countries with respect to newspaper circulation have remained stable in the past fifty years. There is neither convergence nor divergence. Our findings demonstrate that countries in Europe converge with regard to recent media but diverge with regard to the older media or the differences remain stable.

There is a pattern of convergence-divergence. For durable products – in particular those related to income such as passenger cars, television sets and computers – initially, with increased wealth countries converge, but in the developed

---

[7] Telephony, passenger cars, television, radio, the press (newspapers, books), food, mineral water, soft drinks, alcoholic drinks, cigarettes, jewellery, personal computers, Internet, audio, household appliances, watches, cameras, personal care products, household cleaning products and financial products.

world, at a certain level of wealth, convergence reaches a ceiling after which there is no further convergence and differences remain stable or increase. With converging wealth convergence of consumption turns into divergence.

For "old" products such as newspapers and radio that ceiling was reached long ago. New products such as computers have not yet reached a ceiling and differences between countries are still large. The point of convergence lies in the future. But it can be predicted by understanding the process the old products went through.

For all new commodities initially income differences explain differences in ownership across countries. When maximum convergence has been reached, the remaining differences can be explained by culture.

Table 2 presents the means of convergence or divergence per year at the macro-level, for five product categories (telephone main lines, passenger cars, television sets, radios and newspapers per 1,000 population), for the period 1970-1998, for the groups worldwide 44, Developed 26 and for Europe 15.

Table E2:   Convergence-Divergence at Macro Level

Convergence or divergence per year (%) at macro level 1970-1998			
	Worldwide 44	Developed 26	Europe 15
Telephone main lines/1,000 population	1.42	2.16	2.40
Passenger cars per 1,000 population	0.89	1.53	1.74
Television sets per 1,000 population	1.50	1.61	2.26
Radios per 1,000 population	1.18	1.48	**- 0.31**
Newspapers per 1,000 population	0	**- 0.15**	**- 0.37**

Sources: UN Statistical Yearbooks and World Bank Development Reports

In the long term, at macro level, fastest convergence is in the economically homogeneous Europe. Ownership of television sets has converged fastest, while radio ownership and circulation of newspapers diverge. In the figures 1, 2 and 3 the processes are illustrated.

In most cases, if convergence takes place, it is a slow process and convergence is strongest for product categories that are related to economic development (TV sets and telephone main lines). Both for telephony and distribution of television channels, infrastructure is needed, which is linked with economic development of nations.

Data for calculating convergence-divergence at micro level are not readily available worldwide. A few data are available for Europe, but only for shorter time spans. These data provide evidence of divergence.

Figure E1:   TV Sets: Convergence

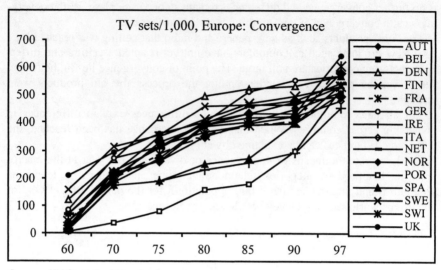

Source: UN Statistical Yearbooks

Figure E2:   Television Viewing: Convergence and Divergence

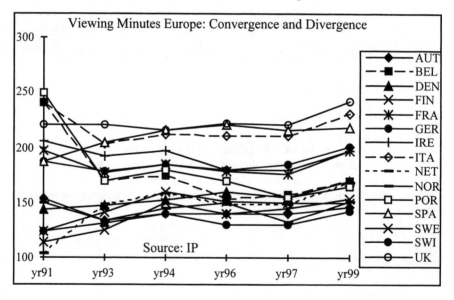

Figure E3: Newspapers: Continuity

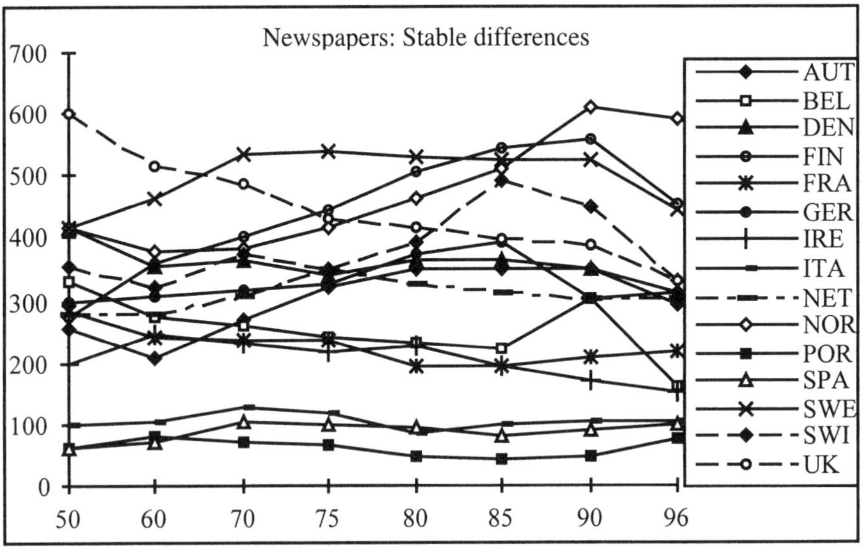

Newspapers: Stable differences

Source: UN Statistical Yearbooks

Table 3 presents divergence at micro-level for numbers of passenger cars per family between 1995 and 1999 (data EMS). Countries first converged for daily viewing minutes (data IP) between 1991 and 1993 and diverged after 1993. In table 2 data on newspaper circulation were used. For table 3 we use readership data, measured by the question "did you read a newspaper yesterday?" (McCann Erickson). Newspaper readership diverged between 1991 and 1996.

Countries also diverged with regard to book readership, measured by the question "did you read more than 8 books (1970) or 12 books (1991) in the past year" (Reader's Digest Surveys).

Table E3: Divergence at Micro Level

Divergence per year (%) at micro level (Europe)	
	Mean divergence per year (%)
Cars: One car in family 1995-1999	2.00
Cars: Two cars in family 1995-1999: stability	0
Cars: Three cars in family 1995-1999	1.74
TV: Daily viewing minutes 1991-1999	.69
Newspaper readership: "Read yesterday" 1991-1996	3.03
Books: Heavy book readership 1970-1991	1.12

Sources: EMS, IP, McCann Erickson, and Reader's Digest Surveys

Differences in media usage are persistent because the media are part of countries' culture. Radio ownership in Europe is related to individualism: in 1997 48 percent of variance was explained by individualism. Over time the significance of the relationship has become stronger. While in the collectivist cultures one radio per family is enough, in individualist cultures everyone wants his/her own radio. In the UK there are 1,400 radios per 1,000 people as compared with 330 in Spain.

Newspaper circulation and readership are correlated with power distance. In 1996 58 percent of variance of newspaper readership was explained by small power distance. In the more egalitarian cultures people read more newspapers.

In 1991 52 percent of variance of heavy book readership was explained by individualism. Measurement of book readership by Eurobarometer in 1992 (answers to question "did you read a book last week?") shows an even stronger relationship: 65 percent of variance is explained by individualism. In individualist cultures people are more verbally oriented, in collectivist cultures people are more visually oriented. In the collectivist cultures television is a more important medium than the press.

New media have not yet reached the point of convergence, so variance across countries can be explained by variance of national income. But the future can be predicted. Our findings suggest that the older the product, the stronger the influence of culture. The new changes fastest, the old changes slowest, if it changes at all. New technology is converging at macro level, but differences at micro level emerged soon after introduction. Internet penetration (numbers of hosts per 10,000 population) converges, but the way the Internet is used varies.

7. Communication Technology: Increasing Influence of Culture

With converging national incomes, the level of infrastructure of countries also converges, which is reflected by the convergence of countries with respect to telephone main lines between 1970 and 1998 in all three country groups. During this time-span, GNP/capita explains between 90 and 63 percent of variance.

In 1980, in all three groups, culture emerges as an explaining variable next to income although the additional percents of variance explained are small. Worldwide (also in the worldwide group of developed countries) individualism is a second predictor. In Europe, in 1980 weak uncertainty avoidance is the second predictor and from 1990 onwards low masculinity is an additional explaining variable. In the feminine cultures (e.g. Scandinavia), a good infrastructure is viewed as important for the quality of life. Table 4 illustrates the increasing influence of culture over time.

Both uncertainty avoidance and low masculinity play a role in understanding differences in use of telephone lines as well as new developments in the category.

Also mobile phone ownership is a matter of quality of life. In Europe in 1997 low masculinity explains 37 percent of variance although in 1998 the relationship is weaker. In 1999, 42 percent of variance of personal ownership of a mobile phone is explained by low masculinity (EMS).

There also is a significant correlation between penetration of telephone main lines and mobile phones (worldwide 44: $r = .78***$; developed 26: $r = .49*$; Europe: $r =$

.48*). This contradicts the general expectation that mobile phones will penetrate faster in countries where the infrastructure of main telephone lines is weak. In contrast: where infrastructure is already strong, it becomes even stronger. New technology makes people do more of what they are used to do.

Table E4:   Telephone Main Lines

Telephone main lines per 1,000 inhabitants							
Year	Predictor 1	R^2	Predictor 2	R^2	Predictor 3	R^2
Worldwide 44						
1970	GNP/cap	0.90				
1980	GNP/cap	0.85	IDV	0.88		
1990	GNP/cap	0.79	IDV	0.83		
1998	GNP/cap	0.85	MAS (-)	0.87	IDV	0.89
Developed 26						
1970	GNP/cap	0.83				
1980	GNP/cap	0.69	IDV	0.75		
1990	GNP/cap	0.72	MAS (-)	0.79		
1998	GNP/cap	0.63	MAS (-)	0.72	IDV	0.76
Europe 15						
1970	GNP/cap	0.74				
1980	GNP/cap	0.72	UAI (-)	0.83		
1990	GNP/cap	0.73	MAS (-)	0.85		
1998	GNP/cap	0.72	MAS (-)	0.87		

Sources: UN Statistical Yearbooks, World Development Reports and Hofstede 1991

How people use the phone also varies across cultures. From EMS data we find that Europe is a homogeneous area with respect to ownership of one telephone line (CV = .03), but there is still heterogeneity with respect to ownership of two or three telephone lines (CVs are .38 and .63). The degree to which the phone is used - for example for international telephone calls - varies and the differences correlate negatively with uncertainty avoidance. In the weak uncertainty avoidance cultures (UK, Scandinavia, the Netherlands) people use the phone more for international calls than in strong uncertainty avoidance cultures (France, Germany). Forty per-cent of variance of the total number of international calls, as reported in EMS99, is explained by weak uncertainty avoidance. GNP per capita explains an additional 18 percent.

This relationship with uncertainty avoidance raises a question that also is of importance for understanding the use of the Internet across countries. Is there a relationship between foreign language speaking (i.e. English by the non-English/Americans) and use of the Internet? Eurobarometer asks questions about foreign language speaking (language spoken apart from mother tongue). The dif-ferences between 13 countries of the EU with respect to English speaking also correlate with uncertainty avoidance (r = -.81***). Variation in foreign language speaking may well be a cause of differences in international telephony. But it is the cultural factor uncertainty avoidance that is the common explaining factor. The same explanation can be given for variation in the use of Internet at home (Euro-barometer Survey #53) that correlates positively with English language speaking and negatively with uncertainty avoidance.

8. The Communication Means of the New Economy

The "new economy" is synonymous with economic development in post-industrial societies. The means of the new economy are concentrated in the developed world. Ninety percent of personal computers are owned by half of our group of 44 countries worldwide and 56 percent are owned by 25 percent of this group. All new communication means belong to one product constellation that is the driver of the new economy: main telephone lines, mobile phones, personal computers and the Internet, they are all very significantly correlated between each other.

The coefficients of variation for the group of countries worldwide (1998) vary between .88 for personal computers and 1.53 for Internet hosts per 10,000 population. The average coefficient of variation for the six categories in 1998 is 1.04 worldwide, .64 in the group developed 26, and .54 in Europe. We find that countries converge with respect to mobile phones and computers although the time-span that can be measured is relatively short. With respect to the Internet convergence is only found in Europe. Worldwide and in the group developed 26 we find divergence. Table 5 summarizes the CVs for six communication means of the new economy.

Table E5:   Communication Means of the New Economy: CVs

CVs Communication means of the new economy per 1,000 population 1998			
	Worldwide 44	Developed 26	Europe15
Fax machines	1.13	0.77	0.48
Telephone main lines	0.64	0.26	0.17
Mobile phones	0.93	0.53	0.52
Cable subscribers	1.11	0.80	0.74
Personal computers	0.88	0.47	0.35
Internet hosts (per 10,000)	1.53	1.03	0.97
Average 6 categories	1.04	0.64	0.54

Worldwide GNP/capita is the main predictor for variance of faxes, telephone main lines, mobile phones, cable penetration, PC ownership and the Internet, while in the developed world culture increasingly explains variance. Table 6 presents the relationships for mobile phones and PCs per 1,000 people (1998) and Internet hosts per 10,000 people (1999).

Table E6: Communication Means of the New Economy: Relationship Income and Culture

Communication means of the new economy: income and culture											
	GDP/cap	PDI	IDV	MAS	UAI	LTO	Pred.1	R²	Pred. 2	R²	Pred. 3	R²
Worldwide 44												
Mobile 98	.76***	-.61***	.63***	-.08	-.35**	-.06	GNP	.58				
PCs 98	.92***	-.63***	.75***	-.06	-.50***	-.25	GNP	.84	UAI (-)	.89		
Internet 99	.67***	-.55***	.63***	-.23	-.43***	-.31	GNP	.45	MAS (-)	.51	IDV	.56
Developed 26												
Mobile 98	.43*	-.40*	.31	-.23	-.42*	.07	GNP	.18				
PCs 98	.79***	-.42*	.57***	-.21	-.76***	-.23	GNP	.63	UAI (-)	.83		
Internet 99	.49***	-.42*	.50***	-.37*	-.49***	-.32	IDV	.25				
Europe 15												
Mobile 98	.43	-.53*	-.38	.38	-.59*	-.19	UAI (-)	.34				
PCs 98	.86***	-.59**	.55*	-.27	-.69***	-.28	GNP	.74	UAI (-)	.86		
Internet 99	.45*	-.46*	.18	-.58*	-.48*	-.31	MAS (-)	.34	PDI (-)	.55		

Source: World Development Reports and Hofstede, 1991

Worldwide, next to GNP/capita, weak uncertainty avoidance is a predictor for PC ownership while variance of the Internet is also explained by both low masculinity and individualism. In the group developed 26, GNP/capita is also the main predictor for mobile phones and PCs, but cultural variables also play a role in explaining variance, for PCs weak uncertainty avoidance that explains acceptance of new technology. Individualism explains variance of Internet hosts per 10,000 population. In Europe weak uncertainty avoidance explains variance of ownership of mobile phones and it is a second predictor for computer ownership. For the Internet low masculinity and small power distance explain much of variance. There is also a significant negative correlation with uncertainty avoidance. Figure 4 illustrates the relationship between uncertainty avoidance and PCs and the Internet for 18 countries worldwide in 1997.

Figure E4:   PCs, the Internet and Uncertainty Avoidance

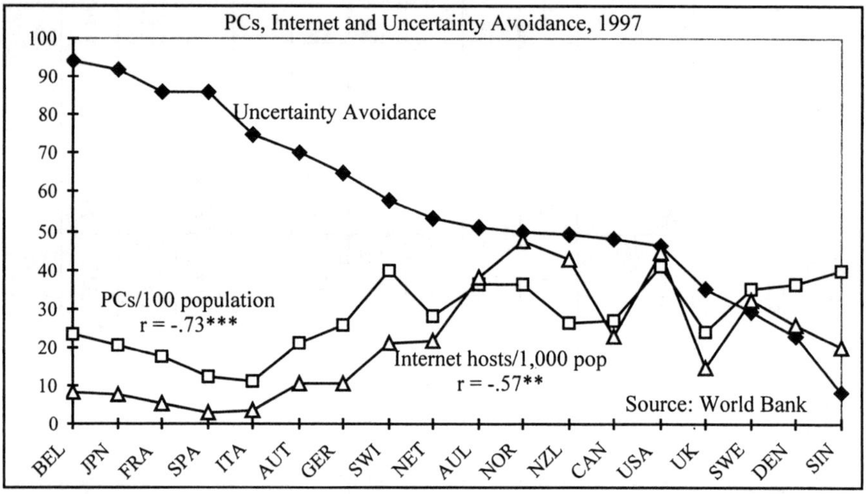

9. The Internet in Europe

The Internet is so new that time series are only available for a short time period. In Europe the CV for the number of Internet hosts per 10,000 population was .80 in 2000, so with respect to the Internet Europe is certainly not a homogeneous area. The number of Internet hosts per 10,000 population in 2000 correlates negatively with masculinity (r = -. 59**), low masculinity explains 35 percent of variance. Likewise, Internet penetration, or "percent access in the Internet in past few weeks", data derived from surveys by Initiative Media, as published in M&M Europe, also correlates negatively with masculinity, with 49 percent of variance explained. This explains the high use of the Internet in the Scandinavian countries, all low on masculinity.

The Internet can be used for various applications: for e-mail and communication, for educational and scientific reasons, for business purposes, for leisure and other personal reasons, for banking, for e-commerce and many others. These differences in usage are culture-bound. Eurobarometer measures the information society by asking people their willingness to pay 10 Euro per month for eleven Internet applications. Six of these are significantly correlated with the cultural variables: to contact a politician on-line in view of participating in political activities, distance learning applications, information for travel, electronic newspaper, e-mail access, and home banking. The coefficients of variation for these six applications vary between .30 for distance learning and .62 for e-mail access. Of the percents answers to the answer category "to contact a politician on-line", 31 percent of variance is explained by low individualism, which fits the need for personal contacts of collectivist cultures. Of the distance learning application 39 percent of variance is explained by weak uncertainty avoidance. Distance learning implies low reliance on the expertise of a teacher and fits better weak uncertainty avoidance cultures. Low masculinity explains variance of the applications electronic newspaper ($R^2 = .36$), e-mail access ($R^2 = .54$) and home banking ($R^2 = .42$). In the feminine cultures all possible applications are embraced to enhance the quality of life.

EMS data on the various applications of the Internet for 1997 and 1999 show that use of the Internet converges, but also that use of the various applications of the Internet vary and are related to culture. The coefficient of variation for daily use of the Internet for business was 1.28 in 1997 and .55 in 1999. This points at convergence. Use of the Internet for three purposes varies strongly in Europe. Of the EMS respondents, 45.4 percent of the Danes said they used the Internet for three purposes; 33.4 percent of the British and the Dutch and only 16.9 percent of the Spanish gave that answer.

Variance of Internet use for *business purposes* is explained by small power distance and weak uncertainty avoidance. In cultures of small power distance and weak uncertainty avoidance the Internet is more used for business than in cultures of large power distance and strong uncertainty avoidance. Small power distance means that values of equality are strong. That is what the Internet stands for: it does not allow for inequality related values such as status, power play, settled positions, rigid structures, authority, and the like.

Variance of daily use for *leisure* is explained by low masculinity and by weak uncertainty avoidance.

Variance of daily use of the Internet for *education* is explained by low masculinity and in 1999 by weak uncertainty avoidance. This confirms our findings for use of the Internet for distance learning from Eurobarometer.

Variance of use of the Internet for *e-mail*, both daily, once a week and once per month, is explained by weak uncertainty avoidance.

Use of the Internet for *e-commerce* is in its infancy. GNP per capita explains variance of use for purchases.

Table 7 presents for 1997 and 1999 the percents explained by the main predictor and the dimension that explains an additional percent of variance (marked by a + sign).

Table E7:   Differences in Use of the Internet

Use of the Internet for four different purposes; Europe 15, 1997-1999								
	Percents explained: Use of the Internet almost daily for							
	business		educa-tion/science		e-mail		leisure, per-sonal reasons	
	1997	1999	1997	1999	1997	1999	1997	1999
Power distance (-)	41%							
Masculinity (-)			39%			+13%	57%	45%
Uncertainty Avoidance (-)	+31%	76%		31%	49%	62%	+14%	+26%

Source: EMS and Hofstede 1991

Thus, after only a decade of Internet existence, in Europe the way it is used appears to vary across countries and variance can only be explained by cultural differences. Understanding the differences will make companies more successful in using the Internet.

Because of egalitarian values implicit in the Internet, its use basically does not fit business practices of cultures of large power distance and strong uncertainty avoidance. It does not fit with centralized control, unless a company finds ways to control the Internet, which will be in conflict with its basic philosophy. The Internet also is a basically unstructured means of communications. This is difficult to accept in cultures of strong uncertainty avoidance. The latter will be late adopters of the Internet for regular communication and mail purposes. This explains a relatively low daily use of e-mail in France and Germany, as compared with the United Kingdom and the Scandinavian countries. Education/science and leisure purposes can be pulled together with respect to the relationship with the configuration low masculinity/weak uncertainty avoidance. The key here is quality of life. In the feminine cultures, people do not restrict their need for quality of life to the private realm of the home. Both time spent in the home and in the office must be quality time as opposed to the performance oriented masculine cultures with a stricter task-orientation in working life. This is reflected in the use of Internet for leisure and personal purposes in the (feminine) Scandinavian countries. In the feminine cultures people also tend to have access to television and Teletext in the office as opposed to the masculine cultures (EMS97). With respect to access to TV channels at work, 56 percent of variance is explained by low masculinity and of variance in use of Teletext at work, 66 percent is explained by low masculinity.

The relationship between low masculinity and usage of the PC at home as well as the relationship between low masculinity and Internet use for leisure and education also explain the relatively low usage of the Internet in Japan. This was related to the low penetration of home computers in Japan, high on both masculinity and uncertainty avoidance. Thus, in Japan the Internet is becoming more representative now that new carriers are introduced such as the WAP phone. Because of its cultural connection, the success of Internet by phone in Japan does not necessarily predict a similar success in Europe and it may be used for different purposes. One popular Japanese I-mode service is downloading cartoon characters, which fits the

Japanese I-mode service is downloading cartoon characters, which fits the Japanese popularity of cartoons. Such a service is not expected to be popular in Europe. In Europe there are high expectations of introducing web technology to the television. Offering Internet via TV is not necessarily a successful option for collectivist cultures because they are more visually oriented. The Internet is still a mainly verbal medium and transferring the current type of Internet service to television will not make the Internet more popular in collectivist cultures. Use of Teletext, for example, a verbal mode used with a visual medium, has from the start been strongly correlated with individualism.

10. Business Application

The major application of our findings for business is the potential for mapping cultures. Figure 5 is an example of such mapping. For understanding the development of the Internet, countries are clustered according to the dimensions masculinity/femininity and uncertainty avoidance. The bottom quadrants include countries that are of weak uncertainty avoidance. These countries are leading in adoption of innovations. The countries in the top two quadrants are laggards. The two quadrants at the left are of low masculinity. Countries in this cluster will adopt new technology for enhancing the quality of life. The countries in the quadrants on the right are high on masculinity and will adopt new technology for enhancing competitiveness.

Figure E5: **Mapping Cultures for Adoption and Application of the Internet**

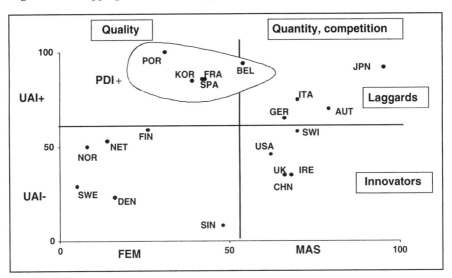

Power distance is introduced as a third dimension that explains variation of government involvement. In the top quadrants are the countries Portugal, Korea, France, Spain, Belgium and Japan that are of large to medium (Japan) power distance. In the bottom quadrant is Singapore that is of large power distance. In large power distance cultures governments can take a leading role in advancing levels of technology. An example is South Korea, where in 2001 the government heavily invested in infrastructure for broadband communications.

11. Conclusions

Nearly four decades after Marshall McLuhan's (1964) phrase "the global village" was coined, there is more evidence than ever of the correctness of his philosophy that the new media are merely extensions and enhancements of ourselves. They allow us to do more of the same, more of what we like to do most and what we have been doing, but in more efficient ways. With the introduction of new technology and with increased wealth no "new" values emerge. Instead, existing "old" values become manifest.

For the development and marketing of Internet and information technology, knowledge and explanation of differences in consumption and consumer behaviour due to cultural differences are indispensable. Expanding operations to countries with different cultural values than one's own without adapting to these differences, can lead to serious losses. This applies to the format and to content. Acceptance and usage of the Internet varies across cultures. The varying success of e-commerce across countries can be predicted. The degree of innovativeness (weak uncertainty avoidance), credit card acceptance and need for convenience (both short-term orientation), all drivers for e-commerce, will be the characteristics to segment markets for developing e-commerce.

If test markets are used for new products, managers must be aware that success in the test market does not automatically mean that other, culturally dissimilar countries will show the same level of acceptance at short term. Success of new technology in test markets like Denmark (lowest on uncertainty avoidance in Europe) or Singapore (lowest in the world) will not guarantee success in other countries, in particular not in cultures of strong uncertainty avoidance. But countries can be grouped according to the type of cultural effect. For each product category, clusters can be formed of countries that are expected to have similar reactions. Hofstede's model of national culture is a powerful instrument for international strategy.

References

ASSAEL, H. (1998), Consumer Behavior and Marketing Action. 6th Edition. Cincinnati, Ohio: South Western College Publishing.

BRADLEY, F. (1991), International Marketing Strategy. UK: Prentice Hall International.

BULLMORE, J. (2000), Alice in Disneyland, A Creative View of International Advertising, in: JONES, J.P. (ed.), International Advertising, Realities and Myths, Thousand Oaks: Sage Publications.

CHAMBERS, J. (2001), The World in 2001, London: The Economist.

CZINKOTA, M.R., RONKAINEN, I.A. (1993), International Marketing 3rd edition. Fort Worth: The Dryden Press.

CRAIG, C.S.; DOUGLAS, S.P., GREIN, A. (1992), Patterns of convergence and divergence among industrialized nations: 1960-1988, Journal of International Business Studies, Vol. 23. No. 4, 773-786.

DE MOOIJ, M. (1998), Global Marketing and Advertising, Understanding Cultural Paradoxes. Thousand Oaks: Sage Publications.

DE MOOIJ, M. (2000), The future is predictable for international marketers: Converging incomes lead to diverging consumer behaviour. International Marketing Review, Vol. 17. No 2, 103-113

DE MOOIJ, M. (2001), Convergence and Divergence in Consumer Behavior. Consequences for Global Marketing and Advertising, Doctoral Dissertation, Pamplona, May 2001, Published by the author.

EMS, the European Media & Marketing Survey (1995, 1997, 1999), A research survey of print media readership and TV audience levels within the upscale consumer group in Europe (EU, Switzerland and Norway), Inter/View International.

EUROBAROMETER, Public Opinion in the European Union, Various years. Public Opinion Surveys and Research, European Commission, Belgium.

EUROSTAT ANNUAL YEARBOOKS (1995, 1996, 1997, 1998/99), Luxembourg: Statistical Office of the European Communities.

HOFSTEDE, G. (1980), Culture's Consequences, Thousand Oaks: Sage Publications.

HOFSTEDE, G. (1991), Cultures and Organizations, Software of the Mind, London: McGrawHill.

HOFSTEDE, G. (2001), Culture's Consequences, second edition, Thousand Oaks: Sage Publications.

HOLLANDERS, H.; SOETE, L., WEEL, B. (1999), Trends in Growth Convergence and Divergence and Changes in Technological Access and Capabilities. Paper pesented at the Lisbon Workshop on "Cliometrics, Econometrics and Appreciative History in the Study of Long Waves in Economic Development", Lisbon, 11-13 March.

HUNT, S.D. (1976), The Nature and Scope of Marketing. Journal of Marketing. Vol. 40, 17-28.

INKELES, A. (1998), One World Emerging?: Convergence and Divergence in Industrial Societies, Boulder: Westview Press Inc.

LEEFLANG, P.S.H., VAN RAAIJ, F. (1995), The changing consumer in the European Union: A "meta-analysis", International Journal of Research in Marketing, Vol 12, 373-387.

LEVITT, T. (1983), The Globalization of Markets, Harvard Business Review (May-June) 2-11.

MCCANN-ERICKSON (1997), The Insider's Report by Robert J. Coen. (June) McCann-Erickson. 750 Third Avenue, New York. Internet: www.McCann. com.

MCLUHAN, M. (1964), Understanding Media: The Extensions of Man. New York: McGraw Hill.

PETERSON, M., MALHOTRA, N. (2000), Country segmentation based on objective quality-of-life measures. International Marketing Review. Vol. 17. No 1, 56-73.

READER'S DIGEST (1970), A Survey of Europe Today, A study of consumption habits and attitudes in 16 European countries, London: The Reader's Digest Association Limited.

READER'S DIGEST (1991), Eurodata Survey, a study of the lifestyles, consumer spending habits and attitudes of people in 17 European countries, London: The Reader's Digest Association Limited.

READER'S DIGEST. (2001). European Trusted Brands. London: Reader's Digest Association Ltd.

ROSSANT, J. (2000), A common identity for Europe? You better believe it. Business Week, November 20, 72.

SARKAR, P. (1999), Theory of convergence and real income divergence 1950-1992, Economic and Political Weekly, February 20, Bombay: A Sameeksha Trust Publication.

SAVITT, R. (1998), Viewpoint: This thing I call Europe. International Marketing Review, Vol. 15. No. 6, 444-446.

SRIRAM, V., GOPALAKRISHNA, P. (1991), Can advertising be standardized among similar countries? A cluster based analysis, International Journal of Advertising, Vol. 10, 137-149.

UN STATISTICAL YEAR BOOKS. (Various Years). New York: United Nations.

USUNIER, J.C. (1996-1997), Atomistic versus Organic Approaches. International Studies of Management & Organization, Vol. 26. No. 4, Winter, p. 90-112.

WILLIAMSON, J.B., FLEMING, J.J. (1996), Convergence theory and the social welfare sector: A cross-national analysis, in: INKELES, A., SASAKI, M., Comparing nations and cultures. Englewood Cliffs: Prentice Hall.

WORLD DEVELOPMENT REPORT. (Various Years), New York: World Bank.

F. E-Commerce: A Paradise for Bargain Hunters?

Christiane Jäcker

The arguments seem clear: When e-commerce customers shop by mouse click, they can compare the prices of the various online suppliers much more quickly than conventional buyers. Market transparency increases. This intensifies inter-firm competition, which then leads to lower prices. The price pressure could spill over from the Internet to conventional channels. However, there is another side to the story of Internet bargain hunting. The market not only becomes more transparent for buyers but also – and maybe to a much greater extent – for sellers. And even if market power does not shift in favor of businesses, online prices can still be higher; if Internet channels offer the customer more value, he will be prepared to pay a higher price. It is therefore by no means clear how e-commerce will affect prices in the long term.

Price comparisons between conventional and Internet retailers support the widespread opinion that customers get a better deal online. According to a US report from 2000, e-commerce books and CDs are between 9 and 16 percent cheaper on the Internet (Cf. BRYNJOLFSSON / SMITH, 2000a). Another study from 2000 shows for the US life insurance market that Internet term life prices were not only lower but also brought down offline prices by 8 to 15 percent within three years (Cf. BROWN / GOOLSBEE, 2000). For Germany the consumer or-ganization *Stiftung Warentest* recently compared the prices of 30 randomly chosen products (Cf. STIFTUNG WARENTEST, 2001). The results: You can in fact save between 10 and 24 percent when shopping on the Internet.

However, do these results really prove beyond a doubt that e-commerce has shifted the balance of power in favor of buyers? Does the online customer indeed have more market power when he lets electronic shopping agents find the best bargain or when he cooperates with other online customers to demand price reduc-tions? Maybe prices posted on the Internet are lower simply because e-commerce suppliers have a more favorable cost structure.

The price studies also allow a different conclusion: It could be argued that Internet channels are using get-acquainted prices to lure reluctant customers onto the web. This strategy is not a bad idea since many customers consider e-commerce to be too unsafe and are thus reluctant to shop online. Another reason why Internet retailers tend to follow an aggressive pricing policy is to ensure a good position for themselves in the still young e-commerce market. The fact that many Internet companies are still in the red speaks for this interpretation of the price spread between online and offline channels. This applies not only to small unknown start-ups but also to big well-recognized brand name companies, which are well-positioned in the e-commerce market.

The theory that the consumer's market power has increased may be faulty for another reason. Suppliers can also use the higher market transparency for their purposes. If price information is available more quickly, it is easier for a company to tune its pricing policy to that of its competitors. The result can be cut-throat price competition – or a consensus high-price policy. The latter is all the more probable, the fewer the number of competitors in the market. It is generally assumed that there is a greater number of suppliers on the Internet than offline. However, this does not necessary always have to be so. At the end of the Internet gold-rush era there seems to be a trend towards few big suppliers who are dividing the market among themselves.

It might sound strange that an aggressive pricing policy could turn out to be an unattractive strategy in this market, precisely because of the short response times which the Internet makes possible. Price competition in traditional trade is implicitly based on the assumption that buyers react more quickly to new prices than competitors. Even if the other suppliers are willing to follow the price cut, they need time to re-label the products on the shelves, to print a new catalogue or to run special offers. For traditional retailers, price cuts therefore promise new customers and higher turnover. In e-commerce on the other hand prices can be adjusted without significant menu costs practically in real time. According to a study, online retailers' price changes are in fact significantly smaller than those of their conventional colleagues (Cf. BRYNJOLFSSON / SMITH, 2000a). If the competition reacts promptly, dumping prices will lead to diminishing margins rather than to new customers in the cyberworld. The incentive to start price competition is accordingly small.

In the long run the consumer's alleged advantage might paradoxically turn into a disadvantage: E-commerce businesses generally know their customers' preferences better than the classic retailers. The Internet enables them to record and evaluate customer data in an heretofore unknown quantity and quality. While the traditional bookseller might know one or the other customer and his interests, big online bookshops can record the individual purchasing habits of millions of customers. Thanks to this mass of data, Internet retailers can strengthen customer loyalty by personalized offers and the building up of one-on-one relationships. And even more importantly, the better a company knows its customers, the easier it is to differentiate prices. In the extreme case, one product can be offered to different customers at different prices, depending on the information the supplier receives from his market research software about how strongly the customer wants the product and how much he is prepared to pay for it (STREITFELD, 2000).[1]

The use of differential pricing to take full advantage of the customers' purchasing power is facilitated by the trend towards mass customization (PILLER, 2001).[2] With the help of different modules, the customer can put the product together on the screen according to his wishes. Mass customization has several advantages for the e-commerce supplier. As there are no price comparisons possible for customized products, it is easy to charge relatively high and differentiated prices. When

---

[1] Amazon.com did in fact try price differentiation but gave it up when customers were outraged.

[2] For more information on mass customization cf. www.mass-customization.de.

customers create their own products, the online business moreover no longer needs to decide what is "in" and what is "out".

Studies on Internet prices in fact show a large price dispersion. What comes as a big surprise is that even prices for homogeneous products such as books and CDs differed by 25 to 33 percent (Cf. BRYNJOLFSSON / SMITH, 2000a). The prices for airline tickets offered by online travel agents also varied by as much as 20 percent (Cf. CLEMONS et al., 1998). The price is obviously not the only criterion by which the customer chooses his Internet channel. Similar to the conventional retail outlets, Internet retailers can justify higher prices if they are well-recognized brand name companies or have a good image, a nifty website or good customer relations (This is empirically confirmed by BRYNJOLFSSON / SMITH, 2000b and SMITH / BRYNJOLFSSON, 2001).

With a roughly 0.5 percent share in retail sales, e-commerce is still a featherweight. The frequently forecast 100 percent annual growth rates over the coming years will not do much to change this. For businesses, e-commerce pricing is still new ground on which they are treading carefully (Cf. BRANDTWEINER, 2001) for the Internet pricing methods). However, the more e-commerce establishes itself, the more it will change the price structure. Although some arguments speak for the fact that the price level will come down, this is by no means certain. The only sure thing is that e-commerce will promote product and price differentiation. Thus the collation of reliable price and inflation statistics will become even more difficult.

References

BRANDTWEINER, R. (2001), Report Internet-Pricing. Methoden der Preisfindung in elektronischen Märkten, Düsseldorf.

BROWN, J.R., GOOLSBEE, A. (2000), Does the Internet Make Markets More Competitive? Evidence for the Life Insurance Industry, NBER Working Paper 7996.

BRYNJOLFSSON, E., SMITH, M.D. (2000a), Frictionless Commerce? A Comparison of Internet and Conventional Retailers, Management Science, 46, 4, 563-585.

BRYNJOLFSSON, E., SMITH, M.D. (2000b), The Great Equalizer? Consumer Choice at Internet Shopbots, MIT Working Paper.

CLEMONS, E., HANN, I.H., HITT, L.M. (1998), The Nature of Competition in Electronic Markets: An Empirical Investigation of Online Travel Agent Offerings, Working Paper, The Wharton School of the University of Pennsylvania, Philadelphia, PA.

PILLER, F.T. (2001), Mass Customization – einen Deckel für jeden Topf, Markus Klietmann (Hrsg.), Kunden im E-Commerce, Düsseldorf.

SMITH, M.D., BRYNJOLFSSON, E. (2001), Consumer Decision-Making at an Internet Shopbot, MIT Working Paper.

STIFTUNG, W. (2001), Keine Mark zu viel – Preisvergleiche im Internet, Test 9, 62-63.

STREITFELD, D. (2000), On the Web, Price Tags Blur: What You Pay Could Depend on Who You Are, Washington Post, September 27.

G. E-Finance: Causing Major Upheavals in the Spatial Organization of the Financial Sector?

Nicole Pohl

> "Clustering develops when the high risks of an activity can be reduced by continuous interchange of information. It is possible, but expensive to communicate by telephone and telex, and many financial functions involving uncertainty are better performed face to face. ... that the central financial district of lower Manhattan minimizes communications costs... While presumably communications costs have declined in the last fifteen years..., they are not likely to be so low as to eliminate all tendency to clustering."
>
> *Charles Kindleberger, 1974*

1. E-Finance: Technological Revolution, Paradigm Shift or Hype?

Like in other sectors, new information and communication technologies have also had a major influence on the financial services sector. They have opened up new possibilities to store, organize and above all transmit and exchange information. For the financial services sector this is essential above all because market access is no longer bound to a presence at a certain location. The sum of the relevant developments that will be outlined in more detail below have been described as electronic or e-finance.

In the same way as there are a number of different definitions of e-commerce, it seems to be difficult to get a standard definition of e-finance. The Gartner Group defines e-finance as "electronically enabled access to financial services". They stress that it is not a delivery (i.e. institution-centric) vehicle, but a vehicle of access and therefore customer-centric. So this point of view would stress the demand-side of financial services. It seems to be to some extent adequate, as most aspects of electronic finance are indeed about new ways of access for the customer and less about the "production-side" of financial services. Whether e-finance can be extended to cover larger parts or even the whole value chain of the financial services sector should be discussed. WITHERELL (2001, p. 2) states that "an e-finance transaction is a financial transaction conducted using the Internet or another open network platform as the distribution channel." This paper will take a rather broad approach to e-finance in simply trying to assess the implications of the Internet for the financial services sector. It will include a broad category of interrelated developments.

The discussions of the last years have shown that the introduction of technological changes especially in the field of information and communication technologies has often induced people to make radical propositions as regards their consequences. This has also been true for the impact of the Internet on the financial sector. This paper will aim at analyzing one field that is deeply concerned by technological changes: the spatial-economic organization of the financial sector. International financial centers are probably the most impressive mirror of the fact that companies in the financial services sector have for a long time tended to cluster certain activities in relatively few locations of the world economy. The paper will discuss to what extent technological changes may have the power to weaken the role of international financial centers, doom them to irrelevance or rather underline the importance of those financial centers that offer special advantages.

We characterize international financial centers as locations where information and interaction advantages are present. This approach as such is not a revolutionary one by itself. Other authors have already chosen the same direction in order to justify the importance of international financial centers and cities in a changing technological environment (GEHRIG, 2001; GASPAR / GLAESER, 1996). An important point of this paper is, however, to argue that – even though the concept is an important one – much of its complexity has not yet been explored. The paper will try to outline reasons for information and interaction advantages in financial centers, such as the possibility of intensive interaction with other companies and agents involved in financial transactions, better access to new information, the opportunity to build and keep connections, a better feeling for market trends, etc. It is vital to distinguish those pieces of information that can be codified and today easily transferred across large distances from information that relies on a physical presence and on face-to-face interaction. The latter type of information would be at the heart of information and interaction advantages of financial centers. This argumentation reflects the state of the art in the literature and has been used to explain why some transactions in the field of financial services are more location-sensitive than others. Although plausible, these arguments remain mostly on the level of assumptions, and they do not take into account the special role of multinational companies in the financial services sector as well as the diverse strategies they may use to expand their international activities and benefit from information advantages.

Ideally, theoretical modeling should be based on empirical observation, and it should therefore be complemented by in-depth interviews with financial service companies in an international context. Interviews should help us to elaborate on the argument both as regards its empirical relevance and theoretical modeling. We will try to set up a research agenda that might help us to analyze whether empirical evidence supports the importance of information and interaction advantages as reasons for the persistence of financial centers.

In the end, the paper will leave the reader with some answers, a survey of the state of the art in the literature, a hopefully convincing survey of questions and hypotheses and a research concept without, however, giving the final answer that will still need more empirical and theoretical research. So altogether we would not claim to have reinvented the wheel. What the paper can hopefully claim is that it sets a starting-point for new research that would clarify the relevance of existing concepts and also provide the empirical knowledge to elaborate on them.

2. The Role of International Financial Centers

The tendency of financial service companies to cluster certain functions in few locations of the world economy has already been analyzed in the literature three decades ago.[1] Kindleberger's explanation is probably the one which has been most quoted:

> Financial centers are needed not only to balance through time the savings and investments of individual entrepreneurs and to transfer financial capital from savers to investors, but also to effect payments and transfer savings between places. Banking and financial centers perform a medium of exchange function and an inter-spatial store value function. ... (T)he specialized functions of international payments and foreign lending and borrowing are typically best performed at one central place that is also (in most instances) the specialized center for domestic interregional payments. (KINDLEBERGER, 1974, p. 6)[2]

New York, London and Tokyo have for some time now formed a relatively stable trio of the world's most important financial centers. They are identified with a large number of financial institutions present and above all also with their stock exchanges and other markets. At least in the case of Tokyo and London we also deal with capital cities, and especially Tokyo is probably the best reflection for the general geographical centralization of activities in one city within a country.

International financial centers are agglomerations of a mix of financial companies such as commercial and investment banks, brokers, stock dealers, specialized business service firms and so forth. Traditionally, they would also host major financial markets like stock exchanges, derivatives markets, etc. In some cases, they are the locations of governmental and regulatory agencies and central banks although – as the example of New York shows – not always. Very often, they are also locations where many companies have situated their global or regional headquarters. For instance, New York as the major U.S. financial center is also the city which hosts with 220 the most headquarters of all U.S. cities.

PORTEOUS (1995, p. 93) states that "a financial center is an area, usually a city, although often more localized within city boundaries, in which high-level financial functions are concentrated." This emphasizes that financial services companies would only locate some of their transactions in these centers. However,

---

[1] For an extensive collection of papers see also ROBERTS (1994).

[2] Kindleberger's work is interesting to read, especially because of its historical perspective. It reminds us of the huge technological changes we have faced in the last decades, but also of some arguments that have kept their truth.

there is a need to further define "high-level financial" functions in order to under-stand the role of financial centers. One approach might be to choose all those functions that are relatively more information-intensive, which is not yet an opera-tional definition either. If information were a localized input factor, this would also mean that high-level financial functions should be more localized. This local-ization might be reflected in the choice of location for branches and subsidiaries that pursue certain activities as well as in the location of global or regional head-quarters. We will elaborate on this argumentation below.

International financial centers have intensive linkages to the world economy, which becomes obvious in the volume of activity in their markets and flows of capital, financial services and without doubt also of information, although the latter is difficult to measure.[3] The literature has paid a lot of attention to the impor-tance of international financial centers, and this has among other things resulted in a hierarchical understanding of these locations.[4] A number of different approaches have been used to identify global, international, supranational and regional finan-cial centers (see e.g. REED, 1980). A related approach is also the literature on world cities that has very much been triggered by Saskia Sassen's contributions (e.g. SASSEN, 1991). Also in her publications the assumption becomes obvious that there are a few cities in the world economy that take a special role. Sassen focuses her analysis on the three world financial centers, New York, London and Tokyo, but her work has fostered a wave of other approaches trying to deal with the relevance of a diversity of cities as world cities.

The importance of financial centers can without doubt be assessed by a com-parative view of certain measurements of their size and volume of activities, some of which might be related to their stock markets (e.g. market capitalization or share turnover). Of course, other measurements can be found regarding other financial activities. Especially for regional financial centers, it is also obvious that the choice of such dimensions for comparison matters a lot as they often have development patterns of specialization that differ from each other. Moreover, financial centers can be understood as important sources of growth for the local and national economy (see e.g. SECURITIES INDUSTRY ASSOCIATION, 2001).

In the case of New York for instance it becomes very obvious that the securities industry is an important source of tax income, and its share of total wages amounts to nearly 20 %. The securities industry has supported local and state development by offering possibilities of finance for the corporate and municipal sector. In gen-

---

[3] Generally, we would also have problems to get information about capital flows to and from locations, as all our statistical standards are country-oriented.

[4] In previous papers the author has expressed her doubts on the adequacy of these hierar-chical points of view, among other things because the notion of a global financial center seems to be related to size rather than openness, which leads to the fact that Tokyo would of course be considered much more global than Singapore. This is without doubt true concerning size, but it also hides important differences between the two concerning the market access of foreigners. Very often size is set equal to importance (HEIDUK and POHL, 2000a and b).

eral financial centers are also attractive sites for foreign banks whose tendencies to cluster may even be stronger than for domestic banks (NACHUM, 2000). The paper will not pursue the aim of comparing financial centers or measuring their importance. This has been done extensively in the literature. We are more concerned with the question why they matter.

In summarizing, the financial geography has traditionally been described by the simultaneous existence of a limited number of locations where a certain set of financial activities and agents were clustered. This poses two questions: firstly, why centers exist at all and which advantages they offer compared to other locations; and secondly, why there are several centers and what the specific competitive advantages of each of them are. These questions are interesting today above all against the background that new technologies might make some financial transactions more footloose, which would imply that only those financial centers will survive that offer advantages that make them "resistant" to these changes.

3. New Technological Developments and the Role of E-Finance

The introduction of new technologies, above all in the information and communication sector, has fueled far-reaching expectations of radical change in a variety of sectors in the world economy. One aspect that has received special interest is its consequences for the spatial organization of the world economy. The potential power of new information and communication technologies to transmit information in real-time and without any friction caused by physical distance has led to their description as space- and time-adjusting technologies. The time of access to information for anybody, from anywhere and at any time seemed to have come. Some people were quick to claim that this would also mean the "death of distance" (THE ECONOMIST, 1995; O'BRIAN, 1992). Time and space seemed to have lost much of their relevance as barriers to interaction. So why should location still matter, if proximity were no longer an advantage? This radical point of view has been refuted by another group of people who pointed out the restrictions of these technologies and the differentiated character of information (GASPAR / GLAESER, 1996). They underline the distinction between standardized information versus information that can only be transmitted face-to-face.

The improved possibilities to transmit information timely and independently from location have also influenced the financial sector in a variety of ways. A few examples, which cover fairly different fields of the financial sector, shall be presented briefly in this paper.[5] This diversity may be justified, as financial centers as well as the financial sector itself are conglomerates of different activities that are partly interrelated. This is nowadays also obvious in the business fields the big investment companies are involved in.

---

[5] We will go as deeply into the different examples as it seems to be necessary in order to get an idea of the impact of changes on financial centers. Of course, each of the fields could still be analyzed in much more depth, which can obviously not be done in this paper.

The following examples will be dealt with in the next paragraphs:[6]
- the rise of online banking
- the improvement of the amount of information available for the individual investor
- new possibilities for online brokerage, online IPOs and other activities that constitute the main pillars of the activities of online investment houses
- the surge of electronic communication networks
- the simultaneous existence of traditional floor-trading at stock-exchanges with electronic trading platforms, and
- the reactions and transformation of traditional stock exchanges that resulted in the demutualization of exchanges and the creation of alliances of stock exchanges[7]

The choice of the examples shows that we adopt a broad definition of the expressions of e-finance. The aspects have been selected, as it will be shown such that all of the trends would, if they were persistent, change the face of international financial centers a lot. What has above all been changed is that access to markets and interaction with customers are in many instances no longer a matter of face-to-face transactions or a local presence in the market.

Access to financial markets can nowadays be granted by a number of access devices that make people independent from location and range from phones to wireless applications. Also the intermediaries in the value chain have changed. Some intermediaries risk being substituted, and new players have entered the field. Internet portals are nowadays the critical link for the customer between access devices and some services. They offer access to a wide range of financial services and even attempt to customize and personalize information. So-called aggregators give us the opportunity to compare products offered by several suppliers along a number of dimensions (CLAESSENS ET AL., 2000). Apart from the traditional players more and more non-bank institutions have entered the financial sector, often via alliances with banks or other non-banks. The competitive face of the financial services sector has changed a lot.

As will be explained in the following paragraphs these changed patterns of contact and access have influenced the way a number of different transactions are done in the financial services sector.

---

[6] For a comprehensive survey of relevant trends see also BANKS (2001).

[7] This tendency is obviously not directly related to new technological opportunities. However, it has resulted as a reaction of stock exchanges to "technological threats", and to some extent alliances also rely on exchange of information and possibilities for access that are based on the use of new technologies.

3.1 Online Banking

At first sight one of the most obvious characteristics of the financial district of a city seems to be the huge number of bank facades of foreign and local banks that serve to some extent as branches for retail banking. Today, however, the Internet is more and more used as a remote delivery channel for banking services. Brick-and-mortar branches have to some degree been substituted by the computer screen. Some banks have offered these services in addition to their traditional services; others have been founded as branchless, Internet-only banks. The latter are able to operate with lower costs and can transfer this advantage to the customer. They have, however, also faced a lot of problems that are among other things related to gaining the trust of the customer. The pervasiveness of click-and-mortar strategies (combining physical branches with online banking) has made it obvious that customers value a hybrid approach that gives them the opportunity to benefit from the freedom of remote access and at the same time have the opportunity to walk into a physical branch of a bank, especially in those cases where non-standardized transactions are concerned. Moreover, a large part of the acquisition of new customers still happens in physical bank branches rather than on the Internet. Some people have also expected that Internet-only services would have to struggle with the problem that customers become less loyal.

Analyses of the U.S. online banking sector have shown that in 1999 about one third of U.S. banks had websites, but under 20 % offered transactional Internet banking. This also reflects the fact that the scope of services that can be provided online is a variable and that the scope of possible changes has probably not yet been exhausted. Interestingly enough those banks that offered online services also had at the same time more offices and were mostly located in urban areas (FURST ET AL., 2000). Moreover, the penetration of OECD-countries by online banking differs strikingly (WITHERELL, 2001).

Bank branches used for retail banking may be an outer characteristic of international financial centers but by no means a constituting feature. However, similar trends towards electronic interaction can also be observed in other fields of the financial services sector.

3.2 Investment Houses: Traditional, Online or Hybrid

One of the most quickly evolving fields penetrated by the Internet has been brokerage of stocks. Online brokerage companies have made customers expect lower commissions and an ease of access to information. Again, the penetration of countries by online brokerage differs with South Korea being one of the most striking examples of success (WITHERELL, 2001). Moreover, online investment firms have been founded that are also involved in securities underwriting. In 1996 Wit Capital created an e-syndicate of investors that got access to IPO shares on a first-come-first-share basis. A major expectation was that online IPOs would facilitate finance for small companies and above all improve the access to shares by individual investors. W.R. Hambrecht has introduced another major change with its

OpenIPO. This is a mechanism that replaces networks of investor relationships that have been central to the pricing and distribution of shares. Investors can place bids of up to 10 % for shares, and settlement in OpenIPO occurs at a price where all the stocks are sold (Dutch auction system). Moreover, road shows can today be done electronically.

Today there are a number of other companies that offer services in this field. Online investment banks have mostly not been lead underwriters in major IPOs, but they have joined traditional investment houses in underwriting syndicates. They offer some potential of disintermediation of traditional intermediaries. Online investment banks have tried to expand their service offerings into investment advice and above all provision of information. Some companies offer their customers e-mail services for instance to make them aware of upcoming IPOs. However, altogether it does not seem as if online companies have reached the scope of services and support traditional investment houses offer. This would probably also be in contrast to their low-cost strategies.

Moreover, we have seen a lot of reactions of traditional investment banks that have created electronic platforms for their services. With their traditional strengths and scope of services, this might well give them an advantage over newcomers. Hybrid players have emerged that rely on both the electronic and the physical channel.

The loads of information that are nowadays provided for investors on the worldwide web (by financial companies and others) seem to hint at an increased transparency: real time quotes, reports, performance Figures, analytical tools, etc. And without doubt, the availability of information is nowadays much better for the individual. However, it has also become much more difficult to filter information. Many people have complained that we live in the age of information overflow and that it is difficult to distinguish qualitatively good from bad information. Investors who want to use this information need a good deal of time and savvyness. This is why instead of disintermediation, we may also experience just the opposite: an increased need for high-quality advice.

Altogether these trends imply changes in the relationships between financial intermediaries and their customers as well as among financial intermediaries. New patterns of competition are introduced; relationships often seem to become less important. The potential of the Internet to allow frictionless communication across long distances might also render proximity among agents less important.

3.3 Alternative Trading Systems and the Competition Between Floor Trading and Electronic Trading

Electronic platforms have penetrated fields of the financial sector that would traditionally concern direct interaction between financial companies and their customers. They have also invaded institutionalized markets like stock and derivatives markets. Electronic trading systems nowadays co-exist with conventional floor trading. In some cases dealers have a choice between the two systems. There are a few studies comparing the different organizational designs of markets in order to make statements about their future. The main differences that are found concern the liquidity of markets, the efficiency of execution and the information available to dealers (FRANKE / HESS, 2000). While "screen-dealers" benefit from the real time information of order books, floor traders are able to "feel" the market (WALL STREET JOURNAL, 2001). Some argue that it is the emotional environment they are lacking when trading from a screen.[8] It is also remarkable that empirical evidence shows that traditional markets gain trading volume in times of important government announcements and similar information.

Basically, the introduction of electronic platforms would make traders independent from location. They could trade in one financial center while being located in another.[9] This is the fate of financial centers like Frankfurt in Germany that has two electronic systems Xetra and Eurex (for derivatives). Frankfurt has had the experience that many of its traders are nowadays located in London.

Without the presence of a trading floor and without dealers being present, we might argue that stock exchanges as main characteristics of financial centers have become very much delocalized. Still the regulatory authorities of the stock exchange may be located in a financial center, but even this is not necessarily the case. Markets have been traditionally understood as issuers of information. Without local physical interaction the creation as well as the diffusion of this information have been fundamentally changed.

In addition to remote trading, there is another tendency that has been relevant above all for NASDAQ. Electronic communication networks (ECNs)[10] nowadays make it possible to directly link buyers and sellers in pure auction markets. They are fully automated and promise their customers best execution, anonymity and the provision of after-hours trading as well as lower costs and the advantage of location-neutrality. Currently there are nine ECNs in the US and all of them trade at NASDAQ, where they constitute as much as 30 % of share volume traded. Instinet is the oldest of them. Some of them are backed by money from top-tier Wall Street firms. Some of the ECNs have also claimed to have achieved the status of a stock exchange (e.g. Archipelago). Archipelago made a deal with the Pacific Exchange in San Francisco / Los Angeles. The San Francisco trading floor was closed in June 2001. Archipelago has taken over its trading business, and the Pacific Exchange will take the role of an in-house regulator.

3.4 Cooperation and Alliances of Stock Exchanges

The invasion of ECNs into the original business of stock exchanges and the possibility to get global access to markets 24-hours a day has been felt to be a threat for

---

[8] Recently a company has brought a product on the market that offers traders the ability to listen to trading noise, while sitting at their computers.

[9] We cannot even be sure whether a central location would be important for traders at all.

[10] ECNs are regulated agency brokers that facilitate off-market auction matching of customers' buy and sell orders, principally in NASDAQ stocks, while providing unmatched orders with direct access to the NASDAQ market.

traditional stock exchanges. They have reacted on the one hand by demutualizing in order to enhance efficiency. On the other hand, we can today observe a wide network of alliances and forms of cooperation between exchanges: shares of NASDAQ are traded in Hong Kong; three European exchanges have founded Euronext; the Singapore and Australian stock exchanges have created an alliance that allows mutual access to markets and information; and many other efforts might be mentioned. NYSE has negotiations with ten of the biggest world exchanges and NASDAQ has promoted the vision of a global exchange as a single marketplace that would offer investors trading in stocks all over the world.[11]

These tendencies towards global markets are still reinforced by the trend of firms to have their shares listed at multiple stock exchanges. The most recent example was the creation of global shares by Daimler Chrysler. These shares are traded on multiple exchanges as well as in multiple currencies (KAROLYI, 1999).

Without doubt the hurdles concerning technological, legal, regulatory and supervisory aspects are still high to realize these visions. At least in the short-term the world does not seem to be ready for any kind of global exchange. However, they seem to indicate that stock exchanges do not only become less local, but also less national. New regimes may have to be found that are based on supranational rules. This expectation is also expressed in the following quotes:

> ... stock exchanges to exist as virtual exchanges without huge buildings, not confined to any country and where shares are defined, listed and traded electronically... (A. Lipp, Pricewaterhouse Coopers, BUSINESS TIMES, 2000)

> What is clear, however, is that the days of each country boasting its own exchange in much the same way as it might have an airline, are gone. It is an expensive status symbol, made irrelevant by the twin forces of globalization and technology. (H. Skeete, Reuters, FISD.NET, 2000)

3.5 Implications for International Financial Centers: Expectations and Perceptions

What these examples show is that in the future, international financial centers may not be defined by the physical presence of markets. We have often used London and the London Stock Exchange interchangeably. This may no longer be justified in a medium-term perspective. The electronization of exchanges might loosen the ties of a number of agents to financial centers. What is generally expected is a consolidation of the number of stock exchanges.

> We will see the future dominated by two, maybe more, electronic exchanges with world-wide coverage and trading, say three hundred of the most liquid global securities. These exchanges will operate twenty-four

---

[11] There is a diverse set of possible legal structures and forms of technological integration for such deals. For an overview of forms, effects and issues see CYBO-OTTONE ET AL. (2000) or also DI NOIA (1999).

hour, seven days a week operation. (J. Friedman, Andersen Consulting, San Francisco, FISD.NET, 2000)

This promises us a seamless world as regards time differences and a new hierarchy of stock exchanges that will be characterized by fewer big players. Besides the idea of a dominance of few big players, we might also imagine the world of stock markets as a world of nodes. The future stock exchange might then be a global exchange in the sense of an inter-market link between current exchanges and alternative trading systems that offers access to multiple markets through one entry point.

Besides that, the physical ties of banks and other companies in the financial sector might be loosened because of the possibility to exchange information on the Internet. This might decrease the importance of local presence and interactions as well as of relationships.

Technically access from anywhere, at any time and for anyone seems to have become much more realistic than before. In many steps of the interaction, location is today replaced by new electronic sites for contact, and information seems to be available in real time. The new developments are supposed to bring cost reductions, enhance efficiency and transparency and should therefore induce growth.[12] Financial centers would in this vision become branchless and disintermediated, with stock exchanges being neither local, nor national, but global.

However, while the vision of more global markets seems to have become a more realistic option today, a lot of barriers certainly remain (legal, supervisory, cultural, etc.). In any case, the increasing delocalization of stock exchanges has induced a changed perception regarding the importance of a local presence in financial centers. The following quote reflects the point that the fate of financial centers is expected to be related to the institutional design of their markets.

The notion of financial service empires tied to certain cities is disappearing. Most of the operations can be domiciled on the dark side of the moon. It's a national, if not global business. ... The concept of a financial center will be less and less meaningful anywhere in the world. When the stock exchange is electronic, it's irrelevant. The notion of needing to come to one place as a financial center becomes far less relevant. (J. Friedman, Andersen Consulting San Francisco, SAN FRANCISCO BUSINESS TIMES, 1999).[13]

---

[12] A discussion of the advantages of electronic platforms in the financial sector would have to go deep into their working mechanisms. This is a task that cannot be performed in this paper. The interested reader may have a look at BIS (2001) or BARCLAY ET AL. (2001) for an evaluation of the performance of electronic trading systems or at FURST ET AL. (2000) for the effects of the Internet on retail banking.

[13] After having closed its trading floor, San Francisco would be an interesting example to study the effects of a delocalization of a financial center's stock exchange. However, the city has already at the end of the last century experienced an exodus of banks and a decrease of importance. It may also to some extent be a special case because of its location near Silicon Valley as a venture capital center and the high dynamics of the region's industry clusters that may also offer alternative growth potentials for San Francisco.

To some extent, this argument makes sense. Stock exchanges were not only visible signs in the financial district of cities. They are also places that have attracted a lot of permanent attention regarding the details of their developments. Their prices are understood as aggregated information. Stock exchanges may to some extent have attracted people and companies to financial centers because they disseminate information. Whether this is still true in the age of electronic exchanges may be debated.

Stock exchanges are only one type of financial markets. Others are less institutionalized and derived from the direct interaction among financial companies and between them and their clients, which may today to some extent also be possible via electronic means. Is market proximity still important and if not what does this imply for the role of international financial centers?

> (The) City of London, the heart of Britain's financial industry, will do fine if the UK remains outside the euro. ...Success, it argues, is determined not by proximity to markets, but by the trading environment – the regulatory regime, infrastructure, the advantages of size, and a critical mass of skilled and qualified staff. (Financial Times, 2001)

Which points remain to justify the clustering of financial activities in centers? The title of this paper has posed the question whether we face an "upheaval" in the spatial organization of the financial sector. Are we approaching a future in which financial centers are not important at all or where we no longer find a set of different financial centers that co-exist? Our argumentation will be that both tendencies are not probable. The next chapter will deal with a line of argumentation that might justify why financial centers are not made irrelevant in the time of increasing possibilities to transmit information and access markets electronically. This argument is concerned with the role of international financial centers as information and interaction centers. We will try to show that "(f)inancial centers are not identical with the financial markets they organize." (SEIFERT ET AL., 2000). It will, however, also be proposed that we still lack empirical knowledge to create a satisfying theoretical basis for this argument.

4. Financial Centers as Information and Interaction Centers

4.1 Delineating the Argument

The argument that agglomeration in financial centers is based on information advantages is not a new one. It is related to the notion that the financial services sector is involved in a number of information-intensive transactions and that information for these transactions is hard to transmit across a distance. Financial centers offer the possibility to have face-to-face interaction with other agents, to listen to "gossip" and to "feel" the market mood. This notion of financial centers as information centers is also expressed in the following quotation by GEHRIG (2001, p. 418):

> To the extent that financial centers are the locations where complex information about the prospects of a region's investment projects is produced and aggregated, they are attractive sites for multinational banks. ... These centers tend to host primarily information-sensitive activities.

Gehrig's analysis is based on the assumptions that on-site information is valuable and that it cannot be communicated perfectly. The fixed costs of a local presence have to be taken into account as well as the costs of communicating information and the value of information. He proposes a model that shows that a local presence may still make sense, even if communication costs drop. He names a few examples for relevant types of information (above all about equities markets) and assumes that financial centers have a regional role.

THRIFT (1994, p. 325) adds that financial centers "are where the stories are. Much of the world's financial press operates from these centers; so does much research and other analysis, information processing and so on."

To some extent the argument of information advantages remains nebulous, above all as regards the type of information, motives and settings for exchange. It seems to be important to complement the existing fragmented set of models by a structured view on the relevant information. Such a view has to take into account the specific need for local information and interaction that is related to different transactions.

The information-intensity of financial transactions has probably best been shown in the field of equities trading. The literature on international finance has illustrated this very impressively by analyzing the equity home bias showing that individuals tend to hold less foreign equities in their portfolios than classic capital market theory (that does not acknowledge friction) would suggest (AHEARNE ET AL., 2000; BRENNAN / CAO, 1997; PORTES / REY, 2000). Other analyses have shown that mutual fund managers differ in their performance depending on their location and have explained this with information asymmetries (SHUKLA / VAN INWEGEN, 1995). We also have papers dealing with the fact that the level of information (based on their location) makes investors react differently in cases of shocks (FRANKEL/SCHMUKLER, 1996). CHRISTOFFERSON/SARKISSIAN (2000) introduce the phenomenon of location overconfidence by less sophisticated investors that are situated in financial centers and thus near more sophisticated ones. Another category of papers has tried to trace the location and dynamic transmission of information (visible in stock prices) for stocks that are traded at several exchanges (GRAMMIG ET AL. 2001). A very interesting paper in this category is the one by CHAN ET AL. (2001) who use the Jardine Group to distinguish location of business from location of trade of the share and try to find out whether news related to one or the other is more important for the price of the share. So what we can certainly say is that the importance of information has been well demonstrated for the equities sector in the literature. The appendix gives a survey of a number of relevant papers without, however, assuming that this list is complete.

While some researchers have stressed the importance of being located in financial centers to gain these information advantages, there have also been critics of this. In his paper HAU (1999) found that location in a financial center does not matter for investor performance, but a location near the headquarters of a firm and language do matter. The evidence on information advantages in financial centers is therefore ambiguous.

Some authors have also argued that financial transactions differ according to their information- and location–sensitivity. WALTER (1998) for instance tries to map the centrifugal and centripetal forces in the financial sector and comes to the conclusion that centripetal forces are strongest for risk management, corporate advisory, securities underwriting, securities trading and sale as well as loan structuring and syndication. Centrifugal forces are above all created by cost considerations. Centripetal forces are those forces that foster the localization of some financial transactions in centers. One reason for this localization might lie in their information and interaction advantages. Without doubt, the class of financial transactions that is more footloose and characterized as back office functions is a variable group. New technologies may allow the decentralization of more transactions, so that more of them may belong to the class of activities that is independent from a location within financial centers.

WILHELM (1999) also underlines that there are some transactions in the financial sector which have for a long time relied on relationships:

The banker's network of personal relationships is perhaps the central element of the production technology of the 20th century investment bank.

He calls this "relationship-based production technology" and names four areas where relationships have been important: IPOs, product innovation, mergers & acquisitions and small firm finance. He describes that the Internet more and more replaces relationships.[14] However, he neither describes how relationships are built, nor whether keeping relationships makes physical proximity necessary.

SEIFERT ET AL. (2000) speak of "sticky financial products" that have a very important local content like M&A, asset management, equity issuance and (to a lesser extent) fixed-income underwriting. They explain this local component with local cultural preferences, legal traditions, specific regulatory frameworks and travel distance[15], the benefits of tailoring a product to local demand and the imperfect substitutability of local talent. Of course, the argument here depends on how we define the local. To some extent local seems to have a broader scale than agglomeration in the narrow financial district of a city. The local content of financial products might be related to the perception of regional markets that dominates the strategic decision-making of banks.

Moreover, we have to acknowledge that the creation of information advantages would finally rely on a process of multiple steps. Once access to information is

---

[14] See also PETERSEN and RAJAN (2000). They deal with changing structures of relationships and proximity in small business lending.

[15] Travel distance should be measured in more dimensions than just kilometers or miles: above all in time costs, inconvenience, distress, opportunity costs, etc.

given, it has to be processed, evaluated and interpreted. Moreover, information can also be actively created within processes of research. Finally, the cumulated information, experiences and learning processes of firms result in special know-how, which shows that information is not just a given endowment of locations that only has to be grabbed.[16]

The literature on equities markets, information asymmetries and the geography of information is relatively extensive. Having a look at other transactions, we find that there are fewer explanations. Some authors refer to the clustering of activities that are subject to joint production of banks (as syndicated loans, M&A and IPOs) and which may require intensive interaction and trust, which would be favored by proximity between intermediaries. In some cases the advice of specialized producer firms (law, consultants) may also be relevant as e.g. in the case of mergers & acquisitions (LO, 2000.).[17] LO / SCHIMMEL (1999) show that local networks of knowledge-intensive services matter. Several authors agree on the importance of trust that is more easily created by continuing local interaction (LO, 2000; CODE, 1991). Moreover, the importance of uncertainty is underlined (see also ROBBINS / TERLECKYI, 1960):

> The uncertainty which those involved in the financial markets are attempting to limit "has a spatial dimension ..., not only because the inherent stability of phenomena may vary from place to place, but also, because communication channels diffuse information unevenly in space, and because perception varies." (WOLPERT, 1964, p. 547)

The point that makes the argument of information advantages nebulous lies in the diverse forms information can take in the financial sector, each of which is accompanied by different problems concerning its acquisition and exchange. The following table tries to list some potentially relevant types of information.[18]

---

[16] Even though we have mostly talked about information here, the distinction between information and knowledge that is usually made in the literature would probably also be useful here. Thus, data alone cannot be a basis for decision-making. Information is dependent on the person who owns it. Information requires perceiving relationships between data. Finally, knowledge is only created if one is able to understand and interpret these patterns.

[17] ECCLES and CRANE (1988) explain the importance of networks in investment banking in detail. Although they do not refer to spatial effects, some proposals can be derived from their explanations, which, however, rely strongly on the assumption whether or not relationship building and trust require spatial proximity.

[18] DIETRICH (1996) distinguishes technical information (concerning transactions), market information (concerning buyers and sellers) and customer-specific information (specifics of individual customers and firms).

Table G1:   Trying to Classify the Relevant Information

TYPE OF INFORMATION	RELEVANCE	ASSOCIATED PROBLEMS IN ACQUISITION AND EXCHANGE
general mentality and culture of a market	general	get involved in the general culture of a market in order to interpret information in the right contextual setting
Short-term news that is valuable as long as it has not become public information	e.g. in equities markets	informal access to information; ability to feel the market mood and to interpret signals; observance of market behavior
knowledge and experience in providing certain services	M&A, IPOs	problem that joint production of service involves different companies; exchange of sensitive information necessary; problem of trust and context-dependent information
aggregated analytical potential that is embodied in human capital and research divisions of companies	can concern variety of markets	Are there spillovers among companies? in the sense that the mere presence of successful companies induces overconfidence in others? because of labor market externalities (human capital changing employers)?
specific information about customers	e.g. credit markets	Do firms collude with regard to this information? Why? When?
relationship-based opportunities	e.g. coming IPOs	get customers because of strong existing relationships and contacts; be better able to see and grab new opportunities
competition-related information	technology research, corporate development	know what competitors are working on; get to know innovative future directions and competitive threats

4.2 Open Questions

The relevance of information in certain sensitive fields of the financial sector seems to be obvious. In the paragraphs above we were also able to gather a few hints on how information might be exchanged, although this part of the argumentation is probably the most nebulous.[19] This is why we would argue that some open questions remain:

---

[19] EGUILUZ and ZIMMERMANN (2000) formulate a stochastic model of the formation of opinion clusters without, however, embedding it into any spatial framework.

1. Externalities

We can expect that agglomeration externalities play a role for the importance of financial centers. Empirical studies have shown that the number of financial companies in a center matters for the location choice of other firms. However, deriving externalities from the mere number of firms present is without doubt only a very rough approach. Some of the above proposals on how information advantages may be created are mere speculations. Finally, these externalities are still to some extent a black box for us. Without doubt, information advantages are also more important for some transactions than for others. There are few analyses that offer an empirical basis for the question how networks of service suppliers work (LO, 2000). However, we know little about the interaction among banks. We do not know with certainty whether and how informal and formal ways of information exchange work between them, nor can we be sure that such an exchange would necessarily be positive.[20] In other knowledge-intensive sectors like high-tech agglomerations (e.g. Silicon Valley) processes of knowledge sharing have been analyzed intensively. However, we can expect that these cannot be compared to those in financial centers, which is already due to the short-term perspective of many types of information and to the special characteristics of the relevant sectors. Whether any parallels can be drawn will have to be analyzed very carefully.[21]

Without doubt the analysis of externalities and interaction in financial centers has to be specific, not only relating to the question which financial activities are concerned, but also as regards the different types of agents involved (banks, lawyers, tax and general consultants and specialized financial service providers, etc.)

We also do not know in which way local atmosphere would be complemented by firm capabilities to create, process and interpret information (firm sophistication) and by the investments firms make in networking. Today we often get the impression that it is not the availability of "raw" information that is the most pressing point, but the interpretation of relevant information. This, however, gives us a different perspective of the information advantages of financial centers that emphasizes the analytical and research potential in these centers rather than the local access to information. This potential could also be understood as a certain degree of sophistication of centers that is determined by the number of experts in the center, their information and communication infrastructure and the related access to information (SEIFERT ET AL. 2000, pp. 8-11).[22] A point that would be very interesting to analyze is whether we can define financial centers by a certain level of expertise, knowledge and information externalities that is not necessarily related to their own national or local markets. Can there be super-ordinate centers

---

[20] Thinking of herd behavior and its potentially negative effects on markets, such an exchange of information might as well be negative. Moreover, if the information exchange mechanism works, it might be possible to distribute pieces of information strategically.

[21] In a different context GEHRIG AND STENBACKA (2001) discuss information sharing in credit markets, which is, however, understood as a long-term commitment and not embedded into any spatial context.

[22] SEIFERT ET AL. (2000) describe these determinants as bums, banks and brains.

whose resources are excellent enough that their information level about other markets is better than in the location of a market itself?

2. Multinational companies and the intra-firm exchange of information

New developments in e-finance have underscored the role of the Internet as an excellent source of information for individual investors. However, we know little about the sources and channels of information for financial companies that are also active in advisory services and investing. We may suppose that local presence and electronic information are complementary to each other and other channels. The power of the Internet might especially be relevant in a sector that is so strongly characterized by multinational companies. If our understanding of finan-cial centers were true, then these companies would have incredible opportunities to share and use this information within their network (KLAGGE, 1997).[23] The literature has pointed out that the firm can be a more efficient channel for informa-tion than the market (internalization of information, COASE, 1990) and that or-ganization matters for the exchange of information. However, we neither know whether this sharing of information within financial companies happens, nor do we know how. We also lack knowledge of patterns of organization of multina-tional banks. The use of information in multinational financial companies is even more important as these increasingly cluster a wide range of services under their roof that may to some extent be interrelated (e.g. a firm providing an extended loan to a customer who later chooses this firm as its leading underwriter and pos-sibly also opts for its support in further transactions like M & A).

The surge of intranets might be one tendency that could also improve the intra-firm communication of financial companies a lot.[24] Moreover, there are a lot of other technologies like e-mail and videoconferencing that should enhance com-munication. Thus, there should also be externalities within the multinational com-pany that depend on its strategy of information sourcing and its capabilities to communicate internally.[25] The analyses of CHOI ET AL. (1986 and 1996) have proposed a way to measure the linkages multinational firms establish between financial centers by analyzing whether banks have offices in other financial cen-ters and the other way around. They have determined unilateral and bilateral link-ages between centers. Although a strong level of linkages would give us an idea

---

[23] In a recent advertisement JP Morgan chose the headline "global strength, local exper-tise". This reflects the importance of a combination of local access and global capabili-ties. Japanese as well as German markets in earlier times have served as proofs for the relevance of this combination in investment banking.

[24] LO (2000) gives information on the use of information and communication technologies by firms involved in M&A services.

[25] GEHRIG (1996) has proposed an approach that analyzes the competition between bro-kers that compete on network size. This approach is certainly useful because it acknowl-edges the local activities of multinational companies. However, it is also based on a very stylized view and does not really touch upon the question of information exchange within the multinational company.

that information advantages might be a reason, the information flows that may be enabled by these linkages remain invisible in this analysis.

However, some people are also skeptical of the potential of electronic exchange of information. They say that its use requires that substantial investments into personal connections have been made before. This is also why traveling and face-to-face meetings still assume an important position in the internal communications by banks.

Figure G1:   New Business Models for Banking

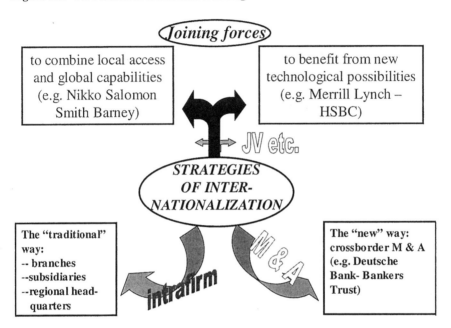

3. New business models

The last decade has moreover been characterized by new business models in the financial services sector (Figure 1). Keywords are consolidation, mergers & acquisitions, alliances, and joint ventures. Some of these have also concerned cross-border transactions. There are a number of different aspects that have been named as reasons for these new strategies (BERGER ET AL. 1999). Market access but also market expertise and the wish to acquire connections can be important motives for this. MOSHIRIAN (2001) presents data that show that a lot of banks choose paths of internationalization where they become shareholders of foreign banks (while the name of the acquired bank often does not change). What we observe are new ways of building networks and exploiting local / global advantages. Concerning the idea of intra-firm information sharing, we should, however, be careful, as the barriers to these synergies may be different than in the case of branches and built-up subsidiaries.[26]

Finally, the possibilities to transmit information between different agents within a company or between different parts of an alliance are also relevant for the possibilities to separate the locations of information collection, decision-making and action (for financial centers as centers of decision-making and action, see Figure 2).

Figure G2:   Information, Transactions and the Role of Financial Centers

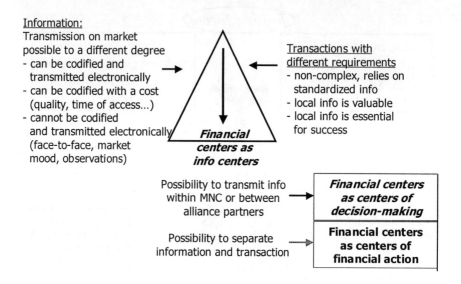

4. How many financial centers do we need?

Our argumentation in the preceding paragraphs was that financial centers are centers that benefit from the agglomeration of localized information, centers of high know-how capacities, centers where products can be tailored to local needs and centers for talent. However, even if we could show that local presence matters for information, we would still not be able to assess what this would mean for the number and hierarchy of financial centers in the world economy. How many financial centers do we need? Which centers might be threatened by decline? Which will remain relevant? Without doubt the simultaneous existence of several financial centers would only be justified if each of them offers a specific set of advantages that cannot be found at any other location; or put differently, only those centers will be resistant to technological change that offer access to a unique set of information or other unique conditions that justify the investment into a local

---

[26] In a recent article about Citibank FT reports how this global banking company has sought to maintain a local touch through dozens of acquisitions and alliances.

presence for financial agents. Such uniqueness might be based on different kinds of advantages. On the one hand, there are certainly borders of information.[27] For instance, information about regional or local conditions will be tied to certain locations. It is easy to imagine that these borders are not exclusively influenced by hard economic variables. Culture, for example, might be an important point in different senses. The literature has shown that high- and low-context cultures have to be distinguished. They differ above all concerning the way they make it easy for foreigners to become insiders or not and concerning their need to be able to read between the lines. Japan is without doubt a good example for a high-context culture. European firms have often complained about their difficulties to enter the Japanese market. This would probably also be relevant for the financial services sector, which might lead us to suspect that proximity may be more important in some markets than in others. This argumentation that certain kinds of information are more easily accessible at certain locations could justify why smaller centers might co-exist with big centers where extraordinary potential and capabilities to create, process, evaluate and interpret information are present. Unique information advantages might also be relevant for centers that have a gateway function for a region (informational hinterland). The custom to establish regional headquarters may be an indicator for the fact that a location may have more than a role in the nation-state but might be seen as a gateway to the region. This is why its geographical position in a wider context and its position to markets would matter. PORTEOUS (1995, p. 113) calls this the information hinterland of a financial center and defines it as follows:

> ...the "information hinterland" of a centre may be defined as the region for which a particular core city provides the best access point for the profitable exploitation of valuable information flows.

He claims that the information hinterland is a function of the natural, institutional, historical and technological environment of the time and that this is a dynamic concept.

5. The interplay between traditional and electronic channels

Altogether we can also expect and already find a financial geography that is characterized by the parallel existence of electronic and "traditional" modes of collect-

---

[27] The relationship between the city of London as Europe's traditional financial capital and the Euro area might be a good research field here. There were fears that London might lose its position as a financial center if the UK does not enter the Euro area. This did not prove right in the first years of the Euro. However, most people expect that a Euro that would be a strong currency in the long-term would harm the position of London as an outsider. Finally, London enjoys tremendous advantages due to size. It has more than 500 foreign banks, more than any other city in the world. Moreover, there are no language problems, and it has a history that may make it easier for foreigners to locate there. Its biggest competitor, Frankfurt, boosted its role as the location of the ECB, but experts stated that this is not an important criterion.

ing and transmitting information and accessing markets. Both modes offer specific advantages that influence the strategies of financial companies and the spatial organization of the financial sector. Empirical research might lead us to a better understanding of the "division of labor" between them (Figure 3). Meanwhile we have to take into account the pace of change with which technological innovations happen nowadays. This new division of labor will also be decisive for the future role and number of financial centers. Especially their number will depend on how new technologies can change their realm of influence.

Figure G3:   E-Finance and Localized Access

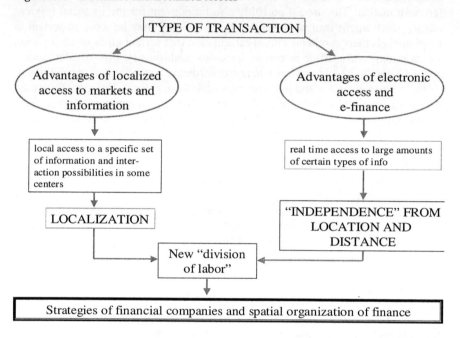

For instance, CODE (1991) assumes that technological and organizational advances have not been sufficient to allow the dispersion of financial center communities. They rather enhance the rate at which relevant information is fed into and disseminated outward from the community. This is because external information is assumed to be standardized which is not true for internal information exchange. If we accept this argumentation, we should expect smaller centers to be endangered, as the bigger ones expand their sphere of influence. In that case only those small centers would survive that are somehow sheltered by frictions.

5. Further Reasons for Agglomeration: Labor Markets and Institutions

Information and interaction advantages have been reviewed as arguments to explain why financial service companies cluster and – as far as access to information not only being localized, but information itself having a local character – why they cluster in several locations. Other types of argumentation can be found in the literature, notably labor market externalities. They can explain clustering, but it is difficult to explain the existence of several centers without taking other reasons into account. The argument of institutions as magnets has above all recently been brought forward in the case of Frankfurt where the ECB has its seat.[28]

5.1 Labor Markets

Labor market externalities are another reason for the agglomeration of some financial activities. This would concern above all high-skill and knowledge-specific activities. Imagine the following "model". It can be argued that both employers and employees in the financial sector have a vital interest in liquid labor markets. Employees incur costs in order to build up a private infrastructure. The higher their investments for this, the less will financial specialists be willing to move geographically because their investments would be sunk costs.[29] This is why it would be interesting to analyze the average mobility of financial experts (in general and within the networks of their company). By clustering together they also have the possibility for collective bargaining. Moreover, employees increase their option of changing employers without moving geographically, when they cluster where a lot of financial institutions are present. This option of changing employers decreases the more employees are specialized or the higher their qualifications are. For experts a location within a cluster would be even the more beneficial. Obviously, the change option is more valuable for them in times of boom, as they can use it to bargain with financial companies about working and payment conditions. Hypothetically, we can also assume that employees have certain social ties that are not necessarily local ties, but above all ties within their profession. Financial specialists might want to pass their leisure time with people from the same profession

---

[28] For some types of markets, market liquidity may be an important force that fosters agglomeration in the center with the biggest market. ECONOMIDES and SIOW (1988) have analyzed the interaction between market liquidity as a centralizing force and market access costs as a decentralizing force that promotes several centers. In times of electronic market access these market access costs would, however, have to be explained carefully.

[29] We may assume that the unwillingness of financial experts to change their living location might also create strong lobbying forces and increase the resistance of centers like Frankfurt to be "eaten" by London. In general it would be interesting to know how strongly locational decisions in banks are influenced by the – potentially irrational – individual preferences of their top-level management.

who speak the same language. Employers in financial centers benefit from a large pool of specialists. KIM (1990) shows similarly that larger centers provide protection against mismatches in case of idiosyncratic shocks.

Differently from our argument of local information the motive of thick labor markets would not tell us which locations become financial centers, as long as we assume that both labor and firms are mobile. It relies first of all on the benefits of agglomeration itself. Moreover, it does at first sight not help us to answer why we need several financial centers and not one world center. This can only be explained when adding arguments like the local content of financial services.

It is interesting that we can observe that a center's labor market is often a reflection of the internationality of its banks. "As cities like London, New York and Tokyo have strengthened their hold on global finance and banking, they have also become global marketplaces for skilled migrant workers" (BEAVERSTOCK / SMITH, 1996, p. 1377). Banking and specialist employment opportunities can be found within corporate headquarters and front-line office networks. To some extent this phenomenon seems to be related to intra- rather than inter-firm labor markets. Interviews by BEAVERSTOCK / SMITH (1996, p. 1392) have also shown that banks could negotiate immigration legislature in part to overcome specific problems concerning the entry of foreign nationals into different countries.

To some extent this argumentation would lead to a process of circular causation whose dynamics depend on the relative mobility of firms and high-skill labor.

What should also not be forgotten is that financial specialists may pose certain requirements regarding the soft environment of their home city. Taking the example of Frankfurt relative to London, problems like the high bureaucratic hurdles have often been named as barriers for foreigners. Moreover, international schools in Frankfurt are crowded with German students, so that there aren't enough openings for children of foreigners. The European Central Bank's (ECB's) staff is to 60 per cent comprised by foreigners. This is why the ECB is actively supporting the establishment of a new European school and its own day-care center. Without doubt, the cultural offerings in a city matter as well. This is why Frankfurt has sometimes been said to be at a disadvantage compared to London, whose metropolitan flair is stronger. "The magnetism of London as a working and living space must not be underestimated in the construction and uneven distribution of skilled international labor migration in the world economy" (BEAVERSTOCK / SMITH, 1996, p. 1381).

The intensive traveling activities of many top-level managers add to the requirements of high-level infrastructure regarding airports in financial centers. Moreover, the strong need for communication sets infrastructure standards. Altogether, we should not underestimate the role of financial centers not only as permanent locations for financial institutions, but also as meeting centers. As THRIFT (1994, p. 336) points out " they have become the meeting places for the global corporate networks of the financial services industry, places that see a larger and constant through-flow of visitors as well as workers from other centers and people in each center simply meeting and talking with each other." This characteristic supports the regular exchange of information by specialists from different locations and the blending of global / local knowledge.

5.2 Institutions

A lot of people have argued that institutions where highly relevant decisions for the financial sector are made matter as a source of local advantage. This argument has persisted with the European Central Bank having chosen Frankfurt for its location. There were expectations that this would serve as a magnet for foreign firms. Basically, this argument can only be grounded on the assumption that there would be possibilities of informal information access and leakages in ECB information. Basically, we can say that the proponents of this argument might have been taught by having a look at the US whose financial centers are not where the Federal Reserve Bank is located. Of course, most banks pay so-called ECB watchers, but these people watch from a far distance. They can be located in New York or at any other location in the world. The run on Frankfurt by foreign banks has not occurred. SEIFERT ET AL. (2000, p. 100) explain this with the fact that

> "the ECB is one of the more secretive central banks. From the refusal to publish minutes in a timely fashion to the secrecy surrounding internal discussions, the European Central Bank gives securities houses precious little reason to try and catch every rumor and casual comment by its officials – because there are so precious few of them."

Some bankers also agree that they do not believe that Frankfurt has an information advantage because of its location with respect to the European Central Bank. This holds on the one hand because the European Central bank does not speak with one voice. On the other hand, there are other centers like New York whose resources may be so good that they possess a worldwide information advantage.

This remark is interesting, as it would lead us to conclude that we cannot assume that institutions do not matter at all. It just results in the statement: "It depends on the type of the institution."

6. Information Strategies and the Special Characteristics of Centers

An interesting question is whether we could be able to find patterns in the information strategies financial institutions apply and in the interaction that occurs in different financial centers. In the following paragraphs we want to propose a matrix-approach to incorporate the question of firm-specific strategies and location-specific patterns in one framework, and complement this with a comparative analysis of differences between different firms and locations (Figure 4).

We claim that our theoretical analysis should ideally be complemented by in-depth interviews with an international set of financial companies located in different financial centers of the world (e.g. starting with the big three: London, New

York and Tokyo). An obvious strategy would be to take the biggest financial institutions of the US, Europe and Asia and analyze them as regards their strategies of localization and information technologies as a tool to source information (rows).[30] These strategies consist of locating within a center, gathering information and using information within the multinational firm. Comparing the different patterns in the horizontal rows may tell us something about the different approaches companies from different countries and regions take, always assuming that there are any patterns to be detected at all.

In analogy to the different "cultural" settings of centers that pose different requirements for firms, firms themselves as well as individuals might have different inclinations to participate in informal social events and to use the informal exchange of information, if this argument holds at all. If this is true, it seems to be vital to explore the reasons.

We might also read the columns from top to bottom. This tells us something about the strategies of foreign financial companies from the point of view of a single financial center (who is present in a center?). Having a look at the linkages from top to bottom, we get information about the interaction between different companies at one location. This is because we assume that part of the attractiveness as an information center is derived from the interaction of financial companies. Comparing the different columns would tell us something about location-specific patterns.[31]

While the comparison of different centers is probably obvious, the comparison of firms from different countries and regions may be disputable, as it is not certain whether nationality or culture is the hint for distinctive strategies. The framework is intended to help us answer the question whether we are able to make out certain patterns concerning information sourcing, location choice and spatial distribution of competencies and activities and to what degree these differ between financial centers.

A final possibility would be that firms from different countries might have alliances and cooperation to alleviate information asymmetries. This is an interesting strategy as local access can be combined with other strengths of the foreign partner.

Asking about how these patterns have changed in the past or which changes are planned in the future will also give us an idea of the dynamics of these patterns.

To test the hypotheses behind this framework empirical (primary and secondary) analysis will have to join theoretical modeling. The knowledge to be gained from in-depth interviews and empirical research should be useful to make propositions about the determinants of financial centers, the effects of e-finance on international financial centers as well as on the implications for the spatial organization of financial intermediaries. We may, however, have to be aware of the strategic

---

[30] Without doubt the range of companies involved in certain transactions is more diverse than just banks. Moreover, more and more non-bank companies get involved in the supply of financial transactions.

[31] It is interesting to note that MOSS (1989) finds that banks of the same nationality cluster together in different parts of Manhattan.

relevance some of the questions about information advantages may have and of the biases we may find in the answers. This is why it is vital to work carefully on the questionnaire.

Figure G4: A Matrix Approach

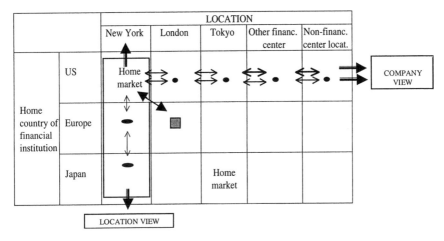

7. Conclusion

The paper has discussed international financial centers as phenomena of agglomeration in the financial sector. It has tried to delineate the state of the art in research and proposed a framework for empirical research, while pointing out those questions that seem to be most relevant to the author. Some of the most interesting and relevant aspects appear to be the role of the multinational company in transferring information as well as alternative strategies to get access to local information and connections (like strategic alliances and joint ventures).

The paper has therefore proposed a framework of research that acknowledges

- transaction-specific differences,
- differences between financial centers,
- multiple strategies of internationalization, and
- the importance of different types of information; the process of collecting, creating, processing, interpreting and transmitting information; as well as different borders of information.

Without doubt a better understanding of this "geography of information" would have to be based on a combination of knowledge from different fields of research on urban dynamics, cities and financial centers as well as approaches from industrial organization and international finance.

Today, technological developments have created opportunities for the financial sector to become more footloose. These opportunities are related to remote access to markets as well as the possibility of electronic interaction with customers. The latter trend is above all visible for standardized types of interaction (execution of decisions, automation of matching systems, transmission of standardized information). The electronic transmission of information can offer the advantage of real time access to a high quantity of information. Moreover, it seems to work independently from location. However, it is still difficult to estimate the scale of activities that may be caught by the e-finance wave. We have also assumed that electronic channels of information and local information sources are not alternatives, but work together. While e-finance may offer advantages for some transactions, access to some types of information still requires a local presence, and some types of transactions require interaction with other agents. These different channels render the question of spatial organization quite complex for multinational financial service companies.

We have proposed reasons for the local clustering of financial information and transactions. Most of them imply that the development of financial centers is to some extent led by self-organizing processes rather than only due to the need to access localized markets. There are indeed good reasons to assume that financial centers are more than the sum of their markets. Our argument would also take into account that "supply-side proximity" (interaction between financial service providers) is as relevant as "demand-led proximity" (the wish to be near to clients). To some extent, this idea of clusters in the financial services sector comes near to other phenomena which we have already observed in the industrial sector: innovative milieus, production clusters etc. More attention should therefore be paid to the question to what degree financial centers as urban phenomena share some characteristics of these clusters and to what extent we should understand them as fundamentally different. Finally, this type of empirical research should open up possibilities for more realistic models.

There is a strong necessity to think about the question what might make a financial center resistant in a world of electronic exchange of information. This is why more empirical research is needed to define the specific set of information that can be accessed in a center and to understand how information and interaction advantages and other local agglomeration advantages are created. It is also interesting to note that these advantages can only partly be influenced politically. Some of them are subject to self-organization. To some extent locally beneficial conditions might, however, be created by guaranteeing an adequate information and communication infrastructure, adequate rules in the labor market and an attractive soft environment as well as a clear regulatory system that fosters transparency for instance. As transactions become more footloose, stronger efforts will be necessary to anchor them, e.g. by providing an adequate soft environment as well as fostering low costs.

Altogether it should have become obvious that the research field still poses a number of interesting and strongly relevant questions whose answers will however have to rely on empirical research that creates the basis for new models. The existing literature has set a solid foundation for further elaboration.

The question of an "upheaval" in the spatial organization of the financial sector can currently be denied. Up to now financial centers have not lost their importance, nor are we very near to the vision of one world financial center. There are, however, hints of possible processes of "consolidation" regarding the number of centers in the medium to long run. Especially for smaller centers it seems to be vital to understand the reasons that explain why – especially foreign – financial institutions would cluster certain activities in several centers worldwide.

Appendix: Tables

Table G2:   Information Asymmetries and the Geography of Information – Selected
Studies from the Literature on International Finance

1. Home Bias	
Ahearne et al. (2000)	Analyze determinants of US holdings of equity across wide range of countries
Tesar and Werner (1995), Cooper and Kaplanis (1994), Gehrig (1993)	Analyze determinants of home bias
Kang and Stulz (1997)	Find evidence for Japan that foreign portfolios are skewed to equities of large firms
Coval and Moskowitz (1999)	Show that preference for investing close to home also applies to portfolios of domestic stocks
Portes and Rey (1999)	Find that geography of information determines cross-border equity flows; do not find special role for financial centers
2. Information Asymmetries and the Performance of Investors	
Kim (2000)	Examines the performance of foreign / local institutional / individual investors
Shukla and Inwegen (1995)	Find that UK open-end mutual fund managers investing in the US underperform US open-end fund managers
Grinblatt and Keloharju (2000)	Find that portfolios of foreign investors out-perform those of locals
Seasholes (2000)	Analyzes whether foreigners transacting overseas are at a disadvantage
Christofferson and Sarkissian (2000)	Find that superior informational advantage and performance of some fund managers in financial centers induce overconfidence among others
Hau (1999)	Compares information asymmetries across the trader population of Xetra; does not find evidence for financial center advantages
3. Locals and Foreigners React Differently	
Frankel and Schmukler (1996)	Find that Mexican locals acted ahead of foreigners in Mexican crisis
Brennan and Cao (1997)	Find that foreign investors tend to engage in trend chasing activities
Kim and Wei (1999)	Find that non-resident foreigners engage in momen-tum or herding strategies more than resident for-eigners do in Korean stock markets
Choe et al. (1999)	Trace momentum and herding behavior by foreign investors

Table G2: (continued)

4. Multiple Listed Stocks and Cross-Listings	
Hasbrouck (2001)	Traces where price discovery occurs for multiple listed securities
Hupperets and Menkveld (2000a)	Test effects of market fragmentation and information flows in case of cross-listed stocks on markets in Central Europe and London
Hupperets and Menkveld (2000b)	Test market integration for Dutch stocks cross-listed at NYSE
Stulz (1999)	Explains cross-listings in countries with higher disclosure standards with positive signals that are given to investors
Pulatkonak and Sofianos (1999)	Examine distribution of trading in NYSE-listed non-US stocks and explain it
Grammig et al. (2001)	Examine where price discovery for interna-tionally traded firms occurs and how stock markets adjust to exchange rate shocks
Bacidore and Sofianos (2000)	Find more that trading volume for ADRs is stronger in home market than in US
Karolyi (1999)	Documents order flow for Daimler Chrysler global share
Froot and Dabora (1999)	Find that stock prices of virtually identical firms differ across geographical locations
Chan et al. (2001)	Analyze stock behavior when location of trade differs from location of business of a company
Pagano et al. (2001)	Analyze pre-listing characteristics and post-listing performance of foreign listed companies

References

AHEARNE, G., GRIEVER, W., WARNOCK, F. (2000), Information Costs and Home Bias: An Analysis of US Holdings of Foreign Equities, Federal Reserve Board, Discussion Paper 691, Washington.

BACIDORE, I.M., SOFIANOS, G. (2000), NYSE Specialist Trading in Non-US Stocks, NYSE Working Paper, 2000-05, New York.

BANK OF INTERNATIONAL SETTLEMENTS (BIS) (2001), The Implications of Electronic Trading in Financial Markets, Basle: BIS Committee on the Global Financial System.

BANKS, E. (2001), E-Finance: The Electronic Revolution, Chichester: John Wiley & Sons.

BARCLAY, M.J., HENDERSHOTT, T., MCCORMICK, D.T. (2001), Electronic Communications Networks and Market Quality, mimeo.

BEAVERSTOCK, J., SMITH, J. (1996), Lending Jobs to Global Cities: Skilled International Labour Migration, Investment Banking and the City of London, in: Urban Studies, Vol. 33, No. 8, pp. 1377-1394.

BERGER, A. N., DEMSETZ, R., STRAHAN, PH. (1999), The Consolidation of the Financial Services Industry: Causes, Consequences and Implications for the Future, in: Journal of Banking and Finance, Vol. 23, 2-4, pp. 135-194.

BRENNAN, M., CAO, H.H. (1997) International Portfolio Flows, in: Journal of Finance, Vol. 52, 5, pp. 1851-1880.

BUSINESS TIMES (2000), E-Trading May Hit Stock Exchanges, www.pwcglobal.com.

CHAN, K., HAMEED, A., LAU, S.-T. (2001), What If Trading Location Is Different from Business Location?, mimeo.

CHOE, H., KOH, B.C., STULZ, R. (1999), Do Foreign Investors Destabilize Stock Markets?, in: Journal of Financial Economics, Vol. 54, pp. 227-264.

CHOI, S.-R., TSCHOEGL, A.E., YU, CH.-M. (1986), Banks and the World's Major Financial Centers, 1970-1980, in: Weltwirtschaftliches Archiv, Vol. 122, pp. 48-64.

CHOI, S.-R., TSCHOEGL, A.E., YU, CH.-M. (1996), Banks and the World's Major Financial Centres, 1990, in: Weltwirtschaftliches Archiv, Vol. 132, pp. 774-793.

CHRISTOFFERSON, S., SARKISSIAN, S. (2000), Location Overconfidence, McGill University Working Paper, Montreal.

CLAESSENS, S., GLAESSNER, T.H., KLINGBIEL, D. (2000), Electronic Finance: Reshaping the Financial Landscape Around the World, World Bank, Washington D.C.

COASE, R. (1990), The Firm, the Market and the Law, reprint, Chicago: University of Chicago Press.

CODE, W.R. (1991), Information Flows and the Processes of Attachment and Projection: The Case of Financial Intermediaries, in: BRUNN, S.D., LEINBACH, TH. R., eds., Collapsing Space and Time, London: HarperCollins Academic, pp. 111-131.

COOPER, I., KAPLANIS, E. (1994), What Explains the Home Bias in Portfolio Investment, in: Review of Financial Studies, Vol. 7, pp. 45-60.

COVAL, J.D., MOSKOWITZ, T. (1999), Home Bias at Home, in: Journal of Finance, Vol. 54, 6, pp. 2045-2173.

CYBO-OTTONE, A., DI NOIA, C., MURGIA, M. (2000), Recent Developments in the Structure of Securities Markets, in: Brookings-Wharton Papers on Financial Services, Washington, D.C.: The Brookings Institution.

DI NOIA, C. (1999), The Stock Exchange Industry: Network Effects, Implicit Mergers and Corporate Governance, in: Quaderni di Finanza, No. 33.

DIETRICH, J.K. (1996), Financial Services and Financial Institutions, Upper Saddle River: Prentice Hall.

ECCLES, R.D., CRANE, D.B. (1988), Doing Deals: Investment Banking at Work, Boston: Harvard Business School Press.

ECONOMIDES, N., SIOW, A. (1988), The Division of Markets Is Limited by the Extent of Liquidity, in: American Economic Review, Vol. 78, No.1, pp. 108-121.

EGUILUZ, V.M., ZIMMERMANN, M.G. (2000), Transmission of Information and Herd Behavior, in: Physical Review Letters, Vol. 85, 26, pp. 5659-5662.

FINANCIAL TIMES (2001), Financial Heart Will Do Fine Outside Single Currency, June 28, p. 8, US edition, New York.

FISD.NET (2000), The Future of Exchanges, www.fisd.net/news/1000reuters.html.

FRANKE, G., HESS, D. (2000), Information Diffusion in Electronic and Floor Trading, in: Journal of Empirical Finance, Vol. 7, pp. 455-478.

FRANKEL, J.A., SCHMUKLER, S.L. (1996), Country Fund Discounts, Asymmetric Information and the Mexican Crisis of 1994, NBER Working Paper, No. 5714, Cambridge/ Mass.

FROOT, K.A., DABORA, E. (1999), How Are Stock Prices Affected by the Location of Trade?, in: Journal of Financial Economics, Vol. 53, pp. 182-216.

FURST, K., LANG, W.W., NOLLE, D.E. (2000), Who Offers Internet Banking, Office of the Comptroller of the Currency, Quarterly Journal, Vol. 19, No. 2.

GASPAR, J., GLAESER, E.L. (1996), Information Technology and the Future of Cities, NBER Working Paper, No. 5562, Cambridge/ Mass.

GEHRIG, TH. (1993), An Information-Based Explanation of the Domestic Bias in International Equity Investment, in: Scandinavian Journal of Economics, Vol. 95, pp. 97-109.

GEHRIG, TH. (1996), Natural Oligopoly and Customer Networks in Intermediated Markets, in: International Journal of Industrial Organization, Vol. 14, pp. 104-118.

GEHRIG, TH. (2001), Cities and the Geography of Financial Centers, in THISSE, J. and HURIOT, J.-M., eds., The Economics of Cities, Cambridge: Cambridge University Press, pp. 415-445.

GEHRIG, TH., STENBACKA, R. (2001), Information Sharing in Banking: A Collusive Device?, CEPR Discussion Paper No. 2911, London.

GRAMMIG, J., MELVIN, M., SCHLAG, CH. (2001), Price Discovery in International Equity Trading, Arizona State University, mimeo.

GRINBLATT, M., KELOHARJU, M. (2000), Individual Behavior and Performance of Various Investor Types, in: Journal of Financial Economics, Vol. 55, pp. 43-67.

HASBROUCK, I. (2001), One Security, Many Markets: Determining the Contributions to Price Discovery, in: The Journal of Finance, Vol. 50, 4, pp. 1175-1199.

HAU, H. (1999), Information and Geography: Evidence from the German Stock Market, CEPR Discussion Paper, No. 2297, London.

HEIDUK, G., POHL, N. (2000a), Asia's International Financial Centers in the Globalized World Economy, paper presented at the international workshop "International Economics and Asia", City University of Hong Kong, mimeo.

HEIDUK, G., POHL, N. (2000b), Asian Hubs – Global or Regional Players?, paper presented at the 17th Annual Meeting of the Euro-Asia Management Studies Association "Globalization and the Uniqueness of Asia", Insead Campus Singapore, mimeo.

HUPPERETS, E., MENKVELD, B. (2000b), Intraday Analysis of Market Integration: Dutch Blue Chips Traded in Amsterdam and New York, Tinbergen Institute Discussion Paper No. 18.

HUPPERETS, E., MENKVELD, B. (2000a), Intraday Analysis of Market Integration, Tinbergen Institute 2000-018/2.

KANG, J.-K., STULZ, R.M. (1997), Why Is There a Home Bias, in: Journal of Financial Economics, Vol. 46, pp. 3-28.

KAROLYI, A. (1999), Daimler Chrysler AG: The First Truly Global Share, Dice Center Working Paper 99-13.

KIM, S. (1990), Labour Heterogeneity, Wage Bargaining and Agglomeration Economics, in: Journal of Urban Economics, Vol. 28, pp. 160-177.

KIM, W. (2000), Do Foreign Investors Perform Better Than Locals?, mimeo.

KIM, W., WEI, S.-J. (1999), Foreign Portfolio Investors: Before and During a Crisis, NBER Working Paper, No. 6968, Cambridge/ Mass.

KINDLEBERGER, C.P. (1974), The Formation of Financial Centers: A Study of Comparative Economic History, Princeton Studies on International Finance, No. 36, Princeton.

KLAGGE, B. (1997), Intrafirm Regional Networks of Multinational Banks, in: Geographische Zeitschrift, Vol. 85, pp. 231-248.

LO, V. (2000), Netzwerke im Mergers & Acquisitions Geschaeft, Johann Wolfgang Goethe Universitaet Frankfurt, mimeo.

LO, V., SCHIMMEL, Y. (1999), Die Vernetzung wissensintensiver Dienste fuer den Bankensektor im Rhein-Main Gebiet, Johann Wolfgang Goethe Universitaet Frankfurt, mimeo.

MOSHIRIAN, F. (2001), International Investment in Financial Services, in: Journal of Banking & Finance, Vol. 25, pp. 317-337.

MOSS, M. (1989), Face to Face: Why Foreign Banks Still Love New York, in: Portfolio, Vol. 2,1.

NACHUM, L. (2000), Economic Geography and the Location of TNC's, in: Journal of International Business Studies, Vol. 31, 3, pp. 367-385.

O'BRIAN, R. (1992), Global Financial Integration: The End of Geography, The Royal Institute of International Affairs, London.

PAGANO, M., ROELL, A., ZECHNER, A. (2001), The Geography of Equity Listing: Why Do Companies List Abroad?, CEPR Discussion Paper No. 2681, London.

PETERSEN, M.A., RAJAN, R.G. (2000), Does Distance Still Matter? The Information Revolution in Small Business Lending, NBER Working Paper 7685, Cambridge / Mass.

PORTEOUS, D. (1995), The Geography of Finance, Aldershot: Avebury.

PORTES, R., REY, H. (2000), The Determinants of Cross-Border Equity Flows: The Geography of Information, NBER Working Paper, No. 7736.

PULATKONAK, M., SOFIANOS, G. (1999), The Distribution of Global Trading in NYSE-Listed Non-US Stocks, NYSE Working Paper 99-03, New York.

REED, H.C. (1980), The Pre-eminence of International Financial Centers, New York: Praeger.

ROBBINS, S.M., TERLECKYI, N.E. (1960), Money Metropolis: A Locational Study of Financial Activities in the New York Region, Cambridge / Mass.: Harvard University Press.

ROBERTS, R., ed., (1994), International Financial Centers, Cheltenham: Edward Elgar Publishing (series of 4 volumes).

SAN FRANCISCO BUSINESS TIMES (1999), In Depth: Banking and Finance Quarterly, San Francisco.

SASSEN, S. (1991), The Global City: New York, London and Tokyo, Princeton: Princeton University Press.

SEASHOLES, M.S. (2000), Smart Foreign Traders in Emerging Markets, mimeo.

SECURITIES INDUSTRY ASSOCIATION (2001), The New York Securities Industry, New York.

SEIFERT, G. ET AL. (2000), European Capital Markets, New York: St. Martin's Press.

SHUKLA, R., VAN INWEGEN, G. (1995), Do Locals Perform Better Than Foreigners?, in: Journal of Economics and Business, Vol. 47, pp. 247-254.

STULZ, R. (1999), Globalization of Equities Markets and the Cost of Capital, mimeo.

TESAR, L., WERNER, I. (1995), Home Bias and High Turnover, in: Journal of International Markets and Finance, Vol. 14, pp. 467-493.

THE ECONOMIST (1995), Turn Up the Lights: A Survey of Cities, 29th of July 1995.

THRIFT, N. (1994), On the Social and Cultural Determinants of International Financial Centres: The Case of the City of London, in CORBRIDGE, S., MARTIN, R. and THRIFT, N., eds., Money, Power and Space, Oxford: Blackwell, pp. 327-355.

WALL STREET JOURNAL (2001), "Open Outcry" Maintains Its Popularity as Many Traders Still Rely on Old Style, June 14.

WALTER, I. (1998), Globalization of Markets and Financial Center Competition, New York University, Salomon Center, Working Paper 98-23, New York.

WILHELM, W. J. (1999), Internet Banking: The Impact of Information Technology on Relationship Banking, in: Journal of Applied Corporate Finance, Spring, pp. 21-27.

WITHERELL, W. (2001), Realizing the Revolution in E-Finance, remarks to the Global Forum for Law Enforcement & National Security, Edinburgh.

WOLPERT, J. (1964), The Decision Process in a Spatial Context, in: Annals of the Association of American Geographers, Vol. 54, pp. 537-558.

H. E-Finance: Causing Major Upheavals in the Spatial Organization of the Financial Sector?
(Some Comments on Paper by Nicole Pohl)

Thomas P. Gehrig

1. Introduction

The paper by Nicole Pohl is a very welcome and timely contribution about the location of financial activity. It fits well into the context of the conference and highlights a particular sector that is probably going to belong to those most dramatically affected by the recent technological innovations in the communication and information technologies largely implemented by the Internet.

E-finance summarizes technological developments that are largely associated with the de-localization of financial activity. E-banking facilitates remote access to banking and savings accounts. E-trading facilities basically allow access to trading accounts from any connected computer terminal worldwide, and, of course, myriads of websites provide potentially useful fundamental information as regards the valuation of securities and the access to electronic public offerings through the net. The paper essentially asks the question, how these developments will affect the performance, and even relevance, of financial centers.

While the Internet has the potential to generate huge centrifugal forces, financial centers are generally perceived as manifestations of the existence of significant centripetal forces, i.e. forces that induce firms to choose locations close to other firms and, in particular, close to their rivals. The very fact that international banks did increase their international presence dramatically in the 1980's and to a lesser extent in the 1990's (CHOI / TSCHOEGL / YU, 1996) demonstrates the size of the amount of costs international banks were willing to invest into the presence in the financial hot spots, such as New York, London, Tokyo and many more. Presumably, these investments were justified by the expectations of economic gains. So this paper is really about the relation between centrifugal and centripetal forces in the financial sector, and how these forces are affected by the Internet and modern communication facilities.

After a short survey of some of the theoretical and empirical literature, the paper argues that our scientific understanding of the contrasting forces in financial markets is still very rudimentary, both from a theoretical as well as from an empirical perspective. The author, therefore, suggests that interviews with practitioners might help to sharpen our understanding and, thus, improve our models and their predictions. While this certainly is a worthwhile approach and any attempt to increase the state of our empirical knowledge about financial activity and financial centers is highly welcome and should be applauded, I would like to use my comments to help and structure such an empirical endeavor. I will first comment on the state of the theoretical literature, then comment on a few key empirical observations and finally suggest some strategies for further empirical and theoretical work.

2. What Does Theory Tell Us?

Interestingly, traditional finance theory does not address the issues of the geographical dimension of financial activity at all. Hence, financial centers do not play any role in this literature, and early scholars of financial centers had to build their arguments on intuitively appealing ad-hoc reasoning without any sound theoretical backing (e.g. KINDLEBERGER, 1974). By design traditional finance theory is cast in a frictionless world of complete markets. In the ideal world of Modigliani and Miller pricing and arbitrage issues are the central questions of analysis but not locational issues. In fact, under the conditions of traditional finance theory location of financial activity is a matter of irrelevance. In this sense, any geographical structure could be in accordance with this theory. Of course, such a view seems to contradict observed patterns of behavior. Why did international banks incur significant costs and increase their market presence in foreign markets? On the other hand, to the extent that cyberspace creates conditions of a perfect market, maybe the traditional paradigm is precisely the vision of the future? Hence, whether geography will become a matter of irrelevance or indifference will depend on whether the Internet can approximate the benchmark model of completely frictionless markets.

On the other hand traditional spatial economics never really ventured into the issue of financial activity but concentrates on trade in real products. Only PAGANO (1989) and ECONOMIDES / SIOW (1988) in their seminal contributions explicitly analyzed spatial decisions in trading frameworks with geographical features. In both frameworks consumers (or investors) incur market access or transportation costs. Both papers show, that in the absence of any other market imperfections the trading activity of otherwise homogenous goods (or assets) can actually geographically segment, such that subgroups of traders deliberately decide to trade goods (or assets) in geographically separated markets. In both papers, due to coordination problems, typically, multiple equilibria arise. In each market participants trade off the benefits of entering the larger and hence more liquid market[1] against the costs of market access. Nevertheless, PAGANO's (1989) segmentation result seems to lack robustness. In general, in his setting one would expect dominance of a single market place and hence concentration of trading in a single market.

GEHRIG / STAHL / VIVES (1996) argue that market access costs need to be complemented by at least one further friction to explain the segmentation of stock

---

[1] In these trading models a liquid market exposes risk-averse market participants to a lower degree of price volatility.

trading and to explain the fragmentation of primary equity markets.[2] Based on vast empirical evidence on anomalous investment behavior, particularly one central assumption of traditional financial theory does seem to be in strong contradiction to reality – market completeness. GEHRIG (1993) argues that informational heterogeneity (in incomplete markets) could explain the domestic bias in equity investment for example.[3] In conclusion, GEHRIG / STAHL / VIVES (1996) and GEHRIG (2000) argue that the combination of both frictions, market access costs and local information could explain market segmentation in financial markets, and, thus, generate a framework on which to construct a model of financial centers. Also a model without market access costs would have trivial implications, since it would imply that all relevant agents should access all markets at the same time. In such a framework geography could not enter meaningfully.

In this comment, therefore, I should emphasize that local information alone is not a sufficient condition for agglomeration of financial activity, or, even, for the existence of financial centers. The paper needs to analyze the impact of the Internet on both market access costs and the communication of local information. Probably, for most financial activities, the Internet will reduce both the costs of market access and the cost of communication. However, the relative impact might differ quite substantially in different types of financial activities causing different implications for spatial redistribution of financial activity.

Will the reduction in communication costs in such a world necessarily lead closer to a frictionless world and ultimately render financial centers irrelevant? As I argue below (and in GEHRIG, 2000) the answer critically depends on the nature of information that can be communicated and the local content of information. To the extent that the relevant local information can be communicated, probably centrifugal forces will dominate for a given financial activity. To the extent that the demand for local information is enhanced by lower communication costs, however, the agglomeration of the corresponding activity may even grow and turn into a (regional) center of information aggregation.

3. What Do Empirical Observations Tell Us?

I have already mentioned an increasing international presence of financial intermediaries in financial centers around the world. This observation is striking since improved communication possibilities would seem to suggest a shrinking need for an international presence. It seems that the international presence of these intermediaries is related to information-sensitive financial activities such as portfolio management and lending but also to international activities of domestic firms, for which domestic banks may have informational advantages relative to international competitors (JEGER / HÄGLER / THEISS, 1995).

---

[2] Likewise GEHRIG (1998) argues in a product market context that modelling "competing markets" does require the introduction of at least two (independent) frictions.

[3] See BRENNAN, CAO (1997) for further implications of the relevance of localized information for portfolio flows.

On the other hand one observes a complete de-localization of less information-sensitive activities. For example, FX-trading basically is completely de-localized and takes place in a cybernet. However, equity trading seems more concentrated on few if not a single market. For example, KAROLYI (1999) documents the migration of the combined trading volume of Chrysler and Daimler stocks to Frankfurt after the merger took place. BESSEMBINDER / KAUFMANN (1997) document for US-stocks that in periods of uncertainty, trading volume in electronic networks dries up and trading basically concentrates on the single market where price discovery takes place (normally the listing exchange).

PAGANO / ROELL / ZECHNER (2000) document some significant trends in firms' listing decisions. In a large international sample they find significant double listings of European firms at the New York Stock Exchange (NYSE) or the National Market (Nasdaq) in the U.S. and a significant degree of de-listing of US-companies in Europe. Given the direct costs of a US-listing and the indirect costs imposed by the accounting requirements for a US-listing, one wonders why firms may still invest in US-listings. Since listings requirements in the US are stricter than in Europe, the authors suggest that the certification role of a US-listing may be an important explanation of both developments in the US and Europe. Moreover, there seems to be also evidence of foreign high-tech and bio-tech firms seeking their first listing at Nasdaq and not even in their home market (e.g. Israel), which makes sense under the assumption that the expertise about the market and technological developments in the high-tech sector, necessary for fair securities valuation, is concentrated at Nasdaq (and possibly only there).

Clearly, all these recent trends document little signs of international equity markets becoming less segmented. In fact, these developments are manifestations of market segmentation and seem to strongly suggest informational explanations. To some extent these observations carry over to fixed income securities, even though their informational complexity seems lower than that of equities.[4]

Hence, in contrast to the underlying paper, the issue is not, whether local information will remain still relevant in the future, but it is about what type of local information will be required for what type of financial activity. What is the nature of the local information that seems to be so important to explain geographical financial patterns? What is it that financial intermediaries are looking for in other financial agglomerations? Is it strategic information or is it some form of inside information?[5] In some sense these issues parallel very similar questions about the

---

[4] GEHRIG (1993) documents for Switzerland and Germany that the domestic bias is more pronounced in equity relative to bonds despite the fact that pension funds were highly regulated to invest in domestic fixed income securities in the 1980s and 1990s.

[5] It may be interesting to observe that in regulated banking markets in Europe, and in particular in countries where price competition was discouraged or prohibited, a certain degree of overbranching could be observed. For example, in Germany you could almost bet that next to the branch of Deutsche Bank you would find a branch of Dresdner Bank or Commerzbank (or both). This type of agglomeration can in principle support collusion since rivals can monitor each other's activities closely. It could, however, also be a mani-

geographical activities of multi-national firms.[6] Why do firms establish a costly presence in foreign countries? Moreover, why do they enhance their international presence in precisely those times when communication and information costs are significantly declining? Given the strategic nature of location decisions I am somewhat skeptical that interviews will ultimately provide clear answers.

4. How Does the Internet Affect Spatial Financial Activities?

The challenge of the basic research issue of the present paper is to disentangle the various financial activities according to their informational characteristics. Various activities seem to exhibit tendencies to cluster, while others may completely de-localize. GEHRIG (2000) argues that financial activities of high informational complexity will tend to cluster, while standard financial activities with a lower degree of informational complexity will become footloose and either completely de-localize (currency trading) or cluster in regions with the lowest regulatory burdens (Euro-money markets). Hence, primary markets for equity and equity-based derivatives but also commodities and their derivative products would be expected to remain highly concentrated. Trading activity per se could de-localize easily, and the emergence of myriads of electronic trading networks (ECNs) is ample proof of this de-localization, but in times of uncertainty, when price discovery is costly, one would expect concentration of trading on the primary issue markets or the main aggregator of payoff-relevant information. This expectation is actually born out in equity markets (BESSEMBINDER / KAUFMANN, 1997).

Moreover, the advent of improved communication possibilities could reinforce the importance of local information aggregation. To the extent that e.g. US-investors value Chinese stocks, US portfolio managers' incentives to produce high quality information about China increases, and hence possibly also their willingness to establish a costly physical presence in the relevant markets. In this case, general information about the Chinese economy and specific local information about particular firms are complements. As the Internet improves the communication of general information it may thus stimulate the demand for specific complex information, and, thus enhance geographic agglomeration (in China). In this sense GEHRIG (2000) argues that the Internet's affects on the geographical agglomeration of financial activities depend crucially on whether standard and complex information are substitutes or complements. It is an empirical challenge

---

festation of competition for market share as predicted from standard spatial competition models when price competition is restricted.

[6] As a smaller point I should correct the statement in footnote 22 of the paper that GEHRIG (1996) does not touch on the issue of information exchange within an intermediary. GEHRIG (1996) establishes that perfect communication within an intermediary does generate strategic advantages. Therefore, in his simple brokerage framework larger networks (i.e. multinationals) enjoy competitive advantages over smaller ones, precisely because of perfect in-house communication.

to identify the various types of information, those that are candidates for Internet dissemination and those that are considered "complex" and less qualified for electronic communication.

While it seems that, in the context of fund management, basic accounting information can easily be transmitted by electronic means, the interpretation of the numbers will depend among other things on conventions, the regulatory and political framework and the behavior of courts. Hence, even the interpretation of standard information may require the help of country experts.

Even, in a simpler trading context, the communication of pricing information necessary for implementing simple arbitrage strategies requires knowledge about specific details of a transaction in order to identify and assess settlement risks, for example.

Finally, how does the Internet affect financial centers? The author hopes to find the key to an answer to this fundamental question by interviewing practitioners. Maybe it is a worthwhile strategy to classify the various financial activities (trading, portfolio management, investment banking, certification, etc.) and market participants (non-financial firms, financial intermediaries, banks, asset management, investors, law firms, regulators, central banks, etc. differentiated according to geographic origin) prior to the interviews to see precisely what kind of activities agglomerate and what kind of activities seem to de-localize. Such information may be useful to target the interviews on the specific forces of agglomeration for each specific activity and to identify the sources of potential spillovers across specific activities, such as primary markets and secondary market trading, for example. The literature provides ample guidance for such an endeavor, even though its size is limited to date.

If the present project could ultimately illuminate our understanding of the informational complexity of financial transactions, and their interrelations, it could generate tremendous momentum, both for theoretical and empirical research. So I am looking forward to the prospective results.

References

BESSEMBINDER, H. and KAUFMANN, H. (1997), A Cross-Exchange Comparison of Execution Costs and Information Flows for NYSE-listed Stocks, Journal of Financial Economics 46, 293-319.

BRENNAN, M. and CAO, H. (1997), International Portfolio Investment Flows, Journal of Finance, 52, 1851-1880.

CHOI, S.-R., TSCHOEGL, A.E., and YU, Ch.-M. (1996), Banks and the World's Major Financial Centers, 1990, Weltwirtschaftliches Archiv 132.

ECONOMIDES N. and SIOW, A. (1988), The Division of the Market is Limited by the Extent of Liquidity, American Economic Review 78, 108-121.

GEHRIG, T. (2000), Cities and the Geography of Financial Centers, in THISSE, J. and HURIOT, J.-M. (eds.), The Economics of Cities, Cambridge University Press, 415-445.

GEHRIG, T. (1998), Competing Markets, European Economic Review, Vol. 42(2), 277-310.

GEHRIG, T. (1996), Natural Oligopoly in Intermediated Markets, International Journal of Industrial Organization, 14, 101-118.

GEHRIG, T. (1993), An Information-Based Explanation of the Domestic Bias in International Equity Investment, The Scandinavian Journal of Economics, 1/1993, 97-109.

GEHRIG, T., STAHL, K. and VIVES, X. (1996), Competing Exchanges: Do Large Drive Out Small?, mimeo.

JEGER, M, HAEGLER, U., THEISS, R. (1992), On the Attractiveness on Financial Centers, in: BLATTNER, N., GENBERG, H., Swoboda, A. (eds.), Competitiveness in Banking, 1992.

KAROLYI, A. (1999), DaimlerChrysler AG: The First Truly Global Share, mimeo, Ohio State University Working Paper.

KINDLEBERGER, C.A (1974), The Formation of Financial Centers: A Study of Comparative Economic History, Princeton.

PAGANO, M. (1989), Trading Volume and Asset Liquidity, Quarterly Journal of Economics 104, 255-274.

PAGANO, M., ROELL, A., and ZECHNER, J. (2000), The Geography of Equity Listings: Why Do European Companies List Abroad?, CSEF-Working Paper No. 28, Universita Degli Studi Di Salerno.

I. How Will the Internet Change the Japanese Financial Perspective?

Mariko Fujii

1. Introduction

The great advancement of information technology has been one of the major driving forces of rapid change and innovation in the financial services sector since the 1980s. These changes include not only the creation of new products but also changes in the delivery and distribution channels of the financial products traded. As well, the electronic marketing of financial services and electronic payment and settlement of financial transactions are widely used with the resulting enhancement of economic efficiency. In this broad sense, information technology is surely affecting the perspectives of the financial services sector in major markets around the world and influencing global economic activities as well.

Among these broad categories of IT and electronic technology-related financial services, this paper focuses on e-finance at the retail level, particularly those services that have grown with the advent and prevalence of the Internet. The Internet offers a new channel for marketing and selling financial products as well as a new channel for executing and delivering financial services. Although e-finance is in its early stage as far as the size of transactions is concerned, it will potentially change the market structure and thus the pricing of services and welfare of the consumers, provided that security concerns are satisfactorily resolved.

The paper will first review the current state of the development of e-finance in Japan and discuss the challenges facing further development. Issues related to the impacts on market structure will then be examined. The final section draws some policy implications and provides some concluding remarks.

2. Current State of the Development of Electronic Financial Services in Japan

At the end of 2000, the number of Internet users in Japan is estimated as 47.08 million, which is 1.74 times greater than a year ago.[1] Among them, 37.23 million users access the Internet via PC, while 23.64 million gain access via cell phones, the latter figure indicating that cell phones have been a prime factor in the surge in the overall number of Internet users since access via cell phone first became possible in February 1999. About half of the residential PC Internet connections use ordinary phone lines, with the other half using ISDNs (128Kbps) or faster circuits.

---

[1] INFORMATION AND COMMUNICATIONS IN JAPAN WHITE PAPER 2001 (2001).

Twelve percent of residential users who connect to the Internet via PC do so using broadband. Most financial institutions offer both PC and cell phone channels, and I begin with a review of the current state of the development of online securities trading and e-banking in Japan.[2]

2.1 Securities Businesses on the Internet

The online trading of securities was initiated in 1996 by traditional, full service securities firms such as Nomura, Daiwa, and others. Since 1999, the Japan Securities Dealers Association has conducted a survey of online trading twice a year. According to the most recent survey of September 2001, 66 securities firms out of 289 member firms currently offer Internet trading services for retail customers (Table 1 and Figure 3). The number of accounts for online trading amounts to 2.48 million, which has been increasing by almost double every six months in 1999 and 2000 with a slightly slower growth rate in 2001 (Table 1).

Table I1 :   Survey on Internet Transactions (as of the end of March 2001)

A: The Number of Security Companies those Offer Internet Channels

	number of member compa- nies sur- veyed	number of companies offering Internet channels			not offering					
							under preparation		under considera- tion		no plan to offer	
1999 October	284	47	(16.5%)	237	(83.5%)	14	(4.9%)	46	(16.2%)	177	(62.3%)
2000 March	291	51	(17.5%)	240	(82.5%)	21	(7.2%)	48	(16.5%)	171	(58.8%)
2000 September	288	64	(22.2%)	224	(77.8%)	7	(2.4%)	36	(12.5%)	181	(62.8%)
2001 March	290	67	(23.1%)	223	(76.9%)	8	(2.8%)	19	(6.6%)	196	(67.6%)
2001 September	289	66	(22.8%)	223	(77.2%)	7	(2.4%)	16	(5.5%)	200	(69.2%)

Note: Figures in parenthesis are share to the total number surveyed.
Source: Survey on Internet Transactions, Japan Securities Dealers Association, September 2001

---

[2] Cross-border transactions and e-insurance are not discussed herein because of the difficulty of data compilation and its relatively lower popularity in Japan at present.

Table I1 :   Continued

B: The Number of Accounts for Internet Transaction (in millions)

	1999 October	2000 March	2000 September	2001 March	2001 September
number of accounts	0.30	0.75	1.33	1.93	2.48

Source: Survey on Internet Transactions, Japan Securities Dealers Association, September 2001

Despite this very rapid growth of the number of online accounts, it is interesting that about 200 securities firms, that is, roughly two-thirds of all securities firms, do not have any plan to offer an Internet trading channel. Although online trading is growing very rapidly, transaction amounts through the Internet are still small making up only 7 per cent of the total transactions in shares (Table 2).[3]

Table I2 :   Transaction Amounts of Online Securities Trading (in billion of yen)

	Stocks			Domestic Investment Funds	
	Internet channel		share to the total transactions	Internet channel	share to the total transactions
	cash transactions	on credit transactions			
1999 October	223	—	—	30	0.4%
2000 March	969	197	1.9%	60	0.8%
2000 September	856	278	3.8%	67	1.5%
2001 March	1254	570	5.8%	257	3.6%
2001 September	1006	684	7.6%	121	2.2%
1999 October - 2000 March	3785	749	1.8%	237	0.5%
2000 April - 2000 September	5500	1437	3.6%	465	1.1%
2000 October - 2001 March	5696	2374	6.3%	863	2.9%
2001 April - 2001 September	7194	3979	7.3%	841	2.3%

Source: Survey on Internet Transactions, Japan Securities Dealers Association, September 2001

Online securities services usually include trading in shares and sales of investment trust funds, and most firms provide only brokerage service over the Internet.

---

[3] It should be noted that the total amount of transactions in shares sometimes decreased despite an increase of the traded amount of online trading. Exact figures will appear in a later section as Table 4.

Online securities services usually include trading in shares and sales of investment trust funds, and most firms provide only brokerage service over the Internet. Full-service securities firms use the Internet as either an alternative trading channel for customers or for developing discount brokerage activities; several firms provide deep discounts for Internet use. New entrants are using the Internet to establish their discount brokerage businesses, and some of them are Internet-only firms. According to a survey conducted by a private research company, 14 firms are regarded as online-only brokers in Spring 2001.

The levels of brokerage commissions have diversified after the full-scale deregulation of October 1999. Introduction of electronic trading is furthering this trend. At present, the brokerage fee charged for online channels is sometimes less than half of that of a traditional face-to-face transaction (Figure 1). For example, for a transaction amount of 5 to 10 million yen, online commissions cost almost 1/3 of that of traditional channels for individual investors.

Figure I1:   The Rate of Commission Fee Charged by Security Companies: via Different Channels for Stock Transactions

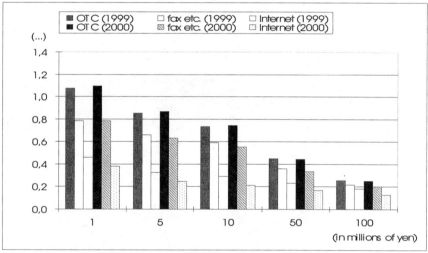

Sources: Survey on the stock transaction commission fees conducted by Japan Securities Dealers Association in October 1999 and December 2000, respectively.

2.2 E-Banking

Internet banking was started in early 1997 by Sumitomo Bank, and nowadays not only all city banks but also almost 40 percent of all depository institutions offer Internet and / or cell phone channels for such services as account inquiry, real time fund transfer, and time deposit.[4] Regarding e-banking, official statistics describing its current state of development are not available; however, the total number of accounts for Internet and cellular phone banking is at least as many as 3.4 million as of June 2001 according to a survey conducted by a private institution (Figure 2). These figures reflect only the numbers of accounts of traditional banks that publish data and thus surely understate the actual number. Even this indicates that the number of accounts has almost doubled in the first half of the year 2001. An article in an economic newspaper reported that the number of contracts for Internet and cellular phone channels reached more than 9 million for only those of city banks.[5] Some banks are offering foreign currency deposit, purchase of investment trust funds, and card loan applications in addition to the services described above.

Figure I2:   Number of Accounts for On-line Trade and Banking

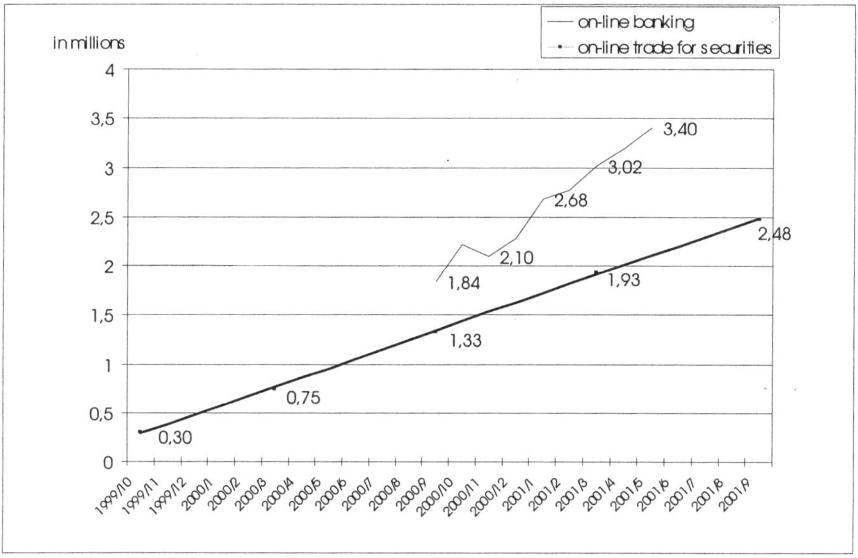

Source: on-line trade for securities; 2001 Survey on Internet Securities Transactions, Japan Securities Dealers Association; on-line banking; "Trader's Databank" by Ichiro Sunada in Internet Magazine, various number. These number represent only for those banks publishing data.

There are two types of electronic service providers. Traditional bankers regard e-banking as another delivery channel that operates side-by-side with the real delivery channel. The second type of e-banking service providers are those close

---

[4] White Paper on Financial Industry Information Systems 2001. In Japan, there are 15,970 branches of all 144 depositary institutions, among which 3,042 branches are of 9 city banks, consisting of 43 percent of the total amount of deposits of all domestically licensed banks as of the end of March 2000.

[5] Article appeared on the 27th of May, 2001 in the Nihon-Keizai Shinbun.

to the idea of virtual banks, which do not have real branches but offer all services through Internet channels. As of December 2001, four of these new types of banks began doing business in Japan, and they are basically Internet-only banks. Table 1 shows the outline of these four banks. All of them obtained banking licenses and incidentally, the first, the Japan Net Bank, which was licensed in September 2000, was also the first bank in the Japanese banking industry to acquire a new license in the last half of the century.

It is interesting that each bank announced a different business strategy, and it is important to recognize which of them will experience the most growth in the coming years, since for all of them size is quite important due to the nature of the businesses they provide. Japan Net bank is an online-only bank, and its cash points are mainly ATMs of Mitsui-Sumitomo banks, servicing small amount card loans. Sony Bank is similar except that Sony offers a full range of banking services to retail customers. E-bank is another category of online-only banks since they do not have their own cash points but use transfers from the accounts of traditional banks, focusing heavily on real time, small amount payments and settlement services via PCs and cell phones. IYbank is unique in the sense that it has a network of customer bases in the Seven-Eleven and Ito-Yokado supermarket groups.[6]

As major shareholders, these banks have non-financial entities. The entries by such non-financial entities into e-banking are expected to have an impact on the market structure in the future.

In regard to service fees, online services charge roughly half those of real cash transactions or ATMs.[7] The interest rate on time deposits offered by online-only banks sometimes appears to be slightly higher than that offered by traditional banks. Most of these providers offer free accounts as means of promoting initial sales. As stated above, banks of this new type all focus on payments and settlement services, and thus scale consideration is the key to success regardless of their differences in business strategy. Against this background, it is quite uncertain how the online fees and the interest rates offered will ultimately converge.

---

[6] Seven-Eleven is a network of about 8,900 convenience stores around the nation. Ito-Yokado, the shareholder of Seven-Eleven Co. Ltd., is managing supermarkets of 182 stores, and Ito-Yokado is the second largest retailer in Japan.

[7] Fees through ATMs are cheaper than those through face-to-face handling.

Table I3: Outline of New Banks

Name of the bank	Day of service started	Day of license approved	Major share owners (percentage in parenthesis)	Paid-in capital in billions	Services offered
The Japan Net Bank, Limited	2001.6.11	2000.10.12	Sumitomo Mitsui Banking Corporation (60), Nippon Life Insurance Company (10), Fujitsu General Limited (10), The Tokyo Electric Power Company, Incorporated (5), MITSUI & CO., LTD. (5), NTT DoCoMo,Inc. (5), NIPPON TELEGRAPH AND TELEPHONE EAST CORPORATION (5)	20	· Internet only (no branches); · cash transactions are mainly through ATMs of Sumitomo Mitsui Banking Corporation, · offering small amount cash-loans
IY Bank Co.,Ltd	2001.5.7	2001.4.25	Ito-Yokado Co.,Ltd. (51), Seven-Eleven Japan Co.,Ltd. (49)	30,85	· Internet only (no branches);· providing ATM at Seven-Eleven chain stores in corporation with Sumitomo Mitsui Bank and others;· focusing on clea-
Sony Bank Inc.	2001.6.11	2001.4.25	Sony Corporation (80), Sumitomo Mitsui Banking Corporation (16), J.P. Morgan Chase & Co. (4)	37,5	· Internet only (no branches);· offering full retail financial services;· cash transactions are mainly through ATMs of Sumitomo Mitsui Banking Corpo-
eBank Corporation	2001.7.23	2001.7.6	ITOCHU Corporation, Sumitomo Corporation, Japan Telecom Co., Ltd	8,9	· Internet only (no branches); · focusing on small amount transactions

Sources : press releases of each bank, as of July 2001

2.3 Challenges to the Development of Electronic Financial Transactions

2.3.1 Internet Access

Several challenges face the further development of electronic financial transactions. Many argue that the lack of high speed Internet access and the high costs associated with Internet usage are presently the largest impediments for the private sector to take businesses into Internet-related areas.

It is expected that the provision of high speed and cost-effective network access, for example, through optical fiber networks will promote the further use and development of electronic commerce in general. The Ministry of Public Management, Home Affairs, Posts and Telecommunications intends to designate the year 2001 as the "First Year of Broadband", and when such broadband functionality becomes more easily available with constant monthly charges in coming years, online businesses in general may grow and accordingly online payment and settlement demand will grow as well.

2.3.2 System Security

In regard to financial services, there may be some concerns for operational risk, security concerns, and reputational risks in managing online operations. To meet these concerns, Financial Service Authority issued operational guidelines regarding licensing and ongoing supervision of e-banking activities in August 2000.[8]

In this regard, the following points were made. First, most of the processes of settlement procedures seem to be unchanged since the new banks acquired banking licenses and are connected to the same network as the traditional banks. Only the initial stages of access from the customer to the financial network are different. Although there are concerns regarding the general capacity and reliability of the electronic system as a whole to process transactions, the basis of the financial clearing and settlement system could be as secure as that of the traditional system.

Second, the unbundling of businesses through outsourcing has not yet become popular. This may have some implications for security as well as for the cost structure in providing electronic financial services, since it is often argued that the outsourcing of technical services is one of the principles essential to realizing cost savings. Until now, Japanese banks do not outsource mainframe computer systems except to their affiliated companies or companies with which they have a long-term relationship. This may be contrasted with experiences of heavy dependence on a third party in other economies. As far as the system security is concerned, this may provide more stability than a rather dispersed system.

---

[8] Further technical issues are discussed in the report of the study group on "Electronic Sales of Financial Services and Supervisory Policy" of April 2000, Financial Supervisory Agency.

2.3.3 Growth Potential for Online Brokers

Although new entrants seem to have flexibility in expanding their businesses, one of the important factors for success is said to lie in maintaining a large enough customer base. For this to happen, the impact of new channels on the size of the market is another important issue.

As CHOI, LAIBSON, and METRICK (2000) have pointed out, even if the emergence of the Internet has coincided with a rise in trading activity, it is difficult to determine whether the Internet's role is causal. The paper cited above reported that at first glance the opening of web trading brought with it a 60 per cent shift of transactions to the new web channel, and that trading rate has quadrupled from its pre-web level. However, all this web trading is not necessarily "new" trading, and is affected as well by various factors such as recent increased volatility in the U.S. securities market.

In Japan, the very limited experience of the last one-to-two years of online transactions in shares shows that the amount traded through new channels does not seem to affect the total amount of transactions, which has been sometimes decreasing because of bear market conditions and other factors.

Table I4:   Amount Traded in Transactions of Shares (in Trillions of Yen)

	Internet trade (A)	Total amount of transactions (B)	(A)/(B) %
Oct. 1999~ Mar. 2000	4.53	258.4	1.8
Apr. 2000~ Sep. 2000	6.94	192.1	3.6
Oct. 2000~ Mar. 2001	8.07	128.1	6.3
Apr.2001~ Sep.2001	11.17	153.2	7.3

Source: Japan Securities Dealers Association (2001b)

In addition, some people argue that because of the relatively conservative attitude of Japanese investors towards risky investments, the growth potential for Internet brokers is seen as limited. In Japanese household portfolios, investments in shares consist of only 4.8 percent of the total outstanding financial assets (Table 5). Since Fall 2001, the defined contribution system of corporate pensions (the so-called "Japanese 401k") has been introduced, and this may enhance the usefulness of Internet channels.

Table I5:   Financial Assets and Liabilities of the Household Sector

	1999cy (Trillions of yen)	2000cy (Trillions of yen)	Share to the total amount (%)	2000/1999 (%)
Total Financial Assets (A)	1.386,2	1.390,2	100,0	0,3
Cash and deposits	751,9	762,9	54,9	1,5
-Transferable deposits	117,3	128,0	9,2	9,1
-Time and savings deposits	594,9	592,0	42,6	-0,5
Securities other than shares	91,7	91,2	6,6	-0,6
-Central government securities	7,3	9,2	0,7	25,6
-Investment trust beneficiary certificates	29,4	33,7	2,4	14,7
-Trust beneficiary rights	36,5	30,7	2,2	-15,8
Shares	91,9	66,5	4,8	-27,6
Insurance and pension reserves	379,5	388,5	27,9	2,4
Total Financial Liabilities (B)	388,7	384,9	100,0	-1,0
Loans by private financial institutions	228,4	225,1	58,5	-1,5
-Housing loans	104,3	106,6	27,7	2,2
-Consumer credit	36,9	37,3	9,7	1,2
Loans by public financial institutions	91,1	90,9	23,6	-0,2
-Housing loans	76,7	77,1	20,0	0,6
Financial Surplus (A-B)	997,5	1.005,3	-	0,8

Note: Figures are outstanding amount at the end of each year.
Source: Financial and Economic Statistics Monthly, No.27 (2001), Bank of Japan.

Reflecting these developments, some foreign capital-owned online security firms are reported to have closed their businesses in Japan, partly because they believe that heavy investments are a burden and will not pay enough.[9]

---

[9] For example, it has been reported that Schwab-Tokyo Marine Securities will liquidate their business in January 2002, with only one-year of operation of online securities booking. Several other foreign capital-owned securities firms are also reportedly closing their business in brokerage services regarding Japanese stocks (Dec. 2001, Nikkei Shinbun).

Figure I3: Number of Security Firms Offering the On-line Trade

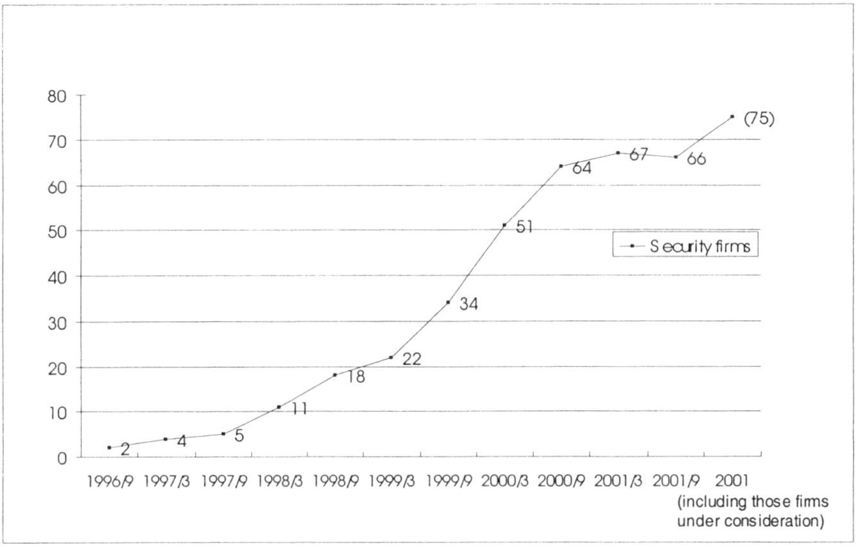

Source: 2001 Survey on Internet Securities Transactions, Japan Securities Dealers Association

3. Impacts of Electronic Financial Transactions on Market Structure

3.1 Direct Effects: Transaction Costs

As typically shown in the cases of brokerage commissions on securities trading, electronic financial services are generally providing more cost-effective transaction methods to the consumers, partly reflecting reductions in the costs of providing those services and partly reflecting the change in competitive conditions in the market. Obviously, reductions in the costs of undertaking transactions benefit participants involved in these transactions and thus result in the increased efficiency of economic activities as a whole. This type of transaction cost issue can be seen as having a direct effect on the economy. The reductions in brokerage fees, fees for electronic fund transfers, and other related e-banking services are examples, and the size of these effects may be captured quantitatively.

Regarding Japanese clearing and settlement practices, electronic bank transfer is already widely used. In contrast to the U.S., check payments are not popular. Most regular payments such as bill payments to utilities are electronically handled by contracts between customers and utility companies through automatic bank transfer systems. Thus, services such as online bill payment are not expected to grow, implying that marginal gains from shifting channels from traditional systems to online transfers are relatively small in comparison with a check-dominated economy. Nevertheless, the potential gains from the reduction of fees and charges of such financial services could be large if the cost and market structure of those services are changed.

More importantly, e-commerce should produce great benefits if further developments in less costly payment and settlement tools, especially those for micropayments, are made widely and securely available. In this regard, e-banking may develop side by side with the development of electronic commerce in a broad category. Some banks clearly use this strategy to enlarge their customer base by cooperating in establishing e-malls for various goods on their sites.

The dynamic interaction between virtual and physical providers' price setting behavior and the resulting price changes are of particular interest. Since most e-finance in Japan is in its early stages, competition has driven down prices so as to take market shares. More time is required to evaluate the process; however, if the current level of prices of online bankers and brokers were maintained, gains for consumers would be not negligible in its size.

3.2 Possibility of Changing Market Structure: Cooperation and Competition

An important question is whether or not the extensive use of Internet channels enhances competition in the financial services industry. It is generally noted that the network economy has several implications for market structure depending on the nature of the goods and services traded on the web. For goods and services having homogeneous characteristics, online channels usually lower search costs, and consumers are thus able to compare prices more cheaply than in the physical world. Thereby the availability of new channels reduces prices and makes markets more competitive. On the other hand, if the traded goods and services have the characteristics of so-called network externalities, a more oligopolistic market structure would eventually emerge. Although there seems to be small network effects in some cases of financial services such as fund transfers, most electronically offered financial services are rather standardized.[10] This implies that more competition is expected in the marketplace dealing with standardized financial services. In particular, fees for banking services through both online and physical channels will be reduced by further competition.

One of the very interesting aspects of e-banking businesses is the new style of competition and coordination. All of the new online-targeted banks involve non-financial capital, and this may produce some new forms of cooperation in their business development. It is often said that the strategy in the network market is distinct from the strategy in traditional markets. The cases of online-only banks are especially useful to illustrate this point.

---

[10] Usually a bank charges higher fees for transfers to the accounts of other banks.

In the banking business, all banks first needed to cooperate with others in collaboration with a central bank in order to establish a secured network system of settlement; this is called the Zengin system. Then, groups of banks and/or financial institutions were formed to set up ATM networks for inter-institution fund transfers such as BANCS. These systems described above are already established by traditional banks.

For new entrants into the banking industry, creating a real branch network is almost impossible in view of the cost consideration unless they use an existing bank network by means of merger or acquisition. Providing online services is usually less costly than establishing a real branch network; however, still they need cash points. In this regard, each of the four online-only banks has cooperated with traditional banks.

Furthermore, the case of the IY bank suggests more room for cooperation between financial and non-financial partners. Because the Ito-Yokado group is Japan's second largest retailer and has a national network of supermarkets and convenience stores, they can utilize their store network as physical points for ATMs, and they also can cooperate with traditional banks in order to provide a greater variety of service content for these ATMs. This expresses a strategy of pursuing economy of scale in operating their ATM networks.

Under the traditional regulated system, competition occurred in very limited areas, such as in the amount of deposits taken, and dynamic interactions could hardly be observed either among financial institutions or between financial and non-financial entities. The new non-financial shareholders of online banks are from the telecommunications industry, retailers, IT manufacturers, and international retailers (Sōgō-Shōsha). They potentially can cooperate with financial capital in a different way than traditional financial companies cooperate with each other. Because e-banking business requires both financial and IT-related technologies and a broad customer base, they may be able to create a great opportunity to work with.

At the same time, the traditional banks and online banks are rivals. Online banks could survive only with economy of scale since the profitability of most of their businesses depends on the volume they handle. Payments and fund transfer services are rather simple businesses, and there may not be much room for innovation. One possibility for a breakthrough in new services is a digital card such as the smart card. It is understood that such digital card technology enables banks to offer a greater range of value-added services to their customers through online services, and to enhance the value of online banking by means of digital money downloading services, thereby providing tools for micro-payments.

4. Policy Implications and Concluding Remarks

4.1 Policy Challenges

A cashless economy will not emerge within the now foreseeable future. The issues that we should address are economic implications, rules and policy considerations in the world of the multi-channel system of financial transactions. Unless cash disappears, even online banking needs cash points, and thus the traditional branch network continues to play an important role. For the securities business, it is still important to sell advisory services and have face-to-face communication. This all implies that we should prepare ourselves for the world of diversified channels of marketing, delivery, execution, and so on, rather than for the online-only world.

From this point of view, a pressing concern is how consistently to apply the same principles and rules of capital markets to these mixtures and combinations of investors and transaction channels. The above development implies that we are offered a variety of execution channels, marketplaces, and delivery channels. In other words, the regulators are facing a variety of channels and marketplaces, as well as different types of investors that do not fit into traditional classifications. In its 1999 report, the U.S. SECURITIES AND EXCHANGE COMMISSION (1999) discussed in detail the issue of the applicability of a well-established doctrine of suitability, the rule of the best execution, and other basic rules in cyberspace, emphasizing that consistent applications of the rules is one of the challenges for the policymakers.

In order to keep up with the development of new technologies, it may be necessary for regulators to follow a step-by-step approach. Most of the measures now undertaken are those for avoiding obstacles for new technological developments. Close monitoring has to follow accordingly. A third step will be the consistent application of market rules and regulations toward a wide variety of channels and markets.

More fundamentally, costs associated with information processing and coordination may reduce the costs arising from informational incompleteness and asymmetries. Information costs are particularly important in financial transactions and have affected the forms of contracts, organizations, market structures, and many others aspects of financial systems.[11]

Improvement of the quality of information and/or services provided will not be necessarily guaranteed even with enhanced competition. As is often noted, lower costs for providing information and services may cause fraud and other types of misconduct in easily accessible markets. Monitoring by the authorities to ensure a

---

[11] These broad changes brought about by electronic transactions may be analyzed in the context of organization and marketplace, as discussed in GARICANO and KAPLAN (2000).

reliable marketplace is another important task for the development of Internet-related financial activities.

4.2 Implications for the Banking Business

For the Japanese financial sector, keeping apace with the development of new technologies is quite important. Although the allocation and distribution of risk and capital has not been well managed in the last decade, especially by the banking sector because of its prolonged bad loan problems, the facilitation of trades by the efficient provision of information and financial services through the Internet should support economic activities in many fields. Since 1997, extensive deregulation has been undertaken in the financial sector. In this spirit, it has been greatly expected that innovations using Internet technology would enhance consumer welfare.

In the last couple of years we have seen an upsurge of mergers in the banking industry. It may be true as many economists have pointed out that Japanese banks are facing problems of capital deficiency and over-banking; however, mergers do not provide a complete solution to the problem. More importantly, the definition of a good, clear strategy is necessary for producing profits in the banking industry.

Whether the multi-channel strategy succeeds or not depends critically on how well banks can clearly define their business strategies. In particular, a multi-channel approach to the customers requires thorough review of the existing system. If a well-defined management policy does not exist, there may arise problems related to so-called channel conflicts in the pricing and marketing of new services and products. Some banks are establishing separate entities that engage primarily in e-finance; however, as new services replace conventional ones, the potential for conflict in many aspects of businesses always exists. In this regard, restructuring of the whole service strategy of traditional institutions is crucial in order to realize the gains provided by new technologies.

Clearly, the impact of the Internet on the economy is yet to be fully realized, and a complete picture of its development has yet to emerge. Although the impact of the electronic channel of financial services is by no means clear, it is expected that the Internet will bring a clearer perspective of a well-functioning financial service sector by changing market structure and redefining the banking business.

References

CHOI, JAMES J., LAIBSON, DAVID, and METRICK, ANDREW (2000), Does the Internet Increase Trading? Evidence from Investor Behavior in 401(k) Plans, NBER Working Paper 7878.

GARICANO, LUIS and KAPLAN, STEVEN N. (2000), The Effects of Business-to-Business E-Commerce on Transaction Costs, NBER Working Paper 8017.

JAPAN SECURITIES DEALERS ASSOCIATION (2001a), Survey on Brokerage Fees.

JAPAN SECURITIES DEALERS ASSOCIATION (2001b), Survey on Internet Transactions.

MINISTRY OF PUBLIC MANAGEMENT, HOME AFFAIRS, POSTS AND TELECOMMUNICATIONS, THE JAPANESE GOVERNMENT (2001), Information and Communications in Japan 2001 White Paper—The Accelerating IT Revolution: A Broadband-Driven IT Renaissance.

THE CENTER FOR FINANCIAL INDUSTRY INFORMATION SYSTEMS (2001), White Paper on Financial Industry Information System 2001.

U.S. SECURITIES AND EXCHANGE COMMISSION (1999), Special Study: Online Brokerage: Keeping Apace of Cyberspace.

J. How Will the Internet Change the Japanese Financial Perspective?
(Some Comments on Paper by Marico Fujii)

Christian Thygesen

In her paper, Dr. Mariko Fujii asks the interesting question of how the internet will change financial perspectives in Japan and arrives at the conclusion that although the impact of the internet on the economy has as of yet not been fully realised, the internet will change the market structure and redefine the banking business. Although I share the view that the internet will have an impact on financial perspectives in Japan as it has had and will continue to have in other parts of the world, I believe that the impact will be much less drastic than a redefinition of the banking business.

Will the internet change the basic function of banks and other providers of financial services in society and the economy? I clearly think not, and I believe Dr. Fujii would agree on this point. Then more modestly, will the internet change the basic structure of the financial services industry and/or will the internet seriously influence competition in the financial services industry? I see the effects of the internet as rather marginal, and this is possibly the core of where I would disagree with Dr. Fujii and thus where I choose focus my remarks.

In my view, the effect of the internet on banks and other providers of financial services will in the end not be much different than the effect of IT on e.g. accounting, dematerialization of securities and payment systems. The automation of accounting allowed the processing of significantly higher levels of transactions with fewer resources. It affected the customer by replacing the savings book by automatically generated account statements received periodically by mail. The dematerialization of securities also allowed for the processing of volumes unthinkable if securities had stayed in paper- and bearer-form. Again, it affected the customer by replacing the physical securities, possibly kept at home in a safe, with account statements. Within payment systems, the single item that has possibly had the largest impact on the customer has been the introduction of payment cards. Among the many benefits, payment cards mean that rather than having the home bank as the only source of cash, one has access to cash from just about any ATM or bank branch anywhere in the world. One can, of course, say that the internet is by nature different than the three examples mentioned above in that its potential scope is broader than any of the other three. It can act as a distribution channel, allowing the customer to access a fairly wide range of services and to do so from anywhere in the world. However, in the end, it will mainly be a cost-saving device, which will allow for a continuation of the gains in efficiency within the financial sector. It will not change the financial business, structure or perspectives in any fundamental way.

This claim I make is based mostly on developments in banking in the Nordic countries. I believe they serve as a valid benchmark, as these countries have the highest per capita rates of internet access and users anywhere in the world as well as the highest frequency of using financial services over the internet. Virtually all banks in all the Nordic countries offer web-based bank services to their customers. These are widely used for two purposes: simple services such as transfers and securities trading and for information-gathering on anything from developments in mortgage interest rates over surveying your portfolio to finding out about new products. However, once more complicated transactions come under consideration – such as buying property, planning investments or pensions – a visit to the local bank branch and a face-to-face discussion with your bank advisor remains the most common form of bank interaction. In fact, a number of pure internet banks that do not offer this possibility have opened in the Nordic countries, but they have been unable to make any profits and most have gone bankrupt. It would thus seem that the traditional business "brick and mortar" model with a branch network will continue to be viable and that the internet will "only" serve as a complement for distributing and accessing the simpler traditional financial services.

My first conclusion would be that the internet will not change the structure of financial services by allowing new entrants. It will of course change the structure to the extent that having a web-bank as a complement to your traditional branch network is necessary to remain competitive. One can say that the structure has changed, from "brick and mortar" to a "click and mortar" model, but in my view, to compete with other incumbent players on having the better webbank is not particularly different than competing e.g. on payment cards, mortgage loans, pensions, insurances etc.

I acknowledge, that the internet has so far actually brought new entrants to the Japanese financial industry, but as Dr. Fujii notes, it is still too early to say whether they will have any particular impact on competition. To the extent that experiences in the Nordic countries are generally valid, I would think not. I do however find it noteworthy, that some of the new entrants have teamed up with retailers to provide customers with a branch-like network providing rudimentary bank services. The idea of retailers entering the banking business is another example of a new distribution channel, which may or may not have an impact on the business. I remain sceptical for the same reason "click-only" is a viable business model for banks. Basically, I believe that customers will continue to regard financial matters as matters of trust, and it will be a long time before you trust a system not anchored in a person whom you know and trust. For example, it is fine to use your webbank or credit card for virtually all your transactions, but when something goes wrong and/or when something important, like the financing of your house is at stake, customers want to be able to contact someone they know and trust, and someone who knows them. There is, of course, a group of customers that are very price sensitive and who will prefer the low-cost, low-service model of banks based either on the internet, the network of a retailer or on a combination of the two. However, I believe they will remain sufficiently few in numbers for it would be difficult to base a business model on them.

Of course, competition can also change without new entrants. Dr. Fujii notes that the introduction of electronic trading has furthered the trend of diversifying brokerage commissions originally prompted by deregulation. I believe this to be generally true for the internet and financial transaction fees. Again, turning to the Nordic experience, this diversification of fees related to the internet even takes place within the individual institution. An account accessed exclusively over the internet may pay higher interest rates than an ordinary account with the same bank. Furthermore, fees for the same transaction, e.g. securities trading, will be different depending on whether they are initiated over the internet, by a fax, a phone-call or a visit to the branch. This price differentiation attempts to reflect the costs borne by the financial institution: the more the institution does for the customer, the more expensive it is. This again illustrates that the internet is only one new channel among others, and it is unlikely that it will in itself introduce more competition and thus a general lowering of fees in any other sense than the one just mentioned: the more the customer does for him or herself, the cheaper it is. One can of course find areas where the possibility to perform some transactions over the internet has lead to a quite significant, downward impact on fees, but as in the case mentioned by Dr. Fujii, this may be in areas where margins have been excessive and where they come down, just as much due to deregulation as to the arrival of the internet. The case of securities brokerage, on which Dr. Fujii focuses parts of her paper, lends credibility to my claim that the internet is unlikely to lead to lasting, new entrants in the financial services sector. Beyond the Nordic experience – the most successful retail internet broker – which did indeed offer much lower fees than its bank-based competitors, is currently in the process of being absorbed by a large French banking group.

Although this is not claimed explicitly in Dr. Fujii's paper, one could possibly say that the impact of the internet on the Japanese financial sector may be different from what has happened elsewhere, because the Japanese financial structure differs from what you find in the rest of the world. For one thing, I doubt that the Japanese financial system is really so much different from what you find elsewhere, for another – as Dr. Fujii points out in the example of the brokerage business – the main impetus for change in the industry came from deregulation. The arrival of the internet helped to accelerate developments but was not the reason for them taking place per se.

In conclusion, I agree with Dr. Fujii that the internet will have an impact on financial perspectives. However, I see this impact as more marginal than a redefinition of the banking business. The internet is an easy, cheap, fast and flexible distribution and access channel. It can help take advantage of changes in regulation or competition faster than traditional channels. However, this does not mean that it will redefine banking per se. Rather it is yet another step in the long development from plumes and parchment to the modern banking business we know today.

K. Internet Dynamics and Expansion of European Financial Markets: Issues from a Behavioral Finance Perspective

Matthias Bank

1. Introduction

The Internet is one of the most dynamic sectors in nearly every developed country. It is closely linked to the information and communication technology (ICT) sector, which has been the driving force for the recent outstanding productivity and growth figures, especially in the U.S. The rate of path breaking innovations in the last years is very high, and so is the uncertainty of future marketability of these innovations. Many of these innovations were developed in small start-up firms, which need huge capital infusions for completing and marketing the resulting products. The process from innovations to final ICT products or services normally needs a very long time without positive net cash flows. That time period needs to be bridged with external cash infusions. The main problem here is the high uncertainty about the long-term success of the underlying business plans. Indeed, risky projects must be undertaken in the first place in order to make profits. It is especially the very dynamic character of the competition in the Internet and ICT-sectors that made reliable mid to long-term forecasting for both – the entire market and individual firms – almost impossible. On the other hand, the uncertainty made short-term speculation based on past developments "reasonable". In recent years the capital markets have stood ready to finance prospects, which seemed "reasonable" in the first place. There was virtually no shortage of capital until March 2000. The high valuation level in the secondary markets attracts a lot of firms to get external equity finance by business angels, venture capitalists and initial public offerings. Other firms want to broaden their capital base with seasoned equity offerings in order to get "acquisition currency", i.e. to pay in acquisitions with one's own high valued stocks. Moreover, most of the cash proceedings were invested in mergers and acquisition activities in order to reach larger market share. This contributed to the rapid expansion of the world capital markets in terms of listed firms, market capitalization and share turnover. Especially the European Financial Markets benefited from these developments. There is now a change underway which will transform continental Europe from a more bank-oriented financial system into a more market-oriented system (see e.g. ALLEN / GALE, 2000). Anglo-American investment banks stood ready to offer their services in the course of creating a single European market and the introduction of the euro. Moreover, the competition among the leading exchanges in Europe fostered the creation of the so-called New Markets for young innovative growth firms. A very positive sentiment for the potential success of Internet and ICT firms was created in this environment. Last but not least, everybody wanted to have the "new Micro-soft" in the own portfolio. This mobilized huge amounts of risk capital in the IPO-market. However, there may be major shortcomings with that development. When assets are mispriced the available funds are allocated inefficiently. Moreover, firms rush to go public or offer additional capital in seasoned offerings when stocks are overvalued; this situation is called a "hot issue"-market. In the short run there are high growth rates because of tons of money being available, which may lead to overinvestment. However, the high growth rates may not be sustainable in the long run when eventually the bubble bursts and funds dry up as they did in 2001.

The paper is organized as follows: After a short overview of the development of the Internet economy and the recent trends in the European Financial Markets, the current situation is analyzed from the viewpoint of the Behavioral Finance Approach. The approach will be used to explain and understand the recent devel-opments of Internet stocks. Finally, a short conclusion is provided.

2. Recent Trends in the Internet and the Internet Economy

The available data suggest that the Internet Economy is growing at a strong pace.[1] The Internet hosts per 1000 inhabitants have grown by about 67% per year on average in all OECD countries between July 1995 and January 2000. In January 2000 about 60 hosts per 1000 inhabitants were installed. On the country level the number of hosts per 1000 inhabitants in January 2000 range from 148.1 in Finland and 141.5 in the US to 34 in Germany and 25.8 in Japan (OECD, 2000, p. 60).

The figures are similar with respect to secure servers, which handle e-commerce transactions over the World Wide Web. The growth of the number of secure servers in the OECD per 1 million inhabitants was about 114% per year between September 1997 and March 2000 (OECD, 2000, p. 62). It is interesting to note that the EU average in March 2000 is about 29.1 compared to the US with about 170.4 (OECD, 2001). According to NETSIZER (2001) as of July 2001 the absolute number of hosts and Internet users worldwide was about 124 million hosts and 464 million people, respectively.

Research done by the Graduate School of Business, University of Texas at Aus-tin (INTERNET ECONOMY INDICATORS, 2001) shows that it is useful to divide the Internet Economy into four layers: (1) the Internet Infrastructure Layer, (2) the Internet Application Infrastructure Layer, (3) the Internet Intermediary Layer and (4) the Internet Commerce Layer. Their analysis shows that job growth and revenues increased considerably for all layers. From an overall revenue of $64,000 million in the first quarter of 1998 the amount jumped to $173,601 mil-lion in the first quarter of 2000. That represents an increase of about 170%.

---

[1] For recent overviews on the development of the Internet, consult e.g. WELFENS / JUNGMITTAG (2000), EITO (1999), WELFENS (1999).

As one can see from Table 1 the overall Internet Economy employment jumped approximately 25% during the first two quarters of 2000. It is interesting to note that layers 3 and 4, which include firms like Yahoo, Commerce One, Dell, or Amazon, show a considerably lower growth of employment than the other layers.

Table K1:   Employment in the Internet Economy

Internet Economy Indicators Quarterly Employment Figures Summary by Layer and Total Internet Economy				
	Quarter 1 2000	Growth over Q1 1999	Quarter 2 2000	Growth over Q2 1999
Layer 1- Infrastructure Indicator	877,245	51.8%	932,484	37.7%
Layer 2 – Application Indicator	711,396	62.3%	740,673	51.9%
Layer 3 – Intermediary Indicator	457,876	5.5%	468,689	3.9%
Layer 4 – Internet Commerce Indicator	1,020,416	12.6%	1,033,159	8.2%
The Internet Economy (After removing overlap)	2,986,913	29.1%	3,088,497	22.6%

Source: http://www.internetindicators.com/keyfindings.html (as of July 11, 2001)

Similar to the employment figures, the revenues grew at a very high rate by about 60% per year. More timely data will show if these growth rates have survived the recent burst of the Internet bubble. Indeed, the bulk of daily news suggests that there are huge layoffs in the last six months in Internet-related firms, especially in the e-commerce sector.

Finally, "Dot Com" companies, which are the true face of the Internet Economy, account only for a small part of employees and revenues. These are firms with 95% or more of their revenues generated from the Internet. Only about 10% of the revenues of the Internet Economy can be attributed to "Dot Coms". Likewise, only about 12% of the employees in the Internet Economy are "Dot Com" employees (INTERNET ECONOMY INDICATORS, 2001).

As the available data shows the Internet is truly one of the most dynamic sectors in the Economy. But there are signs that the growth of Internet traffic will be slower than in the last years and than expected (KRAUSE, 2001).

Table K2:   Revenues in the Internet Economy

	Internet Economy Indicators Quarterly Revenue (in $ millions)			
	Quarter 1 2000	Growth over Q1 1999	Quarter 2 2000	Growth over Q2 1999
Layer 1 – Infrastructure Indicator	$67,656	69.3%	$75,211	57.4%
Layer 2 – Application Indicator	$33,930	73.5%	$38,925	58.9%
Layer 3 – Intermediary Indicator	$27,295	63.8%	$36,704	84.6%
Layer 4 – Internet Commerce Indicator	$60,341	66.7%	$66,956	57.8%
The Internet Economy (After removing overlap)	$173,601	64.2%	$200,219	58.8%

Source: http://www.internetindicators.com/keyfindings.html (as of July 11, 2001)

Table K3:   "Dot Com" Summary

	Internet Economy Indicators "Dot Com" Summary				
	Quarter 1, 2000	Percent of Total Internet Economy	Quarter 2, 2000	Percent of Total Internet Economy	Growth Q1 – Q2
"Dot Com" Revenue ($ Millions)	$16,144	9.3%	$19,125	9.6%	18.7%
"Dot Com" Employees	362,487	12.1%	360,718	11.7%	-.5%

Source: http://www.internetindicators.com/keyfindings.html (as of July 11, 2001)

3. The Expansion of the European Financial Markets

3.1 European Financial Markets as a Source of Risk Capital for SMEs

Besides the various effects of the Internet on financial markets in terms of transaction cost reduction, electronic banking and trading or securitization (see e.g. VARIAN, 1998), the focus here is on the supply of risk capital to Internet firms. The Internet is mainly ICT-driven and as a consequence capital intensive. This results typically in large amounts of initial investments in both technology and human knowledge. Moreover, it usually takes a lot of time (up to years) to expect positive and stable cash flows from those investments. Finally, because of the huge past and projected growth rates for Internet-related business, Internet firms hope to get a "slice out of the cake".

It is long recognized that developed equity markets play a major role in providing risk capital for young and innovative growth firms. The main example is the Nasdaq market, which was created in 1971. Special rules and regulations are imposed which mainly protects investors from fraud and misrepresentation. In Europe, the Nasdaq was long seen as a blueprint for setting up one's own stock exchange for high growth firms. However, especially in continental Europe the stock markets played a minor role in providing risk capital. At the beginning of the 1990s more and more European high-tech firms got listed on the Nasdaq because they did not receive risk capital in Europe on adequate terms. The increasing competition among European Stock exchanges finally has led to the creation of various stock markets and stock market segments for growth firms, which include Easdaq in Brussels, the Neuer Markt in Frankfurt, the Nouveau Marché in Paris and the Alternative Investment Market (AIM) in London (EUROPEAN COMMISSION, 2000).

The markets came at the right moment to provide financing for capital-hungry high-tech firms, most of them directly or indirectly connected to the Internet. Moreover, the "new markets" helped indirectly to finance start-ups in the seed financing stage before going public. Business angels and venture capitalists were eager to finance start-ups because from their point of view the "new markets" are attractive as exit channels to divest. Table 4 contains an overview of a couple of specialized markets in Europe and the US for financing high growth firms as of June 2000. It should be noted that the NASDAQ is still by far the most liquid market for equity in small and medium-sized enterprises (SME). But the new European markets for financing young high-growth firms have gained importance in terms of capital raised and number of companies.

Table K4:   Main Markets Specializing in SME Financing (as of June 30, 2000)

	Euro. NM					EASDAQ	AIM	Tech-MARK	NASDAQ
	Le Nouveau Marché	Neuer Markt	NMAX	Euro. NM Belgium	Nuovo Mercato				
Launch	Mar 96	Mar 97	Mar 97	Mar 97	June 99	Nov 96	June 95	Nov 99	Feb 71
Number of listed companies	140	281	467 15	16	15	62	429	220	4843
Market capitalization (billion €) (B)	27	191	240 1.7	0.5	20	50	22.6	1006	5818
Capital raised (current year, billion €)	1.2	9.5	13.4 0.4	0	2.3	0.3	1.6	3.1	33.2
Average capitalization per company (million €) (B)/(A)	192	678	513 116	31	1340	806	53	4574	1201
Capital exchanged (million €/day)	37	442	537 5	0.2	53	32	48	3633	76680
Performance of index since 30 December 1999	+26%	+17%	+17 +4%	+14%	+2%	-8%	-11%	-8%	-3%

Source: EUROPEAN COMMISSION (2000), p. 4.

In the meantime, as of June 30, 2001, 341 companies are listed on the German Neuer Markt with a market capitalization of about only € 32 billion. According to the segmentation of the Deutsche Börse AG, 18.7% of the companies are in the Internet sector with 20.8% in the technology sector, 11.1% in the IT services sector, 14.3% in the software sector and 5.8% in the telecommunications sector. To sum up more than 70% of all firms listed in the Neuer Markt are part of the Internet Economy with a market capitalization of about € 12.1 billion. The average market capitalization of a company listed on the Neuer Markt is now € 93 million, which is a decrease of about 86% compared to June 2000. The average daily trading volume is now about € 169 million/day, a reduction of about 60% (DEUTSCHE BÖRSE, 2001).

The figures are similar for the French Nouveau Marché. As of June 30, 2001 the market capitalization had shrunk to € 18 billion. 166 companies were listed with an average market capitalization of € 108 million, a reduction of nearly 44% from the previous year. The average daily trading volume decreased slightly to € 33.7 million / day (EURONEXT, 2001).

The total market capitalization of the British AIM was about € 22.2 billion at the end of June 2001. With a total of 576 companies listed, the average market cap was about € 38.5 million. The average daily trading volume was about to € 35.3 million/day (LSE, 2001).

Venture Capital

Venture capital financing was an extremely fast growing business in European countries and especially in Germany. Specialized intermediaries provide venture capital particularly in the start-up stage after the product has been test-marketed successfully and full-scale production and marketing has begun. Suppliers of venture capital are independent private and public venture capitalists or corporate (technology watching) venture capital firms. The total volume of investment of private equity and venture capital firms in the EU reached € 34.9 billion in 2000, an increase of 39% compared to € 25.1 billion in 1999 (EVCA, 2001). In the U.S. for comparison, more than 3,600 companies received venture capital of approximately US$ 58.8 billion in 1999 and amazingly US$ 103.3 billion in 2000. In the first half of 2001 only US$ 19 billion was invested. The total investment in Internet-related firms was about US$ 5 billion in the first half of 2001 (VENTURE ECONOMICS, 2001).

As Table 5 for 1999 data shows, VC investment in the European Union scaled by GDP is still lagging behind the United States.

Table K5:   **Venture Capital in the EU and in the USA in 1999 (in Percent of GDP)**

Financing Stage	EU	US
Early Stage	0.03	0.14
Expansion Stage	0.105	0.23
Overall	0.135	0.37

Source: EUROPEAN COMMISSION (2000), p. 5.

In 2000 the amount of private equity invested in venture capital (seed, start-up and expansion) reached € 19.6 billion, which is a significant increase over 1999, where only € 10.6 billion was invested in venture capital. Figure 1 shows the development of the last six years. The amount invested in the early stage (seed and start-up) in 2000 was about € 6.7 billion going to 4,676 companies (EVCA, 2001).

The development for the German venture capital market was similar (Figure 2). Since 1996, there is an extraordinary growth in new investments, which reached € 4.8 billion invested in about 3000 companies in 2000 (BVK, 2001).

The newest available data for Germany indicate new investments of about € 700 million for Quarter 1, 2001, about € 870 million for Quarter 2, 2001 and about € 570 million for Quarter 3, which is about € 2.2 billion for the first nine months (BVK, 2001). Compared with the previous years that development can be termed a "normalization" in the venture capital market. It is interesting to note that in 2000 about 272 firms received an amount of € 390 million in the seed financing stage. In comparison to the first three quarters of 2001 only 80 firms received an amount of about € 70 million in the seed stage. One has to wait for the data of Quarter 4, but it is safe to say that 2001 will show a remarkable decline compared to 2000.

Figure K1:   Investments in Venture Capital (Seed, Start-up and Expansion) in Europe (in Billion €)

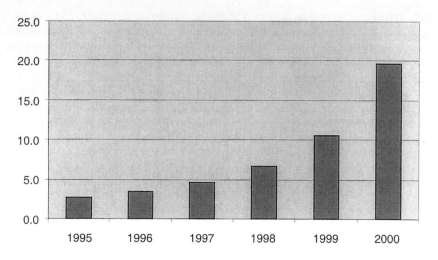

Source: EVCA (2001)

Figure K2:   New Investment of Venture Capital Firms in Germany

amount (in mio. €)

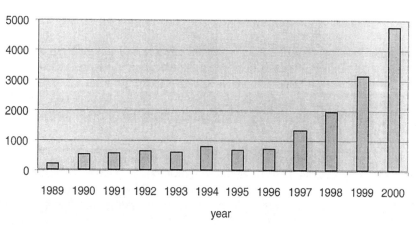

Source: BVK (2001)

Business Angels

Finally, a very dynamic field in Europe is angel financing. So-called Business Angels finance SMEs especially in the seed stage. They are private wealthy investors who, in addition to cash injections, typically provide specific business and management know-how they have gained through work experience or from past investments. The angel finance market is informal and highly intransparent. There are no formal rules of conduct or codices. The number of active angels in Europe is estimated at 125,000, and the number of potential investors at 1,000,000. The available investment pool in Europe is estimated to be between € 10 and € 20 billion. The average amount of investment per business angel is about € 75,000. Business angels are typically organized in networks. From 1998 to 2000 the number of business angel networks (BANs) increased from 62 to 110. In 1998 80% of BANs were located in the UK; in 2000 the share was only 45% which implicitly shows the development in continental Europe (EBAN, 2001).

3.2 Mergers, Acquisitions and Corporate Debt Markets

Beside the new role of the European financial markets providing risk capital for innovative growth firms, two other aspects are worth mentioning: the increased merger and acquisitions activity and debt markets.

Merger & Acquisition Activity

The merger and acquisitions activity in Europe got a lot of momentum from the introduction of the euro and the establishment of the single market. In the course of globalization and focused business strategies, many firms are reorganizing their business which leads to spin-offs, initial public offerings or sales. Moreover, with the introduction of a new tax law on capital gains for corporations in Germany from 2002 on, a break up of the so-called "Deutschland AG" is on the agenda (see. e.g. GERKE / BANK / STEIGER, 1999). This will broaden and deepen the European Financial Markets, despite the recent decrease in the merger and acquisition activity. For the first half of 2001 the worldwide number of deals has fallen 25% compared with the same period last year, from 21,548 to 16,251 deals. Values have fallen 53% from about US$ 21,300 billion to US$ 10,000 billion in the same period last year (WALL STREET JOURNAL, 2001).

Debt markets

There was a remarkable recent evolution of the corporate bond market in Europe, which might be directly linked to the creation of the euro (see e.g. SANTILLIÁN / BAYLE / THYGESEN, 2000). Up to the mid-1990s, the corporate bond market for continental companies did virtually not exist. Financing needs of telecommunication companies for investments in infrastructure, mergers, acquisitions and especially in licenses for the third-generation cellular phones had forced them to raise billions of € in the debt markets. The size of the European corporate bond market in terms of outstanding market value was about € 700 billion in 1999 (U.S.: € 3,500 billion). In only a very short time the market for corporate bonds had become relatively liquid (SANTILLIÁN / BAYLE / THYGESEN, 2000). Of course, there are nevertheless only few multinational companies with good credit ratings which use the organized European corporate debt markets to reduce their cost of capital.

4. An Assessment of the Recent Developments

In the following an assessment of the recent developments is provided from the viewpoint of the Behavioral Finance Approach (DE BONDT / THALER, 1995; BANK, 2000; HIRSHLEIFER, 2001). One key point is, that the high growth rates in the businesses around the Internet **cannot** necessarily be translated into high valuations for Internet firms. What really counts is generating a sustainable positive net cash flow from Internet-related businesses. The hypothesis is that there was and perhaps still is a far too much positive sentiment on possible profits generated through Internet-related business, which resulted in the crash of the so-called Internet bubble.

Figure K3:   The Internet Bubble

Source: ALLEN (2001). All indexes are normalized to 100 on 12/31/1997.

The experience with Internet stock, represented by the CBOE Internet Index, compared to the Nasdaq and S&P 500 indexes may serve as a good illustration. Figure 3 shows that the valuation of Internet stocks in March 2000 were seven times higher than twenty-seven months before at the end of 1997. At the end of 2000 the valuation level – after the bubble burst – came down to more or less the same level as at the start.

Another good illustration is the Internet e-commerce Webvan. Webvan was the leading US-grocery on the World Wide Web. Since the initial public offering in 1999 the firm "burned" $1 billion in cash. Its highest market capitalization was about $8 billion on December 3, 1999 or about eight times its book value. On July 9, 2001 Webvan went into bankruptcy procedures. (DER SPIEGEL, 2001; BUSINESS WEEK, 2001). A similar example of a highly mispriced and failed e-commerce firm is eToys, established in 1997 (SHILLER, 2000). eToys went public in 1999 and reached only a short time later a market valuation of $8 billion. In comparison, the long-established "brick-and-mortar" retailer Toys "R" Us had at this time only a $6 billion market value. An eye opener is the difference in accounting data for the two firms in 1998. eToys' profits were negative at $28.6 million, while the profits of Toys "R" Us were positive at $376 million. Moreover, the sales of Toys "R" Us were $11.2 billion compared to only $30 million in the case of eToys. As SHILLER (2000, p. 176) put it: "The valuation the market places on stocks such as eToys appears absurd to many observers, and yet the influence of these observers on market prices does not seem to correct the mispricing."

Why could such an overoptimistic sentiment develop over the last years? What are the reasons for such an obvious mispricing? At this point the Behavioral Finance Approach (BFA) may offer some answers. However, before that, a short examination on the valuation of Internet-related firms is provided.

4.1 Shortcomings in the Valuation of Internet-Related Firms

The valuation of a firm should be generally based on its business plan. The business plan roughly describes how firms will make sustainable profits. The evaluation of a business plan is a difficult task for external investors when new firms act in new markets, a situation typical of Internet-related firms. That is because such business plans are not directly comparable to already proved successful or unsuccessful ones. In a very dynamic environment with a high innovation rate, even successful business plans may be flawed in the very short run. A further problem arises when it takes a considerably long time (up to many years) before positive net profits can be expected as in the case of Amazon (see SCHWARTZ / MOON, 2000 for a case study about Amazon and see BOND / CUMMINS, 2000 for a macroeconomic perspective on the valuation of the New Economy, i.e. Internet-related firms).

From an investor's view there may be also an information asymmetry about the quality of business plans among competitors for capital (AKERLOF, 1970). When there is no mechanism to separate high-quality firms from low-quality firms, all firms are pooled which leads to an average valuation. So it is very likely that "bad" firms will get a much too high valuation and, as a consequence, high proceeds from selling equity.

Valuation generally depends on future profits, dividends or cash flows (see e.g. COPELAND / KOLLER / MURRIN, 1996; GERKE / BANK, 1998), but expected profit growth is the most celebrated variable for Internet firms. Within the dividend discount model the value of a company depends on its future dividends and the risk adjusted cost of capital. A variant, the Gordon Growth Model, links the current dividend, the cost of capital and the dividend growth in a simple formula:

$$p_0 = E_0 \left[\frac{1}{(1+k)^{t-1}} \frac{d_t}{k-g} \right] \qquad \text{with } k > g,$$

p_0 as the present value of a share, d_t as the dividend per share at the end of the period t, k as the risk adjusted cost of capital, g as the dividend growth rate and E_0 as the expectation operator. It is assumed that a firm starts paying dividends in Period t and that the dividends are growing after this with rate g forever. It is interesting to look at the price/earnings-ratio, which is one of the most popular measures to compare firm valuations:

$$\frac{p_0}{e_\tau} = E_0 \left[\frac{d_t}{e_\tau} \frac{1}{(1+k)^{t-1}} \frac{1}{k-g} \right] \qquad \text{with } \tau \le t, e_\tau > 0, d_t > 0$$

and e_τ as the expected earnings in the first period when they are positive. The formula for P/E-ratio consists of three factors. The first factor is a payout ratio that links the first dividend payment in period t to the expected (positive) earnings in period τ. The second factor is a discount factor and the third a capitalization factor.

The discount factor is clearly lower than one. Because of the high risk of Internet firms k is typically quite large (e.g. 0.35 or 35%, or even higher). Suppose further that $t = 5$, which means that the first dividend payments will be made at the end of the fifth year, then the discount factor is about 0.3 ($\approx 1/(1 + 0.35)^4$). What about the payout ratio? Because earnings per share are typically very low for Internet firms (or even negative), the expected ratio may be rather quite high. Suppose for the moment a ratio at a (reasonable) value of about four. Finally, the capitalization factor for Internet firms may also be quite large. The factor depends on the expected growth rate of dividends. Suppose that the growth rate is about (an extraordinary) 0.25 or 25% per year after t periods. It follows that the implied P/E-ratio with all the assumption together is only about 12. Variations of the input factor cannot account for the extreme high P/E-ratio of Internet firms even for today's "post bubble" valuations. Only when the growth rate of dividends is very close to k does the capitalization factor dominate the valuation and the P/E ratio may be very high (more than 100 or even 200). However, such P/E ratios are simply not reasonable at all. It would, for example, take about two hundred years based on the actual estimated earnings (when the P/E ratio is 200) to regain the present valuation.

In a recent article, Eduardo Schwartz and Mark Moon (SCHWARTZ / MOON, 2000) applied real-options theory and capital-budgeting techniques to the problem of valuing Internet firms. They conclude that the high valuation of Internet firms may be rational provided that the growth rate of revenues and the volatility of expected growth rate of revenues – their most critical parameter – is high enough. Depending on a set of specific parameters it may indeed be the case that the high valuation of Internet firms can be grounded on rationality. However, their analysis is very sensitive to variations of the underlying assumptions. For example, Schwartz and Moon made the assumption that the cost of goods sold (COGS) and other variable components of other expenses are in a fixed proportion to the revenues. Moreover, they assume that the fixed component of other expenses is constant over time (25 years!). As a consequence, their main conclusions are highly questionable. However, their model can serve as good starting point for further research.

4.2 The Behavioral Finance Approach (BFA)

The term "Behavioral Finance" was introduced in the mid-1980s. The BFA can be considered as an answer to empirical findings which standard finance theory, i.e. neoclassical theory with perfectly rational agents, cannot explain. Among them there are the equity premium puzzle (MEHRA / PRESCOTT, 1985), the size effect (BANZ, 1981), the value effect (FAMA / FRENCH, 1992), the momentum effect (JEGADEESH / TITMAN, 1993) and the mean reversion effect (DE BONDT / THALER, 1985). Attempts to explain these anomalies within standard finance theory are simply not convincing (for such attempts, see CAMPBELL, 2000; FAMA, 1998).

The BFA assumes that people act in a not perfectly rational manner; i.e. they do not have smooth standard preferences exhibiting risk aversion (KAHNEMAN / TVERSKY, 1979) and they do not process information correctly (TVERSKY / KAHNEMAN, 1974). Moreover, arbitrage by (truly) rational agents – the cornerstone of the standard finance model – may fail in very "normal" circumstances with obvious arbitrage opportunities (LEE / SHLEIFER / THALER, 1991; SHLEIFER/VISHNY, 1997; DE LONG ET AL., 1990b). One celebrated example is the so-called closed-end fund puzzle. The market price of closed-end funds should be near the value of their net assets (NAV) to prevent arbitrage. Empirical research shows, however, that the difference between market price and NAV can be unreasonably large (a discount of about 10% or more) over a quite long time (LEE / SHLEIFER / THALER, 1991).

Departures from rationality emerge both in judgment and in choice. Examples include overconfidence, loss aversion, mental accounting, anchoring, and making judgments of frequency or likelihood based on salience (availability heuristic) or similarity (representativeness heuristic) (for an overview, see KAHNEMAN / SLOVIC / TVERSKY, 1982; RABIN, 1998; or HIRSHLEIFER, 2001).

One of the best-established facts of departure from rationality is overconfidence (DE BONDT / THALER, 1995). Overconfident people tend to underestimate the range of possible outcomes. They think they make fewer mistakes in judgment than they actually do. Overconfidence can cause asset prices to over- or underreact to new information, which makes positive or even negative bubbles likely (DANIEL ET AL. 1998; ODEAN, 1998; BANK, 2000). Research done by GRIFFIN / TVERSKY (1992) indicates that especially professionals, such as lawyers or bankers, are well calibrated in transparent situations but exhibit substantial overconfidence in opaque settings.

4.3 A Behavioral Finance Interpretation for the Internet Bubble

The Behavioral Finance Approach blames the unreasonable valuation of Internet-related firms (telecommunication firms included) to shortcomings in information processing, overconfidence and reference point dependence.

Reference point dependence may be illustrated with a specific example. In the second half of 1999 the Internet-related cellular telephone company Vodafone made a successful attempt to buy Mannesmann, a German cellular telephone company. Vodafone offered the shareholders of Mannesmann an extraordinary high share price (at least compared with the stock price of Mannesmann before the offer). The point here is that this price and the implied expectations may serve as a very salient reference point for investors in the course of valuating other Internet-related firms. The battle between the two telecommunication "giants" can be viewed as a starting point for revaluation of the telecommunication firms which lead to record highs in stock prices in the whole technology sector. The investors learned that (historically) very successful professional managers, i.e. the top management of Vodafone, – "who should really know what they are doing" – are willing to pay such a high price. Indeed, in the meantime we all learned that such prices were unsustainable. The share price of Vodafone went down more than 60% (as of December 2001) since the time of the Mannesmann acquisition.

The shortage of reliable information for future developments made investors, analysts and the (mass) media dependent on historic trends and figures. Moreover, good news was weighed more heavily than more reliable "base rate" information, which includes relatively hard facts (for example, the reasonableness of the underlying business plans of Internet firms). In addition, the momentum in stock prices gave support to further price increases. The availability of specific information, representativeness of information and valuation patterns (extrapolation) make investors believe in further capital gains. More realistic or "rational" professional investors ("arbitrageurs") did not bring the prices down because of at least two reasons (see also SHLEIFER / VISHNY, 1997). First, it might be the case that their belief of an overpriced market may be simply not true. As a consequence, they thus were getting increasingly less confident as stock prices only went up. Moreover, not being invested in a soaring market might be worse when all competitors are invested because the money flows to (in the past proven) "successful" asset managers (GRUBER, 1996). Second, it might be very rational to jump on the market momentum, even when the market is overvalued (DE LONG ET AL.,

1990a). What is important is only to leave the market early enough before the bubble bursts, which is a very difficult task.

Flawed information processing is interconnected with overconfidence. News which is in line with given expectations tends to be overweighted. On the other hand, when the news is not in line with expectations, it is likely that it tends to be underweighted. Especially overweighted "good" news may be one major reason for the ongoing overreaction in the course of the inflating asset prices (BANK, 2000).

5. Conclusions

The dynamic development of the Internet and Internet-related firms strongly contributed to the broadening and deepening of the European Financial Markets in terms of newly listed firms, capital raised, seasoned offerings, corporate debt financing, turnover ratios and increased liquidity. However, the major downturn in asset prices of Internet-related stocks leaves many investors without faith in the market. This may lead – and surely has already led – to an exit of many investors and a severe lack of risk capital needed. Investments to develop the Internet environment further may be simply not available.

In hindsight, the raised capital was sold at inflated prices to investors. There is every reason to assume that this had caused overinvestment in the behavior of the firms, which in turn supported the inflated asset prices. With the step-by-step deflation of the so-called Internet bubble the question arises how such a long-lasting mispricing could develop in the first place. To answer this question, the Behavioral Finance Approach was used. Among the reasons might be overconfidence, reference point dependence and flawed information processing of professional and private investors. As investors lose faith in fair asset valuation, the danger lies in the decreased ability to further finance the growth of the Internet and Internet-related innovations. Moreover, it may be the case that asset prices are now too low compared with market efficiency. That might induce firms to wait before raising new capital and investing. As a consequence there may be underinvestment, which in turn reinforces the downturn. Last but not least, such a development will probably slow down growth figures in the overall economy.

"Irrational Exuberance", to quote Robert SHILLER (2000), isn't good in both directions: inflated or deflated asset prices. What is needed is much more stability in the financial markets, which should be in line with the fundamentals to improve the conditions for Internet-related firms to get risk capital at adequate terms.

References

AKERLOF, G.A. (1970), The Market for "Lemons": Quality Uncertainty and the Market Mechanism, in: Quarterly Journal of Economics, Vol. 84, p. 488-500.

ALLEN, F. (2001), Do Financiall Institutions Matter? in: Journal of Finance, Vol. 56, p. 1165-1175.

ALLEN, F. and GALE, D. (2000), Comparing Financial Systems, MIT Press.

BANK, M. (2000), Behavioral Finance und Marktmanipulation, unpublished, Habilitationsschrift, Nürnberg.

BANZ, R.W. (1981), The Relation between Return and Market Value of Common Stock, in: Journal of Financial Economics, Vol. 9, p. 3-18.

BOND, S.R. and CUMMINS, J.G. (2000), The Stock Market and Investment in the New Economy: Some Tangible Facts and Intangible Fictions, Brookings Papers on Economic Activity, Macroeconomics, www.nber.org/~confer/ 2000/efcosi00/bond.pdf

BUSINESS WEEK (2001), July 23, 2001, p. 43.

BVK (2001), http://www.bvk-ev.de/fakten01/fakten.cfm?page=10

CAMPBELL, J.Y. (2000), Asset Pricing at the Millennium, in: Journal of Finance, Vol. 55, p. 1515-1567.

COPELAND, T., KOLLER, T., MURRIN, J. (1996), Valuation: Measuring and Managing the Value of Companies, 2nd ed., New York et al.

DANIEL. K., HIRSHLEIFER, D., SUBRAHMANYAM, A. (1998), Investor Psychology and Security Market Under- and Overreaction in: Journal of Finance, Vol. 53, p. 1839-1885.

DE BONDT, W.F.M., THALER, R.H. (1995), Financial Decision-making in Markets and Firms: A Behavioral Perspective, in: JARROW, R.A., MAKSIMOVIC, V., ZIEMBA, W.T., eds., Handbook in Operations Research and Management Science, Vol. 9, Finance, Amsterdam.

DE BONDT, W.F.M., THALER, R.H. (1985), Does the Stock Market Overreact?, in: Journal of Finance, Vol. 40, p. 793-805.

DE LONG, J.B., SHLEIFER, A., SUMMERS, L.H., WALDMANN, R.J. (1990a), Positive Feedback Investment Strategies and Destabilizing Rational Speculation, Journal of Finance, Vol. 45, p. 379-395.

DE LONG, J.B., SHLEIFER, A., SUMMERS, L.H., WALDMANN, R.J. (1990b), Noise Trader Risk in Financial Markets, in: Journal of Political Economy, Vol. 98, p. 703-738.

DER SPIEGEL (2001), Rapides Artensterben, No. 29, July 16, p. 88-89.

DEUTSCHE BÖRSE (2001), http://www.deutsche-boerse.com/nm .

EBAN (2001), http://www.eban.org .

EITO (1999), European Information Technology Observatory 1999, Frankfurt/M.

EURONEXT (2001), http://www.bourse-de-paris.fr/en/index_fs.htm?nc=3&ni=1 &nom=indice .

EUROPEAN COMMISSION (2000), European Economy, Supplement A, Economic Trend, No. 8/9, August/September 2000, Progress Report on the Risk Capital Action Plan http://europa.eu.int/comm/economy_finance/document/ eesuppa/a2000_0809_en.pdf .

EVCA (2001), Record Levels Invested and Raised in 2000, Press Release, Rome, 6/14/2001, http://www.evca.com .

FAMA, E.F. (1998), Market Efficiency, Long-term Returns, and Behavioral Finance, in: Journal of Financial Economics, Vol. 49, p. 283-306.

FAMA, E.F., FRENCH, K. (1992), The Cross-Section of Expected Stock Returns, in: Journal of Finance, Vol. 47, p. 427-465.

GERKE, W., BANK, M. (1998), Finanzierung, Investitions- und Finanzierungsentscheidungen in Unternehmen, Stuttgart.

GERKE, W., BANK, M., STEIGER, M. (1999), The Changing Role of Institutional Investors – A German Perspective, Working Paper, Nürnberg.

GRIFFIN, D., TVERSKY, A. (1992), The Weighting of Evidence and the Determinants of Confidence, in: Cognitive Psychology, Vol. 24, p. 411-435.

GRUBER, M.J. (1996), Another Puzzle: The Growth in Actively Managed Mutual Funds, in: Journal of Finance, Vol. 51, p. 783-810.

HIRSCHLEIFER, D. (2001), Investor Psychology and Asset Pricing, in Journal of Finance, Vol. 56, p. 1533 – 1597.

INTERNET ECONOMY INDICATORS (2001), Key Findings, July 2001 http://www.internetindicators.com/keyfindings.html (as of 7/11/2001).

JEGADEESH, N., TITMAN, S. (1993), Returns to Buying Winners and Selling Losers: Implications for Stock Market Efficiency, in: Journal of Finance, Vol. 48, p. 65-91.

KAHNEMANN, D., SLOVIC, P., TVERSKY, A., eds. (1982), Judgement Under Uncertainty: Heuristics and Biases, Cambridge: Cambridge University Press.

KAHNEMAN, D., TVERSKY, A. (1979), Prospect Theory: An Analysis of Decision Under Risk, in: Econometrica, Vol. 47, p. 263-291.

KRAUSE, J. (2001), Has the Net Stopped Growing? http://biz.yahoo.com/st/010629/27394.html .

LEE, C.M.C., SHLEIFER, A., THALER, R.H. (1991), Investor Sentiment and the Closed-end Fund Puzzle, in: Journal of Finance, Vol. 46, p. 75-109.

LSE (2001), http://www.londonstockexchange.com .

MEHRA, R., PRESCOTT, E.C. (1985), The Equity Premium Puzzle, in: Journal of Monetary Economics, Vol. 15, p. 145-161.

NETSIZER (2001), http://www.netsizer.com, July 2001.

ODEAN, T. (1998), Volume, Volatility, Price, and Profit When All Traders Are Above Average, in: Journal of Finance, Vol. 53, p. 1887-1934.

OECD (2000), Local Pricing and E-Commerce, July 2000, http://www.olis.oecd.org/olis/2000doc.nsf/linkto/dsti-iccp-tisp(2000)1-final.

OECD (2001), Internet and Electronic Commerce Indicators Update, July 2001, http://www.oecd.org/dsti/sti/cm/stats/newindicators.htm .

RABIN, M. (1998), Psychology and Economics, in: Journal of Economic Literature, Vol. 36, p. 11-46.

SANTILLIÁN, J., BAYLE, M., THYGESEN, C. (2000), The Impact of the Euro on Money and Bond Markets, Occasional Paper Series No. 1, European Central Bank, July 2000.

SCHWARTZ, E., MOON, M. (2000), Rational Pricing of Internet Companies, in: Financial Analyst Journal, May/June 2000, p. 62-75.

SHILLER, R. (2000), Irrational Exuberance, Princeton.
SHLEIFER, A., VISHNY, R. (1997), The Limits of Arbitrage, in: Journal of Finance, Vol. 52, p. 35-55.
TVERSKY, A., KAHNEMAN, D. (1974), Judgment under Uncertainty: Heuristics and Biases, in: Science, Vol. 185, p. 1124-1131.
VARIAN, H. (1998), Effects of the Internet on Financial Markets, School of Information Management and Systems, University of California, Berkeley, http://www.sims.berkeley.edu/~hal/people/hal/papers.html .
VENTURE ECONOMICS (2001), http://www.ventureeconomics.com/stats/2001 Q2/us.html .
WALL STREET JOURNAL (2001), Mergers Snapshot, July 18, 2001, p. C14.
WELFENS, P.J.J. (1999), Internet Market Dynamics in Germany: Moving From a Small Market to a Strategic Sector of the Economy, Discussion Paper No. 59 of the EIIW at the University of Potsdam.
WELFENS, P.J.J., JUNGMITTAG, A. (2000), Effects of an Internet Flat Rate on Growth and Employment in Germany, Discussion Paper No. 81 of the EIIW at the University of Potsdam.

L. Competition in Telecommunications and Internet Services: A Dynamic Perspective

Günter Knieps

1. The Internet as the Prime Driver of Convergence of the Telecommunications, Media and Information Technology (IT) Sectors

Convergence of the telecommunications, media and information technology sectors has been increasing in recent years with the emergence of the Internet and with the increasing capability of existing networks to carry both telecommunications and broadcasting services. Developments in digital technologies and software are creating large innovative technological potential for the production, distribution and consumption of information services. Convergence, characterized as the ability of different network platforms to carry essentially similar kinds of services, may have different faces: telecommunications operators may offer audiovisual programming over their network; broadcasters may provide data services over their networks, cable operators may provide a range of telecommunication services (cf. EUROPEAN COMMISSION, 1997, p. 1). Up to the present time the most relevant evolution and adaptation of such platform independence is that of the transmission control protocol / Internet protocol (TCP / IP). TCP / IP allows information packets to be transported across different networks despite differences in bandwidth, delay, and error properties associated with different transport media (e.g. fiber, radio, satellite) (cf. FRISHMANN, 2001, p. 4).

The Internet as the prime driver of convergence is displacing traditional isolated computer networks; it is providing an alternative means of offering telecommunication services (e.g. Internet telephony) and is also becoming a significant platform for broadcasting services. Moreover, technological convergence makes possible innovative services which combine product characteristics from the traditionally distinct branches of telecommunications, IT and the media, thereby enlarging the scope of voice, data, multimedia and audio-visual services.

The role of government intervention and regulations has strongly different traditions in the media, IT and telecommunication sectors. The media industry is traditionally attributed a function as the bearer of social, cultural and ethical values within our society. Whereas private communication has traditionally been unregulated, broadcast content has traditionally been regulated to some extent (public broadcast). The computer / IT industry developed in an unregulated manner, under the application of general competition law. In contrast, the telecommunications sector had for many years been organized as a legal monopoly.

In the meantime the recent process of gradually opening the telecommunications markets to competition has been coming to an end. Since 1998 in most countries of the world market entry has been allowed to all parts of the telecommunications networks, including both cable-based infrastructure and telephone services. Nevertheless, sector-specific regulations still play an important role. In many countries the telecommunications sector is still a heavy-handedly regulated sector. Remaining sector-specific regulations concern not only technical regulations (e.g. allocation of radio frequencies) or politically desired universal services objectives, but there also exists a complex set of ex ante regulations of end user tariffs, and interconnection and access charges in long distance as well as local networks (cf. KNIEPS, 1999, 2001). These different approaches of government intervention may be challenged by the convergence of the telecommunications, media and IT sectors. On the one hand convergence may outpace existing sector-specific regimes. On the other hand sector-specific regulation may even be extended in the future to include markets not yet regulated, e.g. mobile telephony and new markets, or e.g. Internet services (cf. UNGERER, 2000, pp. 227). The question arises how to achieve the proper role of government intervention in a comprehensive institutional framework, leaving markets as much freedom as possible.

2. Internet Periphery Versus Internet Service Provision

Internet service provision requires several complementary elements belonging to the Internet periphery, which are viable on their own, even in the absence of the Internet. In contrast to the elements of the Internet periphery, the elements of Internet service provision are an inalienable part of the Internet and would not exist without the Internet (see Figure 1).

Terminal equipment (PCs, cellular phones) can be used either without or with access to the Internet although obviously the use of the Internet is not possible without any terminal equipment. *Content* (including broadband) may be provided via the Internet (e.g. video on demand, customized music and video libraries), but there are also other distribution channels available (e.g. cinemas, traditional video libraries, traditional broadcasting). Internet service provision would be possible even without any content provision, by specialising in interactive services (e.g. e-mail). *Access* to the Internet may take place via local telecommunications networks, cable networks or wireless local loop. In order to provide Internet services, capacity of long distance telecommunications networks (bandwidth) is required. Although in the meantime investments in long distance telecommunications infrastructure are strongly motivated by Internet demand, telecommunication transmission capacity has many alternative purposes.

Internet service providers (ISP) offer their customers a spectrum of different services (cf. ELIXMANN / METZLER, 2001, p. 14 ff.) which are classified according to O'Donnell (O'DONNELL, 2000, p. 13 ff.) as fundamental networkking and internetworking, application services and customer relations. Examples of fundamental networking and internetworking are IP number assignments, directory services, in particular domain name service (DNS), outgoing / incoming

Figure L1:   Internet Periphery Versus Internet Service Provision

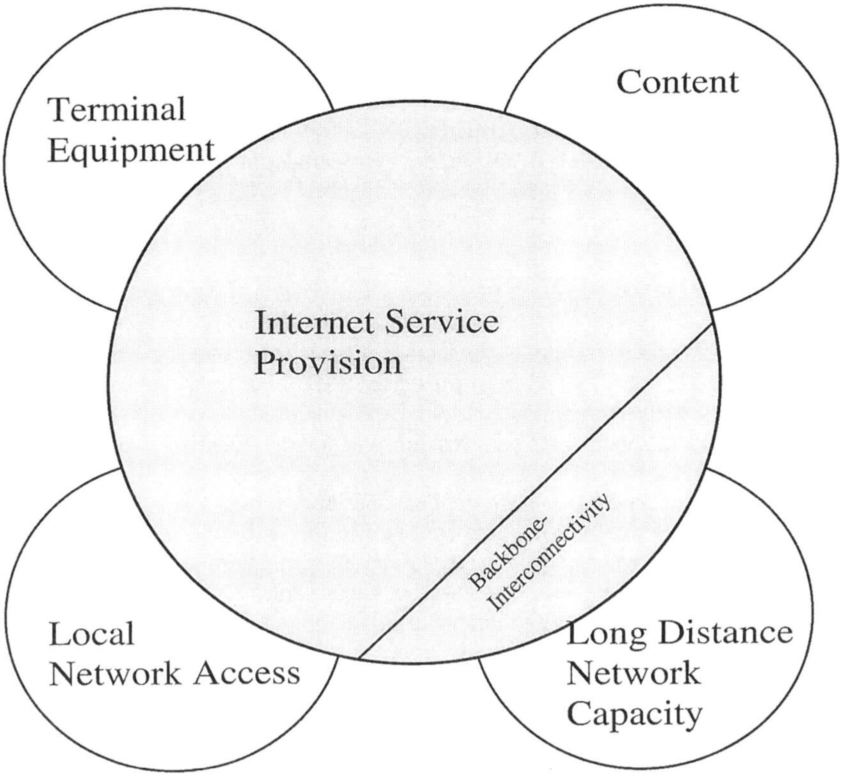

packet routing and connectivity (among different ISP), quality of service and network management. Via their servers ISP offer different kinds of application services to their customers. Examples for application services are file transfer (FTP), e-mail, web-browsing, newsgroups and chat-rooms, IP-telephony, IP-fax and video on demand. By means of client-server architecture and different client-programs, a large number of value added services such as incoming and outgoing mail services, mail list services, online banking, portals and web hosting are realized. The borderlines between content provision and service provision are obviously blurring. Customer relations may be divided into technical support, billing and accounting, and security and confidentiality.

The focus of this paper is on those elements of the Internet periphery and Internet service provision which are strongly based on telecommunications, in particular Internet access (Section 3) and Internet backbone (Section 4). Fundamental networking and internetworking may be divided into Internet-governance (IP number assignments and domain name service) and Internet backbone services; the latter is considered in Section 4.2. There are many other highly relevant questions related to the Internet which are not the subject of this paper: for example, is there still a future role for content regulation given the enormous scope of content production and distribution in the converging markets? (cf. MESTMÄCKER, 2001); is there still a serious applications barrier to entry problem in the microprocessor market given the enormous potential for middleware threats due to innovations on the browser market? (cf. ECONOMIDES, 2000; FISHER, 2000; SIDAK, 2001); what is the potential and limits for self-regulation in the organization of access to IP number assignments and domain name systems? (cf. KESAN / SHAH, 2001; HILLEBRAND / BÜLLINGEN, 2001); how are Internet safety (cf. MÜLLER / RANNENBERG, 1999) and the enforcement of property rights within the Internet to be guaranteed? (cf. MÖSCHEL, 1999; ENGEL, 1999).

3. Access to the Internet

Access to the Internet requires a connection between the Internet user and the interface to the Internet (ISP point of presence / POP). Public switched access to the Internet primarily requires access to a local telecommunications network. In addition, a (long-distance) link between the originating (local) network and the ISP is required.[1]

Several access technologies exist: copper, fiber optics, two-way cable TV infrastructure (CATV network), powerline communication and radio in the loop. One may differentiate between narrowband and broadband Internet access. Narrowband Internet access takes place on two-pair copper cables via analog modem and ISDN (integrated services digital network). Broadband Internet access can be provided either by upgrading two-pair copper cables by means of xDSL (digital subscriber line) technologies – the most popular one being ADSL (asymmetric DSL) technology –, CATV-based broadband Internet access, or broadband wireless technology (e.g. UMTS). Convergence and platform independence, however, does not mean that these broadband access technologies have the same cost characteristics, and they also have different access quality attributes (e.g. mobility, reliability, start-up speed, etc.).

There are particularly strong quality differences between low-speed access (narrowband) and high-speed access (broadband). For example, transmission of 100 text pages takes 120 sec. via modem, 25 sec. via ISDN and 0.4 sec. via ADSL; five color photos take 22 min. via modem, 5 min. via ISDN and 4-5 sec. via ADSL; a 30-minute video takes 38.8 hours via modem, 8.7 hours via ISDN and 8 min. via ADSL (cf. FESENMEIER, 2001, p. 17). This already indicates that narrowband Internet access does not provide an economically sensible way to consume data-intensive Internet services like streaming video and interactive entertainment. On the other hand, dial-up (analog modem) access is sufficient for managing an e-mail account and surfing the Internet for a few hours a week. At the moment narrowband Internet access still plays the dominant role. According to Oftel:

---

[1] OFTEL (2001), p. 41, differentiates between "wholesale call origination" and the "wholesale Internet call termination market".

> The importance of dial-up Internet is crucial. Analysts and market research widely predict that dial-up access will remain the dominant method of connecting to the Internet among residential consumers and small businesses for the foreseeable future. Broadband access will be attractive for some users and some applications. (OFTEL, 2001, p.11)

From this rather short-run perspective the local loops of the established carriers are still – at least to some extent – monopolistic bottlenecks, with a consequent need for sector-specific regulations (price caps, accounting separation, discriminatory free entry).[2] Alternative providers of broadband access (e.g. CATV networks) are not yet able to discipline the market power of the established provider of the local loop. Line sharing obligations, focusing on the stimulation of broadband access are, however, superfluous from the perspective of this low-speed access market.

However, line sharing regulations also do not seem justified from the perspective of broadband Internet access. From the longer-run dynamic perspective of convergence, the separation of the Internet into a large narrowband part on one hand and a rather marginal broadband part on the other seems artificial. For the development of the innovation potential for data-intensive Internet services broadband access is indispensable. Whereas the local loop of copper pairs can provide, via xDSL, one broadband access possibility, there also exist economically feasible access alternatives (see Table 1). In particular, mobile Internet access based on GPRS (General Packet Radio System Standard) as well as UMTS demonstrate the large innovation potential and evolution of mobile technologies for the Internet (e.g. BÜLLINGEN / STAMM, 2001; BÜLLINGEN / WÖRTER, 2000).

---

[2] Even from the traditional perspective of narrowband access there does exist a potential for phasing out sector-specific regulation in local telecommunications networks due to the gradual disappearance of monopolistic bottlenecks (cf. KNIEPS, 1997, p. 331). It is traditionally assumed that local networks, in contrast to long-distance networks, constitute monopolistic bottlenecks, for which neither active nor potential substitutes are available. To the extent and as long as local networks constitute monopolistic bottlenecks, ex ante regulation seems justified. Non-discriminatory access to essential facilities has to be guaranteed. However, it is important to view the application of the essential facilities doctrine in a dynamic context. Therefore, an objective in the formulation of access conditions must be to not impede infrastructure competition, i.e., to not destroy incentives for either research and development activities or innovation and investment. In this way a balance between service and infrastructure competition is reached. Competitive conditions cannot be expected to change simultaneously in all local loops. Therefore it is necessary to examine at regular intervals which subclasses of local loops still constitute monopolistic bottlenecks and in which subclasses of local loops there is already workable active and / or potential competition, e.g., because of wireless local loop facilities.

Table L1:   Narrowband and Broadband Access

Low-speed Access or Narrowband	Dial-up modem (up to 56 Kbit/s over analog connection) ISDN Internet on TV GSM dial-up (e.g. using WAP) and GPRS mobile access (the latter not available yet) Leased lines (up to 128 Kbit/s)
High-speed Access or Higher Bandwidth ("broadband" by some definitions)	Leased lines (over 128 Kbit/s) Satellite (upstream usually on lower-speed dial-up) xDSL Cable modem Broadband fixed wireless access UMTS mobile access (not available yet)

Source: OFTEL (2001, p. 56).

From the perspective of high-speed broadband access, the local loops of the established telecommunication carriers therefore lose the characteristics of a monopolistic bottleneck. Alternative broadband access technologies (cable modem, UMTS, mobile access, etc.) create economically sensible alternatives to xDSL. Due to the increasing role of product differentiation, based on different network characteristics of these access technologies, the long-run convergence towards a single globally dominating access technology seems unrealistic. As a consequence, sector-specific regulation of broadband access – in particular line sharing obligations – seems superfluous.

Neither from the (short run) perspective of narrowband Internet access nor from the (longer-run) perspective of broadband Internet access does the recent introduction of line sharing regulation by the FCC as well as the European Parliament therefore seem justified. The provision of xDSL-based service by a competitive local exchange carrier (LEC) and voiceband service by an incumbent LEC on the same loop is called "line sharing" by the FCC. The FCC decision to unbundle the high frequency portion of the loop was issued in December 1999.[3] The regulation of the European Parliament and the Council of December 5, 2000 on unbundled access to the local loop[4] also entails line sharing:

> "shared access to the local loop" means the provision of access to the non-voice frequency spectrum of a copper line over which the basic telephone service is being provided to the end-user by the incumbent operator allow-

---

[3] FEDERAL COMMUNICATIONS COMMISSION, In the Matters of Deployment of Wireline Services Offering Advanced Telecommunications Capability (CC Docket No. 98-147) and Implementation of the Local Competition Provisions of the Telecommunications Act of 1996 (CC Docket No. 96-98); Third Report and Order in CC Docket No. 98-147; Fourth Report and Order in CC Docket No. 96-98, Washington, D.C., December 9, 1999.

[4] Regulation on unbundled access to the local loop (EUROPEAN PARLIAMENT AND COUNCIL 2000/0185 (COD), Dec. 5, 2000).

ing a new entrant to deploy technologies – such as asymmetrical digital subscriber line (ADSL) systems – to provide the end-user with additional services such as high-speed Internet access.

The question whether broadband Internet access and narrowband Internet access belong into one large Internet access market was controversial in recent antitrust cases dealing with AT&T-Media One and AOL-Time Warner mergers. Here the controversy was not whether the traditional local loop of telecommunications carriers would constitute a monopolistic bottleneck, but whether DSL or satellite-based Internet service will be able to offer close substitutes for cable-based Internet services in the short run (within a two-year time horizon). The proponents of the one large Internet access market approach argued that "residential broadband cable modem Internet access" is not a relevant market because of the intense deployment of DSL by both incumbent and competitive local exchange carriers (LEC's), and additional competition from providers employing other technologies and networks (such as satellite and fixed wireless) (ORDOVER / WILLIG, 1999, p. 7). Since the existing digital loop carrier (DLC)[5] cannot support DSL service without additional investment – the carrier must install digital subscriber line access multiplier (DSLAM) termination at the DLC – it has been argued by the opponents of the one large Internet access market approach that this additional investment may impede DSL's ability to compete with cable-based broadband Internet access within a two-year time horizon (HAUSMAN / SIDAK / SINGER, 2001, p. 150). Due to the economically feasible alternatives of access to the Internet, this controversy did, however, not come to the conclusion that residential broadband cable modem Internet access creates a bottleneck monopoly that is an essential facility in the relevant market of Internet access.

4. Internet Backbones

In the following we shall differentiate between Internet service providers (ISPs), Internet backbone providers (IBPs) and suppliers of long distance network capacity (communications bandwidth). IBPs may be vertically integrated into the market for telecommunications inputs that underlie the services that backbones provide on one hand and with ISPs on the other hand. IBPs may be differentiated by the reach of their networks. There are regional and national backbones which may number from one to many in any given country. At the top level or tier 1 level of IP-connectivity only a limited number of companies (such as MCI / WorldCom, Sprint, AT&T and GTE) are operating (cf. EUROPEAN COMMISSION, 2000, p. 5).

---

[5] As early as the 1970s, local exchange carriers in the US began using a new type of loop, a digital loop carrier (DLC).

4.1 Long Distance Network Capacity (Communications Bandwidth)

Access to the IP-based backbone network is impossible without access to tele-communications transport capacity, delivered e.g. by high-speed fiber optic networks, coaxial cables and satellite. The performance-price ratio for leading-edge optical communications technology has been improving rapidly. Developments in optical technology unquestionably have made massive increases in bandwidth possible. New transmission technologies work most effectively over new fiber strands that have enhanced optical properties. Growth of bandwidth in use for Internet traffic has been dramatic since 1995. However, expectations of a bandwidth revolution similar to Moore's Law on the performance-price ratio for computers have not yet been fulfilled. Costs and benefits of additional investment into bandwidth have to be counterbalanced. This also includes exploiting the benefits of substitution among bandwidth, storage and CPU cycles (cf. GALBI, 2000).

The market for long distance transmission capacity is competitive (cf. LAFFONT / TIROLE, 2000, p. 98) . There have been a large number of newcomers building transnational network infrastructure as input for Internet backbone capacity (cf. ELIXMANN, 2000, p. 7). Another possibility is to lease transmission capacity from several alternative providers of network infrastructure. In Germany a larger number of carriers possess their own fiber-optic networks (IMMENGA / KIRCHNER / KNIEPS / KRUSE, 2001, Table 1, pp. 14). The telecommunications transport capacity is readily available today from a variety of providers (KENDE, 2000, p. 25).

4.2 Internet Backbone Services

IBPs own or lease communications bandwidth that is connected by routers which the backbones use to deliver traffic to and from their customers. The underlying network logistics is the TCP/IP protocol. Whereas the IP (Internet protocol) is responsible for shifting the data packets from router to router, the TCP (transfer control protocol) is responsible for the reliability of transmission, including error correction. IBPs are also responsible for quality of service and network management, including the capacity control of the backbone network. An additional dimension of Internet backbone services is the organization of interconnectivity with other IBPs by means of peering and transit arrangements.

4.3 Organization of Interconnectivity: Transit and Peering

Each IBP forms its own network that enables all end users and content providers connected to it to communicate with each other. End users, however, often want to be able to communicate with a wide variety of end users and content providers, regardless of which IBPs are involved. In order to provide end users with such universal connectivity, IBPs must interconnect with one another to exchange traffic destined for each other's end users. It is this interconnection that makes the Internet the "network of networks".

One may differentiate between peering and transit arrangements. Peering partners exchange traffic on a settlement-free basis (bill and keep type); that is, each peer terminates without charge the traffic originating with other peers. In contrast, with transit arrangements one IBP pays another IBP to deliver traffic between its customers and the customers of other IBPs (e.g. KENDE, 2000, p. 5). Peering used to occur in the U.S. at public peering points, NAPs (network access points)[6], where different backbones could exchange traffic. As the result of the increased congestion at the NAPs, IBPs turned to bilateral peering arrangements (private peering). Because each bilateral peering arrangement only allows backbones to exchange traffic destined for each other's customers, backbones need a significant number of peering arrangements in order to gain access to the full Internet. The alternative to peering is a transit arrangement between IBPs in which one IBP pays another IBP to deliver traffic between its customers and the customers of other backbones. Many IBPs have adopted a hybrid approach to interconnection, peering with a number of backbones and paying for transit from one or more IBPs in order to have access to the backbone of the transit supplier as well as the peering partners of the transit supplier.

Transit and peering arrangements among IBPs are not subject to sector-specific regulations, neither by the Federal Communications Commission, nor by the regulatory agencies in Europe. The agreements that cover interconnection between IBPs are characterized by private negotiations and are subject to non-disclosure rules. From the economic theory of regulation it follows that there is indeed no need for ex ante regulation due to the absence of network-specific market power. The input market of communications bandwidth is competitive, and each IBP can develop its own logistics concept to optimize its own backbone and set of transit and peering arrangements.[7]

---

[6] In 1993, the U.S. National Science Foundation, NSF, designed a system of geographically dispersed NAPs (see KENDE, 2000, p.5).

[7] Of course, general competition law also applies to transit and peering arrangements. However, antitrust proceedings are geared towards handling concrete conflicts case by case and not towards designing a new ex ante regulatory policy.

References

BÜLLINGEN, F., STAMM, P. (2001), Mobiles Internet – Konvergenz von Mobilfunk und Multimedia, Wissenschaftliches Institut für Kommunikationsdienste (WIK), Bad Honnef: Diskussionsbeitrag Nr. 222.

BÜLLINGEN, F., WÖRTER, M. (2000), Entwicklungsperspektiven, Unternehmensstrategien und Anwendungsfelder im Mobile Commerce, Wissenschaftliches Institut für Kommunikationsdienste (WIK), Bad Honnef: Diskussionsbeitrag, Nr. 208.

ECONOMIDES, N. (2000), The Microsoft Antitrust Case, Stern School of Business Working Paper 2000-09, New York: New York University.

ELIXMANN, D. (2000), Wettbewerbsintensität auf dem Markt für Übertragungskapazität, Wissenschaftliches Institut für Kommunikationsdienste, Bad Honnef: WIK Newsletter, No. 41, December, 6-9.

ELIXMANN, D., METZLER, A. (2001), Marktstruktur und Wettbewerb auf dem Markt für Internet-Zugangsdienste, Wissenschaftliches Institut für Kommunikationsdienste (WIK), Bad Honnef: Diskussionsbeitrag Nr. 221.

ENGEL, C. (1999), Das Internet und der Nationalstaat; Gemeinschaftsgüter: Recht, Politik und Ökonomie, Bonn: Preprints aus der Max-Planck-Projektgruppe Recht der Gemeinschaftgüter.

EUROPEAN COMMISSION (1997), Green Paper on the Convergence of the Telecommunications, Media and Information Technology Sectors, and the Implications for Regulations, COM(97)623, Brussels.

EUROPEAN COMMISSION (2000), Internet Network Issues, Directorate General Information Society, ref: internetreg-sk-sep00.

FESENMEIER K.-H. (2001), Plötzlich wollen alle ADSL, Badische Zeitung, July 14, 17.

FISHER, F.M. (2000), The IBM and Microsoft Cases: What's the Difference?, American Economic Review, Papers & Proceedings, Vol. 90/2, 180-183.

FRISHMANN, B. (2001), Privatization and Commercialization of the Internet: Rethinking Market Intervention into Government and Government Intervention into the Market, SSRN Telecommunications and Regulated Industries Law Working Paper, 2/1, March.

GALBI, D.A. (2000), Growth in the "New Economy": U.S. Bandwidth Use and Pricing Across the 1990s, FCC Working Paper, July 9.

HAUSMAN, J.A., SIDAK, J.G., SINGER, H.J. (2001), Residential Demand for Broadband Telecommunications and Consumer Access to Unaffiliated Internet Content Providers, Yale Journal on Regulation, Vol. 18/1, 129-173.

HILLEBRAND, A., BÜLLINGEN, F. (2001), Internet-Governance – Politiken und Folgen der institutionellen Neuordnung der Domainverwaltung durch ICANN, Wissenschaftliches Institut für Kommunikationsdienste (WIK), Bad Honnef: Diskussionsbeitrag Nr. 218.

IMMENGA, U., KIRCHNER, C., KNIEPS, G., KRUSE, J. (2001), Telekommunikation im Wettbewerb – Eine ordnungspolitische Konzeption nach drei Jahren Marktöffnung, München: Verlag C.H. Beck.

KENDE, M. (2000), The Digital Handshake: Connecting Internet Backbones, Federal Communications Commission, Washington: OPP Working Paper No. 32.

KESAN, J.P., SHAH, R.C. (2001), Fool Us Once Shame On You – Fool Us Twice Shame On Us: What We Can Learn From the Privatizations of the Internet Backbone Network and the Domain Name System, University of Illinois College of Law, Urbana Champaign: Law and Economics Working Paper No. 00-18.

KNIEPS, G. (1997), Phasing out Sector-Specific Regulation in Competitive Telecommunications, Kyklos, Vol. 50/3, 325-339.

KNIEPS, G. (1999), Market Entry in the Presence of a "Dominant" Network Operator in Telecommunications, in WELFENS, P.J.J., YARROW, G., GRINBERG, R., GRAACK, C., eds., Towards Competition in Network Industries, Berlin et al.: Springer Verlag, 131-144.

KNIEPS, G. (2001), Sector-Specific Regulation of German Telecommunications, forthcoming in MADDEN, G. and SAVAGE, S.J., eds., The International Handbook of Telecommunications Economics, Cheltenham: Edward Elgar, Vol. III.

LAFFONT, J.-J., TIROLE, J. (2000), Competition in Telecommunications, Cambridge, Massachusetts, London: MIT Press.

MESTMÄCKER, E.-J. (2001), Unternehmenskonzentrationen und Urheberrechte in der alten und "neuen" Musikwirtschaft, Zeitschrift für Urheber- und Medienrecht (ZUM), Vol. 3/2001, 185-194.

MÖSCHEL, W. (1999), Wettbewerbsrechtliche und urheberrechtliche Aspekte der Internet-Benutzung, in Der Einfluss des europäischen Rechts auf die Schweiz (Festschrift zum 60. Geburtstag von Roger Zäch), Zürich: Schulthess Polygraphischer Verlag, 377-391.

MÜLLER, G., RANNENBERG, K., eds. (1999), Multilateral Security in Communications – Technology, Infrastructure, Economy, München et al.

O'DONNELL, S. (2000), Broadband Architectures, ISP Business Plans, and Open Access, paper presented at the 28th Annual Telecommunications Policy Research Conference, Alexandria, Virginia, September 5.

OFTEL (2001), Oftel's 2000/01 Effective Competition Review of Dial-Up Internet Access, issued by the Director General of Telecommunications, London.

ORDOVER, J.A., WILLIG, R.D. (1999), Declaration on the Matter of: Applications for Consent to the Transfer of Control of Licenses (MediaOne Group, Inc. vs. AT&T Corp.) before the Federal Communications Commission, CS Docket No. 99-251, Washington, D.C.

SIDAK, J.G. (2001), An Antitrust Rule for Software Integration, Yale Journal on Regulation, Vol. 18/1, 1-83.

UNGERER, H. (2000), The Case of Telecommunications in the EU, in EHLERMANN, C.D. and GOSLING, L., eds., European Competition Law Annual 1998: Regulating Communications Markets, Oxford and Portland, Oregon: Hart Publishing, 211-236.

M. Persistence of Monopolistic Bottlenecks in Telecommunications and Internet Services
(Some Comments on a Paper by Günter Knieps)

Torsten J. Gerpott

1. Summary of Key Conclusions of Knieps

Günter Knieps provides a concise description of the service convergence in the telecommunications and electronic media industries and of some of the regulatory challenges implied by this trend. Service convergence means that specific services (e.g., video streaming) are made available to end customers over different networks (e.g., coax cable broadcasting and point-to-multipoint radio infrastructures). *Service* convergence has to be differentiated from the *network* convergence notion (cf. GERPOTT, 1998a, p.1). The latter implies that different telecommunication services (e.g. voice and picture transmission) are no longer provided via separate networks, but rather that a single integrated infrastructure platform is used to supply the different services to end customers. *Knieps* convincingly shows that the diffusion of decentralized IP/TCP-based client-server-computer networks (i.e., the so-called Internet) is a key driver of both service and network convergence.

A crucial thesis of *Knieps* is that IP/TCP-based networks convergence does *not* mean that a single converged multi-service (access) telecommunications network run by one dominant operator is likely to emerge in the foreseeable future (KNIEPS, 220th page). Instead, according to *Knieps*, it is economically feasible that several access and backbone networks are run in parallel by various competing operators. Based on the assumption that the (German [?] Internet) access and backbone bandwidth markets are or will become competitive, *Knieps* concludes that there is no need for sector-specific ex ante regulation for each of the two markets.

Regrettably, a differentiated analysis which considers technical facts and empirical observations of service offerings and pricing behavior of the incumbent *Deutsche Telekom* (*DT*) as well as of alternative carriers and of market shares of access and bandwidth suppliers in Germany reveals that, at least for Germany, the major conclusion of *Knieps* is not flawless. In the remainder of this paper I will provide evidence to support this argument.

2. Availability of Competing (Internet) Access Technologies

For the (broadband Internet) access market, *Knieps* asserts that there are powerful alternatives to the copper-based ubiquitous *DT*-platform. In particular, he refers to the mobile GPRS- and UMTS-standards as innovative technologies with promising potential to overcome monopolistic bottlenecks in the local loop. Both claims are not tenable for technical and economic (cost) reasons.

For mobile GPRS and UMTS access alternatives *Knieps* disregards the obvious fact that the bandwidth of these technologies is much too limited to provide *broadband* Internet access which he himself classifies as "indispensable" "for the development of the innovation potential for data intensive Internet services" (KNIEPS, 219th page). Current GPRS offerings of mobile operators in Germany do not exceed 40.2 kbit/s – a (shared) bandwidth that is lower than the (unshared) transmission speed of 56 kbit/s delivered by a standard analog fixed line narrowband modem access to the Internet. Although the GPRS specification technologically allows for a maximum (shared) bandwidth of 171.2 kbit/s, frequency availability constraints have the impact that this bandwidth will not be supported by mobile carriers in real-life settings.[1] In a similar vein, UMTS will supply mobile users with Internet access speeds in the magnitude of 128–144 kbit/s. This is approximately equal to the bandwidth provided by two bundled fixed network ISDN channels. However, it is far below the (downstream) transmission rates of 768–1024 kbit/s already delivered in 2001 by copper-based fixed line DSL-technologies. In conclusion, GPRS and UMTS mobile radio technologies do not provide an alternative platform with the capability to overcome the monopolistic bottleneck in the German fixed line local loop market, neither from a short nor from a longer run perspective.

At least from a mid-term perspective (i.e., until 2006–2008), the competitive potential of other mass market (Internet) stationary access solutions partially enumerated by *Knieps* (e.g., point-to-multipoint [PMP] radio systems, powerline communications, interactive cable broadcasting infrastructures) is also very limited due to the typical investment/cost disadvantages of such alternatives against the copper-based DSL-Internet access platform run by the German incumbent. Detailed evidence for these comparative cost disadvantages of various access alternatives is well documented in academic publications (e.g., GERPOTT / MEISSNER, 1997; GERPOTT, 1998b; WALKE, 1999; URBAN, 2000) and in publicly available conference presentations (e.g. ZUNDL, 1999) which appear to be not known by *Knieps*.

Furthermore, a mere look at the recent development of various groups of access platform operators in the German market also reveals that broad- or narrowband

---

[1] A mobile GSM network run with four GPRS radio frequency channels is able to simultaneously supply only four users per radio cell with the maximum GPRS transmission rate of 171.2 kbit/s. Therefore, the mobile operator is likely to limit the maximum bandwidth delivered to a single customer to ensure that mobile Internet access services can be provided to a sufficient number of his customers.

access solutions/operators which provide sensible alternatives to copper-based DSL-offerings are not on the horizon. For instance, firms holding licences to deploy fixed PMP radio access systems either went bankrupt (e.g. *Callino, First Mark, Deutsche Landtel, Viatel, Winstar*) or announced their withdrawal from this technology (e.g. *ArcTel, BT Ignite, Broadnet, Star21*). Similarly, in Germany powerline access systems are run by only three companies in regionally limited field trials which are unlikely to be expanded to a nationwide scale. Fortunately, there is a vague hope that the new foreign majority shareholders of the German cable broadcasting networks formerly controlled by *DT* will aggressively market TV and Internet access service bundles to a large number of residential customers in the mid-term future. However, due to the internationally unique and complex structure of the German coax cable networks industry and due to tight media regulation constraints this access alternative to copper-based DSL may still turn out as practically irrelevant for Germany. In any case, coax cable upgrade investment of *Callahan/ish* and *NTL/iesy Hessen* (1) will take at least another 4-6 years before a larger number of German homes has the option to use this platform for Internet access and (2) will never reach at least about one third of all German households.

To summarize, both from a mid- and longer-term perspective there are no (broadband) Internet access technologies which create economically attractive alternatives to DSL-platforms based on the existing copper access network rolled out by *DT* under a monopoly shield. Hence, for the foreseeable future the local loops of the incumbent keep the characteristics of a monopolistic bottleneck. The incumbent aggressively deters newcomers from entering the German residential DSL-market by high installation charges and monthly rentals for a local copper loop that other competitors have to pay while at the same time setting low end-customer prices for DSL-access services. At the end of the year 2001, the result of this "two-front-strategy" of *DT* was that the incumbent controlled about 98% of the 2.1–2.3 million (A)DSL-lines sold to residential customers in Germany. As a consequence, industry-specific regulation of broadband (Internet) access which is symmetric to the market power of local loop operators obviously remains a critical requirement to promote a transition of the German telecommunications and Internet services industry toward self-sustaining competition. In particular, DSL-line sharing obligations of incumbents are yet indispensable to ensure that innovative technology developments (e.g. voice over DSL-frequencies) and service offerings (e.g. DSL-services with bandwidths far above the speed provided by the incumbent targeted at specific customer segments such as online gaming enthusiasts) are not prevented by the market power of an incumbent local loop operator.

3. Competitive Intensity on the German (Internet) Backbone Bandwidth Market

With regard to the (Internet) backbone bandwidth/connectivity market *Knieps* correctly points out that there is "… a large number of newcomers building transnational network infrastructure as input for Internet backbone capacity" (KNIEPS, 222nd page). Unfortunately, he does not point out that these newcomers operate only a limited number of routes linking a few major metropolitan centers only a limited number of routes linking a few major metropolitan centers in Germany (e.g., Berlin – Hamburg) and Europe (e.g., Frankfurt – Brussels) (cf. IMMENGA et al., 2001, pp. 14-15). Especially, there is a very limited supply of leased line connectivity for Internet Service Providers and other corporate customers demanding a bandwidth of less than 34 Mbit/s to connect locations in less densely populated areas of Germany.

Empirical evidence supporting the preceding arguments can be easily gained by taking a somewhat closer look at *DT*'s price adaptations for standard leased lines (i.e. "Standardfestverbindungen") during the period from late 1997 to mid-2001 (see GERPOTT / WALTER, 2001 for details). This look reveals that *DT* drastically lowered its bandwidth prices for 34 and 155 Mbit/s leased lines particularly between 10 German urban centers where the dominant operator faces fierce competition. However, *DT* price cuts were much lower for 64 kbit/s and 2 Mbit/s bandwidth services and for leased lines linking rural locations where no competitor has or very few alternative bandwidth suppliers have entered the market.

Thus, although on an overall basis the German market for communication bandwidth beyond the local loops is clearly more competitive than the access market, the (general) claim that "the input market of communications bandwidth is competitive" (KNIEPS, 223rd page) is too undifferentiated to allow any far-reaching conclusion regarding changes in the end user leased line price regulation of *DT*. Quite to the contrary, in Germany the time to phase out the price regulation for leased lines provided by the dominant carrier either to other carriers or to other corporations not holding a telecommunications license (such as pure Internet Service Providers) has yet to come.

References

GERPOTT, T.J. (1998a), Konvergenz von TK & IT: Status und Trends im Überblick, Paper presented at the 2nd EUROFORUM Annual Conference on Convergence Between Telecommunications and Information Technologies, October 1, Königswinter/Düsseldorf: EUROFORUM (24 mimeographed pages).

GERPOTT, T.J. (1998b), Wettbewerbsstrategien im Telekommunikationsmarkt, 3rd. ed., Stuttgart: Schäffer-Poeschel.

GERPOTT, T.J., MEISSNER, P. (1997), Wirtschaftlichkeit von funkgestützten Anschlußnetzplattformen für alternative Carrier, Telekom Praxis, Vol. 74, No. 9, 18-31.

GERPOTT, T.J., WALTER, A. (2001), Preisanpassungen für Standard-Festverbindungen der Deutschen Telekom, Telekom Praxis, Vol. 78, No. 9, 19-24.

IMMENGA, U., KIRCHNER, C., KNIEPS, G., KRUSE, J. (2001), Telekommunikation im Wettbewerb, München: C.H. Beck.

URBAN, T. (2000), Modellierung optimaler Zugangsszenarien für Alternative Netzbetreiber unter betriebswirtschaftlichen Gesichtspunkten, Doctoral Dissertation, Dresden: Technical University of Dresden.

WALKE, T. (1999), Markteintritt in lokale Telekommunikationsmärkte, Aachen: Wissenschaftsverlag Mainz.

ZUNDL, T. (1999), Strategische Bedeutung der Teilnehmeranschlußleitung, Paper presented at the IIR-Conference "Unbundled Access", May 26, Düsseldorf / Frankfurt: IIR (32 mimeographed pages).

N.   Regulatory Economics and the Internet

Friedhelm Dommermuth and Christoph Mertens[1]

1. Introduction

This paper aims to show that there are indeed points of contact between "conventional" telecommunications regulation and the Internet in its different aspects. In this connection it seeks to show the limits of regulation. Section 2 outlines some of the relevant trends in the market and the importance of the Internet. Section 3 then sets out the determinations issued to date by the Regulatory Authority for Telecommunications and Posts (RegTP) with a bearing on the Internet. Section 4 gives a schematic illustration of the impact of the Internet on the PSTN/ISDN. This is significant in that a large proportion of the services connecting to the Internet still use the narrowband telephone network today. More fundamental reflections are set out in section 5. These are concerned with making clear that the RegTP activities referred to in section 3 do not address regulation of the Internet as such. Attention is focused particularly on whether or not it is enough to limit regulation to wholesale products. In conclusion, the paper explores the implications of particular developments for future regulation.

2. Market Trends and the Importance of the Internet

2.1 Importance of the Internet

The economic importance of the Internet is clearly more than its value-added components, since the Internet is becoming all-pervasive. For business, the Internet is a platform that enables transactions to be made more efficiently. Berlecon Research has estimated that B2B – business to business transactions via the Internet – revenues will total between DM 470 and 680 billion by 2004. For home users, the Internet is first and foremost an information and communications platform. Even though it is not possible at this stage to quantify the Internet's economic importance, the experts all agree that it is still growing. From the regulator's point-of-view, the importance of the Internet stems from the convergence processes that technology has made possible.

---

[1] Friedhelm Dommermuth is Head of Department Economic Aspects of Telecommunications Regulation at RegTP. Christoph Mertens is Assistant Head of Section in this Department. This paper reflects the views of the authors.

2.2 Development of Internet Usage / Development of Broadband Internet

There was further strong growth in 2001 in use of the Internet in Germany. Estimates made by RegTP found that over 30 million Germans in the over-14 age group were using the Internet by the end of 2001 – at home, at work or in Internet cafés. The number of users has therefore tripled since mid-1999, i.e. in the space of just two and a half years. This trend is also reflected in the fact that roughly one-third of all fixed line traffic is now accounted for by dial-up Internet connections.[2] But this figure is only part of the picture, as the Internet is increasingly being accessed via DSL lines.[3]

The Society for Consumer Research ("GfK") compared use of the Internet in six European countries in spring and autumn 2001.[4] The study showed the growth dynamic to be unbroken in the UK, Belgium and, most notably, Germany. Growth has slowed in the Netherlands, even if usage levels are still high, while France recorded only moderate growth and Spain stagnation even.

The Internet has long become part of our daily lives: no longer is it the preserve of just a small part of the population. Another GfK study shows just how embedded in our daily lives it has become. Thus the percentage of e-consumers in Germany increased from 29% to 36% between spring and autumn 2001.[5] Only in the UK was this figure higher in autumn 2001 (47%) than in Germany.

At the end of 2001, more than 2.1 million broadband Internet connections were operational in Germany.[6] Of these, 2 million were provided by Deutsche Telekom AG and around 70,000 by the ADSL and SDSL connections of competing companies. In addition, there were some 30,000 broadband connections delivered by the cable network, around 2,000 powerline connections and an unspecified number of satellite connections. Overall, Deutsche Telekom AG held around 95% of the broadband Internet access market. And the broadband access trend is expected to continue.

One of the main reasons for the growing use of the Internet is likely to be today's radically lower prices. Pay-as-you-go Internet prices, for instance, have fallen almost 75% since February 1999. Even lower prices are possible if customers register with their provider. This price trend was also noticeable in 2001. Broadband DSL is likely to be particularly attractive for heavy users. A number of companies offer flat rates for Internet usage with DSL as the access mechanism. Some of these limit the download volumes, however.

---

[2] RegTP's Annual Report 2001.
[3] DSL does not have dial-up connections. Thus DSL as an access mechanism does not increase the volume of calls in the fixed network.
[4] The study focused on age groups between 14 and 69. See www.gfk-webgauge.com/ (February 2002).
[5] GfK defines an "e-consumer" as an individual who has bought at least one product or service over the Internet in the last six months.
[6] RegTP's Annual Report 2001.

2.3 Internet Service Provider Trends

The term Internet Service Provider (ISP) is not clearly defined. It can cover companies of different size and with different business models. This explains why estimates of the number of ISPs can vary widely. While RegTP is currently working on the basis of 1,000 ISPs, another analysis gives a figure as high as 2,100 for July 2000.[7]

The different kinds of ISP can be classified by the activities they perform along the value chain.[8] Smaller ISPs mainly provide Internet access, generally buying the originating service to the point-of-presence (PoP) from Deutsche Telekom AG. These ISP customers are predominantly the self-employed and small companies. National and international ISPs focus more on offering transport services. National ISPs serve mostly small and medium-sized enterprises (SMEs) and provide transport services for smaller ISPs. For connection to the Internet they are reliant in turn on chargeable transit services from the backbone operators. The groups targeted by the international ISPs are primarily national and international ISPs, to whom they sell transit services, and large groups. As so-called tier 1 providers, they are connected to the global backbone via peering arrangements. Online service providers (e.g. AOL) offer Internet access for home users. They usually purchase transport services as well – access to the PoP, and transport on the Internet platform. Access network operators likewise serve end users. They have direct access to the customer, but are usually dependent on transit agreements with larger ISPs to connect to the Internet.

The following trends are becoming apparent. As Internet access tariffs fall, ISPs need to tap new sources of revenue. Portal activities and advertising revenue are becoming more interesting for ISPs serving the retail customer market. As far as the Internet user is concerned, the cost of changing portals is often only minimal, many being free of charge. Customers will only use the portals that are most helpful and interesting for them. Portal operators thus have no option but to keep users loyal to their own portals for as long as possible by providing attractive content. Only thus can a portal operator generate advertising revenue. Yet as the Internet euphoria has faded, so too has the optimism regarding the possibility of generating income through advertising. ISPs are now thinking harder about introducing paid content.[9]

The major - national and international - ISPs are increasingly featuring activities such as web hosting, applications service providing and virtual private networks in their strategically important fields of business. These fields of business are usually opened up through the purchase of small, specialised service providers.

---

[7] Internet / e-commerce startups in Germany: segment analysis: Internet Service Providers, October 2000, www.e-startup.org.

[8] Wissenschaftliches Institut für Kommunikationsdienste (the consultancy "WIK"), Newsletter no 41, December 2000.

[9] For instance, T-Online announced the launch of a paid content service in a press release on 16 January 2002.

One reason for extending the service portfolio in this way is undoubtedly the lower margins for Internet transport services.

A further trend is the takeover of foreign ISPs in particular, providing a potential new customer base. But external growth is also a strategy through which to become a vertically-integrated provider and realise economies of scope and scale. In addition, the capital markets increase the pressure for external growth.

2.4 Convergence

Nor is the term convergence clearly defined. Yet one important facet of convergence is that services can no longer be clearly assigned to any one platform. For instance, both data and voice can be carried over an Internet Protocol (IP) based infrastructure. Voice services, in turn, can be delivered over line-switched and packet-switched networks. The general trend is towards the replacement of line-switched by packet-switched networks with IP networks being used initially in the core networks.[10]

3. RegTP Determinations

3.1 Wholesale Metered Access for ISPs

Even in 1999, it was still the norm for customers to buy Internet usage as such from an ISP and access via the telephone network from – as a rule – Deutsche Telekom AG. However, as time went on, another business model began to gain ground, one in which customers obtained the access and the Internet usage service from their ISP as a complete package. Here, the ISP procures access to its own online service via Deutsche Telekom AG's telephone network as a wholesale product from Deutsche Telekom AG.

In an ex-post rates regulation procedure provided for by section 30(2) of the Telecommunications Act ("TKG"), RegTP in June 1999 set the per-minute rates for the narrowband access service via Deutsche Telekom AG's telephone network. Internet usage itself was not part of the case, being covered by the Teleservices Act and not by the TKG.

The case addressed Deutsche Telekom AG's wholesale connection rates for ISPs ("AfOD" product), the call origination service from the end user to the ISP's primary rate access at its PoP. This is a product for ISPs with an Internet platform of their own. However, the AfOD product is also part of the more comprehensive Deutsche Telekom "T-InterConnect OnlineConnect" ("TICOC") product, intended for ISPs without their own Internet platform. T-Online is one of these. Besides the wholesale access service, it also uses Deutsche Telekom AG's Internet platform.

---

[10] The core network is essentially the same as the carrier, or long distance, network.

Use of the platform is not subject to regulation and was not therefore addressed in RegTP's determination. The fact that neither Internet usage by the end user nor use of the Internet platform is regulated indicates the limitations of telecommunications regulation.

An international price comparison showed that the basic wholesale access rates were only slightly higher than the OECD average. No price abuse as specified in section 24(2) para 1 of the TKG was thus established. As regards the access component of the TICOC service, RegTP established that Deutsche Telekom AG's variable discounts gave its subsidiary T-Online (then called DeTeOnline) unjustified advantages. The outcome of the case was that Deutsche Telekom AG was required to offer wholesale access to all ISPs on a non-discriminatory basis, regardless of whether it was offered directly as the AfOD product or indirectly as part of the TICOC product.

3.2 Wholesale Unmetered Internet Access

It was decided on 15 November 2000, likewise during an ex-post rates regulation procedure, that Deutsche Telekom AG should offer ISPs, from 1 February 2001, a flat rate for its Internet access service ("OVF" product). This wholesale flat rate is the unmetered variant of the AfOD service. RegTP had construed the fact that Deutsche Telekom AG's access service was not offered optionally at a flat rate as discrimination against AfOD users on the grounds of section 24(2) para 3 of the TKG.

Underlying the ruling was the assumption that the risk of a price-cost squeeze could only be avoided by introducing similarly-structured rates at the wholesale and at the retail levels. This price-cost squeeze resulted from Deutsche Telekom AG letting its T-Online subsidiary offer end users a flat rate, but not calculating the access service on a per-minute basis. Other ISPs were thus compelled to offer customers a flat rate, too, running the risk of overuse of the service. On the one hand, they would have a steady flow of income from the retail flat rate, but on the other, they would be faced with costs increasing linearly with the duration of use. With Deutsche Telekom AG, however, even in the case of overuse, T-Online's losses would be offset by mirror-image gains by the parent company as a result of the time-dependent wholesale connection rates.

Meanwhile, T-Online discontinued its retail flat rate on 1 March 2001. The Münster higher administrative court then ruled on 15 March 2001 that the wholesale flat rate RegTP had ordered need not be introduced for the time being. The reason for the immediate enforcement of the order had ceased to apply with discontinuance of the narrowband retail flat rate. The mere existence of the option for T-Online to offer a retail flat rate did not constitute a competitive advantage over other ISPs that justified the introduction of a wholesale flat rate being ordered.

All the same, Deutsche Telekom AG did not withdraw its unmetered access offer. Following this concept, an ISP wishing to be fed traffic from all parts of the country at the flat rate would require connections at 1,622 local exchanges.

How a wholesale flat rate is framed has diverse implications. The questions arising with respect to this are currently being explored in a wide-ranging report.[11] We look at the main issues in section 4.

3.3 DSL

Deutsche Telekom AG's T-DSL prices were investigated in March 2001 in an ex-post rates review. Although some of the T-DSL prices were found not to cover costs, no action was taken since a predatory effect could not be proven. Specifically, it was determined that the price of T-DSL in conjunction with an analogue line overabsorbed costs, but combined with an ISDN line was below cost. No objections were raised, however, since the objectively-justifiable reason referred to in section 24(2) of the TKG were initiated. On the one hand, startup losses were entirely to be expected when new products were introduced, while on the other, this strategy served to exploit economies of scale more quickly. Ultimately, this would also benefit Deutsche Telekom AG's rivals. At the heart of the determination was the aim to grant competitors non-discriminatory access to the network infrastructure. Important here was the requirement placed on Deutsche Telekom AG to enable line sharing. Also, Deutsche Telekom AG had pledged to improve its delivery of local loops, colocation space and carrier leased lines.

The March 2001 determination allowed the case to be reopened if compliance with fundamental aspects of the determination was found to be lacking. The persistent backlog of carrier-leased lines along with the fact that, despite repeated court rulings for immediate enforcement, no line sharing provisioning arrangements had been negotiated, prompted RegTP on 18 December 2001 to reopen its investigation into T-DSL prices.

Finally, Deutsche Telekom AG in January 2002 announced marked price increases in the monthly rental and one-off connection charges.[12] This caused RegTP to close the reopened T-DSL case, as the price dumping suspicions now appeared in a different light.

3.4 Line Sharing

According to industry analysts, Internet usage is set to continue its vigorous growth, with an ever larger number of Internet connections being broadband. T-DSL technology, which builds on the copper pair, is likely to feature prominently. This is the background against which the European Parliament and the Council in December 2000 issued a Regulation on unbundled access to the local loop. The Regulation is directly applicable and has thus been in force in Germany

---

[11] The findings of the report were not available at the time this paper was being prepared.

[12] Deutsche Telekom AG press release of 15 January 2002. The new monthly rentals are applicable from 1 May 2002 onwards, while the connection charges will increase in two stages effective 1 July 2002 and 1 January 2003.

too since 1 January 2001. It commits Deutsche Telekom AG as a dominant company amongst other things to make its competitors a line sharing offer. Competitors are entitled to request just the upper portion of the loop, suitable typically for high-speed Internet access. The remaining lower portion can still be used by Deutsche Telekom AG for voice telephone service.

In March 2001, RegTP ruled on the basic conditions of line sharing. Accordingly, Deutsche Telekom AG was to draw up a standard offer within a period of two months. A further period of three months for technical implementation was then permitted. No decisions were taken on charges, however. Deutsche Telekom AG appealed against RegTP's ruling. To date, customers still have no possibility of obtaining the high frequency portion of the loop from a competitor.

In its ruling of 21 June 2001, Cologne administrative court identified a general obligation to offer line sharing. It established that Deutsche Telekom AG, contrary to the stipulations of the EU Regulation, had not made requesting companies any such offer.

The ruling was confirmed on 23 August 2001 by the Münster higher administrative court. The court found delaying tactics by Deutsche Telekom AG, aimed at strengthening its own position for T-DSL products. This constituted an abuse of its position as an operator with significant market power (SMP). Deutsche Telekom AG's intensive marketing of its T-DSL brand shows how realistic this assessment is. Admittedly, Deutsche Telekom AG did subsequently submit a line sharing offer, but this was rejected by the competitors on account of the level of charges asked.

RegTP then determined in March 2002 that the monthly rental for the high frequency portion of the local loop would be €4.77. This included nothing towards the cost of the loop, a contribution Deutsche Telekom AG had called for. The costs of the local loop are not increased by sharing the line. They are fully covered by the line and call charges and may not be recouped again through line sharing. However, specific line sharing costs – for the splitter on the network side, for any additional fault repair and for product and supply costs, e.g. marketing costs – were taken into account.

Just how much the line sharing option will encourage competition in the local access market remains to be seen. Remembering, however, that the added value of local access provided by Internet usage and especially by DSL is likely to grow strongly, makes line sharing all the more relevant.

3.5 Internet Telephony

Internet telephony (Voice over IP, or VoIP) is assured a rosy future, according to most of the experts. Analysis, for instance, forecast in 1998 that by 2003 some 25% of all international call minutes would be handled over the Internet.[13] Even if the euphoria surrounding the Internet and the assessment of its economic perspec-

---

[13] Analysys, Commercial Strategies for Internet Telephony, May 1998.

tives has been fading for almost two years now, the economic importance of Internet telephony is likely to increase significantly.

At this stage, however, we should point out one frequently neglected aspect. The term VoIP is often reduced to the possibility of telephoning via "the Internet". Thus the emphasis initially was on cost-effective substitution for the then much more expensive line switched phone calls. Liberalisation of the telecommunications markets has made conventional calls much cheaper, however. Hence, other things being equal, the market potential of Internet telephony, understood thus, has diminished. Yet we have another picture if we remember that the term VoIP really only means that voice is transmitted over an IP-based network. And the trend towards IP-based networks is clear (cf 2.4). Tomorrow's networks will be based on packet-switching technology, creating a single platform for the transmission of both data and voice. If we take this more general understanding of VoIP, we see that its economic importance will almost certainly grow.

The first issue for the regulator in respect to Internet telephony is the licence requirement under section 6(2) para 2 of the TKG. Voice telephony provided on the basis of self-operated networks requires a Class 4 licence. To date, it has not been possible to classify Internet telephony as voice telephony according to section 3 para 15 of the TKG since one of the criteria, real time, is not given. This criterion is said not to be realised throughout, even if this may now be the case in individual instances. But even if the real time criterion were deemed met, a licensing obligation would not be given since the criterion of "self-operated network" must also be met. Section 3 para 2 of the TKG refers namely to functions control (legal control) of the network.

If we look at the structure, that is to say the routing of traffic in the Internet, it seems questionable at the very least whether legal control of the network(s) can be assumed. The Internet is a mesh of networks forming one vast network. Data transmitted from A to B are routed over the capacity that is free at the time. These can be quite different paths. Data packets can also travel along different paths even if they are part of the same logical connection. As a result, the question of whether there is a self-operated network can only be answered on a case-by-case basis.

In the past, the European Commission had referred primarily to the criterion of real time in support of its finding that Internet telephony was not to be regarded as voice telephony. It held a public consultation in order to accommodate technical and market changes. The outcome of the consultation process[14] was that, while the previous classification was in essence confirmed, there was now a shift of emphasis away from the real time criterion. Instead, it was determined that Internet telephony, in most cases, did not provide the usual reliability and sound quality the average consumer had come to expect. True, there were tailored offerings for business customers, yet these could not be classed as voice telephony since voice transmission was only part of the package.

Earlier in this section we said that a narrow interpretation of the term VoIP referred to telephoning over "the Internet". VoIP in the wider sense, however, means

---

[14] 2000/C 177/03.

that voice is transmitted over an IP-based network. This distinction is significant in that the TKG links the licensing requirement of section 6(1) para 2 in conjunction with section 6(2) para 2 with the criterion of a "self operated network". Yet in respect to whether a self-operated network can be identified, it is not important, whether line switching or packet switching is used. The difference in emphasis in the EU's argumentation is thus of no consequence as far as the criterion "self-operated network" is concerned.

So far, Voice over DSL (VoDSL) has only appeared on the fringe of the regulatory debate. This could change with implementation of line sharing as envisaged in the local loop Regulation if competitors also offer voice over the high frequency portion. This would put the spotlight on cost allocation. At the moment, it is not possible to say whether, and if so how rapidly, a mass market for VoDSL could emerge. The question of a possible licensing requirement for VoDSL has to be looked at on a case-by-case basis. RegTP has not made any general classification as yet.

4. Impact of the Internet on the PSTN/ISDN

Most users still access the Internet over narrowband dial-up connections. The extent to which the line switched network is used depends on where the ISP's PoP is located. In any case, Internet traffic is always routed at least through the lowest exchange level before being transferred to an IP platform. Narrowband Internet traffic now accounts for 30% of all PSTN/ISDN traffic – a considerable share. Thus the extent to which continued growth in Internet usage can cause congestion in Deutsche Telekom AG's network is becoming more urgent. Against the background of the debate on flat rates both at retail and at wholesale level (OVF debate) it is particularly relevant.

To begin with, however, let us outline a few fundamentals. A growing proportion of Internet traffic in the total volume of traffic does not automatically lead to bottlenecks. Assuming that Internet traffic behaved in complementary fashion to voice telephony, the daily traffic curves would also be complementary. Capacity would thus be better utilised. Crucial to the question of possible congestion is the effect narrowband Internet traffic has during peak hours, as only peak-hour traffic is relevant to network dimensioning. On the one hand we can assume that, as the Internet penetration rate continues to grow, the number of users of narrowband access technologies will increase further. But on the other, the number of users of broadband Internet connections is likely to grow markedly. This would reduce the strain put on the PSTN/ISDN by Internet traffic, since broadband Internet traffic is transferred to a packet switched network before the first exchange. And even Deutsche Telekom AG's pricing policy is likely to have encouraged Internet users to choose a DSL connection at an early stage, as the combination of a DSL line with a DSL flat rate is only slightly more expensive than an analogue or ISDN line and a narrowband flat rate.[15] Added to this is the fact that it is precisely the heavy users who are the first to switch to a broadband connection. Put differently, the extent to which broadband Internet connections take the pressure off the PSTN/ISDN is disproportionately high. It is already clear that a substantial part of Internet traffic as a whole uses DSL as its access mechanism.

The debate on the introduction of flat rate wholesale access must take all these factors into account. The analysis is rendered more difficult by the complex connections – the interplay between the intensity and the time of day of Internet usage and the provider's pricing, for instance. But the second aspect in particular, the time of day of Internet usage, can only be influenced to a certain extent by the ISP's pricing, since most customers work during the day. And in turn, an ISP's pricing is affected by how a wholesale flat rate is framed.

In terms of network efficiency, it is desirable to transfer Internet traffic from the line switched to a packet switched network as close as possible to its origin. And given the specific characteristics of Internet traffic with its longer average holding times than those of voice traffic, this is all the more desirable.

Yet the picture changes if the aim is to strengthen competition among ISPs. In this case it makes better sense for the competitors to collect the traffic at a higher exchange level. This reduces migration to the local exchanges and provides bundling advantages. Thus there is a conflict of aims between network efficiency on the one hand and competition among ISPs on the other.

Hence an important aspect of the debate about the introduction of a wholesale flat rate is the level of Deutsche Telekom AG's network hierarchy at which an ISP can take over the traffic. We must investigate whether, and if so, where, bottlenecks in Deutsche Telekom AG's network could occur. A rule of thumb is that the higher the PoP is in the network hierarchy, the more likely there is to be congestion in the lower sections. Traffic handed over, say, at a level 2 exchange is more heavily concentrated than if it were handed over at a local exchange. At a level 2 exchange, traffic meets up from a number of access areas, but its distribution among the access areas is still not known. If the traffic is very unevenly distributed and comes mainly from one access area, bottlenecks can occur in this section. This problem could be solved in principle if an ISP wishing to receive Internet traffic at level 2 informed Deutsche Telekom AG of how the traffic is distributed among the access areas.

Deutsche Telekom AG must review its network dimensioning, depending on where the PoP is located. An analysis must be made of whether the expected daily profile of Internet traffic can be handled in the relevant part of the network with the capacity available.[16] Dimensioning is also affected by the following points we have already mentioned: expected development of narrowband Internet usage, less traffic on the PSTN/ISDN as a result of migration to DSL, and ISP pricing. Cru-

---

[15] Deutsche Telekom AG discontinued its narrowband flat rate on 1 March 2001 (press release from Deutsche Telekom AG, 15 February 2001)

[16] If the traffic were handed over at the level 2 exchanges, network dimensioning would also need to include the capacity of the transmission paths between the level 2 exchanges and the local exchanges.

cial ultimately is the impact of all these factors on busy hour traffic (shift in the busy hour / increased peak load).

Finally, let us mention an aspect that is frequently omitted in the debate. The impact of narrowband Internet traffic on the PSTN/ISDN has nothing to do with whether an ISP buys the access service at a wholesale rate or per-minute. Bottlenecks are not caused primarily by flat rates at the wholesale level. Yet a wholesale flat rate can lead indirectly to bottlenecks in the PSTN/ISDN if the ISP offers its customers a flat rate on this basis. Such effects would need to be taken into account in calculating a wholesale flat rate.

5. Questions Arising from Regulatory Practice and Emerging Trends

5.1 Should RegTP Regulate the Internet?

An essential feature of a free market economy is that market processes have priority over state intervention. Thus there must always be a reason for regulatory intervention in the market. This also applies to the Internet. Particularly in a market that is experiencing such rapid growth, the primacy of market forces is especially important. And finally, the Internet is a global phenomenon – not a homogeneous entity but a phenomenon made up of a mass of different networks, market players and services.

Yet this is too global a view for our purposes. There may well be need for – justifiable – regulatory action in places. We are not talking here about subsequently legitimising regulation – on the contrary, RegTP's determinations to date show there to be need for action where there are points of intersection with the "conventional" telecommunications sector. This applies first and foremost to connecting to the Internet, access normally provided by the conventional line switched infrastructure. And second, technological advance is forcing us to rethink some of the legal classifications made in the past (e.g. convergence). Whereas in the first case, the legitimacy of and the need for regulatory intervention (mainly in the absence of competition) is largely uncontested, in the second case (convergence) the matter is altogether more difficult.

The example of Internet telephony shows what the basic options are. First, such a service – given the legal requirements – could be regulated analogously to the conventional voice telephone service. This could mean a licensing requirement for Internet telephony. Second, a conscious decision could be taken not to regulate new services, even if the legal requirements were in principle given. An example is the exemption of value-added service providers (these include ISPs) from the payment of access charges in the US. It could be argued that a burgeoning industry should not be inhibited by regulatory intervention. Theoretically, such an approach, not treating like with like, could lead to biased enterpreneurial decisions and business efficiency and profitability being compromised in order to avert regulatory intervention. Whether these arguments hold up in practice is another matter. The TKG, however, makes no provision for such politically motivated exceptions. Nor should we forget that the measure of market dominance in the TKG represents a not inconsiderable hurdle for regulatory intervention. And third, an attempt could be made to achieve regulatory parity by deregulating the tele-communications sector rather than by regulating the Internet. This, however, is more a long term aim than a concrete option.

5.2   Is Regulation of the Wholesale Service Enough?

In the debate about the future shape of regulation it is sometimes said that the regulation of wholesale and retail charges is unnecessary duplicate regulation. RegTP does not share this view.[17] It is right that competitors have been able to capture a remarkable share of some segments of the market. Yet it should not be forgotten that the competitors have to pay a substantial part of their revenues to Deutsche Telekom AG for its wholesale services, as the majority use the former monopolist's network infrastructure. This understanding of regulation is just as applicable in the traditional telecommunications sector as it is in respect to the Internet.

   One of the central aims of the TKG – the protection of consumer interests – can only be achieved by regulating wholesale *and* retail charges. Without the comple-mentary regulation of retail charges there would be the risk of the dominant com-pany abusing its position. This potential for abuse is a latent threat to competition and the achievements to date. For instance, anti-competitive discounts and dump-ing strategies could make it difficult for new players to enter the market, or could squeeze others out. Cross-subsidising and price-cost squeezing also provide poten-tial for abuse.

   We must ask ourselves whether these arguments are applicable to the Internet as well. Could just regulating wholesale products (eg AfOD, wholesale flat rate) be justified simply by saying that the intention was to intervene in the Internet as little as possible? It could be objected that a price-cost squeeze for instance, by definition, has two sides (level of wholesale *and* retail charges). However, the TKG specifies that telecommunications services not classified as voice telephony are subject only to *ex-post* rates regulation. This clearly shows that the classifica-tion under the TKG of whether we have a telecommunications service in the given instance is of immense importance.

5.3   Regulatory Implications

The future of communications services is characterised by the merging of tele-communications, information technology and media. Regarding the transport of digitised signals, it is consistently becoming less relevant whether the signals are

---

[17] RegTP Activitiy Report 2000/2001, p208f.

ultimately converted into voice, data or images. It is this development in particular that is enabling voice, data and images to be delivered to the end user over different platforms (cable, fixed line, mobile).

More and more data services, as well as voice services, are now carried on the traditional copper pair as a result of DSL deployment. Voice telephony could also be offered on the broadband cable network after a change in ownership and investment in return channel capability. The next generation of mobile communications will also deliver high speed data transfer.

As data continues its dramatic growth, its importance is growing in relation to that of voice telephony. In the long term, voice and data networks will be integrated and the new network will serve as a transport platform for a host of communications services. Pivotal to all these developments will be the Internet as an increasingly central area of the economy. The cost advantages of the packet switching mode the Internet protocol uses compared to line switching are likely to mean that voice and images will be transmitted more and more over the Internet as well as data.

In regulatory terms, Internet content must be distinguished from that part of the Internet which is relevant to telecommunications, that is to say, provision of the infrastructure. The TKG permits regulation solely of the latter. The central regulatory issue is access to the Internet. As long as access to data services is handled over the same infrastructure as access to telecommunications (voice) services – and this is the case until decided otherwise – there is much in favour of treating access in parallel, since the bottleneck is the same in both cases.

The regulatory treatment of access in turn has a bearing on the structure and development of the other levels of value added in the ISP market. The access issue is particularly critical when telecommunications companies merge vertically with content providers, for it raises the risk of leverage in the access market, shutting out rival content providers.

Competition in the local access market can therefore have the important function of ensuring content diversity.

Hence one of the regulator's principal tasks is to identify the relevant bottleneck factors which inhibit or even prevent the development of competition. To do so, all changes in the access technologies must be closely observed. A basic reason is that regulation is linked to the criterion of market dominance. Yet the question of market dominance depends not least on the definition of the relevant product market.[18] Thus different access technologies could only be assigned to one market if, from the point of view of the informed consumer, they were functionally interchangeable. The convergence processes we are witnessing would tend to lead us to regard the different access mechanisms as functionally interchangeable as they are the conduit for both voice and data services. Thus the cable networks for instance can be used in principle for telephony or to access the Internet. The extent to which existing determinations on market dominance will perhaps need to be revised on account of alternative technologies (cable, powerline communications

---

[18] Also, the relevant geographic market must be defined.

or perhaps even UMTS in future) cannot be decided *a priori*, but only in the given case.

6. Conclusion

The past few years have seen a huge increase in Internet usage. The Internet is becoming an established feature of more and more of our lives. Even if its growth rates should flatten out with time, its economic and social importance is likely to rise still further. This paper has shown there to be a number of RegTP determinations connected with the Internet, none of which, however, was or is concerned with regulation of "the Internet" as such. On the contrary, all such action has been aimed at facilitating competition. As a consequence, RegTP rulings can have a great impact on the degree of Internet penetration and the intensity of use. Yet only if a service is established to be a telecommunications service can RegTP act at all. This has to be decided on a case-by-case basis.

The possible contention that the Internet should preferably be left to market forces has no substance. Regulatory intervention is not an end in itself, but a means to an end. Its aims are specified in section 2(2) of the TKG. Fundamental aspects of this are therefore, amongst others, safeguarding users' interests and ensuring fair and effective competition.

"Internet issues" can best be addressed starting from the points of contact with the conventional telecommunications sector. This is the case for instance when the Internet is accessed over line switched infrastructure. Second, technological advances and convergence processes may make it necessary to investigate specific aspects of the Internet. The more traditional telecommunications structures are replaced by IP-based infrastructures, the more urgent the question of a consistent regulatory framework becomes. If we are to posit technological neutrality, it is essential to treat like as like, regardless of the technological infrastructure platform used.

O. The Regulation, Deregulation, and Nonregulation of Telecommunications and the Internet in the United States

Donald K. Stockdale

1. Background and Overview

1.1 Antitrust versus Regulation: A Two-Pronged Approach to Regulating Firms

In 1887, Congress created the first modern federal regulatory agency, the Interstate Commerce Commission ("ICC"), whose original purpose was to regulate railroads.[1] Shortly thereafter, Congress passed the Sherman Act, the first federal antitrust statute.[2] Oversimplifying significantly, these two statutes can be viewed as forming the basis for a two-pronged approach to the regulation of firms in the United States.

Under this two-pronged approach, if law-makers believed that competition in a particular industry was sustainable and would yield relatively efficient results, then they would refrain from applying industry-specific regulation, and instead would rely on the antitrust laws to maintain competition. If, on the other hand, they believed that competition in a particular industry would be unlikely to work efficiently (*e.g.,* because the industry exhibited characteristics of natural monopoly), then they would pass a law subjecting that industry to "industry-specific" regulation administered by a state or federal regulatory body or both.[3] In most

---

[1] Interstate Commerce Act of 1887, 24 Stat. 379, 49 U.S.C. § 1. *See generally* MITNICK, B. (1980), at 173-91 (discussing alternative theories explaining the creation of the Interstate Commerce Commission). Congress subsequently gave the ICC additional authority to regulate other industries, including trucking and, for a time, telephone companies.

[2] 26 Stat. 209, 15 U.S.C. § 1 *et seq.* Section 1 of the Sherman Act provides, in relevant part, that "[e]very contract, combination . . . or conspiracy, in restraint of trade or commerce among the several States, or with foreign nations, is hereby declared to be illegal." 15 U.S.C. § 1. Section 2 of the act provides, in relevant part, that "[e]very person who shall monopolize, or attempt to monopolize, or combine or conspire with any other person or persons, to monopolize any part of the trade or commerce among the several States, or with foreign nations, shall be deemed guilty of a felony. . ." 15 U.S.C. § 2.

[3] Under the principles of federalism embodied in the United States Constitution, responsibility for industry-specific regulation was divided between state and federal regulators.

cases, there were four principle components of such industry-specific regulation: (1) regulation of price; (2) controls over entry (and frequently prohibitions on the regulated firm's entering competitive markets);[4] (3) regulation of the terms, conditions, and quality of services; and (4) an obligation that the regulated firm(s) serve all customers seeking service under reasonable conditions.[5] Following the example set by the Interstate Commerce Commission, state and federal lawmakers subsequently applied industry-specific regulation to a wide range of industries, including airlines and surface transportation, electric, gas, and water utilities, the banking, securities, and insurance industries, and telecommunications.[6]

1.2 Reconsidering Industry-Specific Regulation

Beginning in the late 1950s, economists and others began to evaluate critically the traditional view of industry-specific regulation and how it had been applied to particular industries.[7] Focusing first on the railroad and airline industries, critics pointed out various costs associated with industry-specific regulation and questioned the prevailing view that competition in those markets was inefficient and non-sustainable. For example, in 1959, John Meyer and his collaborators published a study suggesting that railroad regulation encouraged cartel-like behavior that imposed significant costs on society.[8] Similarly, Richard Caves, in 1962, identified several types of harms arising from airline regulation, including higher prices resulting from the need to protect inefficient carriers.[9] Soon, critics expanded this analysis to other industries that were subject to industry-specific regulation, including the telecommunications industry, and to other types of regulation, including environmental and health and safety regulation.[10]

The remainder of this paper considers how these evolving views to regulation and deregulation were applied to the telecommunications industry and to the Internet. As discussed in greater detail below, in the United States the telecommu-

---

In general, federal regulators were responsible for interstate and international services, while state regulators were responsible for intrastate services.

[4] For exaample, during the early years of radio, radio companies opposed the idea of AT&T's entering the radio business. This led to the passage of the Radio Act of 1927, which prohibited cross-ownership of telephone companies and broadcasting stations. *Radio Act of 1927*. 44 Stat. 1162 (1927)

[5] *See, e.g.* KAHN, A. (1970), vol. 1, at 3.

[6] *See, e.g.,* SCHERER, F.M. (1980), at 481. *See generally* VICUSI, W., VERNON, J., & HARRINGTON, J. (2000); BREYER, S. (1982), at 156-61 (comparing industry-specific regulation with regulation under the antitrust laws).

[7] *See, generally.,* WEISS, L. & KLASS, M. (1981); POOLE, R. (1982); VICUSI, W., VERNON, J., & HARRINGTON, J. (2000).

[8] MEYER, J., PECK, M., STENASON, J., & ZWICK, C. (1959).

[9] CAVES, R. (1962), at 398-400, 443-449. *See also* DOUGLAS, G. & MILLER, J. (1974) (developing a theory that carriers simply competed away the benefits of any increase in price by increasing investment in service quality, such as an increased number of flights).

[10] *See, e.g.,* BREYER, S. (1982); WEISS, L. & KLASS, M. (1981); POOLE, R. (1982).

nications industry was viewed as a natural monopoly for much of the twentieth century. In the late 1960s and early 1970s, competition began to be introduced into formerly monopoly telecommunications markets. With the introduction of competition into these formerly monopoly markets, telecommunications regulators realized that two types of regulatory changes needed to be made. First, they realized that it was in the public interest to streamline the regulation of firms that lacked individual market power, either because a firm was a new entrant into a market or because a former monopoly firm had lost its individual market power as a result of competition. At the same time, regulators realized that the introduction of competition also required the imposition of additional regulations that were intended to prevent the regulated incumbent monopolist from using its market power in one market to foreclose competition in markets in which competition was emerging. This paper illustrates these two trends by outlining the federal regulatory responses to the emergence of competition in the long-distance and local telephone markets.[11] The Internet, in contrast, was viewed from the start as a market that was workably competitive and therefore generally was not subjected to industry-specific regulation.

2. Regulation and Deregulation of Telecommunications

2.1 The Communications Act of 1934

When the United States Congress passed the Communications Act of 1934 (the "Communications Act"),[12] it was generally believed that telephony was a natural monopoly and that allowing competition would be both futile and inefficient.[13]

---

[11] Although this paper focuses on regulatory responses to the development of competition in the long-distance and local telephone markets, competition was also being introduced in other related markets. For example, at the same time that competition was developing in the long-distance market, regulators were encouraging the development of competition in the markets for customer premises equipment ("CPE") and enhanced (or information) services. *See, e.g.,* HUBER, P., KELLOGG, M., & THORNE, J. (1999), at 651-730, 1075-1157; BROCK, G. (1981), at 234-55; BROCK, G. (1994), AT 79-101.

[12] 48 Stat. 1070, 47 U.S.C. § 201 *et seq.*

[13] In hindsight, it is far from clear that telephony was, in fact, a natural monopoly. After the expiration of the original Bell Company patents in 1894, thousands of independent telephone companies began offering telephone service, and by 1902, 451 of the 1002 cities with telephone service had two or more companies providing it. *See,* HUBER, P, KELLOGG, M. & THORNE, J. (1999), at 12; BROCK, G. (1994), at 65; LAVEY, A. (1987), at 179. After 1907, AT&T aggressively began to try to regain its monopoly through patent infringement suits, targeted price reductions in markets subject to competition, refusals to interconnect with independent telephone companies, and purchases of independent companies. BROCK, G. (1981), at 109-122, WEIMAN, D. & LEVIN, R. (1994). AT&T's response to competitive entry was so aggressive that, in 1912, the U.S.

Accordingly, the Communications Act created a regulatory framework for regulating a natural monopoly, under which regulatory responsibility was divided between the Federal Communications Commission ("FCC) and the state public utility commissions.[14] Consistent with principles of federalism embodied in the U.S.Constitution and past regulatory practice, the FCC was given jurisdiction over interstate and international telecommunications services, while state public utility commissions were given jurisdiction over intrastate services, including local telephone service.[15] Both federal and state regulators had the power to control the prices charged by monopoly telephone providers, and both required that regulated firms file tariffs. In addition, both sets of regulators had the authority to control the entry and exit of firms.[16]

The goals of telecommunications regulation were to: (1) prevent the imposition of excessive prices for telecommunications services; (2) prevent undue discrimination in the provision of such services; and (3) encourage universal access to telephone service.[17] Federal and state regulators cooperated to achieve the last goal by creating a system of implicit subsidies,[18] including subsidies from long-distance services to local services, from business customers to residential customers, and from low-cost urban areas to high cost rural areas.[19]

Department of Justice ("DOJ") threatened to bring suit under the antitrust laws. The DOJ dropped its threat of suit after AT&T offered the Kingsbury Commitment. Under the Kingsbury Commitment, AT&T agreed to: (1) connect its long-distance network to the remaining independent local telephone companies; (2) refrain from acquiring any more independent telephone companies, and (3) divest itself of Western Union. The effect of this agreement was to reduce competition between AT&T and independent local telephone companies, and basically to confirm a market structure of local telephone monopolies and a single long-distance monopoly telephone provider. *Id.,* at 154-158; HUBER, P., KELLOGG, M. & THORNE, J. (1999), at 16-17.

[14] Prior to the creation of the FCC, Congress, in 1910, had passed a law that brought interstate telecommunications within the jurisdiction of the Interstate Commerce Commission ("*ICC*"). *Mann-Elkins Act of 1910*, ch. 309, 36 Stat. 539 (1910). The ICC did not take an active role in regulating rates for interstate telecommunications services, however. HUBER, P., KELLOGG, M., & THORNE, J. (1999), at 214-16; BROCK (1981), at 159-60.

[15] 47 U.S.C. § 152. *See generally* HUBER, P., KELLOGG, M., & THORNE, J. (1999), at 220-22.

[16] Not only did regulation prevent new firms from challenging the regulated monopolies, but it also prevented the regulated monopolies from entering other competitive businesses. For example, AT&T was prohibited from owning broadcast stations and movie studios and, later, from participating in the emerging computer business.

[17] 47 U.S.C. §§ 151, 201, 202.

[18] An implicit subsidy occurs when regulators force a regulated firm to charge rates for certain services or customer groups that are above competitive levels, in order to charge below-competitive rates for other services or customer groups.

[19] *In the Matter of Federal-State Joint Board on Universal Service,* First Report and Order, 12 FCC Rcd 8776, 8784-85, at paras. 10-12 (1997).

For several decades, federal and state regulators pursued these goals through the regulation of a series of monopoly providers. These regulated monopolies included AT&T, which was the sole provider of long-distance service, and various AT&T local operating companies as well as several thousand independent incumbent local telephone providers, which had monopoly franchises to provide local telephone service.

2.2 The Introduction of Competition into the Long-Distance Market

2.2.1 Opening the Long-Distance Market to Competition

The first crack in this monopoly paradigm was created by AT&T itself, when its Bell Laboratories subsidiary developed a commercial microwave system that could provide high-volume voice communication or transmit video signals over the airwaves. Although the FCC, in its early spectrum licensing decisions, initially foreclosed competitive entry, it subsequently concluded, in its 1959 *Above 890* decision, that there was sufficient spectrum for both existing monopoly common carriers and for private microwave users who could use it for their own end-to-end private connections.[20]

In 1963, Microwave Communications, Inc. (which later became MCI), filed a request for authorization to build a microwave communications system between St. Louis and Chicago. The application indicated that MCI intended to use this system to provided voice service and other telecommunications services, on a common carrier basis, over "private lines" in competition with AT&T. In 1969, the FCC, over opposition from AT&T, granted MCI's request.[21] This approval encouraged others to file hundreds of applications. Rather than holding separate proceedings on each individual application, the Commission, initiated a rulemaking proceeding to establish a general policy governing new entry into the "specialized communications field." In its *Specialized Common Carriers* decision, the Commission adopted a general policy favoring competition in the provision of intercity, private line connections.[22]

In 1974, MCI filed revisions to its tariffs that included a new service, called Execunet. This service allowed a subscriber who dialed a local MCI number to reach any telephone number in any city served by MCI. After AT&T filed a protest, the Commission rejected the tariff. Following an appeal by MCI to the federal court of appeals, and a remand to the Commission (where it again supported

---

[20] *Allocation of Frequencies in the Bands Above 890 MHz,* Decision, 27 F.C.C. 359 (1959). *See generally* BROCK, G. (1981), at 202-10; HUBER, P., KELLOGG, M. & THORNE, J. (1999), at 737-38.

[21] *See generally* BROCK, G. (1981), at 210-14; BROCK, G. (1994), at 111-16; HUBER, P., KELLOGG, M., & THORNE, J. (1999), at 734-41.

[22] *Establishment of Policies and Procedures for Consideration of Application to Provide Specialized Common Carrier Services in the Domestic Public Point-to-Point Microwave Radio Service,* First Report and Order, 29 F.C.C. 2d 870 (1971).

AT&T), the court of appeals, in *Execunet II*, held that AT&T must interconnect with MCI and provide local exchange facilities for MCI to use in providing Execunet service.[23] By requiring AT&T to provide interconnection to competing long-distance carriers and to allow competitors to use its local network facilities, the court of appeals opened the market for long-distance, switched-access services to competition.

2.2.2 Regulatory Responses to the Introduction of Competition

The introduction of competition into the long-distance market necessitated numerous changes in the FCC's rules and regulations. One of the most important regulatory changes made by the FCC was to streamline its regulations for carriers that do not possess individual market power. While these streamlining efforts were initially targeted to new entrants into the long-distance, they were later extended to the original monopoly long-distance provider, AT&T, as competition eroded its market power. A second important area of regulatory change was the Commission's adoption of regulations to prevent incumbents that possessed market power in certain markets from leveraging that market power into emerging competitive markets. These changes are described briefly below.

Competitive Carrier Proceeding: In 1979, the FCC initiated the *Competitive Carrier Proceeding*[24] to consider how its regulations should be modified for new firms entering formerly monopoly markets. In a series of orders, the Commission distinguished two kinds of carriers – those with individual market power (dominant carriers) and those without market power (nondominant carriers).[25] The Commission found AT&T's Long Lines Department, which provided interstate

---

[23] *MCI Telecomms. Corp. v. FCC*, 580 F.2d 590 (D.C.Cir. 1978) (*Execunet II*). *See generally* BROCK (1981), at 224-30; HUBER, P., KELLOGG, M., & THORNE, J. (1999), at 748-56.

[24] *Policy and Rules Concerning Rates for Competitive Common Carrier Services and Facilities Authorizations Therefor*, CC Docket No. 79-252, Notice of Inquiry and Proposed Rulemaking, 77 FCC 2d 308 (1979); First Report and Order, 85 FCC 2d 1 (1980) (*First Report and Order*); Further Notice of Proposed Rulemaking, 84 FCC 2d 445 (1981) (*Further Notice of Proposed Rulemaking*); Second Further Notice of Proposed Rulemaking, FCC 82-187, 47 Fed. Reg. 17,308 (1982); Second Report and Order, 91 FCC 2d 59 (1982) (*Second Report and Order*); Order on Reconsideration, 93 FCC 2d 54 (1983); Third Report and Order, 48 Fed. Reg. 46,791 (1983) (*Third Report and Order*); Fourth Report and Order, 95 FCC 2d 554 (1983) (*Fourth Report and Order*); *vacated, AT&T v. FCC*, 978 F.2d 727 (D.C. Cir. 1992), *cert. denied, MCI Telecommunications Corp. v. AT&T*, 113 S.Ct. 3020 (1993); Fifth Report and Order, 98 FCC 2d 1191 (1984) (*Fifth Report and Order*); Sixth Report and Order, 99 FCC 2d 1020 (1985), *vacated MCI Telecommunications Corp. v. FCC*, 765 F.2d 1186 (D.C. Cir. 1985) (collectively referred to as the *Competitive Carrier* proceeding).

[25] The Commission defined market power as "the ability to raise prices by restricting output" and as "the ability to raise and maintain prices above the competitive level without driving away so many customers as to make the increase unprofitable." *See Competitive Carrier Fourth Report and Order*, 95 FCC 2d at 558, para. 7.

long-distance services, to be dominant in the interstate, long-distance market (including the long-distance private line market). It also found AT&T's 23 local telephone companies as well as independent, incumbent local telephone companies to be dominant, because they "possess control of essential facilities."[26] The Commission further found that specialized common carriers and resale carriers, both of which provided interstate, long-distance services in competition with AT&T, to be nondominant.

The Commission determined that nondominant carriers were unable to charge unreasonable rates or engage in discriminatory practices that contravene the requirements of the Communications Act, both because they lacked market power and because affected customers always had the option of taking service from an incumbent dominant carrier whose rates, terms, and conditions for interstate services remained subject to close scrutiny by the Commission.[27] Accordingly, the Commission gradually relaxed its regulations of nondominant carriers. Specifically, the Commission eliminated rate regulation for nondominant carriers and presumed that tariffs filed by nondominant carriers were reasonable and lawful. It also streamlined tariff filing requirements, which, *inter alia*, had required dominant carriers to file tariffs with notice periods of up to 120 days, and to submit cost support with their tariffs. For nondominant carriers, in contrast, the Commission required only that tariffs be filed on 14 days notice and did not require any cost support. Finally, the Commission reduced existing Section 214 requirements, which required dominant carriers to file a request for authorization before constructing new lines; under the Commission's streamlined rules, nondominant carriers only had to file a simple, semi-annual report on circuit additions, but did not have to obtain preauthorization.[28]

---

[26] *Competitive Carrier First Report and Order*, 85 FCC 2d at 22-24. The Commission specifically noted that it would "treat control of bottleneck facilities as prima facie evidence of market power requiring detailed regulatory scrutiny. *Id.*, at 21. The Commission also found Western Union, domestic satellite carriers, and miscellaneous common carriers that relay video signals to be dominant in various relevant markets. *Id.*, at 24-28. It acknowledged, however, that market developments were likely to erode the market power of these carriers over time.

[27] *Id.*, at 31.

[28] *Competitive Carrier First Report and Order*, 85 FCC 2d at 31-37, 39-44. Subsequently, the Commission announced a policy of permissive "forbearance," under which it would forbear from applying the tariff filing requirements of Section 203 and the entry, exit, and construction authorization requirments of Section 214 to nondominant carriers. *See Competitive Carrier Second Report and Order*, 91 FCC 2d at 73; *Competitive Carrier Fourth Report and Order*, 95 FCC 2d at 557; *Competitive Carrier Fifth Report and Order*, 98 FCC 2d at 1193, 1209. In 1985, the Commission decided to shift from "permissive" to "mandatory" forbearance, thus requiring detariffing by all nondominant carriers. *Competitive Carrier, Sixth Report and Order*, at 99 FCC 2d at 1030-32. A federal court of appeals reversed this finding, holding that the Commission lacked statutory authority to prohibit the filing of tariffs, and in a subsequent appeal, the court further found that the Commission lacked the authority to allow permissive detariffing.[28] *See MCI v. FCC*, 765

Streamlining the Regulation of AT&T: As competition developed in the inter-state, long-distance market, the Commission initiated two proceedings to deter-mine whether it should streamline its regulation of AT&T, the sole dominant long-distance carrier. In 1990, the Commission initiated the *Interstate Interexchange Competition* proceeding to consider streamlining the regulation of certain AT&T services.[29] After analyzing the level of competition for particular classes of long-distance service, the Commission found that certain services provided by AT&T had become "substantially competitive," and accordingly, it streamlined the regu-lation of those services.[30] Specifically, for services that it found to be subject to substantial competition, the Commission removed those services from price cap regulation (*i.e.*, eliminated rate regulation), reduced the notice period for tariff filings relating to those services; and eliminated the cost-support requirement for those tariffed services.[31] In addition, the Commission permitted AT&T and other interstate long-distance carriers to offer services pursuant to individually negoti-ated contracts (*i.e.*, to offer contract tariffs).[32]

Subsequently, AT&T filed a petition to be reclassified as a nondominant carrier in the provision of both interstate, interexchange services. In 1995, the Commis-sion granted AT&T's motion, based on its finding that "AT&T lacked individual market power in the interstate, domestic, interexchange market."[33] Thus, the Commission freed AT&T from price cap regulation for all of its domestic, inter-state, interexchange services, subjected it to the same streamlined tariffing and Section 214 regulations that applied to its nondominant competitors, and elimi-nated certain accounting and reporting requirements applicable only to dominant

---

F.2d 1186 (D.C. Cir. 1985); *AT&T v. FCC,* 1993 WL 260778 (D.C. Cir. 1993), *aff'd MCI v. AT&T,* 512 U.S. 218 (1994).

[29] *Competition in the Interstate Interexchange Marketplace,* Notice of Proposed Rulemak-ing, 5 FCC Rcd 2627 (1990); Report and Order, 6 FCC Rcd 5880 (1991) (*First Interstate Interexchange Competition Order*); Memorandum Opinion and Order, 6 FCC Rcd 7569 (1991); Memorandum Opinion and Order, 7 FCC Rcd 2677 (1992); Memorandum Opin-ion and Order on Reconsideration, 8 FCC Rcd 2659 (1993); Second Report and Order, 8 FCC Rcd 3668 (1993) (*Second Interstate Interexchange Competition Order*); Memoran-dum Opinion and Order, 8 FCC Rcd 5046 (1993); Memorandum Opinion and Order on Reconsideration, 10 FCC Rcd 4562 (1995) (collectively referred to as the *Interstate In-terexchange Competition* proceeding).

[30] In the *First Interstate Interexchange Competition Order,* the Commission found that services provided to large- and medium-size business customers had become "substan-tially competitive, while in the *Second Interstate Interexchange Competition Order*, the Commission found that, with the introduction of 800 number portability, the market for 800 services (except for 800 directory assistance where AT&T had a monopoly) had be-come substantially competitive. *See First Interstate Interexchange Competition Order,* 6 FCC Rcd at 5911, para. 188; *Second Interstate Interexchange Competition Order,* 8 FCC Rcd at 3668, para. 1.

[31] *See First Interstate Interexchange Competition Order,* 6 FCC Rcd at 5894, para. 74.

[32] *Id.*, at 5897, at para. 91.

[33] Motion of AT&T Corp. to Be Reclassified as a Nondominant Carrier, Order, 11 FCC Rcd 3271, para. 1, 3356, para. 164 (1995).

carriers.[34] In 1986, the Commission reclassified AT&T as nondominant in the market for international services.[35]

Competitive Safeguards: Where a regulated, vertically integrated firm serves multiple markets, and competition is introduced into some, but not all, of those markets, two sorts of problems may arise. First, if the regulated firm's monopoly services are subject to rate regulation that is responsive to cost changes (such as rate-of-return regulation), while its competitive services are not rate regulated, then the firm has an incentive to shift costs from its competitive services to its monopoly services in order to raise regulated rates.[36] Second, because the regulated firm generally will have an incentive to resist entry by competitors that seek to serve some of the incumbent's customers, it may try to raise rivals' costs in competitive markets through various forms of price and non-price discrimination.[37] It is these two concerns that caused both the U.S. Department of Justice ("DOJ") and the FCC to impose a number of rules designed to prevent or deter such conduct. The examples of the various types of safeguards by the DOJ and the FCC that are briefly discussed below illustrate the kinds of safeguards regulators have adopted to prevent or deter incumbent monopoly telephone firms from engaging in improper cost shifting or from leveraging their market power in one market into a related competitive market.

Prohibition on the Provision of Competitive Services: One approach to preventing leveraging is simply to prohibit the incumbent monopolist from participating in the provision of the competitive services. The *Modification of Final Judgement* ("MFJ"),[38] which ended the government's ten-year antitrust suit against AT&T illustrates this approach.[39] A major condition of the MFJ was that AT&T divest its

---

[34] *Id.,* at 3281, para. 12.

[35] *Motion of AT&T to Be Declared Non-dominant for International Service,* 11 FCC Rcd 17,963 (1996).

[36] This incentive to misallocate costs becomes less important if the firm's monopoly services are subject to pure price cap regulation, since, in that case, a shift of costs to regulated services will not increase the price of those regulated services. Where, however, price cap rules include a provision for profit sharing or a low-end adjustment, or if the price cap or productivity factor (also known as the X factor) is periodically adjusted, then there may still be an incentive to shift costs among services in order to increase regulated rates.

[37] *See, e.g.,In the Matter of Implementation of the Non-Accounting Safeguards of Sections 271 and 272 of the Communications Act of 1934,* First Report and Order and Further Notice of Proposed Rulemaking, *("Non-Accounting Safeguards Order"),* 11 FCC Rcd 21,905, at paras. 10-12 (1996) *In the Matter of Regulatory Treatment of LEC Provision of Interexchange Services Originating in the LEC's Local Exchange Area,* Second Report and Order in CC Docket No. 96-149 and Third Report and Order in CC Docket No. 96-61 *("LEC Classification Order").*12 FCC Rcd 15756, at para. 98 (1997)

[38] *U.S. v. AT&T,* 552 F. Supp. 131 (D.C. 1982)

[39] In 1974, the DOJ filed an antitrust suit against AT&T alleging that AT&T had used its bottleneck control over local networks to monopolize or attempt to monopolize the market for long-distance services. That suit was settled when the parties entered into a con-

local operating companies, which were reorganized into seven Regional Bell Operating Companies ("RBOCs"). AT&T was to retain its long-distance business, its manufacturing arm and its Bell Laboratories research branch. The RBOCs were to retain the local monopoly telephone operations, but were barred from providing interLATA long-distance services and information services[40] and from manufacturing customer premises equipment.[41]

Structural Safeguards: Another approach to preventing leveraging is to impose structural safeguards, such as requiring the incumbent monopolist to provide competitive services through a structurally separate subsidiary. Structural safeguards may vary significantly in the degree of separation required between the incumbent monopolist's regulated services and competitive services. For example, the Telecommunications Act of 1996 ("1996 Act"), which detailed procedures whereby Bell Operating Companies ("BOCs") could obtain authorization to provide Inter-LATA telecommunications services, required that BOCs that sought to provide such services must do so through a separate subsidiary or affliliate that complied with the provisions of Section 272 of the Act.[42] Section 272 requires that the separate affiliate must: (1) operate independently of the BOC; (2) maintain separate books and records (in a manner prescribed by the Commission); (3) have separate officers, directors, and employees; (4) not obtain credit under any arrangement that would permit the creditor, upon default, to have recourse against the BOC; and (5) conduct all transactions with the BOC "on an arm's length basis with any such transactions reduced to writing and available for public inspection."[43] In addition, Section 272 contains non-discrimination safeguards that prohibit BOCs from discriminating in favor of its affiliate "in the provision or procurement of goods,

---

sent decree. The consent decree, as approved by the federal district court, was the MFJ. *See, e.g.,* BROCK, G. (1994), at 152-167.

[40] Under the MFJ, the United States was divided into over a 100 Local Access and Transport Areas ("LATAs"). Each state contained one or more LATAs. InterLATA telecommunications services are defined as services that involve "telecommunications between a point located in a local access and transport areas and a point located outside such area." 47 U.S.C. § 3(21).

[41] BROCK, G. (1994), AT 162; HUBER, P., KELLOGG, M., & THORN, J. (1999), at 372-73. In 1991, the district court modified the MFJ to permit the RBOCs to provide intra-LATA information services. *Id.,* at 412.

[42] The Act also required BOCs that sought to manufacture customers premises equipment or to provide interLATA telecommunications services or interLATA information services to do so through a separate subsidiary that complied with Section 272. *See* 47 U.S.C. § 272(a)(2).

[43] 47 U.S.C. § 272(b). *See also Implementation of the Non-Accounting Safeguards of Sections 271 and 272 of the Communications Act,* First Report and Order and Further Notice of Proposed Rulemaking, *("Non-Accounting Safeguards Order")*11 FCC Rcd 21905, at paras. 146-193 (1996); *Accounting Safeguards Under the Telecommunications Act of 1996,* Report and Order, *("Accounting Safeguards Order"),* 11 FCC Rcd 17,539 (1996).

services, facilities, and information, or in the establishment of standards." Finally, the section requires the BOC to conduct a biennial audit.[44]

In contrast, the Commission imposed much less stringent separate subsidiary requirements on smaller, independent incumbent LECs (*i.e.,* non-BOC incumbent LECs) that provided interstate, interexchange services. In that case, the Commission likewise required that the independent LEC create a separate subsidiary for the provision of interstate, interexchange telecommunications services. The separate subsidiary, however, was only required to: (1) maintain separate books of account; (2) not jointly own transmission or switching facilities with the LEC; (3) acquire any services from its affiliated local exchange companies at tariffed rates, terms, and conditions; and (4) comply with the Commission's accounting rules governing transactions between affiliates.[45] Thus, there can be significant variations in the degree of required separation between the incumbent provide of monopoly services and its affiliate that provides competitive services.[46]

Equal Access Requirments: Fearing that the RBOCs would continue to favor AT&T over its competitors even after divestiture, the DOJ through the MFJ, and the Commission, through its *Equal Access* proceeding, adopted various rules intended to ensure that AT&T's long-distance competitors had the same access to local telephone networks as AT&T.[47] Among other things, these equal access requirements included a requirement that customers be able to reach their presubscribed long-distance carrier by simply dialing a "1" rather than having to dial an access code.[48] They also required incumbent LECs to provide to all long-distance carriers exchange access, information access, and related services on an unbundled tariffed basis and on non-discriminatory rates terms and conditions.[49]

Other Safeguards: The Commission has adopted numerous other types of safeguards, as well. For example, dominant carriers are subject to extensive accounting rules, which include rules for allocating costs between regulated and nonregulated services and between an incumbent and its affiliates.[50] Similarly, the

---

[44] 47 U.S.C. § 272(c) and (d). *Non-Accounting Safeguards Order*, 11 FCC Rcd at paras. 194-236.

[45] *Competitive Carrier Fifth Report and Order*, 98 FCC 2d at 1198, para. 9. *See also LEC Classification Order*, 12 FCC Rcd at para. 162.

[46] *See also Amendment of Section 64,702 of the Commission's Rules and Regulations, Second Computer Inquiry*, Final Decision, 77 FCC 2d 384 (hereinafter *Computer II), modified on recons.,* 84 FCC 2d 50 (1980), *further modified on recons.,* 88 FCC 2d 512 (1981), *aff'd sub nom. Computer and Communications Indus. v. FCC,* 693 F.2d 198 (D.C. Cir. 1982), *cert. denied,* 461 U.S. 938 (1983) (imposing strict separate subsidiary requirements AT&T (before divestiture) if it wished to provide "enhanced" services.)

[47] *U.S. v. AT&T,* 552 F.Supp. at 225-28; *MTS and WATS Market Structure Phase III,* Report and Order, 100 FCC 2d 860 (1985). *See generally* BROCK, G. (1994), at 162-64; HUBER, P., KELLOGG, M. & THORNE, J. (1999), at 423-24, 771-75.

[48] *Id.,* at 772-73; BROCK, G. (1994), at 163.

[49] *Id.*

[50] *Separation of Costs of Regulated Telephone Service from Costs of Nonregulated Activities,* Report and Order, *(Joint Cost Order),* 2 FCC Rcd 1298 (1987), *on recons.,* 2 FCC

Commission imposed various sorts of reporting requirements on certain dominant local carriers, including quality of service reports.[51]

2.3 The Introduction of Competition into Local Telephone Markets

In 1996, the United States Congress passed, and the President signed into law, a statute that fundamentally changed telecommunications regulation in the United States. Rejecting the view that local telephone markets were natural monopolies,[52] the *Telecommunications Act of 1996 (the "Act" or the "1996 Act"),*[53] sought to introduce competition into local telephone markets and to facilitate increased competition in telecommunications markets already subject to competition. The Act also sought to encourage deregulation as competition rendered regulation unnecessary, and thus contained provisions intended to encourage deregulation. The Act divided responsibility for introducing local competition between the FCC and state regulators.

2.3.1 The Local Competition Provisions

The Act contains a number of detailed provisions designed to open up local telephone markets to competition. These local competition provisions impose on all carriers, but particularly incumbent local exchange carriers (LECs), additional regulatory obligations necessary to foster and sustain local competition.

In brief, the Act imposes certain obligations on *all telecommunications carriers*, the most important of which is the obligation "to interconnect directly or indirectly with the facilities or equipment of other telecommunications carriers."[54] In addition, the Act imposes certain, more stringent obligations, on *all local exchange carriers*. These obligations include: (1) the duty not to prohibit, or to im-

---

Rcd 6283 (1983) (*Joint Cost Reconsideration Order*); *on further recons.*, 3 FCC Rcd 6701 (1988) (*Joint Cost Further Reconsideration Order*). *See* § III.A *infra*.

[51] *Automated Reporting Requirements for Certain Class A and Tier 1 Telephone Companies (Parts 31, 43, 69, and 60 of the FCC's Rules),* Report and Order, 2 FCC Rcd 5770 (1987), *on recons.*, 3 FCC Rcd 6375 (1988).

[52] In rejecting the view that local telephony was a natural monopoly, Congress was influenced in part by the development of competition in other telecommunications markets, and in other markets that had previously been thought to be natural monopolies. It was also influenced, however, by the development of "competitive access providers" ("CAPs"), which had built facilities to bypass local telephone companies in order to avoid the payment of access charges, by various state regulatory commissions that had begun to introduce regulations intended to open up local telephone markets to competition; and by statements by cable television companies that claimed that they were planning to provide local telephone service over their cable networks. *See, e.g.,* HUBER, P., KELLOGG, M. & THORNE, J. (1999), at 58-59.

[53] *Telecommunications Act of 1996*, Pub. L. No. 104-104, 110 Stat.56, 47 U.S.C. §§151 *et seq.*

[54] 47 U.S.C. § 251(a)(1).

pose unreasonable or discriminatory conditions on the resale of the LEC's tele-communications services; (2) the duty to provide number portability; (3) the duty to provide dialing parity to competing providers of local telephone service and to provide non-discriminatory access to telephone numbers, operator services, and directory assistance; (4) the duty to afford access to poles, ducts, conduits, and rights of way of such carrier to competing carriers; and (5) the duty to establish "reciprocal compensation arrangements for the transport and termination" of tele-communications traffic.[55]

Finally, and most importantly, the Act imposes certain additional obligations on *all incumbent local exchange carriers* (*i.e.,* the current local telephone monopolies). First, the Act requires incumbent LECs to provide to requesting carriers physical interconnection with the incumbent's network at "any technically feaisble point" in the incumbent's network. The interconnection must be at least equal in quality to that provided by the incumbent to itself , to any subsidiary, or to any other party to which the incumbent provides interconnection, and the interconnection must be provided on rates, terms and conditions that are "just, reasonable, and non-discriminatory.[56] Second, the Act requires incumbent LECs to provide "nondiscriminatory access to network elements on an unbundled basis at any technically feasible point on rates, terms, and conditions that are just, reasonable, and nondiscrimintory."[57] Third, the Act addresses specific methods of interconnection that are particularly important to the development of local competition. Specifically, the Act requires incumbent LECs to provide *physical collocation* of equipment necessary for interconnection or access to network elements at the incumbent's premises, on rates, terms, and conditions that are just reasonable, and nondiscriminatory.[58] Fourth, incumbent LECs are required to "offer for resale at wholesale rates any telecommunications service that the carrier provides at retail to subscribers who are not telecommunications carriers."[59] Finally, the Act imposes on incumbent LECs a duty to negotiate in good faith the terms and conditions of interconnection agreements with requesting carriers.[60]

The 1996 Act also sets forth rules governing the procedures for negotiation, arbitration, and approval of agreements between requesting carriers and incumbent

---

[55] 47 U.S.C. § 251(b).

[56] 47 U.S.C. § 251(c)(2). *See also In the Matter of Implementation of the Local Competition Provisions in the Telecommunications Act of 1996*, First Report and Order (hereinafter *Local Competition First Report and Order*), 11 FCC Rcd 15499, at paras. 172-225 (1996)

[57] 47 U.S.C. § 251(c)(3). *See also Local Competition First Report and Order*, 11 FCC Rcd at paras. 226-541.

[58] 47 U.S.C. § 251(c)(6). The incumbent LEC may provide for virtual collocation, however, if it demonstrates to the state commission that physical collocation is not practical for technical reasons or because of space limitations. *See also Local Competition First Report and Order*, 11 FCC Rcd at paras. 542-617.

[59] 47 U.S.C. § 251(c)(4). *See also Local Competition First Report and Order,* 11 FCC Rcd at paras. 863-984.

[60] 47 U.S.C. § 251(c)(1). *See also Local Competition First Report and Order*, 11 FCC Rcd at paras. 138-143.

LECs. Basically, under the Act, if the parties can voluntarily negotiate terms and conditions of an agreement, the agreement need not comply with the specific local competition provisions of the Act, and state commissions must approve such negotiated agreements as long as they do not discriminate against third parties and are in the public interest.[61] If the parties cannot reach agreement, then either party can seek mediation or arbitration from the state commission. Arbitrated agreements must be approved by the state commission, which must find that the agreement complies with the statute and the Commission's implementing rules, does not discriminate against third parties, and is in the public interest.[62]

In designing the local competition provisions, Congress recognized that, even with the removal of regulatory barriers to entry, economic barriers to entry would still remain. These economic barriers arose from the large sunk investments required for entry, the economies of scale, scope and density associated with local telephone networks, and the incumbent telephone companies' control over inputs that are essential to new entrants. For example, without interconnection between the incumbent and a new entrant, the entrant's customers would be unable to call the vast majority of telephone subscribers who subscribe to the incumbent. Similarly, Congress recognized that incumbents possessed economies of density, connectivity and scale that would allow it to offer service at a lower incremental cost than could new entrants.[63] Finally, Congress expressly recognized that "it is unlikely that competitors will have a fully redundant network in place when they initially offer local service, because the investment necessary is so significant."[64] For these reasons, the Act imposed new wholesale obligations on incumbent LECs, with respect to interconnection, unbundled network elements, collocation, and resale, so that entrants could obtain the inputs necessary for them to offer service. Morevoer, in light of these wholesale obligations imposed on incumbent LECs, it is clear that the Act contemplates three alternative paths for competitive entry: the construction by the entrant of an entirely new network; reliance by the entrant on the incumbent's network elements; and resale by the entrant of the incumbent's services.[65]

Congress further recognized that incumbent LECs are likely to have little incentive to assist competitors in entering local markets. Instead, incumbents are likely to have both the incentive and ability to raise rivals' costs by raising the price of essential inputs or by engaging in non-price discrimination. To address this potential for discrimination and anticompetitive foreclosure by incumbents, the Act contains a number of competitive safeguards. For example, to constrain the ability of incumbents to raise rivals' costs in this manner, Congress specified that the price for interconnection and unbundled network elements should be "cost-based," "just and reasonable," and "nondiscriminatory."[66] These require-

---

[61] 47 U.S.C. § 252(a).

[62] 47 U.S.C. § 252(b).

[63] *Local Competition First Report and Order*, 11 FCC Rcd at paras. 10-11.

[64] Conf. Rep. No. 104-230, 104th Cong., 2d Sess.1 (1996).

[65] *Local Competition First Report and Order*, 11 FCC Rcd at para. 12.

[66] 47 U.S.C. §§ 251(c); 252(d). In implementing the local competition provisions, the Commission adopted rules requiring that the price of interconnection and unbundled

ments resemble the equal access safeguards that the Commission adopted when competition was introduced into the long-distance market.

Despite these statutory safeguards, there is considerable evidence that incumbent LECs have continued to try to discriminate against entrants in the provision of these inputs. For example, there have been numerous complaints that incumbent LECs have denied requests for collocation space or have provided such space only after significant delays. Similarly, there have been complaints that incumbent LECs have failed to provision, delayed in provisioning, or made errors in provisioning network elements requested by entrants. Finally, competitors have complained that incumbent LECs have attempted to charge unreasonable rates for interconnection and network elements. For this reason, a number of state commissions have imposed various types of performance reporting requirements and performance standards. In addition, the FCC recently issued a notice of proposed rulemaking seeking comment on whether it should adopt federal performance reporting requirements.[67] Finally, some state commissions have considered requiring structural separation between the incumbent LEC's retail and wholesale operations. Thus, in introducing competition into local markets, both Congress, which drafted the legislation, and the regulators, which are attempting to implement it, have recognized and attempted to deal with the problem that incumbents may exploit their control over bottleneck facilities and services to disadvantage new and emerging competitors

2.3.2 Deregulation

As previously noted, another major goal of the Act is to encourage deregulation where appropriate, and the Act contains specific provisions designed to facilitate deregulation. Thus, the Act authorizes the Commission to forbear from applying any regulation or provision of the Act if it finds that three statutory criteria are satisfied. These criteria are that: (1) "enforcement of such regulation . . . is not necessary to ensure that the charges, practices, classifications by, for, or in connection with that telecommunications carrier or telecommunications service are just and reasonable . . .;" (2) "enforcement of such regulation . . . is not necessary for the protection of consumers;" and (3) "forbearance . . . is consistent with the public interest." With respect to the third criterion, the Act further directs the Commission to "consider whether forbearance from enforcing the provision or regulation will promote competitive market conditions, including the extent to which such forbearance will enhance competition among providers of telecommu

---

network elements be based on forward-looking economic cost. *Local Competition First Report and Order*, 11 FCC Rcd at paras. 618-984.

[67] *In the Matter of Performance Measures and Standards for Unbundled Network Elements and Interconnection*, Notice of Proposed Rulemaking, CC Docket No. 01-318 (released Nov. 19, 2001).

nications services."[68] The Act specifically prohibits the Commission, however, from forbearing "from applying the requirements of section 251(c) [which details the obligations of incumbent LECs] or 271 [which specifies the requirements BOCs must satisfy before they can provide interLATA services] . . . until it determines that those requirements have been fully implemented."[69]

In addition, the Act requires the Commission, every two years, to review all regulations under the Act, and to determine whether each such regulation "is no longer necessary in the public interest as a result of meaningful competition between providers" of telecommunications services.[70]

The Commission has employed both these provisions in streamlining its existing regulations. For example, in 1996, the Commission used its new forbearance powers to order mandatory detariffing of rates by nondominant interexchange carriers.[71] In 1999, the Commission adopted an order that streamlined the regulation of certain interstate access services by incumbent LECs subject to price-cap regulation.[72] The order was designed to grant greater pricing flexibility to incumbent LECs whose services were subject to increasing competitive pressures, while at the same time ensuring that the incumbents did not use this flexibility to deter efficient entry or engage in exclusionary conduct or to raise rates to unreasonable levels for customers that lack competitive alternatives. More specifically, the order streamlined the introduction of new services and allowed greater geographic deaveraging of rates for transport services. It also established a framework for granting price-cap incumbent LECs greater pricing flexibility with respect to interstate access services in specific geographic areas, once the LEC demonstrates that certain competitive indicia have been achieved. A final example of the Commission's deregulatory efforts has been its efforts to simplify the accounting requirements imposed on incumbent LECs, by reason of their classification as dominant carriers.[73]

Thus, as with the introduction of competition into the long-distance market, the introduction of competition into local markets required two types of regulatory

---

[68] 47 U.S.C § 160.

[69] 47 U.S.C. § 160(d).

[70] 47 U.S.C. § 161.

[71] *Policy and Rules Concerning the Interstate, Interexchange Marketplace; Implementation of Section 254(g) of the Communications Act of 1934, as Amended,* CC Docket No. 96-61, Second Report and Order, 11 FCC Rcd 20730 (1996), *stay granted, MCI Telecommunications Corp. v. FCC,* No. 96-1459 (D.C.Cir. Feb. 13, 1997), Order on Reconsideration, 12 FCC Rcd 15014 (1997), Second Order on Reconsideration, 14 FCC Rcd 6004 (1999).

[72] *In the Matter of Access Charge Reform,* Fifth Report and Order and Further Notice of Proposed Rulemaking, 14 FCC Rcd 14221 (1999)

[73] *See, e.g., In the Matter of Comprehensive Review of the Accounting Requirements and ARMIS Reporting Requirements for Incumbent Local Exchange Carriers: Phase I,* CC Docket No. 99-253, Report and Order, (rel. Mar. 8, 2000); *In the Matter of 2000 Biennial Regulatory Review – Comprehensive Review of the Accounting Requirements and ARMIS Reporting Requirements for Incumbent Local Exchange Carriers: Phase 2,* CC Docket No. 00-199 (rel. Nov. 5, 2001).

adjustments. First, Congress and the FCC adopted new regulations to open local markets to competition and to prevent incumbent monopoly providers from using their market power to foreclose emerging competition. Second, the introduction of competition into local markets permitted the Commission to streamline or eliminate certain regulations as competition rendered those regulations unnecessary.

3. The Non-Regulation of Enhanced Services and the Internet

3.1 The Non-Regulation of Enhanced Services

In 1966, long before the birth of the Internet, the FCC foresaw the convergence and increasing interdependence of computer and telecommunications technologies. Accordingly, it opened a formal inquiry, the *Computer I Inquiry* into the use of computer-based services over telephone lines, and the regulatory and policy issues posed by this convergence.[74]

In *Computer I,* the Commissions made two decisions that laid the foundation for its regulatory approach to services provided by computer data processing service providers. First, the Commission concluded that the public interest would not be served by regulating such data processing services, since the provision of such services is "essentially competitive."[75] Second, while the Commission determined that the participation of common carriers in the data processing market would benefit consumers, it expressed concern that common carriers might engage in unfair competition. The dangers of unfair competition, the Commission explained, relate "primarily to the alleged ability of common carriers to favor their own data processing activities by discriminatory services, cross-subsidization, improper pricing of common carrier services, and related anticompetitive practices and activities."[76] Accordingly, the Commission concluded that there was a need for competitive safeguards; and it required common carriers seeking to offer data services to do so through a structurally separate affiliate.[77] These safeguards were intended to ensure that carriers would not "give any preferential treatment to their data processing affiliates" and that competing data service providers would there-

---

[74] *In the Matter of Regulatory and Policy Problems Presented by the Interdependence of Computer and Communications Services and Facilities,* (hereinafter *Computer I Inquiry),* 7 FCC 2d 11 (1966). *See generally,* HUBER, P., KELLOGG, M., & THORNE, J. (1999), at 1086-1103; OXMAN, J. (1999).

[75] The Commission specifically found "that there is ample evidence that data processing services of all kinds are becoming available . . . and that there are no natural or economic barriers to free entry into the market for these services." *Computer I,* Tentative Decision, 28 FCC 2d 291, at para. 20 (1970)

[76] *Computer I,* Final Decision and Order, 28 FCC 2d 267, at para. 12 (1971).

[77] *Id.,* at paras. 12 *et seq.*

fore have nondiscriminatory access to the underlying communications components used in providing their services.[78]

The Commission continued its examination of these issues in the *Computer II* proceeding, which it initiated in 1976.[79] In *Computer II*, the Commission reaffirmed its basic regulatory approach to the provision of computer data services, but refined its analysis. In particular, the Commission, attempting to define and distinguish regulated telecommunications services and unregulated data services, created the categories of "basic" services and "enhanced" services.[80] The Commission also specified in greater detail the extent of structural separation required between the incumbent telephone provider and its enhanced services affiliate.[81] Specifically, the enhanced services separate subsidiary was required to: (1) obtain all transmission facilities from the parent under tariff; (2) elect separate officers; (3) maintain separate books of account; (4) employ separate operating, installation, and maintenance personnel; (5) perform its own marketing and advertising; (6) enter into transactions with any affiliated manufacturing company only on an arm's length basis; (7) utilize separate computer facilities in providing enhanced services; and (8) in general develop its own software or contract with non-affiliates for such software.[82]

Thus, in *Computer II*, the Commission reaffirmed its commitment to its essential policy of regulating only the common carrier "basic" transmission service, while exempting "enhanced" services from common carrier regulation. The Commission also continued to emphasize the need for competitive safeguards to ensure that common carriers did not compete unfairly against unaffiliated computer data services providers.

In 1986, the Commission, in its *Computer III* decision,[83] offered an alternative set of competitive safeguards to protect competitive providers of enhanced services. Specifically, the Commission gave AT&T and the BOCs that sought to

---

[78] *Id.,*at para. 21.

[79] *In the Matter of Amendment of Section 64.702 of the Commission's Rules and Regulations (Second Computer Inquiry),*(hereinafter *Computer II*), Notice of Inquiry and Proposed Rulemaking, 61 FCC 2d 103 (1976).

[80] The Commission defined the term "basic" service, which referred to traditional common carrier telecommunications offerings as "the offering of transmission capacity for the movement of information." *Computer II*, Final Decision, (*Computer II Final Decision*), 77 FCC 2d 584, at para. 93 (1980). The Commission defined "enhanced services" as:
services, offered over common carrier transmission facilities used in interstate communications, which employ computer processing applications that act on the format, content, code, protocol, or similar aspects of the subscriber's transmitted information; provide the subscriber additional, different or restructured information; or involve subscriber interaction with stored information.
46 C.F.R. § 64.702(a).

[81] *Computer II Final Decision*, 77 FCC 2d at paras. 190-266.

[82] *Id.*, at paras. 233-260.

[83] *In the Matter of Amendment of Section 64.702 of the Commission's Rules and Regulations,* Report and Order, (*Computer III*), 104 FCC 2d 958 (1986), *vacated California v. FCC*, 905 F.2d 1217 (9th Cir. 1990).

provide enhanced services the option of continuing to comply with *Computer II's* strict separate subsidiary requirements, or of complying with new "nonstructural safeguards."

There were two primary components to these nonstructural safeguards: Open Network Architecture ("ONA") requirements, and detailed cost allocation requirements.[84] Under the Commission's ONA requirements, carriers opting for the nonstructural approach were required to submit a plan demonstrating how they would unbundle the basic telecommunications services used to provide enhanced services and make them available to competing enhanced service providers.[85] Because ONA was a long-term program that would take time to implement, the Commission also established a transitional program, known as Comparably Efficient Interconnection ("CEI"). Under the Commission's CEI rules, a carrier, before it could offer a new enhanced service, had to submit a plan to the Commission, explaining how it would make available to all competing enhanced service providers the basic services used in the provision of that enhanced service.[86]

Finally, in order to prevent any improper shifting of costs from unregulated to regulated activities, the Commission, in its *Joint Cost* proceeding,[87] also adopted new, and more detailed, accounting rules that applied to all incumbent local exchange carriers and to dominant interexchange carriers. The *Joint Cost Order* established two sets of separate, but complementary, rules. The first set establishes a process to separate the costs associated with the provision of regulated services from the costs associated with the provision of nonregulated services. The second set of rules governs transactions between a carrier and its affiliates.[88]

Thus, in the *Computer Inquiries*, the Commission made clear that it would not subject enhanced services to common carrier regulation, since it believed that those services were competitive. At the same time, the Commission acknowledged the possibility that dominant telecommunications carriers might attempt to leverage their market power in certain telecommunications markets into the competitive enhanced services market, and accordingly, it established competitive safeguards to prevent or deter such leveraging.

3.2 The Non-Regulation of the Internet

The Origins of the Internet: The current Internet can be traced back to ARPANET, a network developed in the late 1960s and early 1970s by the Advanced Research

---

[84] *See* BROCK, G. (1994), at 224-28.

[85] *Id.*, at paras. 201-222.

[86] *Id.*, at paras. 111-193.

[87] *Separation of Costs of Regulated Telephone Service from Costs of Nonregulated Activities*, Report and Order, (*Joint Cost Order*), 2 FCC Rcd 1298 (1987), *on recons.*, 2 FCC Rcd 6283 (1983) (*Joint Cost Reconsideration Order*); *on further recons.*, 3 FCC Rcd 6701 (1988) (*Joint Cost Further Reconsideration Order*).

[88] In *Computer III*, the Commission also aimposed new rules governing disclosure of network changes and the handling of customer proprietary network information. *Computer III Order*, 104 FCC 2d, at paras. 241-65.

Projects Administration of the U.S. Department of Defense. ARPANET was designed to connect the computers of universities and defense contractors.[89] In 1986,
the U.S. National Science Foundation ("NSF") initiated the development of the
NSFNET, which was intended to encourage more academic institutions to interconnect their computer networks. The NSFNET included funding for a national
backbone to connect academic institutions across the United States. Because the
NSFNET was intended for academic purposes, the NSF enforced an "Acceptable
Use Policy," which prohibited use of the NSFNET national backbone for commercial purposes.[90] At the same time, the NSF encouraged regional networks to
seek commercial customers, in order to exploit economies of scale and thus lower
unit capacity costs.[91] This encouragement of commercial traffic at the local and
regional levels, combined with the prohibition on the use of the NSF national
backbone for commercial purposes, created significant incentives for construction
of private, long-haul networks, such as PSI, UUNET and others.[92]

By the early 1990s, the NSF began to recognize the commercial opportunities
offered by the Internet and began considering the possibility of ending its support
of NSFNET and relying instead on the development of private, interconnected
backbones. The NSF believed that a competitive market for Internet services,
including Internet backbone services, could function and be sustained, and it recognized that its continued support of NSFNET, which provided backbone service
at no cost, might actually be deterring the development of private backbones.[93]
Accordingly, in 1993, the NSF initiated the transition to a private Internet by re-
leasing Solicitation 93-52, which described its view of the future structure of a
private Internet that did not rely on government support.[94] In 1995, the NSF ended
its funding of NSFNET.[95]

Since the NSF ended its support of NSFNET, the Internet in the United States
has experienced steady and rapid growth. According to a recent report by the U.S.
General Accounting Office ("GAO"), there are now 41 backbone providers with a
national network and many other regional networks.[96] This growth is also seen in
the substantial investments made by Internet backbone providers, the explosion in
Internet applications and content, and the rapid increase in the number of Internet
users. For example, according to another recent GAO report, the number of Internet users in the country increased from 27 million in 1996 to 86 million in 2000.[97]

---

[89] LEINER, B. *et al. (2000)*

[90] *Id.;* CERF, V. (2001); MARCUS, J.S. (1999), at 274..

[91] LEINER, B., *et al.* (2000)

[92] *Id.*

[93] MARCUS, J.S. (1999), at 274.

[94] In order to facilitate the growth of overlapping, competing national backbones, Solicitation 93-52 sought to create a system of geographically dispersed Network Access Points
("NAPs"), each of which was to have a shared packet switch that was to be used to exchange traffic. *Id., at 276;* KENDE, M. (2000), at 5.

[95] *Id.,* at 274; LEINER, B., *et al.* (2000).

[96] U.S. GENERAL ACCOUNTING OFFICE (2001), at 6. Of the 41 national backbone
providers, between five and eight are considered "Tier 1" backbone providers. *Id.*

[97] U.S. GENERAL ACCOUNTING OFFICE (2000), at 8.

Finally, it appears that, with the increase in the number of Internet backbone providers and innovations in fiber and electronics technologies, the price of backbone connectivity has decreased significantly in recent years.[98] Moreover, this growth has taken place in the absence of any industry-specific regulation of the Internet.[99]

Thus, it appears that the Government's prediction that the Internet could become a robustly competitive market that did not require industry-specific regulation appears to have proved accurate. In light of this, the FCC has continued to resist calls for regulating this dynamic and technologically innovative market.

4. Summary and Conclusions

Historically, the United States has applied the antitrust laws to markets that it believed to be workably competitive, and industry-specific regulation to markets where competition was viewed as ineffective or non-sustainable. The telecommunications market was generally considered to be a natural monopoly and therefore subject to industry regulation by both the FCC and state regulators.

In recent decades, as policy-makers have become more aware of the costs and inefficiencies associated with industry-specific regulation, and as competition has developed in markets where competition was thought to be non-sustainable, there has been an increased interest in introducing competition into traditionally regulated markets and reducing regulation as competition renders it unnecessary. The introduction of competition initially into the long-distance telephone market and later into local telephone markets illustrates this trend.

This change in FCC's approach to regulating telecommunications markets necessitated two types of regulatory changes. First, to the extent that the incumbent regulated monopoly has control over bottleneck facilities or services, the FCC has found it necessary to adopt new regulations in the form of competitive safeguards to prevent the incumbent from leveraging its market power so as to foreclose emerging competition. Second, as competition has taken hold in previously monopolized markets, the FCC has gradually deregulated and allowed the discipline of the market to ensure efficient prices and choices for consumers and to encourage rapid innovation.

Three principles appear to underlie the Commission's approach to deregulating telecommunications markets. First, new entrants that do not possess individual market power need not be subjected to the same level of regulatory control as incumbent regulated firms that do possess market power. Second, even dominant carriers need to be given some regulatory flexibility to respond to emerging competition. This is particularly true where implicit subsidies, such as those implemented to further universal service, created incentives for cream-skimming. At the same time, however, the regulator needs to ensure that the incumbent will not use

---

[98] U.S. GENERAL ACCOUNTING OFFICE (2001), at 17.

[99] Of course, the antitrust laws continue to apply to the Internet. For example, mergers of Internet backbones are reviewed by the U.S. DOJ and the FCC. *See, e.g., Application of WorldCom, Inc. and MCI Communications Corp. for Transfer of Control of MCI Communications Corp. to WorldCom, Inc.*, 13 FCC Rcd 18,025 (1998).

this new flexibility to engage in predatory strategies (such as attempting predatory price squeezes or using their control over bottleneck facilities to discriminate against rivals) or to charge unreasonably high rates to customers that lack competitive choices. Finally, regulation of dominant carriers can and should be relaxed when competition has eroded their market power.

In contrast to telecommunications markets, which developed in the nineteenth and early twentieth centuries, the Internet is a new market. By the time that the Internet had begun developing, policy-makers had changed their views and believed that competition, and not regulation, should generally be relied on to ensure efficient prices and rapid innovation. Accordingly, the United States has avoided regulation and instead relied on the antitrust laws, including merger law, to protect the competitiveness of the Internet. This regulatory restraint has enjoyed enormous success to date.

References

Books and Articles
BREYER, S. (1982), Regulation and Its Reform.
BROCK, G.W. (1994), Telecommunications Policy for the Information Age: From Monopoly to Competition.
BROCK, G.W. (1981), The Telecommunications Industry: The Dynamics of Market Structure.
CAVES, R.E. (1962), Air Transport and Its Regulators: An Industry Study.
CERF, V.G. (2001), A Brief History of the Internet and Related Networks, http://www.isoc.org/internet/history/cerf.shtml
DOUGLAS, G.W., MILLER, J.C., III, (1974), Economic Regulation of Domestic Air Transport: Theory and Policy.
HUBER, P.W., KELLOGG, M.K., THORNE, J. (1999), Federal Communications Law, (2d ed.).
KAHN, A.E. (1970), The Economics of Regulation: Principles and Institutions, Vol. 1.
KENDE, M., (2000), The Digital Handshake: Connecting Internet Backbones, OPP Working Paper Series No. 32/2000.
LAVEY, A.S., (1987), The Public Policies That Changed the Telephone Industries into Regulated Monopolies: Lessons from 1915, 39 Fed. Comm. L.J. 171.
LEINER, B., CERF, V.G., *et al.* (2000), A Brief History of the Internet, http://www.isoc.org/internet/history/brief.shtml
MARCUS, J.S. (1999), Designing Wide Area Networks and Internetworks: A Practical Guide.
MEYER, J.R., PECK, M.J., STENASON, J., ZWICK, C. (1959), The Economics of Competition in the Transportation Industries.
MITNICK, B.M. (1980), The Political Economy of Regulation: Creating, Designing, and Removing Regulatory Forms.
OXMAN, J. (1999), The FCC and the Unregulation of the Internet, OPP Working Paper Series No. 31/1999.
POOLE, R.W., JR., ed. (1982), Instead of Regulation.
SCHERER, F.M. (1980), Industrial Market Structure and Economic Performance, 2d ed.
UNITED STATES GENERAL ACCOUNTING OFFICE (2001), Characteristics and Competitiveness of the Internet Backbone Market, October 2001.
UNITED STATES GENERAL ACCOUNTING OFFICE (2000), Technological and Regulatory Factors Affecting Consumer Choice of Internet Providers, October 2000.
VICUSI, W.K., VERNON, J.M., HARRINGTON, J.E. (2000), Economics or Regulation and Antitrust, 3d ed.
WEIMAN, D., LEVIN, R. (1994), Preying for Monopoly: The Case of Southern Bell, 102 J. Pol. Econ. 103.
WEISS, L.W., KLASS, M.W., eds. (1981), Case Studies in Regulation: Revolution and Reform.

Statutes, Commission and Court Decisions, and other References

Access Charge Reform, Fifth Report and Order and Further Notice of Proposed Rulemaking, 14 FCC Rcd 14,221 (1999)

Accounting Safeguards for Common Carriers Under the Telecommunications Act of 1996, First Report and Order, 11 FCC Rcd 17,539 (1996).

Allocation of Frequencies in the Bands Above 890 MHz, Decision, 27 F.C.C. 359 (1959).

Amendment of Section 64,702 of the Commission's Rules and Regulations (Computer II), Notice of Inquiry and Proposed Rulemaking, 61 FCC 2d 103 (1976); Final Decision, 77 FCC 2d 384 (hereinafter *Computer II*), *modified on recons.*, 84 FCC 2d 50 (1980), *further modified on recons.*, 88 FCC 2d 512 (1981), *aff'd sub nom. Computer and Communications Indus. Assn. v. FCC*, 693 F.2d 198 (D.C. Cir. 1982), *cert. denied*, 461 U.S. 938 (1983)

Amendment of Section 64.702 of the Commission's Rules and Regulations, Report and Order, (*ComputerIII*), 104 FCC 2d 958 (1986), *vacated, California v. FCC*, 905 F.2d 1217 (9th Cir. 1990).

Application of WorldCom, Inc. and MCI Communications Corp. for Transfer of Control of MCI Communications Corp. to WorldCom, Inc., 13 FCC Rcd 18,025 (1998).

Automated Reporting Requirements for Certain Class A and Tier 1 Telephone Companies (Parts 31, 43, 69, and 60 of the FCC's Rules), Report and Order, 2 FCC Rcd 5770 (1987), *on recons.*, 3 FCC Rcd 6375 (1988).

Competition in the Interstate Interexchange Marketplace, Notice of Proposed Rulemaking, 5 FCC Rcd 2627 (1990); Report and Order, 6 FCC Rcd 5880 (1991) (*First Interstate Interexchange Competition Order*); Memorandum Opinion and Order, 6 FCC Rcd 7569 (1991); Memorandum Opinion and Order, 7 FCC Rcd 2677 (1992); Memorandum Opinion and Order on Reconsideration, 8 FCC Rcd 2659 (1993); Second Report and Order, 8 FCC Rcd 3668 (1993) (*Second Interstate Interexchange Competition Order*); Memorandum Opinion and Order, 8 FCC Rcd 5046 (1993); Memorandum Opinion and Order on Reconsideration, 10 FCC Rcd 4562 (1995) (collectively referred to as the *Interstate Interexchange Competition* proceeding)

Conf. Rep. No. 104-230, 104th Cong., 2d Sess.1 (1996)

Establishment of Policies and Procedures for Consideration of Application to Provide Specialized Common Carrier Services in the Domestic Public Point-to-Point Microwave Radio Service, First Report and Order, 29 F.C.C. 2d 870 (1971)

Federal-State Joint Board on Universal Service, First Report and Order, 12 FCC Rcd 8776 (1997)

Implementation of the Local Competition Provisions in the Telecommunications Act of 1996, First Report and Order, 11 FCC Rcd 15499 (1996)

Implementation of the Non-Accounting Safeguards of Sections 271 and 272 of the Communications Act, First Report and Order and Further Notice of Proposed Rulemaking, 11 FCC Rcd 21905, (1996)

Mann-Elkins Act of 1910, ch. 309, 36 Stat. 539 (1910)*MCI Telecomms. Corp. v. FCC*, 580 F.2d 590 (D.C.Cir. 1978)

MCI v. FCC, 765 F.2d 1186 (D.C. Cir. 1985)

Motion of AT&T Corp. to Be Reclassified as a Non-dominant Carrier, Order, 11 FCC Rcd 3271 (1995).

Motion of AT&T to Be Declared Non-dominant for International Service, 11 FCC Rcd 17,963 (1996).

MTS and WATS Market Structure Phase III, Report and Order, 100 FCC 2d 860 (1985)

Performance Measures and Standards for Unbundled Network Elements and Interconnection, Notice of Proposed Rulemaking, CC Docket No. 01-318 (released Nov. 19, 2001).

Policy and Rules Concerning Rates for Competitive Common Carrier Services and Facilities Authorizations Therefor, CC Docket No. 79-252, Notice of Inquiry and Proposed Rulemaking, 77 FCC 2d 308 (1979); First Report and Order, 85 FCC 2d 1 (1980) (*First Report and Order*); Further Notice of Proposed Rulemaking, 84 FCC 2d 445 (1981) (*Further Notice of Proposed Rulemaking*); Second Further Notice of Proposed Rulemaking, FCC 82-187, 47 Fed. Reg. 17,308 (1982); Second Report and Order, 91 FCC 2d 59 (1982) (*Second Report and Order*); Order on Reconsideration, 93 FCC 2d 54 (1983); Third Report and Order, 48 Fed. Reg. 46,791 (1983) (*Third Report and Order*); Fourth Report and Order, 95 FCC 2d 554 (1983) (*Fourth Report and Order*); *vacated, AT&T v. FCC*, 978 F.2d 727 (D.C. Cir. 1992), *cert. denied, MCI Telecommunications Corp. v. AT&T*, 113 S.Ct. 3020 (1993); Fifth Report and Order, 98 FCC 2d 1191 (1984) (*Fifth Report and Order*); Sixth Report and Order, 99 FCC 2d 1020 (1985), *vacated MCI Telecommunications Corp. v. FCC*, 765 F.2d 1186 (D.C. Cir. 1985) (collectively referred to as the *Competitive Carrier* proceeding).

Policy and Rules Concerning the Interstate, Interexchange Marketplace; Implementation of Section 254(g) of the Communications Act of 1934, as Amended, CC Docket No. 96-61, Second Report and Order, 11 FCC Rcd 20730 (1996), *stay granted, MCI Telecommunications Corp. v. FCC*, No. 96-1459 (D.C.Cir. Feb. 13, 1997), Order on Reconsideration, 12 FCC Rcd 15014, Second Order on Reconsideration, 14 FCC Rcd 6004 (1999).

Radio Act of 1927. 44 Stat. 1162 (1927)

Regulatory and Policy Problems Presented by the Interdependence of Computer and Communications Services and Facilities, (Computer I Inquiry), 7 FCC 2d 11 (1966); Report and Further Notice of Inquiry, (*Computer I Report and Further Notice*), 17 FCC 2d 587 (1969); Tentative Decision, (*Computer I Tentative Decision*) 28 FCC 2d 291 (1970); Final Decision and Order, 28 FCC 2d 267 (1971)

Regulatory Treatment of LEC Provision of Interexchange Services Originating in the LEC's Local Exchange Area, Second Report and Order in CC Docket No. 96-149 and Third Report and Order in CC Docket No. 96-61 12 FCC Rcd 15756 (1997)

Separation of Costs of Regulated Telephone Service from Costs of Nonregulated Activities, Report and Order, (*Joint Cost Order*), 2 FCC Rcd 1298 (1987), *on recons.*, 2 FCC Rcd 6283 (1983) (*Joint Cost Reconsideration Order*); *on fur-*

ther recons., 3 FCC Rcd 6701 (1988) (*Joint Cost Further Reconsideration Order*).

Telecommunications Act of 1996, Pub. L. No. 104-104, 110 Stat.56, 47 U.S.C. §§151 *et seq.*

U.S. v. AT&T, 552 F. Supp. 131 (D.C. 1982)

P. Deregulation of Telecommunications and Non-Regulation of the Internet in Japan[*]

Koichiro Agata

1. Introduction

This title shows a typical situation on the Japanese infocommunications market: the telecommunications field is deregulated, while the Internet is not regulated. The purpose of this paper is to describe today's situation in deregulating telecommunications and non-regulating the Internet in Japan to provide a discussion framework for further development. For this purpose, in Chapter 2, we shall attempt to define actors on the Internet market generally to lay a basis for further description in this paper. In the third chapter, we will analyze the deregulated situation in the Japanese telecommunications market to show a possible orientation for the further policy development. In the fourth chapter, we will go on to describe the non-regulated situation of the Japanese Internet to show issues that need to be cleared.

The deregulation of telecommunications in Japan can be represented by a one-go reform in 1985 which almost completed the formal liberalization of the market and privatization of monopolistic public enterprise. Combined with some modificatory measures in the 1990s, the Japanese telecommunications market was further activated. More liberalization measures have been discussed and partially decided on. A certain clear policy might have to be determined to promote competition on the market. On the other hand, the no regulations on the Internet content in Japan can be marked with the principle of self-imposed control based on the guidelines issued by a certain legally incorporated organization of related industries under the influence of concerned ministries. The discussion on possible regulations must be continued to find reasonable solutions considering some pending issues.

2. Actors on the Internet Market

Actors on the Internet market could be classified into at least seven groups: (1) content creators, (2) content providers, (3) content aggregators, (4) service providers, (5) network providers (6) consumers with appliances and (7) regulator(s) (based on NTT 2001). The first group is those who actually create several contents

---

[*] This paper discusses the situation until the summer 2001, as the concerned symposium in Germany was held. In May 2002 the Law of the Providers' Responsibility was issued in Japan. The recent regulation of the internet in Japan must be newly analysed.

for provision on the Internet with copyright for the respective content, namely authors, musicians, cameramen, scenario writers, so on. The content providers, on the other hand, integrate the created content for a united program also with an own copyright for the program, such as editorial firms, movie studios, record companies, etc. The content aggregators commercialize such programs for supply on the Internet, so they are broadcasters, publishers, and portal sites. These three groups hold responsibility for every content, either positively or negatively. The fourth group, the service providers, is those who function as retailers of digital contents for consumers, such as Internet service providers (ISP), while the network providers play the role of transporting the content from the service providers to consumers. Appliance makers supply the sixth group, namely the consumers, with terminal units and software. Even if individual consumers, technologically well furnished and technically well trained, could naturally also create, provide, or aggregate contents, they should only be observed as a functional part in this classification. The last group can, if necessary, regulate the market to put things in order.

Some of these groups can be further classified into larger groups according to each aspect of the Internet. The first two groups could be called *content providers in a broader sense* who hold principally their own copyright for the respective content such as music, games, application software, movies, TV programs, etc. The third and fourth actors build another larger group called *platform providers* for the consumers; they not only function as a united group but also as integrated enterprise such as a provider aggregating Internet content. Platform providers like content aggregators collect and edit the content, organize the content supply, manage the related copyright and buy the televising rights. Platform providers as service providers supply the actual Internet services, collect fees for the service consumption either for themselves or as an agency for related content providers, and manage the E-commerce system. The other three groups should remain, when functionally observed, as previously discussed. *Network providers* hold and manage the networks and secure the Internet connection, while *consumers* can be supplied by appliance makers with the receiving apparatus, receiving software and network interface at home, etc. The *regulator*(s) could stand outside the market for its order. Therefore, five groups of actors are involved with the Internet in the narrower sense: content providers, platform providers, network providers, consumers, and regulator(s).

This classification of Internet actors based on five categories can contribute to a discussion of possible regulation in the global Internet. Every actor has its rights and responsibilities for functioning on the Internet, although not all areas of their actions must be regulated from some viewpoints on the Internet. In the following two chapters, we shall mainly discuss the above-mentioned classification of Internet market actors. The market of telecommunications in Japan has been deregulated over the last 16 years, while any explanation of the actual regulation on the Japanese Internet market must start from awareness that it is not regulated by the government at all.

3. Deregulation of Telecommunications in Japan

3.1 Concrete Actors

To analyze the situation of the telecommunications market we should examine some concrete actors other than those in the previous chapter: (1) the Ministry of Public Management (MPM) as the regulator for the market, (2) the Cabinet and its advisory committees, (3) telecommunications companies as network providers, and (4) USA as an international actor.

A large administrative reform was realized in Japan on 6 January 2001. The twenty-four former ministries and agencies were reshuffled into the present twelve ministries and agencies, although some remained almost unchanged, for example the Ministry of Foreign Affairs and the Ministry of Justice (see AGATA 1998 on the administrative reforms in Japan). The MPM is an integration of three different ministries: the Ministry of Post and Telecommunications (MPT), the Ministry of Home Affairs, and the Agency of General Coordination. Therefore, the MPM plays the role of the regulator for today's telecommunications market in Japan. If we observe the process of administrative reforms in Japan, the significance of advisory committees of the Cabinet or the ministries must be underlined, although the effects of their expert opinions were each very different. The important committees for telecommunications reform in Japan were the Second Provisional Administrative Reform Committee (SPARC) and the Advisory Committee for Telecommunications (ACT).

The largest Japanese telecommunications company is the Nippon Telegraph and Telecommunications (NTT), organized through privatization of the former Nippon Telegraph and Telecommunications Public Corporation (NTTPC) as a public enterprise in 1985. NCCs, or new common carriers, are private telecommunications companies that have entered into the telecommunications market after NTT's privatization.

The US has played an important role as an international catalyst with a lot of influences on the Japanese telecommunications market in some aspects. Its influence on the initial telecommunications deregulation in Japan was so decisive that the motive for original reform almost depends on it.

3.2 Stages of the Telecommunications Deregulation

The telecommunications deregulation in Japan might be characterized as a one-go reform in which most aspects necessary for telecommunications deregulation were realized in one reform in the year 1985, while the German telecommunications deregulation could be observed as gradual, composed of three steps in 1989, 1995, and 1998 (AGATA 1998).

The guideline for the Japanese one-go deregulation was first proposed by the SPARC 1982. As a background to this proposal, we can observe the fact that the technology of the information and telecommunications field had greatly developed and that the American telecommunications market underwent reform as the first case in the world. The Japanese reform included both liberalization of the tele-communications market and privatization of NNTPC into NTT (AGATA 1996). Market liberalization meant the end of the telecommunications monopoly through the NTTPC and was realized by a new categorization of telecommunications car-riers, namely Type I and Type II, in the provisions of Telecommunications Ser-vices Law. The former is a telecommunications carrier establishing an original telecommunications network and providing telephone services using that network. Type I carriers must be approved by the MPM to enter the market. On the other hand, Type II carriers supply enhanced telecommunications services, for example data banks or Internet services, over the networks of Type I carriers. Type II carri-ers must register for or report their entry into the market. The difference between the registration and report depends on the extent of Type II services of the carrier. Based on the above-mentioned classification, Type I and Type II carriers could be observed respectively as network and platform providers. Through liberalization, the MPT at that time got the jurisdiction for regulating the market after liberaliz-ing it (reregulation). This categorization of telecommunications carriers might be described as a vertical one in the sense that carriers intended to supply telephone services must be approved as Type I carrier and set up as an original network at the same time. This system may have to be changed so that the approvals for tele-phone services and networks could be separated (horizontal categorization), as in Germany's case (AGATA 2001(1)).

The NTT privatization was carried out simultaneously with other privatizations of the Japan National Railways and the Japan Tobacco Monopoly. Through its privatization by disposing its stocks, the NTT became one of other telecommuni-cations carriers on the market. During its period of monopoly, the NTT has en-joyed autonomy as the public enterprise on the market, and also independence of the influence of the MPT at that time. In this reform, a new NTT Law was passed. After its privatization the NTT stands under the regulation of the MPM. Some NCCs were soon founded by related companies of other network economy, for example the privatized Japan Railways and the Japan Highways. In this context, it must be emphasized that foreign capitalists were restricted to participate in the capital market of telecommunications, for not only NTT but also NCCs. In the case of the NTT it was forbidden, while two thirds of the entire stocks of Type I carrier must be owned by domestic capitals. In my opinion, this measure truly contributed to the protection of Japanese telecommunications carriers within the market competing against foreign capitals, but it prevented a potential activation of the competition in the Japanese telecommunications market. Due to the restric-tion of foreign capital participation, the diversity and number of telecommunica-tions carriers were reduced on the market.

In the 90s some modificatory deregulation measures were adopted to improve competition on the telecommunications market, namely deregulation of foreign capital participation in the market and reorganization of the NTT. In 1992 the restriction of foreign capital participation was abolished for NCCs, while the NTT Law was so amended that 20% of the entire stock holding of the NTT could be held by foreign capitalists. This measure led to activating alliances or fusion among domestic and foreign telecommunications carriers for closer competition.

Another amendment of the NTT Law was passed in 1997: the NTT was reorganized into a share holding company, an affiliated one for distant calls (NTTCom) and two subsidiary companies for local calls (NTT West and East) in 1999. This measure was intended to weaken the relative competitiveness of the entire NTT against other domestic telecommunications carriers. On the other hand, in my opinion, it may also have weakened the global competence of the NTT through its division into four smaller companies. The real effect of these modificatory measures should be evaluated several years from now.

3.3 Further Discussions and Reforms

In 2001 after the extensive reform of the Ministries, the Japanese Cabinet made a decision for telecommunications regulation leading to some changes of the related legislation in April. Mainly composed of six measures, they can be classified into two competing orientations of regulatory philosophy, namely closer domestic competition or greater international competitiveness of the NTT (AGATA 2001(2)).

There are three points in the orientation for enhancing domestic competition: (1) compulsory announcement of access charges for other carriers by carriers with market shares over 25%, (2) compulsory opening of NTT networks for other carriers, and (3) deregulation of foreign capital participation in the NTT. The first point provides a so-called regulation of dominant carriers: they must clearly announce the level of access charges to other carriers. They should truly be regulated so that their access charges could be open for sound competition on the telecommunications market. One question remains as to who will decide the criteria of the compulsory announcement. Based on the topical cabinet decision, the Ministry of Public Management should make a decision by its own discretion. On the other hand, it should be a more neutral proceeding if the Cartel Committee were involved in the decision. The second and the third measures are convincing. The different NTT networks as dominant carriers should be made more widely available than ever. The present restrictions on foreign participation in the NTT should be raised from 20% to 33% in order to enhance domestic competition.

On the contrary, in the orientation to greater competitiveness of the NTT there are three measures for reinforcing its competitiveness on the international market: (1) extending NTT's business fields such as L-Mode; (2) sharing universal services with other carriers; Universal Service Funds; and (3) non-regulating NTT's participation in its subsidiaries. The NTT has supplied Internet services through mobile phones since some years ago, namely by I-Mode through NTT-DoCoMo., also for simplified web services. This ISP of the NTT will be extended to a fixed telephone base via the L-Mode; the NTT may also play a role of platform providers based on the above-mentioned classification. This business can expect a great reaction from the users. Moreover, compulsory universal services based on the NTT Law have been laid only upon the NTT as the dominant carrier in effect. The topical Cabinet decision proposed a sharing of the universal services together with

other carriers through building universal service funds. This is a measure for easing the NTT's burden in this field. Non-regulation on NTT's participation in its
subsidiaries, for example NTTDoCoMo as a mobile telephone company, continues to keep the unity of the NTT family as an international actor on the global
market.

No clear priority between the two regulation philosophies has been established
yet, at least in the latest Cabinet decision for telecommunications regulation. This
can be a compromise among the concerned actors, especially between the concerned Ministry plus new common carriers and the NTT, however, not an extreme
measure on the polarized spectrum between closer domestic competition and
greater competitiveness of the NTT. The past reform phases show a swing between both poles. Now that the Japanese telecommunications market is relatively
mature in the sense of telephone charges and the market share, a clear priority
should be laid for the next reform.

4. Non-regulation of Internet Content in Japan

4.1 Concrete Actors

An analysis of the Japanese Internet market should be based on the fact that Internet content in Japan is not regulated by legal measures specific to the Internet, but
we must apply the principle of self-imposed control. In this context, at least two
actors related to the self-imposed principle must be mentioned: (1) two ministries
as possible regulators for the Internet market, and (2) related industries as platform
providers, some of which are legally organized under the appropriate ministry.

The Ministry of Trade and Industry (MITI) was renamed the Ministry of Economy, Trade and Industry (METI) in the above-mentioned reform of the Japanese
Ministries in January 2001. The jurisdiction for the fields of computers, information and the concerned industry formally belonged to the MITI and now belongs
to the METI, while the MPT or the MPM is responsible for the field of telecommunications and the related industries, as already discussed. In the process of the
reform it was argued that the jurisdiction for information and telecommunications
should be integrated into a single ministry, but in vain. Therefore the METI is
mainly concerned with problems of the Internet, although the MPT or the MPM
has been also involved into the discussions on the Internet matters.

The Electronic Network Consortium (ENC) was a private organization established in 1992 composed of about 80 corporative bodies such as ISPs, computer
industries, software companies, mass media, and so on, as well as about 20 mu-
nicipalities interested in public communications networks for the sake of mutual
adjustment of problems concerning the Internet. It was one of the founding members of the Internet Content Rating Association (ICRA) and had a close relationship with the New Media Development Association as an agency of the METI.

The ENC was integrated in 2001 with the Internet Association of Japan (IAJ) into the Internet Association Japan (IAjapan). The IAJ was also a private organization composed of about 300 companies and institutes concerned rather with technological aspects of the Internet and its diffusion. The IAjapan is organized as a legally incorporated foundation under the METI to serve former functions of the ENC as well as the IAJ. The establishment of IAjapan as such an organization authorized and helped develop the role of the ENC and IAJ.

The Telecom Services Association (TELESA) is also a legally incorporated foundation under the MPM organized in 1994 and has about 400 platform providers as its members. The organization of legally incorporated foundations is an important method for controlling the power of Japanese ministries against affiliated actors under them. Therefore not only the METI but also the MPM utilize the influencing method through the IAjapan and the TELESA, respectively.

4.2 Process of Discussions

In 1995 the MPT has issued a report on the results of the "Working Group for Electronic Information and Its Usage on the Internet" (MPT 1995) that only suggested problems of information on the Internet under the valid laws, but did not demand a certain regulation for the world of Internet.

In February 1996, the ENC published the "General Ethical Guidelines for Running Online Services" (ENC 1996(1)) and "Recommended Etiquette for Online Service Users" (ENC 1996(2)), while the MITI announced on the same day "About the Independent 'General Ethical Guidelines for Running Online Services'" that recommended the independent guideline method for self-imposed control on Internet problems among the concerned. The publication of three documents on the same day must be no coincidence, but the ENC might have been influenced by the MITI. The purpose of the ENC Guidelines was to propose instructions for domestic platform providers supplying communications services through the Internet to prevent ethical problems in Internet communications. Therefore it has greatly affected the concerned actors to evoke a heated discussion on rule making for Internet services through either self-imposed control or legal regulation.

In June 1996, the MPT emphasized the necessity of legal reform considering the convergence of telecommunications and broadcasting in its "Report on the Working Group for the Convergence of Telecommunications and Broadcasting in the 21st Century" (MPT 1996). In this direction, the ministry analyzed some serious Internet problems in its "Midterm Review on the Working Group for the Convergence of Telecommunications and Broadcasting and Its Development" in order to cooperate with other ministries to suggest a special legislation named by Cyber Law (MPT 1997(1)). This aspect was also pointed out in the "Vision for the 21st Century of Infocommunications" by the APT (MPT 1997(2)). These steps might be observed as positive reaction of the MPT for legal regulation for Internet problems.

On the other hand, this ministry also perceived the significance of a self-imposed control method, especially shown in its "Report on Information Traffics on the Internet" (MPT 1997(3)). This orientation was reflected in another "Guideline for Providers Concerned with Internet Access Services" of the TELESA (TELESA 1998). However, this subtle guideline is so hard to distinguish that platform providers could declare the deletion of problematic content on the Internet. The guideline attracted criticism for this reason in spite of its self-imposedness.

In 1999 a working group under the MPT proposed an institution for protecting the victims of the Internet problems; the information on wrongdoers on the Internet, i.e. their names and addresses, should be published under certain conditions (MPT 1999). In the same year the ruling Liberal Democratic Party showed a great interest in enacting a law for measures against criminality on the Internet. Yet no concrete action whatever has been taken for legal regulation of Internet problems in Japan.

From the above-mentioned process of discussing possible regulation of the Internet in Japan, the principle of such self-imposed control has been applied, although a certain orientation toward legal regulation has been expressed. As far as the orientation of the actors is concerned, it can be said that the METI prefers a system of self-imposed control, whereas the MPM is searching instead for a solution through legal regulation.

4.3 Pending Issues

Based on the above-described observations on the process of the Japanese discussions on the Internet regulation, issues to be cleared can be classified into at least three categories: (1) quality of Internet content, (2) institutions and (3) international cooperation.

The aspect of *Internet content's quality* may be analyzed according to three aspects, namely (x) decency, (y) publicity, and (z) individuality. Abusive behaviors to be avoided on the Internet exemplified by the European Commission (EU 1997) could be classified into these three categories: decency infringed by behavior against national security (instructions on bomb-making, illegal drug production, terrorist activities), protection of minors (abusive forms of marketing, violence, pornography), and protection of human dignity (incitement to racial hatred or racial discrimination). The field of publicity includes economic security (fraud, instructions on pirating credit cards), information security (malicious hacking), and intellectual property (unauthorized distribution of copyrighted works, such as software or music). Individuality concerns the protection of privacy (unauthorized communication of personal data, electronic harassment) and protection of reputation (libel, unlawful comparative advertising).

In order to clear these Internet content quality concerns, some concrete *institutional measures* must be taken. In this context the MPT once summarized some important aspects (MPT 1997(1)), while the METI also recently announced a proposal of necessary reform actions for the network infrastructure (METI 2001).

Based on these reports, institutional viewpoints may be classified into at least four categories, related to the classification of actors on the Internet described earlier in this paper: (a) rules for content providers, namely copyright of and responsibility for the content, (b) control of Internet content through platform providers, (c) self-defense or self-responsibility on the consumers side, and (d) complaint procedures.

If we combined both classifications, namely (x) to (z) for quality and (a) to (d) for institutions, then we have a 3 by 4 matrix for discussing the issues to be cleared. We could set the latter against the former classification to make a framework for future discussions.

For the protection of decency, content providers should be responsible for the Internet content they provide (the principle of self-responsibility). As long as the anonymity of the concerned content providers could be avoided, it is clear who is responsible for it. Content providers must be responsible for avoiding their own anonymity. Otherwise it would be very difficult to put the responsibility on a certain content provider especially on the global Internet. In this context, platform providers can either restrict the anonymity of content providers contrary to decency or be responsible for the indecent content. It would be difficult to define the criteria for restriction through platform providers on the anonymity of content providers, but the guidelines of the ENC or the TELESA can be regarded as a good example for such criteria. Platform providers and even content providers can make independent decisions according to such guidelines. The responsibility of platform providers can either be blamed only because of the fact that they have put indecent content on the Internet as was the case in Germany, or fulfilled through a system of rating or filtering such content platform providers organize (ENC 1999). If such a rating or filtering system could be established, it would be easier for consumers to defend themselves from indecent content, especially using certain sorts of appliances. These devices give consumers a chance to choose freely which content to see and which one to avoid. In this sense, the principle of self-responsibility also applies to the above issues. Complaint procedures against indecent Internet content could be institutionalized, after the German model of Bundesprüfstelle für jugendgefährdende Schriften (BPJS). The philosophy behind such a procedure is that the information on the responsible providers should be published in order to prevent further diffusion of the indecent content.

In the context of publicity, related copyright must be guaranteed to content providers. Their copyrights can be secured on the Internet through technological measures such as code keys or authorization system, on their own or through platform providers who have a certain limit to complete. Therefore, consumers in this framework must be self-conscious and responsible for the use of copyrighted content. Although rigid legal measures are possible for protecting copyright unique to the Internet, technological security seems to be a better way for the protection of copyright. This will satisfy the responsibility for economic and information security on the side of content providers as in the case of decency, as long as their anonymity is avoided. Otherwise, consumers must defend themselves with such security.

For individuality, content providers and platform providers must be responsible for the protection of privacy and reputation. If the anonymity problem is cleared, the responsibility will be clearly defined. In this case, too, both actors should be aware of the responsibility. In this sense, the above-mentioned guidelines can play an important role for maintaining self-responsibility. On the other hand, consumers have the rights to privacy and reputation that ought to be guaranteed through content providers and platform providers. Complaint procedures for infringed privacy or reputation should be institutionalized. In this field, existing procedures for protection can play an important role, when the anonymity problem is cleared. The conflicting points in this chapter are put together in the following table.

Table P1:   Framework for Discussions on Pending Issues

Concerning Internet Regulation

	(x) Decency	(y) Publicity	(z) Individuality
(a) Content Providers	Responsibility for Content	Copyright to Content and Responsibility for Economic/Information Security	Responsibility for Privacy and Reputation
(b) Platform providers	Restriction on Anonymity and /or Responsibility for Content	Protection of Copyright	Protection for Privacy and Reputation
(c) Consumers	Self-defense against Content	Self-responsibility for Content and Self-defense to Economic/Information Security	Right to Privacy and Reputation
(d) Complaint Procedures	To be institutionalized	Rather through Technical Security	To be institutionalized

Source: Author

To discuss **international cooperation**, some points analyzed in the former paragraphs should be highlighted: the principle of self-responsibility, independent control from the side of platform providers based on some guidelines and the development of devices for free choice of Internet content. Though these aspects are interrelated with each other, international cooperation could perhaps contribute most in developing selection devices, because they can overcome the differences in legal regulations between countries. For this purpose, there are at least two prerequisites for the collaborating countries: standardization of devices and criteria for filtering. As far as they are concerned with the technical standardization, they can be said to be already well established through the PICS (Platform for Internet Content Selection) that the World Wide Web Consortium has developed.

ENC introduced it for filtering its content in 1997, and the system continues to the present (ENC 1997 and 1999).

Criteria for filtering have certain significance to a kind of international guideline for platform providers. Countries can cooperate together in order to form such guidelines. For example, the RSACi by RSAC (Recreational Software Advisory Council) provides a well-organized criterion. It is also fundamentally important that concerned countries share the principle of self-responsibility on both sides between content providers and consumers. Content providers must be conscious of the responsibility for and risks from the Internet content, while consumers must also be aware that some Internet content can be less than reliable or even criminal in order to defend them from such content. In this sense, we suggest a global informational cooperation in protecting the Internet content.

5. Perspectives

In the telecommunications context, the MPM announced in June 2001 an important guideline to abolish the approval system for the market entry of Type I carriers for telephone services and networks, in order to further activate the competition in the telecommunications market. This measure could thoroughly change the map of Japanese telecommunications marketing. Those who would like to set up networks could only register in the MPM without its official approval. This would be especially profitable for today's Type II carriers who would like to and are financially able to set up their own networks already the current system. On the other hand, to set up networks without approval means to withdraw from the market without approval. The approval system for Type I carriers has the function for security of universal services; type I carriers in unprofitable areas must not withdraw from the networks. Therefore a possible measure for abolishing the Type I carrier approval system must be well combined together with the planned system of universal service funds.

Moreover, the MPM decided in July 2001 another measure that terminal circuits of the NTT in every household must be opened to other Type I carriers. It may be considered as an extension of the above-mentioned measure for compulsory opening of NTT networks for other carriers. A big bottleneck for a sound competition on the Japanese telecommunications market lies in the fact that the NTT enjoys most of the monopoly of the terminal circuit market. Therefore, the NTT exclusively collects a basic charge from every telecommunications user. Based on this measure, NCCs can lease terminal circuits of the NTT to collect basic fees from the users. This step can contribute to lowering the entire telecommunications prices and help further distribute Internet services.

Such measures in the field of Japanese telecommunications can influence the current situation concerning the Internet, especially for increased diffusion of Internet content through the growing number of Internet users combined with the higher availability of ADXL. What we should do now as an institutional measure in Japan is to discuss further about the legal possibility to publish information on content providers who have supplied problematic content on the Internet. Then it must be legally determined in which conditions, in which procedure, and by whom such decisions could be made and realized.

References

BPJS (Bundespruefstelle fuer Jugendgefaehrdende Schriften), Organisation und Aufgaben usw., in: http://www.bmfsfj.de/dokument/sonstiges/ix6682_440 81.htm (German version).

ENC (1996/1), General Ethical Guidelines for Running Online Services, Electronic Network Consortium, in: http://www.nmda.or.jp/enc/guideline.html.

ENC (1996/2), Recommended Etiquette for Online Service Users, Electronic Network Consortium, in: http://www.nmda.or.jp/enc/etiquette.html.

ENC (1997), To Establish a Filtering System on the Internet, Electronic Network Consortium, in: http://www.nmda.or.jp/enc/rating/ratingdb-press.html (Japanese version).

ENC (1999), Start of 'Rating/Filtering System' for the Next Generation on the Internet", Electronic Network Consortium, in: http://www.nmda.or.jp/enc/rating/rating2nd-press.html (Japanese version).

EU (1997), Action Plan on Promoting Safe Use of the Internet, on 26 November 1997, European Commission, in: http://www2.echo.lu/legal/en/Internet/act plan.html.

JANN, W., KOENIG, K., LANDFRIED, C., WORDELMANN, P., hrsg., (1998), Politik und Verwaltung auf dem Weg in die Transindustrielle Gesellschaft, Baden-Baden.

METI (2001), Institutional Reform for Promoting Competition on the Network Infrastructure and Adapting to the Age of Information and Communications Technology, Ministry of Economics, Trade and Industries, in: http://www.meti.go.jp/feedback/ downloadfiles/i00818ej.pdf (Japanese version).

MITI (1996), About the Independent 'General Ethical Guidelines for Running Online Services, Ministry of Trade and Industries, in: http://www.nmda.or.jp/enc/press.html (Japanese version).

MPT (1995), Report on the Working Group for Electronic Information and Its Usage on Internet, Ministry of Post and Telecommunications, Tokyo, 65p., N19960003 (Japanese version).

MPT (1996), Report on the Working Group for the Convergence of Telecommunications and Broadcasting in the 21st Century, Ministry of Post and Telecommunications, in: http://www.yusei.go.jp/policyreports/japanese/group/tsusin/kankyou/index.html (Japanese version).

MPT (1997/1), Midterm Review on the Working Group for the Convergence of Telecommunications and Broadcasting and Its Development, Ministry of Post and Telecommunications, in: http://www.yusei.go.jp/policyreports/japanese/group/tsusin/70616x01.html (Japanese version)

MPT (1997/2), Vision for the 21st Century of Infocommunications, Ministry of Post and Telecommunications, in: http://www.yusei.go.jp/policyreports/japanese/telecouncil/vision21-9706/v21-9706.html (Japanese version)

MPT (1997/3), Report on Information Traffic on the Internet, Ministry of Post and Telecommunications, in: http://www.mpt.go.jp/policyreports/japanese/group/Internet/kankyou-1.html (Japanese version)

MPT (1998), Report on the Rules for Information Traffic on the Internet, Ministry of Post and Telecommunications, in: http://www.yusei.go.jp/pressrelease/japanese/denki/980105j601.html (Japanese version)

MPT (1999), Report on Inappropriate Usage of Infocommunications and Complaint Procedures, Ministry of Post and Telecommunications, in: http://www.joho.soumu.go.jp/pressrelease/japanese/tsusin/990201j501_01.html (Japanese version).

MURAMATSU, M., NASCHOLD, F., eds. (1996), State and Administration in Japan and Germany, Berlin.

NAKAMURA, K., AGATA, K., eds., (2001), Convergence of Telecommunications and Broadcasting in Japan, United Kingdom and Germany, Richmond.

NTT East and West (2001), Outlines on Broadband Content Services, Nippon Telephone and Telegraph East Inc. and West Inc., not yet published paper for a discussion held on 17 July 2001 in the Institute of Information and Communications Research, Tokyo (Japanese version).

TELESA (1998), Guideline for Providers Concerned with Internet Access Services, Telecom Services Association, in: http://www.telesa.or.jp/fuiede.html (Japanese version).

AGATA, K. (1996), Three Contentious Issues in the Liberalisation Process of the Japanese Telecommunications Market, in; MURAMATSU et al., 223-243.

AGATA, K. (1998/1), Reform of the Administrative Organization in Japan after the War - Consequences of Committee-Oriented Organizational Reforms and Political Leadership, in: Waseda Political Studies No.29, 17-46.

AGATA, K. (1998/2), Zur Telekommunikationspolitik in Deutschland und Japan, in: JANN et al., 565-574 (German version).

AGATA, K. (2001/1), Public Policy for Telecommunications and Broadcasting: Japan and Germany in Contrast, in: NAKAMURA et al., 131-140.

AGATA, K. (2001/2), Aktueller Kabinettsbeschluss zur Telekommunikationsregulierung in Japan, noch nicht veroeffentliches Referat im Japanisch-Deutschen Symposium "Herausforderungen fuer die Informationsgesellschaft im 21. Jahrhundert" vom 17. Mai 2001 in Muenchen (German version).

Q. Electronic Commerce and the Gats Negotiations

Claude E. Barfield

1. Introduction

The aim of this paper is to spark discussion and debate over issues raised by the integration of electronic commerce into the rules governing the international trading system. Negotiations regarding E-Commerce will play a prominent role in the GATS 2000 round, and at this point a number of countries, private sector organization and academics have voiced opinions and suggestions concerning the path forward. While substantial agreement has been reached in a number of areas, there is still no consensus on some important questions reflecting both disagreements over the proper path or option as well as the need for more study and analysis. The paper does not attempt to include all of the issues, and does not exhaustively treat the issues it does cover – again the aim is to provide enough information to elicit debate as the serious negotiations on electronic commerce and other service sectors begin in Geneva over the coming months.

The issues described in this paper were developed from a variety of sources, including the WTO secretariat's 1998 study, Electronic Commerce and the Role of the WTO (WTO 1998a); the subsequent "Note on the Work Program on Electronic Commerce" (WTO, COUNCIL ON TRADE IN SERVICES, 1998b) developed by the WTO secretariat and interim reports by the Council on Trade in Services; submissions to the work program by the U.S., the EU and Japan; recommendations by private sector organization such as the U.S. Coalition of Service Industries and the Alliance for Global Business; and academic studies by scholars and trade experts interested in E-Commerce and in the functioning of the GATS.

The paper will discuss six issues: classification, taxation, scope or modes of supply, regulation (Article VI, the Telecommunications Annex and Reference Paper), privacy and intellectual property. It should be noted that not all of these issues will be dealt with directly in the GATS 2000 negotiations, but each will affect or be affected by the outcome of these negotiations.

2. Classification

Electronic Commerce presents difficult challenges to the traditional trade classification system of goods and services. Oversimplifying somewhat, when does an electronic transmission assume the characteristics of a service; when does it seem more like a product; and when do some transmissions actually represent a kind of hybrid, fitting uncomfortably into either of the existing designations. How these issues are resolved will have major consequences for future rulemaking and the settlement of electronic commerce trade disputes. As the WTO secretariat stated in its 1998 study: "For historical reasons, rules on trade in goods and trade in services evolved separately. The two sets of rules are similar in many ways, but they contain important differences." (WTO, COUNCIL ON TRADE IN SERVICES, 1998a). These differences between the GATT and GATS regimes include the general national treatment obligation in the GATT, as opposed to sector specific national treatment obligation in the GATS; the general prohibition against quantitative restrictions in the GATT, as opposed to less stringent limitations on quantitative restrictions in the GATS; use of customs duties on imports where GATT members have not bound themselves to zero tariffs, as opposed to virtual silence on this issue in GATS; and focus in GATT on cross-border trade in goods, whereas GATS deals not only with cross-border transactions but also commercial presence or establishment and movement of natural persons as components of trade in services.

The U.S. February 1999 submission to the work program also acknowledges that there are no easy or simple answers to the classification questions. It states: "While some have suggested that all commerce based on electronic transmission is a service, this conclusion needs further examination. For example, are there products which tend to be distributed electronically and generally are not marketed in tangible form... (G)reeting cards, clip-art, Web-pages, Java-based "applets," and certain industrial designs might be created, distributed and used entirely within a network, without even acquiring a tangible form. While the transmission of these products can certainly be characterized as a service, the products themselves are not consumed in their transmission, but rather retain a permanence analogous to the goods world. And yet, some may argue that these are not quite goods or services." (WTO, COUNCIL ON TRADE IN SERVICE, 1999a).

In attempting to sort out these questions and their implications for GATS 2000 negotiations, a classification model for E-commerce presented by the EU is a helpful starting point. The EU submission pointed out that there are three different kinds of transmission involved in electronic commerce: (1) electronic transmissions that consist solely of telecommunications, such as electronic mail and internet telephony; (2) electronic transmissions used for ordering goods, which subsequently are delivered physically or downloaded physically, e.g., flowers or books; and (3) electronic transactions in which the entire process is conducted electronically, e.g., legal advice or financial services ordered and delivered electronically. (WTO, COUNCIL ON TRADE IN SERVICES, 1999b) (Some observers have also suggested a further refinement or distinction: that is, if the traffic over the Internet is what might be termed an 'off the shelf good' [a movie or book] then it should be treated as a good for WTO purposes; but if the traffic is a service tailored specifically for a purchaser or client [i.e., architectural drawings or a financial plan], then even if downloaded into a physical form, it should be counted as a service.)

Harking back to the EU classification system, clearly, the difficult questions lie in the intersection between the second and third types of transmissions described above. And the matter is further complicated by the fact that the WTO has never developed a comprehensive definition either of goods or services. As the WTO secretariat points out in its "Note on the Work Program": "There is no classification which would permit us to say that all intangible products, even all electronically delivered products, are services by definition." (WTO, COUNCIL ON TRADE IN SERVICES, 1998b)

Behind these definitional complexities lies one important reality: a decision to treat certain forms of electronic transmissions as "hybrid" within the WTO legal system could trigger a separate set of negotiations to create a trade regime between GATS and GATT for these hybrids. To many, particularly for the private sector services organizations, this is an unacceptable solution that could produce chaos and friction for years to come. Both the U.S. Coalition of Service Industries, and the Alliance for Global Business have come out strongly against acknowledging "hybrids" and forcing a new round of rulemaking and negotiations. The AGB states: "Certain digital products may not fall cleanly with the traditional classification systems of "tangible goods" and "intangible services," although they will fall into one category or the other...It also seems clear...that all transmissions can be categorized as either a good or a service." (INTERNATIONAL CHAMBER OF COMMERCE: ALLIANCE FOR GLOBAL BUSINESS, 1999)

And the CSI states: "CSI rejects the idea that there is a class of services that can be labeled electronic commerce and thus be negotiated separately." (U.S. COALITION OF SERVICE INDUSTRIES, 1999).

The WTO secretariat has been ambivalent on the hybrid issue. In its 1998 study, the secretariat noted: "If certain transactions over the internet were to be seen neither as trade in goods nor trade in services, new rules may be required or existing ones may need to be revisited." (WTO, COUNCIL ON TRADE IN SERVICES, 1998a) Subsequently, however, in the November 1998 background note on the work program, the secretariat, while still acknowledging that "the existing classification systems are often imperfect or incomplete," basically ignored the hybrid transmission issue. The chief concern was clearly to keep all transactions within the existing WTO legal framework. Thus, the secretariat stated: "Any suggestion that electronic transmissions as such should be regarded as outside the scope of the GATS would of course fundamentally damage the entire Agreement and undermine a wide range of existing commitments, since the vast majority of cross-border trade in many sectors is done electronically." (WTO, COUNCIL ON TRADE IN SERVICES, 1998b)

Business organizations, however, are wary of aiming for quick solutions to classification questions. The AGB argues that moving to clear distinctions in the immediate future would risk distorting "the mode of distribution chosen by an industry still in its infancy" and without adequate knowledge "affect how lines are drawn in other areas, such as the sale and use of intellectual property." (INTERNATIONAL CHAMBER OF COMMERCE: ALLIANCE FOR GLOBAL BUSINESS, 1999)

In this area, then, the negotiations will likely take some time, with decisions reached only after further study and analysis of specific cases such as classification of computer software, books and music sold and used on the Internet. The negotiations will also have to wrestle with question of hybrid transmissions and whether, despite the strong reservations of both the private sector and some governments, certain transmissions and transactions cannot be fitted into existing goods and service modes.

3. Taxation

Customs Duties are border measures that are rarely applied to services – although there is no reason in principle why customs duties could not be applied to services, whether supplied electronically or any other way. In May 1998, the WTO agreed to a temporary standstill agreement not to impose customs duties on electronic transmissions. Both the United States and the EU have announced that permanent extension of this moratorium (and making it legally binding) will be a major priority at the WTO Ministerial Meeting in November, 1999. During the course of discussions in the electronic commerce study program, though, other WTO members have resisted this suggestion. Some developing countries have stated that because of the large potential impact on revenues and fiscal policies more time is needed to study the question. Thus, while it is likely that the moratorium will be extended in November, this outcome is not foreordained.

In a 1999 submission to the WTO Council on Services, then-U.S. WTO Ambassador Rita Hayes pointed out that internationally there is no precedent for taxing electronic transmissions per se. There are no customs duties on telephone calls or on fax messages. The issue becomes more complicated, however, when one is dealing with internet transmissions that consist of content that could either be a good or a service, i.e., as noted above, a book, song, set of architectural drawings or legal advice that can be ordered over the Internet and then either downloaded into hard copy or used entirely in its electronic form.

In her presentation, Ambassador Hayes tried to draw a clear distinction between duties and taxes. She stated emphatically that "I am not discussing the tax policies of any country. I am not suggesting that we discuss or take decisions on any measure that would affect the way in which our tax authorities treat electronic transmissions." And she states further: "I am not discussing how we define what is an electronic transmission, that is, whether it is a good, a service or something in between." (HAYES, 1999)

The problem here is that one must discuss – even concede – that if the internet transmission is downloaded as a good or service, or used as either a good or a service in electronic form, then issues related to internal sale taxes or value-added-taxes immediately present themselves. As the WTO secretariat pointed out in its 1998 study: "If Internet transactions are not taxed, this would give the medium a considerable advantage over other means of commerce that are taxed. If a VAT of 20 percent, or corporate income tax of 30-50 percent, could be circumvented via the Internet, the latter would be made more attractive for sellers and buyers alike.

This is not, however, in the interest of the general public." (WTO, 1998a) The challenge the Council on Services faces on taxation is whether a tax on either the downloaded internet product or service or that good or service in electronic form is covered by the proposed moratorium. The WTO secretariat has presented the reasons why they should not be covered, but the issue remains unresolved at the moment (It should be noted that an EU submission to the E-Commerce work program also is silent on the tax status of downloaded or electronically utilized goods. It states merely that "[The moratorium] does not include...tariffs on goods ordered electronically and delivered physically.") (WTO, Council on Trade in Services, 1999b)

Though they are not likely to become a large part of WTO trade negotiations, it should be added that major problems arise for the administration of sales taxes and the VAT on Internet transactions, because taxable online transactions will be difficulty to trace, particularly if payment records are encrypted. In principle, for instance, VAT or sales taxes should be collected in the country where the product is consumed. In practice, however, governments have adopted a policy of taxing the final seller under the assumption that consumption takes place close to this sale. Internet sales blow apart this assumption. It has been suggested that for Internet transactions, the place of supply might be defined as the place where the customer is established. What this would mean is that a U.S. company selling in many countries would have to register for VAT purposes in all of these countries. Alternatively, companies would enlist fiscal agents in each of the countries. None of the suggested solutions is entirely satisfactory, particularly for small and medium-sized companies, which would face major transaction costs coping with the system.

4. Scope: Modes of Supply

The GATS Agreement defines trade in services according to the supply of a service through any of four modes. These modes of supply are defined as follows: (1) cross-border, where the service is supplied from the territory of one WTO member into another; (2) consumption abroad, where the consumer purchases a service which is delivered in the territory of another WTO member; (3), commercial presence, where the service supplier of a WTO member establishes a subsidiary or branch in another WTO member to supply a service; and (4) presence of natural persons, where the service is supplied by a a person working in the territory of a WTO member. As is evident, these modes of supply distinguish between services transactions on the basis of the territorial presence of the supplier and of the consumer of the service. In the GATS Agreements, WTO members made national commitments (as to market access and national treatment, for instance) both by sector and by mode of supply related to the sector.

It should be stated up front that at the moment there is a great deal of confusion and disagreement about the practical consequences of the advent of electronic commerce on this mode of supply system. The two modes of delivery most relevant for electronic commerce are cross-border supply (Mode 1) and consumption abroad (Mode 2). Many observers contend that the technological realities of electronic commerce have blurred, if not erased, crucial distinctions between the modes of supply, particularly with regard to modes 1 and 2.

From the outset, the WTO secretariat has taken note of the ambiguities introduced by the Internet. The secretariat pointed out in its 1998 study that: "The modes of supply are essential defined on the basis of the origin of the service supplied and consumer, and the degree and type of territorial presence within the territory of the (WTO) Member...The distinction between the two modes is not always clear. Since the physical presence of the consumer is not a criterion for determining the place of delivery of a service, it sometimes becomes difficult to determine in an unambiguous manner where the service is delivered." (WTO, 1998a)

A recent exchange between trade experts regarding examples of Modes 1 and 2 illustrates the lack of consensus at the operational level. The following situations were offered as examples of Mode 2 by one group. A student via the Internet contacts a university in another country and goes on to complete a university degree online without having left his or her home territory. The student's consumption, according to one interpretation, should be viewed as an example of Mode 2 of supply. Similarly, a consumer decides to purchase the services of an architectural firm by contracting for architectural designs of new homes. The consumer never leaves his home territory but conducts the transaction entirely over the Internet, using the designs for construction of a house in his own country. Once again, under one interpretation this would be considered an example of Mode 2 supply. This interpretation has been directly challenged, however, by other trade experts who argue that these are is in reality an examples of Mode 1, cross-border supply of services – largely because the consumer did not physically move into the supplier's territory. As one analyst stated: "The Modes in the GATS are defined using the criterion of presence in a territory, and thus Mode 2 involves the movement of the consumer himself (i.e., natural person) into the territory of the supplier...If the supplier does not move from the home territory and the consumer is not in that territory, then the supply is Mode 1. There seems to be no good reason to argue that some cases of Mode 1 supply...should be arbitrarily treated as Mode 2 by conjuring a new form of travel called electronic visiting, such as adduced for the examples given of distance learning (and) architectural designs sent over the Internet." (Julian Arkian, E-mail to author, May 10, 1999)

In a recent paper, Geza Feketekuty of the Monterey Institute of International Studies, describes other situations which even introduce the possibility of Mode 3 (establishment) as the correct mode in the above circumstances. He notes: "Some have argued that direct marketing to consumers in a particular (foreign) country should be considered as local establishment, subjecting the production of the service to the local regulatory jurisdiction of the country of the consumer. Alternatively, if the purchaser acquires a service from a foreign producer who does not engage in targeted marketing, the sale might be consider as cross-border trade...But what if the consumer in question intends to consume the service abroad? Should the buyer's physical location determines whether it is foreign consumption...?" Feketekuty also points out that the physical location of the Internet service provider might be a criterion for deciding modal distinctions. (FEKETUKUTY, 2000)

Finally, one noted trade in services commentator, Julian Arkell, president of ITSP Consulting, has suggested that, because of the numerous complications in distinguishing between Modes 1 and 2, consideration should be given to merging them by "collapsing" Mode 2 into Mode 1 – in other words both types of transaction would be treated as cross-border. He has also pointed out that until countries conclude Mutual Recognition Agreements regarding consumer protection and other matters, there will inevitably be jurisdictional conflicts as both home and host countries attempt to discipline errant suppliers. (ARKELL, 1999)

As several of the above quotation indicate, for trade negotiators the "rubber hits the road" at two places: (1) in the national schedules where nations signed on to either Mode 1 or Mode 2, or signed up for both but agreed to more liberalization in one mode than the other; and (2) in questions involving regulatory authority where the decision on the site of the E-Commerce transaction will determine where regulatory authority will be exercised.

On national schedules, the problem faced by GATS 2000 negotiators is that in the Uruguay Round, for better or for worse, nations signed up by mode; and the danger with shifting definitions is that it could well jeopardize the ability to hold WTO members to their GATS' commitments. This is a particular problem (which he acknowledges) with Arkell's suggestion to collapse Mode 2 into Mode 1. It is also a problem for a suggested solution by the WTO secretariat which, in the Note for the Working Program, admitted that there was great confusion over the boundaries of Modes 1 and 2 but then asserted that the real problem was that trade officials were focused "on the wrong questions...The real function of the modes is to categorize commitments in national schedules. The question of the mode under which a transaction takes place only becomes important if there is disagreement about the legitimacy of a measure taken by a Member affecting...the Member's commitments...In the context of electronic commerce, it means that in considering the consistency with national commitment of measures affecting electronic supply, one would ask first on whom the measure impinged – the provider or the consumer – and judge its consistency in the light of commitment under Mode 1 and Mode 2." (WTO, COUNCIL ON TRADE IN SERVICES, 1998b)

The problem with this approach is that it begs the question of where transaction actually take place, and thus if the matter went to dispute, Dispute Settlement panels would be just as much at sea in resolving the underlying questions as trade experts are today. The WTO secretariat's solution seems merely to postpone the muddle and could ultimately end up damaging the system more than attempts to settle the issues now would do.

Defining the relationship between Modes 1 and 2 also has a direct impact on issues of legal jurisdiction and regulatory authority. As the WTO secretariat also admits in the "Note on the Work Program": "Issues concerning the country of legal jurisdiction of a transaction have already begun to arise in e-commerce, especially in relation to consumer protection, policing of illegal activities such as on-line gambling and obscenity, and perhaps most importantly, determining the jurisdiction of validity and enforceability of commercial contracts and obligations.

(In some case) the parties concerned draft contracts, indicating the agreed locale of jurisdiction for the matters concerned. But for other transactions, the locus of legal jurisdiction is an open question." (WTO, COUNCIL ON TRADE IN SERVICES, 1998b) Though these questions are beyond the scope of GATS negotiations, solutions in the trade areas will have important consequences on questions of regulatory authority and legal jurisdiction.

In the current GATS 2000 negotiations, the following options will have to be considered – none is entirely satisfactory. First, negotiators could commission the WTO secretariat to assemble blocks of illustrative examples such as those briefly described above; and then create in the negotiations more detailed and precise criteria for distinguishing between Modes 1 and 2 – for instance, coming down one way or the other on the question of whether Mode 2 would require the physical movement of the consumer. Second, the negotiators could attempt to follow original suggestion of the WTO secretariat and work through the national commitments, determining which national reservations constricted the supplier and which constricted the consumer. The working party delegations may be moving in this direction, for the interim report of the secretariat states that at a December 1998 meeting: "Several delegations expressed interest in the suggestion in the Secratariat's paper...that the real function of the modes is to classify commitments and measures taken under them rather than to classify transactions, and that the essential distinction between modes one and two would be made according to whether the measure in question restricts the ability of suppliers to supply the service on a cross-border basis or whether it restricts the ability of domestic consumer to buy the service abroad." (WTO, COUNCIL ON TRADE IN SERVICES, 1999c)

A third option would be to explore Arkell's suggestion of folding Mode 2 into Mode 1. As he acknowledges, there would need to be further study of how this would affect WTO members commitments and obligations. (ARKELL, 1999)

Finally, Feketekuty has suggested that consideration be given to creating a fifth mode just for electronic commerce. He states: "It may well be that honing the definition of the four modes is not the best way of addressing the issues posed by the Internet and E-Commerce. An alternative approach may be to create a fifth mode for the sale of services through the Internet. Governments might agree for an interim period to let the market sort out regulatory issues through private codes, or through declarations by sellers as to whose regulations apply with respect to a particular transaction, and what the rights of consumer are under such regulations. Alternatively, government could decide to negotiate a common regulatory framework for such transactions." Operationally, Feketukuty sees a fifth mode working on an opt-in basis: that is, a group of companies along with a group of countries could voluntarily agree to a fifth mode regime in which rules affecting the supplier and consumer would be applied. Such an opt-in arrangement would have the advantage, he argues, of not creating disruption by overturning the existing modes. (FEKETUKUTY, 2000)

Feketekuty's proposal has merit, but there are two caveats which should be noted: first, it does not deal with very real possibility that quite soon the WTO disputes settlement process may be challenged to rule on national commitments, particularly with regard to Modes 1 and 2; and second, creation of fifth mode would go a long way toward creating a separate regime for E-Commerce, a course that many governments and private sector associations have been adamantly against over the past several years.

5. E-Commerce: The Impact of Regulation

Though electronic commerce has flourished in a largely non-regulated environment, there are a number of places where the regulatory elements of the GATS will exert substantial influence over future patterns of growth. Specifically, Article VI (Domestic Regulation); Articles VIII and IX (Monopolies and Exclusive Service Suppliers; Business Practices), in conjunction with the Annex and Reference Paper on Telecommunications; and Article XIV (Exceptions)

The unresolved issues in the area of regulation and E-Commerce are: (1) the degree to which the negotiations should attempt to refine and deepen existing regulatory rules, not only for the Internet but also for other service sectors; and (2) whether, and on what specific issues, there is the necessity to establish particular rules for E-Commerce, or revise existing regulatory principles to achieve a closer fit for the Internet.

Article VI: Article VI of the GATS requires that all regulations affecting trade in services be administered in a reasonable, objective and impartial manner. In addition, Article VI tasks the Council on Services to develop necessary disciplines that would ensure that national domestic regulations do not constitute "unnecessary barriers to trade in services." These disciplines would require that regulations are based on objective and transparent criteria, and not "more burdensome than necessary to ensure the quality of the service."

In the submissions to the Work Program and in meetings informal discussions related to the Work Program, a number of suggestions for further study and negotiations have been put forward. The EU and a number of other WTO members have pointed out the Article VI does not specify the criteria by which one judges whether particular national regulations meet the "reasonable," "unnecessary barriers to trade," and "not more burdensome than necessary" provisions would be decided. They have recommended that as a part of the upcoming negotiations the Council on Services consider formulating a list of regulatory objectives that would serve as a model for WTO member government when considering the regulation of E-Commerce. (WTO, COUNCIL ON TRADE IN SERVICES, 1999b) In a recent meeting of the Work Program participants, the following proposition was put forward by one delegation: "Three issues required consideration in the area of domestic regulation: 1) whether it would be desirable to agree under Article VI on a group of regulatory policy objectives justifying the imposition of regulatory restrictions in electronic commerce, with a view to minimising unnecessary barriers to trade; 2) whether it would be advantageous to distinguish between regulations applying to content and regulations applying to transport; and 3) whether it would be desirable to request an Internet service provider to make inaccessible to consumers a web site which does not comply with domestic regulations." (WTO, COUNCIL ON TRADE IN SERVICES, 1999c)

Other trade policy experts have advanced proposals which go substantially beyond what is currently under discussion in the Work Program. Thus, Geza Feketukuty argues that Article VI needs to be strengthened and deepened with the addition of new principles to guide sectoral commitments on regulatory barriers, including:

- transparency of regulatory objectives: WTO members would provide a clear statement of the regulatory goals of a particular law or regulation, and the measure would be judged as to whether it achieved this goal by the least burdensome means.
- appropriate use of market mechanism: WTO members would be required to use a market mechanism wherever possible in the promotion of social goals. Economic incentives and disincentives would provide a more economically efficient method of accomplishing desired social goals in allowing market forces ultimately to determine the means of reaching those goals.
- minimizing the scope of regulations: As a principle, governments would agree to minimize the regulatory burden by reducing the scope of any regulation to what is absolutely necessary to achieve a desired social objective. It would hold governments to the test of regulating activities directly related to the achievement of a desired social objective.
- use of international regulatory standards: government would be bound to use accepted international standards where feasible to achieve the desired social goal. This laudable goal may in practice be difficult to attain because WTO has little experience in dealing with standards issues, including questions relating public/private conflicts of interest (i.e., in US, for instance, standards are set by bodies composed of public officials and representatives of leading producers) and a process by which the WTO would decide just which standards constituted the international norm. (FEKETUKUTY, 2000)

Julian Arkell has suggested several other elements should be considered, including:

- a necessity test, that would clarify the exceptions for the protection of consumers, quality of services, professional competence and the integrity and fitness of managers and experts;
- a clear definition of universally service obligations, that is transparent, non-discriminatory and competitively neutral;
- publication of licensing criteria
- a clearly worded, binding ban on cross-subsidization. (ARKELL, 1999).

Articles VIII and IX (Combined with the Annex to the Telecommunications Agreement and Reference Paper): The central importance of Article VIII, the Telecommunications Annex and the Reference Paper to E-Commerce stems from the rules they establish for non-discriminatory access to telecommunications networks. Article VIII requires that WTO members ensure that monopoly suppliers of a service do not "in the supply of the monopoly service in the relevant market" act in a manner inconsistent with the MFN obligation and the Member's specific commitment in that sector. Article VII has a direct impact on E-Commerce in two respects: (1) in those countries where basic telecommunications services are still monopolized, Article VIII requires that the monopoly not discriminate against rival Internet access providers; and (2) Article VIII also requires that exclusive Internet providers not thwart commitments made on other services which are bing supplied over the Internet. Both the Telecommunications Annex and the accompanying Reference paper extend and deepen protection of the rights of users of telecommunications services. For instance, the Annex requires non-discrimination as a general proposition and does not depend upon whether a WTO member has undertaken a national treatment commitment in the sector. In addition the Annex provides greater specificity in certain areas, particularly with regard to transparency obligations on such matters as conditions affecting access to and use of public telecom transport networks.

The Reference Paper establishes additional obligations or regulatory principles for major suppliers of telecoms services including the terms of interconnection, misuse of information, licensing criteria, cross-subsidization and other provisions relevant to the prevention of the abuse of dominant position. As the WTO secretariat detailed in its 1998 study: "Major suppliers are obliged to provide interconnection on non-discriminatory terms, conditions and rate and of a quality no less favourable than that provided to all other suppliers of like services...Interconnection must also be granted in a timely manner, on terms and conditions and at cost-oriented rates that are transparent and reasonable...The right of governments to provide for universal service is recognized, but this must be done in a way that does not confer a competitive advantage to any supplier." (WTO, 1998a)

In the deliberations associated with the electronic commerce Work Program, some nations have argued that an expanded version of the Reference Paper, or some kind of combination of the Reference Paper and the Telecoms Annex, could form the basis for a possible model for domestic regulation of electronic commerce. What is not clear and must be sorted out whether the GATS Council on Services should build upon the general Article VI regulatory principles, or turn to the more specific rules for access and competition embodied in the Annex and the Reference Paper. Arkell has suggested that a general Annex on Domestic Regulation become the vehicle for a consolidated set of regulatory principles and guidelines.

Before completing this section, two other points should be introduced, one substantive and one political. On the substantive point, it should be noted that work in the OECD has demonstrated, many key issues are outside the jurisdiction of the WTO, including privacy, public decency and cultural policies, protection of minors, authentication of documents, secure payments systems, encryption, domain names and protection of intellectual property, among others.

On the political front, though largely unpublicized thus far, it is certainly true that the private sector in major industrial nations (but particularly in the United States) has very mixed feelings about new regulatory rules and the inclusion of E-Commerce within the WTO. On the one hand, there is a strain of thought which argues that the Internet is too revolutionary and important to attempt to bind within existing WTO rules and that a regime especially tailored to electronic commerce issues should be established. On the other hand, there is the strong awareness that one of the reasons – beyond the technological breakthroughs – for the astonishing growth of the Internet over the past half decade is the very lack of public regulation, either domestic or international. This leads to a great wariness about all efforts to rein in Internet activities, and an ambivalence about the upcoming GATS 2000 negotiations. U.S. corporate leaders, especially, have become nervous about what they perceive as the expansiveness of the EU desires with regard to new regulatory rules and structures – EU Trade Commissioner Sir Leon Brittan's advocacy during his tenure for new competitive rules of Internet Service Providers (ISPs) being a case in point. (EUROPEAN COMMISSION, 1999)

5. Intellectual Property Issues

As knowledge-based industries are the engines driving many of the world's economies and accompanying economic growth, a strong intellectual property rights (IPR) regime has become increasingly important. The advent of electronic commerce, however, portends future challenges. On the one hand, to promote electronic commerce, sellers need to know that their intellectual property will not be stolen and consumers want to know that they are obtaining authentic products. On the other hand, though, governments face significant challenges in reconciling tensions between a strong IPR regime and a business environment increasingly dominated by electronic transactions. This is not to say that the two systems are inherently at odds but specific tensions exist for all three major forms of intellectual property including copyright, patent, and trademark.

Industries critically dependent on copyright protection are arguably the most concerned about a business environment increasingly dominated by electronic commerce. With the advent of digital technology, for example, it is now possible to download perfect reproductions of works such as compact discs at a minimal cost. Similarly, in the book publishing industry, it is possible to download and disseminate entire manuscripts at virtually no cost, thereby greatly undermining the incentive to engage in the creative process. Other problems abound as well. Some countries, for example, provide an exception to the right of communication to the public for teaching purposes or scientific research. If a university in one country, though, posts a copyrighted work on its site, individuals in a different country where that right is still protected, would be able to access the site, thereby infringing upon the right of the author. More broadly, many copyright holders sell distributors exclusive rights to sell a product in a particular territory. The 'borderless' nature of the internet, of course, fundamentally conflicts with such territorially-based rights.

The international community has taken steps to redress this problem through the World Intellectual Property Organization (WIPO). Specifically, in December 1996, WIPO updated the Berne Convention for the Protection of Literary and Artistic works to reflect the challenges of a digital environment through the signing of two treaties: the WIPO Copyright Treaty; and the WIPO Performances and Phonograms Treaty. While some countries have not yet ratified them in their domestic legislatures, these treaties contain provisions relating to technological protection, copyright management information, and the right of communication to the public, three pillars of a strong IPR regime to protect copyright holders in a digital environment. (WTO, 1998a)

Private sector initiatives are also being developed to bolster the protection of copyright material in an electronic commerce environment. Companies are designing a number of technical solutions to track copyright products including 'digital object identifiers', which consist of a string of numbers attached to a copyrighted text. Despite these innovations, however, it is widely believed that for every protective device developed, another device will develop in response that is capable of bypassing said protections. At some point then, the international community will have to reconcile two competing objectives – strong copyright protection and the efficiencies gained through transacting electronically.

Another challenge for the world community is the adequacy of the definition of IPR in an electronic networking environment. A strong argument can be advanced that computer programs, currently protected under copyright provisions, should also be protected under patent law because the programs contain specific algorithms. This 'blurring' of mediums with technology will require a synchronization of IPR laws, regardless of whether the transaction is conducted electronically or not. Some steps in this direction are already being made. Currently, one hundred countries and international governmental organizations participate in WIPO's permanent committee on industrial property formation (PCIPI), which is taking up this task. One specific task for the international community is to discourage compulsory licensing of internet-related technology except as a remedy to anticompetitive practices. (WTO, 1998a)

The trademark field faces unique challenges as well with regard to regulation and oversight of the domain name system (DNS). Courts have begun to attribute IPRs to domain names, which essentially service as source identifiers. Those trying to conduct business electronically, of course, want consumers to easily find their web site. In many countries, though, the practice of 'domain-squatting' has emerged, where an individual or group will register a domain name of a company which has yet to do so. The 'squatter' or 'domain-shark' as the individual is also called, will the sell the rights to that name to the company in question. (WTO, 1998a) Some have no interest in doing so. Several opposed to the presidential candidacy of Albert Gore in the United States, for example, have been buying up domain names related to the vice-presidents last name.

To date, these disputes have been resolved through negotiations and litigation or both. (WTO, 1998a) Currently, an interagency working group is working to determine what input, if any, the government or international organizations such as the WTO (through TRIPs) should take to help redress this problem.

In terms of future action by the WTO, one positive step would be to consider establishing provisions within the TRIPs agreement, which currently is silent on this matter. This is not to slight the important work of WIPO, but the WTO is likely a better forum in which to handle these matters, in light of its ability to link issues through the form of side payment (or sanctions).

6. Privacy & Security

In a world of electronic commerce, both buyers and sellers alike have a strong interest in the protection of availability, confidentiality and the integrity of data that is stored and transmitted. Electronic commerce will only grow if buyers and sellers are confident that transactions are conducted with minimal risk of deceit and abuse. Specifically, the minimally sufficient base for safe transactions are: 1) the identification of the sender and recipient of a message; 2) the authentication of the message; 3) non-repudiation; 4) encryption of payment information (Matlick, 1999)

Steps to ensure these four prerequisites are being made on both the technological and regulatory front. Companies are now setting up systems whereby they can imprint a 'digital watermark' or 'digital signature' on a transaction to guarantee both authenticity and lack of alteration of a message. Similarly, companies are increasingly relying on "double-blinded encryption" which allows for online payment with the seller seeing the credit card number. Some banks and financial institutions, for example, hold and issue "keys" between two parties which allow the other to decrypt messages.

On the regulatory front, the GATS agreement already has provisions in Article XIV which provides guidelines on the protection of privacy and prevention of fraud. Like most international agreements, however, there is an exception clause which some find troublesome. As these guidelines can be interpreted in a variety of ways, both the United States and the European Commission are emphasizing private sector industry-developed solutions to the problem. Synchronizing these policies though is difficult in light of different national traditions. The EU, for example, has adopted a directive that prohibits the transfer of personal data to countries that do not in its view extend privacy protection to EU citizens. Such directives potentially impede trade, however, and thus require, like intellectual property, a balancing of goals. (EUROPEAN COMMISSION, 1999; LUKAS, 2001)

Interestingly, while encouraging private sector initiatives to promote the privacy and security of data, it is not lost upon governments that this can be taken too far. Governments, particularly the United States, are concerned about the proliferation of highly advanced cryptography technology, which might threaten national security interests and foster the growth of organized crime. Cryptographic technology uses a complex algorithm to render data unintelligible to anyone who does not have the cryptographic 'key' or 'code.' Developed in the 1970s, this technology was widely used by the military for national security purposes. While cryptography may well contribute to a well-functioning electronic commerce environment, it might well help protect data privacy that could be used by criminal elements to avoid detection by law enforcement agencies. For example, if large transfers of money are being made through a variety of dummy corporations (in order to launder money), it would be difficult for law enforcement agencies to monitor these activities if the nature of the transactions were protected by highly complex codes. While European countries have taken less restrictive approach with regard to the export and use of encryption technology, the United States has taken a much more hard-line position on the proliferation of this technology. Again, though, as we have so often said – a balancing act needs to be struck, which will require not just an understanding of the technologies involved, but a delicate weighing of sometimes conflicting but important public policy goals. (MATLICK, 1999)

References

ARKELL JULIAN (1999), E-mail to the author, May 10, 1999.

EUROPEAN COMMISSION (1999), 1999 Communications Review: Toward a New Framework for Electronic Communications Infrastructure and Associated Services, Brussel, Belgium.

FEKETUKUTY, G. (2000), Assessing and Improving the Architecture of GATS, in: SAUVE, P., STERN, R.M. (2000), GATS 2000: New Directions in Services Trade Liberalization, Center for Business and Government, Harvard University and Brooking Institution, Boston and New York, 2000, pp. 85-111.

HAYES, R., U.S. Ambassador to the WTO, (1999), Presentation to WTO General Council on Global Electronic Commerce: Duty Free Treatment for Electronic Commerce, February 19, 1999, Geneva, Switzerland.

INTERNATIONAL CHAMBER OF COMMERCE: ALLIANCE FOR GLOBAL BUSINESS (1999), A Discussion Paper by the Alliance for Global Business on Trade-Related Aspects of Electronic Commerce, New York, N.Y.

LUKAS, A. (2001), Safe Harbor or Stormy Waters? Living with the EU Data Protection Directive, Trade Policy Analysis No. 16, October 30, 2001, Cato Institute, Washington, D.C.

MATLICK, J. (1999), Governing Internet Privacy: A Free Market Primer, The Pacific Research Institute, San Francisco, Calif., 1999.

U.S. COALITION OF SERVICE INDUSTRIES (1999), Position Paper on Electronic Commerce (Submission to the U.S. Trade Representative), Washington, D.C.

WORLD TRADE ORGANIZATION (1998), Electronic Commerce and the Role of the WTO — Special Studies 2, Geneva, Switzerland.

WORLD TRADE ORGANIZATION, COUNCIL ON TRADE IN SERVICES (1998), Work Program on Electronic Commerce: A Note from the Secretariat, (November 16), Geneva, Switzerland.

WORLD TRADE ORGANIZATION, COUNCIL ON TRADE IN SERVICES (1999a), Work Programme on Electronic Commerce—Communications from the United States, (February 12), Geneva, Switzerland.

WORLD TRADE ORGANIZATION, COUNCIL ON TRADE IN SERVICES. (1999b), Work Programme on Electronic Commission: Communication from the European Communities and Their Member States, (February 23), Geneva, Switzerland.

WORLD TRADE ORGANIZATION, COUNCIL ON TRADE IN SERVICES (1999c), World Programme on Electronic Commerce: A Program Report to the General Council (March 31, 1999), Geneva, Switzerland. This report contains an Annex by the Chairman that consists of the minutes of interim meetings of the Council on Trade in Services between November 1998 and March, 1999.

WORLD TRADE ORGANIZATION, GENERAL COUNCIL (1998), Work Programme on Electronic Commerce, (September 30), Geneva, Switzerland.

R. Electronic Commerce and the GATS Negotiations
(Some Comments on a Paper by Claude E. Barfield)

Harald Sander

1. Introduction

Electronic commerce is not only expected to change the ways of doing business dramatically but also to have a tremendous impact on the rules and regulations under which international trade will be conducted in the future. Many studies highlight the enormous potential of e-commerce. For example, International Data Cooperation has estimated that e-commerce will amount to US$ 2.5 trillion in the year 2004[1]. Since e-commerce is in essence "borderless", much of this electronic commerce will result in electronic trade. FORRESTER RESEARCH (2000) argues that in 2004 US $1.4 trillion of exports will be traded online, which would constitute about 18% of global exports[2]. Even if one does not believe fully in such projections – estimates often vary widely – the relevance of global e-commerce is obvious.

Despite its importance it is still unclear under what international trading rules electronic trade will be conducted in the future. The most important reason for this uncertainty is the very nature of e-commerce: it blurs the dividing line between goods and services. As a result, it is unclear what international trading rules should be applied to it. In other words, the subject of Claude Barfield's paper is among the most pressing and important unresolved issues in international trade negotiations. The paper's aim is "...to provide enough information to elicit debate". Although the author indicates that he does not have the aspiration to include all issues arising in the coming negotiations on electronic commerce and to treat them exhaustively, I find that the author covers most of the relevant issues in an impressively compact paper. I also find these issues being covered comprehensively, though – as said by the author himself – not exhaustively. In sum, I have benefited a lot from the paper, and it truly deserves to be read by a broad audience.

My comments are directed more towards "extending" the scope of the paper rather than criticizing its content. I have two types of comments. The first one deals with some – but not all – of the "six issues" related to e-commerce as raised

---

[1] Quoted from NIELSON and MORRIS (2001). The report "The Internet Economy" was originally published in September 2000 by International Data Cooperation and is available on www.idc.com.

[2] All data are quoted from HAUSER and WUNSCH (2001).

by the author. The second one is more general in respect to the author's aim to "provide enough information to elicit debate".

2. Issues in E-Commerce and Trade

The author distinguishes six issues of importance regarding e-commerce in the GATS negotiations: classification, taxation, scope or modes of supply, regulation (Article VI, the Telecommunications Annex and Reference Paper), privacy, and intellectual property. I will restrict my comments to the first three issues: classification, taxation, and modes of supply.

Claude Barfield discusses *classification* and *taxation* separately. I will, however, discuss both issues jointly for a very simple reason: classification determines taxation. From the point of view of trade negotiators classification is not just an intellectual exercise, but also, if not predominantly, instrumental in determining market access. As Barfield rightly points out, the problem cases for classification are "hybrids", or "fuzzy goods", i.e. e-commerce activities that can be classified either as goods or as services. In principle, the classification of e-commerce could have four different outcomes:

1. E-commerce is treated as goods trade and GATT rules apply.
2. E-commerce is treated as either goods trade subjected to GATT rules or trade in services subject to GATS rules depending on the nature of the transaction under consideration.
3. E-commerce is completely treated as trade in services and as such subject to GATS rules.
4. E-commerce is treated by a completely new multilateral discipline.

While the author has discussed the pros and cons of each classification extensively, I will have a closer look at the consequences of such classifications. If e-commerce were treated as goods trade, this would eventually lead to a situation of complete free trade in Internet transactions given the present moratoria on customs duties for electronic transmissions. Consequently, exporters interested in maximizing market access would eventually prefer e-commerce to be treated this way. However, nobody is really advocating this option for at least three reasons. First, bringing e-commerce under GATT rules would require reconsidering the moratoria explicitly. Secondly, applying GATT rules would in many cases conflict with the service character of e-commerce activities and thus meet resistance from trade negotiators. And finally as Claude Barfield has rightly pointed out, the WTO is eager to at least partially bring e-commerce under the umbrella of GATS. The latter point also speaks against establishing a completely new multilateral discipline for e-commerce, a position which is also taken by business groups such as CSI and AGB. While option #1 and #4 can therefore be considered to be unrealistic, the real choice is between option #2 and #3.

Arvind PANAGARIYA (2000) has strongly argued in favor of option #3, i.e. bringing e-commerce completely under the umbrella of the GATS agreement. Why does he want to override the classification debate? His main argument is that treating e-commerce across the board as services "...is clean and minimizes possible disputes that may arise from countries wishing to have certain transmissions classified as intangible goods and others as services. Under a mixed definition, in any trade dispute involving Internet trade, panels will have to decide whether the subject of dispute is a good or a service to determine whether the rules of GATT or GATS are to be applied in evaluating the dispute." (PANAGARIYA, 2000, p.5). While this suggestion has simplicity and clarity on its side, it also has its drawbacks:

- In the case of hybrid goods which can be delivered either electronically or physically this could eventually result in differential treatment. This leaves arbitrage possibilities to the market which may result in inefficiencies and subsequent welfare losses. Panagariya clarifies this point by contrasting a tariff/tax-free Internet import of a book by means of downloading with the physical import of the same book which is subject to import duties. Provided the Internet import has a lower price tag than the physical import this would lead to a complete switch to e-commerce. In this case one would buy from the most efficient source and subsequently experience welfare gains. If, however, Internet imports are carrying a relatively higher price tag or (particularly relevant in a developing country context) are subject to increasing marginal cost, e.g. caused by Internet congestion, the tariff/tax free status of e-commerce would lead to trade diversion and thus efficiency losses resulting from buying from a more expensive source, while at the same time the state will lose tax/tariff revenues.

- Given the virtual absence of tariffs in trade in services, subjecting all e-commerce to GATS rules could lead to substantial tariff revenue losses. In particular, developing countries may suffer from such losses (which – of course – need to be weighed against the benefits of cheaper imports). However, because under the current moratoria the duty free status is already there, this implies no additional losses.

- GATS allows for quantitative restrictions which are generally regarded as more harmful than tariffs.

- Given the potential loss in tariff revenues, taxation of Internet transactions might become an important issue. Since GATS allows discriminatory treatment of supply from abroad (unless the country has adopted "national treatment")m higher excise taxes or VAT on e-imports are possible means of trade policy and sources of government revenues. It is needless to say that collecting such taxes is difficult to administer, particularly in B2C-relations (while less so in B2B-relations)[3].

It is clear from this discussion that the debate will continue to revolve around option 2 and 3. Despite some drawbacks of option 3, its appealing feature is clarity and minimisation of possible trade conflicts. However, maybe it is just this particular feature that makes it less attractive from the point of view of trade negotiators and interest groups. We may therefore most likely continue to witness an "intellectual" debate on the hybrid character of e-commerce.

---

[3] The loss of tax revenues is a recurrent theme in the debate on e-commerce, at times resulting in a call for a general Internet tax, also known as a "bit tax".

In chapter 3 Claude Bárfield gives a very good account of the discussion evolving around the *modes of supply* in the GATS agreement and its application in e-commerce. Again, I do not have to add much to the discussion provided by Barfield other than referring to the likely consequences of classifying e-commerce under the different modes of supply. Barfield lists the 4 modes of supply according to GATS:

1. Cross-border, i.e. the service is supplied from the territory of one WTO member into the territory of another WTO member country.
2. Consumption abroad, i.e. the consumer purchases a service which is delivered in the territory of another WTO member.
3. Commercial presence, where the service supplier of a WTO member establishes a subsidiary or branch in another WTO member to supply a service.
4. Presence of natural persons, where the service is supplied by a person working in the territory of a WTO member.

For most e-commerce activities the choice is between Mode 1 and 2. However, once again, the applicable proper classification is not always beyond any doubt as the dividing line is often fuzzy. Consequently, it is likely that the choice made will be the result of negotiations which will take into consideration the likely outcome from adopting one or the other position. In this respect it is important to realize that in the Uruguay Round countries made the strongest liberalization commitments under Mode 2 and 3 (ALTINGER and ENDERS, 1996; PANAGARIYA, 2000). Given this situation, filing e-commerce under Mode 1 or Mode 2 has a direct influence on the extent of market liberalization. If e-commerce is considered to be Mode 2 the liberalization impact will be the largest. Thus businesses interested in market access may favor this solution. Consumer organizations, however, often favor a filing under Mode 1. Here the transaction is considered to have taken place in the country where the buyer resides. The buyer's residence is therefore also the country of jurisdiction. Consequently, Mode 1 will provide better consumer protection. The coming negotiations on Mode 1 to 4 will therefore most likely revolve around these two central issues: market access versus consumer protection.

3. Towards an Informed Debate on E-Commerce

Claude Barfield's paper provides a detailed and informed discussion of the most pressing issues regarding trade and e-commerce. While trade policy has always been controversial as it directly benefits and hurts interest groups, the perceived threat from "unrestricted e-commerce" is even more disputed[4] (and not at least

---

[4] For illustrative purposes just have a look at the following statements on e-commerce by the Telecommunication Workers Association of Canada found on the Internet at www.twa.ca as the first (!) website listed by GOOGLE, a search engine that sorts websites by "relevance". The document is entitled "E-Commerce and the General Agreement on Trade in Services (GATS): The Expanding Threat of Free Trade": "If the deregulation of electrical commerce is integrated into the GATS agreement, however,

reflected visibly in the protests surrounding recent WTO ministerials). Consequently, Barfield's objective to "...provide enough information to elicit debate" should therefore be highly welcomed, given the controversial nature of the issue, let alone the often uninformed publicly given opinions on e-commerce. However, one can never do enough to "elicit an informed debate". While I think that the paper could gain from discussing more explicitly the diverging positions of and consequences for countries and interest groups involved in the ongoing discussion, I am fully aware that my request is far beyond what one can reasonably expect from Claude Barfield's paper here. However, in the presence of the increasingly public discussion on trade policies and the impact of such discussions on the negotiation strategies in WTO ministerials, my dream of a (so far – to my knowledge – unwritten) paper on e-commerce would be one that comparatively analyzes the position of the various stakeholders in the negotiation process: developed countries that are mainly net e-exporters, e-exporting developing countries, e-importing developing countries, e-business, workers organizations and consumer (protection) organizations. Claude Barfield's paper already goes a long way in providing deep insights into a complicated, controversial and important issue. However, because of the relevance of the matter it is also clear that even more needs to be done to facilitate an informed(!) debate on e-commerce as this will ultimately influence and determine the future of one-fifth of world trade.

companies would be able to challenge any contract provisions or government action which limited their ability to engage in such cross-border activity as a violation of the agreement — and to have such challenges backed by the threat of trade sanctions. ...This scenario poses a profound threat to a wide range of jobs. Corporations would be able to have telephone, hydro, insurance, airline, banking, postal and other work currently done in Canada carried out far more cheaply in far flung, low-wage areas of the world, by utilizing telecommunications capacity to link their widely dispersed operations. If the corporate position on e-commerce is integrated into the GATS, corporations would be able to shift any activity that is carried out online to jurisdictions where labor is cheap and submissive or where they find tax and environmental laws more to their liking."

References

ALTINGER, L., ENDERS, A. (1996), The Scope and Depth of GATS Commitments, The World Economy, May.

FORRESTER RESEARCH (2000), Sizing Global Online Exports, Forrester Research, Report Series.

HAUSER, H., WUNSCH, S. (2001), A Call for a WTO E-Commerce Initiative, Swiss Institute for International Economics and Applied Economic Research, University of St. Gallen.

NIELSON, J., MORRIS, R. (2001) E-Commerce and Trade: Resolving Dilemmas, OECD Observer, March 30.

PANAGARIYA, A. (2000), E-Commerce, WTO and Developing Countries, Geneva: UNCTAD.

TINAWI, E., BERKEY, J.O. (1999), E-Services and the WTO: The Adequacy of the GATS Classification Framework, Paris: OECD Forum on Electronic Commerce, Paris, 12-13 October, available at: www.oecd.org.

S. The Internet and Society

William H. Dutton[1]

1. Technological Determinism and Conflicting Visions of the Internet

Rapid, continuing advances in computer technology, and the related convergence of computing and telecommunications, has enabled the development of an array of information and communication technologies (ICTs), from the cell phone to the Internet. The significance of these innovations, and their application across all sectors of society, made ICTs like the Internet key defining technologies of the late twentieth century. Widespread fascination with their technical ingenuity and growing capabilities has been a consistent focus of attention: from the emergence of the "computer age" in the 1950s and 60s, through the "microchip revolution" in the 1970s, to the Internet-based "superhighway" and "information society" of the 1980s and 90s, on to twenty-first century Internet-enabled "e-everything" digitized globalization.

The social implications of ICTs have been viewed mainly in terms of conflicting utopian versus dystopian perspectives. For example, the classic dystopian novel of the twentieth century, George Orwell's *1984*, pivoted around the emergence of two-way television – the telescreen – as an instrument of propaganda and electronic surveillance. Half a century after its first publication, the growing centrality of the Internet and World Wide Web has generated up-dated Orwellian visions of multimedia surveillance, together with fears that new Internet-based networks and services are isolating individuals, undermining democratic processes, and destroying jobs. On the other hand, many influential protagonists have argued that the Internet and Web promote global community, "electronic democracy", and an information economy which would bring fulfillment, empowerment, and jobs for the twenty-first century (NEGROPONTE, 1995; GATES, 1995). Still others dismiss the importance of ICTs.

These diverse views of the technology oversimplify its role and fail to provide an understanding of the "actual mechanism by which technology leads to social change" (MESTHENE, 1969). The continuing debate between utopian and dystopian perspectives has illuminated the social and economic issues at stake, but has failed to inform policy and practice. There is much evidence to show that complex social processes can result in many different outcomes for the same technology, depending on choices made by people involved in the production, use, consumption and governance of ICTs (DUTTON, 1996). Developing perspectives on the

---

[1] This chapter is an up-dated and revised version of Dutton (forthcoming). My thanks to Malcolm Peltu for his comments on this chapter.

relationship between computers and society to illuminate these processes is therefore a vital step in addressing broad social, economic, and political issues - and to provide guidance on social and technical choices about ICTs in a variety of contexts. Understanding the Internet in this wider context is essential when assessing its societal implications.

2. Limitations of the "Social Impacts of ICTs" Approach

There are four major limitations of the technologically-driven traditional view of ICTs and society: an over-simplified depiction of how outcomes are determined; too narrow a focus; bias towards long-term predictions; and failure to recognize that technology is implicitly social.

2.1 An Over-simplified View of the Processes Determining Societal Outcomes

Dystopian and utopian scenarios appear highly plausible because they are often based on the technical capabilities of ICTs, which are treated as having "social impacts" as drivers of change. However, the actual implications of the development and use of ICTs - for example in relation to issues such as privacy, freedom of speech, and employment - are more difficult to forecast because they are shaped by social and political choices, not simply by features of the technology. However, the view that social impacts followed technologically-driven trajectories has been prevalent from the earliest research into social aspects of ICTs, which were led by specialists involved directly in developing the technology.

The social-impact approach was usually based on rational forecasts of the social opportunities and risks created by particular features of the technology, such as the way a computer's storage capacity enables organizations to create huge databanks of information about individuals. However, empirical research usually found that rational expectations based on such capabilities were seldom realized (KLING, 2000). For example, when computers were first introduced to organizations, they did enable the creation of huge databanks - but managers and professionals tended to use them within prevailing data processing paradigms that aimed simply to improve the efficiency of existing practices. It took decades before the emergence of new ICT paradigms changed information collection in ways that opened potentially major new threats to privacy and surveillance.

This poor track record in forecasting the implications of technical change led to fundamental criticisms of theories based on assumptions that particular real or potential technical features will have predetermined "impacts". Instead of trying to predict the impacts of technical change, alternative approaches to social research on the design and implications of technologies have therefore emphasized ways of exploring broader psychological, organizational, political, geographical, economic, and other social processes and choices which determine outcomes of innovation (DUTTON, 1999; KLING, 2000). Such research on the "social shaping" of technological change has been highly critical of the simplified, linear models of cause and effect used by technological determinists (WILLIAMS and EDGE, 1996). In examining the Internet and society, this broader perspective is vital because the Internet touches so many everyday social, organizational, and individual activities.

2.2 Narrowness of the "Information Age" Thesis

By focusing on the technology, social-impact research naturally gave high priority to the functions for which ICTs were designed: processing and communicating information. For example, American sociologist Daniel Bell (1999 [1973]) wrote a seminal work on the "information society", which he called the "post-industrial society". He saw information as the key economic resource in this new era - not raw materials or financial capital, as in earlier agricultural and industrial societies.

The most significant trend towards an information society was the shift in the majority of the labor force from agriculture and manufacturing to services, largely through the growth of "information work". This includes a broad array of jobs related to the creation, transmission, and processing of information, ranging from programmers and Web designers to teachers, researchers, consultants, journalists, game designers and call-center staff. Increasing importance has also been attached to knowledge created from information and to the power shifts involved in the growth of a knowledge élite who understand how to work with data, knowledge, information systems, simulation, and related analytical techniques.

These conceptions of the information society have increasingly defined the public's understanding of social and economic change tied to ICTs. However, the changes in work, technology, and power posited by this thesis have all been challenged (FREEMAN, 1996), as has the general identification of information as the key resource of the economy (DUTTON, 1999). The emphasis given to the information sector has also risked shifting attention away from other still-important parts of the economy, such as agriculture, manufacturing and healthcare.

Information is a highly variable currency: it is not always wanted or valued. As a resource, information can lose its value, such as in the case of a day-old newspaper, or retain its value after repeated use, as with a literary classic. If defined narrowly in the sense of being about "facts", the term "information" becomes far too limiting as a depiction of the social role of ICTs. But if defined very broadly, for instance as anything that "reduces uncertainty", then information seems to be so all encompassing that it becomes virtually meaningless. Moreover, information can create, rather than reduce uncertainty. For example, those more informed about a topic are often less certain about its properties than many who are less informed (MacKENZIE, 1999). And information is not a new resource, as has frequently been suggested. It has been important in every sector of the economy throughout history (CASTELLS, 2000). What is new is how you use ICTs to get access to information, as well as to people, services, and technologies (DUTTON, 1999).

2.3 Bias Towards Long-term Analyses of Staged Development

The information society concept is underpinned by the notion of a staged progression of an economy: from agricultural to industrial, information, and whatever comes next, such as a "knowledge society". An alternative forecast of social and economic evolution is the idea of long economic development cycles caused by successive waves of technological revolutions (FREEMAN, 1996). This argues that the invention of a new technology, like the steam engine or computer, can have applications across the economy that affect many facets of our lives, for instance ICTs having effects well beyond what might be labeled as information work or information processing.

Both the staged and cyclical theories are attractive because they promise some level of predictability. However, there is no consensus on the identification and validation of these stages or cycles. There is a long lag of one to two decades between the invention of a radically new technology and its impact on the way things are done, as it takes time for people to change habits and beliefs before accepting a new paradigm for how they do things. But such lags do not always eventually yield to progress or a new stage of development.

Although these long-term perspectives provide valuable insights, more detailed treatments are needed to identify the precise manner in which the technology is incorporated into everyday life and how the choices made by users and designers affect outcomes. These studies of technology and society, in which ICTs are just one instance - albeit an important one – are needed to identify, analyze, and understand the processes at work in reshaping institutions and practices. Researchers in this field have investigated the uses and consumption of many specific ICTs, ranging from cell-phone text messaging by teenagers to uses of the Internet by political activists and global industries. Such technology assessments bring to the surface a wide range of multidisciplinary issues.

2.4 Failure to Acknowledge that Technology is Intrinsically Social

The "e-society" and other popular conceptions of an information society might capture the social significance of the increasing centrality of the Internet, but fail to provide adequate insights into its role in social change. Social research can move beyond the constraints of such technologically-based viewpoints only by recognizing that technologies are inherently social, in that they are designed, produced, and used by people. Moreover, their design and use involves knowhow, which is itself a social attribute (MacKENZIE and WAJCMAN 1985: 3). And technologies are social in that they define, but do not determine, how people do things, thereby making some paths more economically, culturally, or socially rational than others.

This is exemplified by the way the Internet can shape and reshape many aspects of daily life: how people get information and communicate with one another; what, when, and where things are done; what people know; who they know; and what they consume. These are all issues concerned with access, specifically "tele-access" through the Internet and other ICT networks, rather than the technology as such. Tele-access involves much more than just access to information or ICTs, but to how ICTs shape access - both electronically mediated and unmediated - to a wide array of social and economic resources. A realistic analysis of the Internet's social role therefore requires an understanding of (tele)-access and its multiple dimensions.

3. The Internet and Society: The Crucial Role of Tele-Access

3.1 "Communicative Power" and the Politics of Information

The central role of processes that shape tele-access has become more evident as people understand the limitations of seeing information as the pivotal concept in social studies of ICTs. The tele-access perspective at last challenges the cliché that "information is power", which ignores the degree to which economic resources enable access to the information and expertise that is the basis of creating knowledge. It is not information *per se*, but the ability to control access to information that is key. Access is also shaped not only by technologies, but also by institutional arrangements, public policy, geographical proximity - as in gaining tacit knowledge from direct observation – and other social factors.

The role of ICTs in shaping access to information might be called "information politics" (DANZIGER et. al., 1982: 133-35; GARNHAM, 1999). However, information is only one element in what can be viewed as a far more general politics of access.

3.2 Key Dimensions of Tele-Access

Social and technical choices about ICTs can reconfigure not only electronic and physical access information, as is often suggested, but to four inter-related resources (DUTTON, 1999):

1. Information. ICTs not only change the way people get information, but also alter the whole corpus of what a person knows and the information available at any given time and place. ICTs play a role in making some people information rich and others comparatively information poor.

2. People. ICTs can change more than just the ways individuals communicate with one another. They can also influence whom individuals meet, talk to, stay in touch with, work with, and get to know. ICTs can connect or isolate people. For example, one of the most popular uses of the Internet is for e-mail - for gaining access to people, not for access to information *per se*.

3. Services. ICTs influence what products and services a person consumes and whom an individual purchases them from, as well as changing how people

consume information, products, and services. They can also render obsolete a local business or an entire industry, or create a new business or industry.
4. Technologies. Access to particular technologies - equipment, knowhow, and techniques - shapes access to other technologies, as ICTs interconnect and depend on one another in many ways. For instance, the Internet can provide access to vast numbers of computers around the world, yet it can be accessed only using other ICTs, such as a computer and communications links. The push for digital television requires consumers as well as producers to adopt new technologies.

There are many other ways in which ICTs can reduce, screen, reinforce, or alter tele-access, such as shaping the information content and flow by accident or design. ICTs also change patterns of interaction between people, information, communities, and organizations. The Internet can reduce travel, save time, and extend the geography of human community as a substitute for face-to-face communication, or permit communication among people who might never have an opportunity to meet face-to-face. It may also replace valuable human contact with a much less rewarding form of communication, fostering social isolation (SMITH and KOLLOCK, 1999).

3.3 Social Factors Shaping Choices and their Implications for Access

ICT innovations and their social implications are not random or unstructured. For example, a pattern of tele-access such as the distribution of information "haves" and "have-nots" is enabled and constrained by the social and economic contexts within which relevant actors at all levels make choices. There are a number of major sets of factors that shape such tele-access patterns (DUTTON, 1999). One includes economic resources - such as the size, wealth, and vitality of nations, companies and other actors - that place substantial constraints on the development and use of ICTs.

A second set relates to ICT concepts and practices that become the foundation of powerful belief systems or "paradigms", which create very different ways of interpreting reality and thinking within each paradigm. For instance, information-society visions, like "virtual universities", have been important shapers of social, political, and technological choices in education and other arenas, irrespective of their descriptive validity. At the same time, experience and knowledge about ICTs can influence or create a paradigm shift, which also substantially changes how people design and use ICTs (FREEMAN, 1996).

Another set of factors focus on the conceptions and responses of the wide variety of users - workers, consumers, managers, citizens, audiences, etc - who play an active role in shaping the implications of ICTs, often in very different ways to those expected by simply extrapolating from the perceived potential of the technology. Misconceptions of the user can therefore undermine the diffusion of ICTs (COOPER and WOOLGAR, 1993).

Factors related to the geography of space and place can also facilitate or constrain tele-access. For example, the use of the Internet can depend on where ICTs are placed within a household or around the world. ICTs do not erase geography, as is often argued, but often make geography more important (GODDARD and RICHARDSON, 1996). Since ICTs can be used from many places, they give individuals or firms more flexibility in location decisions, such as enabling a firm to place a higher priority on criteria like easing face-to-face communication with customers or gaining access to skilled or low cost labor, rather than physical proximity to the headquarters of the firm (CAIRNCROSS, 1997).

Finally, choices about access are constrained by a wide variety of institutional arrangements and public policies, because technical, social, policy, and organizational innovation are interdependent (FREEMAN, 1996). For example, the design of an organization influences how the Internet is used within it, but the Internet also creates many new options for radically redesigning organizations and interactions between them.

These kinds of social factors shape, and are shaped by, tele-access in ways that can have both immediate and cumulative long-range consequences on most areas of modern life. However, this focus on the social and technical shaping of access is but one way to understand and study the social implications of the Internet. It is also useful to compare this approach with a number of more conventional perspectives on the "information revolution" that have widely influenced policy and practice by framing what people think about, and what they ignore. The primary focus of the most influential of these perspectives fit one of five broad and overlapping categories: impacts, information, influence, technology and strategy (DUTTON, 1999). The first two have been discussed earlier; influence, technology and strategy in relation to tele-access are examined in the next section.

4. Encompassing Studies of Influence, Control and Management

4.1 Influence and the Mass Media

An early social-impacts perspective evolved out of research after World War II on propaganda and the political implications of mass media, such as newspapers, radio and television. This research created many useful models of media effects, including "agenda-setting" that highlights the critical role of media "gatekeepers", like journalists and publishers, in shaping access to news. It generally focused on the content of messages conveyed through the media, and the messages' influence on those exposed directly or indirectly to them.

Researchers increasingly looked at ICTs within this media "influence" tradition, as awareness grew that all communication media are based on the technologies that have converged into ICTs. One issue raised by some of these researchers is whether the interactiveness of emerging media, such as digital and Web-TV, will make them more engaging and, therefore, more powerful in shaping attitudes, beliefs, and values. Others have focused on the way the profusion of media and channels can segment audiences in ways that might erode their quality and integrative effect in providing the common experiences or shared text of a community.

However, the ICT-based technical change that is reconfiguring access to audiences has challenged the very idea of "mass media" that dominated communication industries and media research throughout the twentieth century. The influence perspective becomes even less applicable outside media studies, such as to assess the implications of ICTs for the economy.

Marshall McLuhan anticipated this problem in the early 1960s, when he argued that there had been too much emphasis on the content of the message. In claiming "it is the medium that shapes and controls the scale and form of human association and action," McLuhan (1964: 9) indicated his belief that television's ability to reconfigure access to messages was more significant than whatever message was conveyed. This resonates more with a focus on tele-access than the media-influence tradition.

4.2 Technology, Expertise, and Social Control

The study of technological change suggests that tele-access should be viewed as the outcome of an indeterminate social and political process, rather than being set on a predetermined technological trajectory. For example, the much promoted view that technological advances are democratizing access to ICTs or isolating individuals are based on deterministic assumptions that are empirically questionable. Deterministic perspectives can also be dangerous if they undermine the political will to make hard choices about achieving positive social and political outcomes.

The design and development of ICTs is not as deterministic of social outcomes as often assumed by early theorists. Neither are they neutral. Advances in ICTs reshape access, but they do not determine access. Technology is like policy, because it tells us how we are supposed to do things, and makes some ways of doing things more rational and practical than another. Also, the biases designed into technological artifacts and systems can be even more enduring than legislation (WINNER, 1986: 19-39), and create a momentum that is difficult to reverse (HUGHES, 1994). For instance, the rise of e-mail is biased toward the speed up of interpersonal communication. Individuals can choose to slow their communication down, but this often takes a conscious effort and strong political will within organizations and networks accustomed to Internet speed.

Technology concerns more than just equipment. It also encompasses the knowledge essential to its use (MacKENZIE and WAJCMAN, 1985: 3). The control of technology is therefore bound up with issues of who has access to the skills, equipment, and knowhow essential to design, implement, and use it. Changes in technology can restrict access to all these resources, but can equally expand access, for example by the way simple Web user interfaces have given easy and quick access to worldwide stores of information. Likewise, social choices, such as the decision to learn a new human or computer language, affect access to technology, jobs, and people.

These perceptions have led to the identification of centralized social control as a significant possible outcome of technological change. Many dystopian novels and films, such as *Jurassic Park*, capture the fear that technology is out of control and is creating an unelected, high-tech élite which increasingly dominates decision-making. This concern has remained a consistent theme of social research on ICTs, from the earliest computer-impacts studies. However, many social researchers observing more recent advances argue the opposite, particularly in relation to the Internet's ability to place more control in the hands of users (De SOLA POOL, 1983; SHAPIRO, 1999).

4.3 Management Strategies Related to ICT Use

A focus on the goals and strategies of actors, instead of the capabilities of the technology, has been most fully developed within the management field. In the early decades of its use, from the 1950s, the computer was seen by management theorists as a strategic tool for enabling executives to boost centralized control by giving them access to information about the organization's resources and everyday operations. Centralization using computers was seen primarily as an extension of, and means for realizing, the prevailing management paradigm of the time. Empirical research indeed discovered that those who control decision-making tend to adopt and use ICTs in ways that follow and reinforce existing centralized or decentralized patterns of control within the organization (DANZIGER et al, 1982).

This highlights the malleability of ICTs. However, top managers are only one of a more complex and interdependent set of organizational actors. Unpredictable organizational and social outcomes emerge from a struggle among these actors over the design and use of ICTs. This does not take place on a level playing field, since inequalities in existing institutions, cultures, and social and technical systems favor some actors and choices over others; but neither does any single actor have a monopoly of control.

From this perspective, the major implications of ICTs grow from management strategies rather than technological characteristics. That view remains central to contemporary management research, but often within a management paradigm that places less emphasis on the value of top management control and more on the virtues of innovation and networking (CASTELLS, 2000; ARQUILLA and RONFELDT, 2001).

5. The Interaction of Strategies within a Broader Ecology of Games

The struggle for control over the design and use of the Internet and other ICTs generally takes place in a variety of different arenas at the same time. All actors are not involved in the same struggle: individuals and groups pursue different goals within their own domains in an "ecology of games" (DUTTON 1999: 14-16). For instance, a specialist might be pursuing a technically elegant network design, while a top manager is primarily seeking cost reductions. This places major constraints on the predictability of outcomes based on assessments of strategic aims, unless the varied goals of different actors in the broader ecology of games is well understood and orchestrated.

Global advances in ICTs, the momentum of technologies already in place, and the widespread application of the Internet place limits on the ability of any individual, household, organization, or nation to control the design and implementation of ICTs in predetermined ways. Tele-access therefore provides a more realistic view of how the outcomes of technological change emerge from processes of social and technical choice involving many different actors, within a variety of separate but inter-related technical, organizational, social, and policy arenas.

Ideas like the information society are important because they shape views about the way the world works and, thereby, influence the decisions of individuals, firms, and governments. That is one reason why alternative perspectives on the role of the Internet in society, such as the shaping of tele-access, are more than competing theories. They are also ideas that can shape decisions in everyday life, and in once-in-a-lifetime choices.

References

ARQUILLA, J., RONFELDT, D. (2001), Networks and Netwars, Santa Monica, CA: RAND.

BELL D. (1999, 1973), The Coming of Post-Industrial Society: A Venture in Social Forecasting, New York: Basic Books.

CAIRNCROSS, F. (1997), The Death of Distance, Cambridge, Massachusetts: Harvard Business School Press.

CASTELLS, M. (2000, 1996), The Rise of the Network Society: The Information Age: Economy, Society and Culture, Volume 1, Second Edition, Oxford: Blackwell Publishers.

COOPER, G., WOOLGAR, S. (1993), Software is Society Made Malleable: The Importance of Conceptions of Audience in Software and Research Practice, PICT Policy Research Paper No. 25, Uxbridge: PICT, Brunel University.

DANZIGER, J.N., DUTTON, W.H., Kling, R., Kraemer, K.L. (1982), Computers and Politics New York: Columbia University Press.

De SOLA POOL, I. (1983), Technologies of Freedom, Cambridge, Mass., and London: The Belknap Press of Harvard University Press.

DUTTON, W. H., ed. (1996), Information and Communication Technologies – Visions and Realities, Oxford: Oxford University Press.

DUTTON W. H. (1999), Society on the Line: Information Politics in the Digital Age (Oxford: Oxford University Press).

DUTTON, W. H. (forthcoming), Computers and Society, in: SMELSER, N. J. and BALTES, P. B. (2001), The International Encyclopedia of the Social and Behavioral Sciences, Oxford: Elsevier Science Limited.

FREEMAN, C. (1996), The Two-Edged Nature of Technical Change: Employment and Unemployment, in: DUTTON, W. H. (ed.), Information and Communication Technologies – Visions and Realities, Oxford and New York: Oxford University Press, 19-36.

GARNHAM, N. (1999), Information Politics: The Study of Communicative Power, in: DUTTON, W. H. (ed.), Society on the Line: Information Politics in the Digital Age, Oxford: Oxford University Press, 77-78.

GATES, B. (1995), The Road Ahead, London: Viking.

GODDARD, J., RICHARDSON, R. (1996), Why Geography Will Still Matter: What Jobs Go Where?, in: DUTTON, W. H. (ed.), Information and Communication Technologies – Visions and Realities, Oxford and New York: Oxford University Press, 197-214.

HUGHES, T.P. (1994), Technological Momentum, in: SMITH, M.R., MARX, L. (eds), Does Technology Drive History?, Cambridge, Massachusetts: MIT Press, 101-13.

KLING, R. (2000), Social Informatics: A New Perspective on Social Research about Information and Communication Technologies, Prometheus, 18 (3), September, 245-264.

MacKENZIE, D. (1999), The Certainty Trough, in: DUTTON, W. H. (ed), Society on the Line: Information Politics in the Digital Age, Oxford: Oxford University Press, 43-46.

MacKENZIE, D., WAJCMAN, J., eds. (1985), The Social Shaping of Technology: How a Refrigerator Got Its Hum, Milton Keynes and Philadelphia: Open University Press.

McLUHAN, M. (1964, reprinted 1994), Understanding Media: The Extensions of Man, London: Rutledge.

MESTHENE, E.G. (1969), The Role of Technology in Society, reprinted in: TEICH, A. H., ed. (1981), Technology and Man's Future, Third Edition, New York: St. Martin's Press, 99-129.

NEGROPONTE, N. (1995), Being Digital, London: Hodder & Stoughton.

SHAPIRO, A. L. (1999), The Control Revolution, New York: The Century Foundation.

SMITH, M. A., KOLLOCK, P., eds. (1999), Communities in Cyberspace, London: Routledge.

WILLIAMS, R., EDGE, D. (1996), The Social Shaping of Technology, in: DUTTON (1996), 53-67.

WINNER, L. (1986), The Whale and the Reactor: A Search for Limits in an Age of High Technology, Chicago and London: The University of Chicago Press.

T. The Internet and Society
(Some Comments on Paper by William H. Dutton)

Guenter Heiduk

Information and communication are basic activities that support and permit the functioning and development of a society. Moreover, patterns of information and communication make it possible to define and distinguish societies. This is true on many levels, starting with the small-scale societal 'family', but also including large-scale societies, such as cultures and possibly – though not always – nation-states.

At the same time, it is only possible for societies to coexist, if some of their members possess communication skills that allow senders and receivers of information to bridge the differences between societies.

The *quantitative and qualitative demand* for information and communication in a society seem to be directly related to its level and speed of development, its size and the degree to which it is geographically spread out. Moreover, the technology that is used to communicate within a society co-evolves with its level of complexity. Complex societies whose members are spread out in large areas have relied more and more upon communication technologies that make it possible to communicate independently from geographical and time restrictions. This has brought about a rise in the speed of information exchange as well as an increase in the volumes of information that are transmitted. This co-evolution has become evident in the consecutive development of print technologies, telephone, radio, television and finally the Internet.

William Dutton is correct in pointing out that the availability of new ICTs in a society does not necessarily justify its characterization as an 'information society'. We also share his opinion that technologically-driven traditional approaches to ICTs and society have limitations that do not make it possible to catch the complexity of this relationship. William Dutton makes 'tele-access' the central term of his argumentation. One way to interpret this focus is to ask to what extent new ICTs can be used to fully exploit the resources of a global society via interactive information and communication processes. He subsumes various aspects of Internet technology under one conceptual headline and points out that the impact of ICTs on society is far from being deterministic. However, the paper does not make it clear how his concept can be used for analytical work. There is little doubt, though, that Dutton has chosen a very ambitious task in this work. To make his concept operational he would have to present a complete picture of interdependences and repercussions between socio-cultural, political and economic levels. All of these levels are crucial when it comes to the impact of ICTs on society. At the same time, as Dutton uses tele-access as his key term, we have to acknowledge that access itself requires specific technological, economic, political and behavioral conditions.

It is obvious that the derivation of elegant deterministic results will always re-quire significant simplifications in assumptions. This type of analysis is of course not qualified to solve questions similar to those asked by Dutton. At the same time, the modeling of complex socio-dynamic processes still presents us with major methodological difficulties. There are currently only a few approaches that provide promising directions.[1]

To analyze the interdependences between new ICTs, access and society on a macro-level the following ideas may be helpful:

I. *We have to distinguish between societies that develop technologies (innovators) and those that are confronted with given technologies (potential adopters).*

    A modern capitalistic society needs a high quantity and quality of information and a high intensity of communication. Such a society has stronger incentives to develop technologies that allow it to satisfy this need for information and communication. The political system as part of this society has to offer the degree of freedom that makes access to such technologies possible.

II. *The use of this access by the members of a society is an evolutionary process that can be called "change of a society".*

    It includes system-specific characteristics on the economic, political and socio-cultural level. After the complete diffusion of a technology there is a new window for the development of another technological generation.

III. *The diffusion of a technology by potential adopters goes along with more friction.*

    A specific characteristic of new ICTs is their potentially rapid global diffusion. For societies that are not developers, but only adopters of a technology, the probability is greater that a given technology fits their needs much less than is the case for the developing society. In other words: The friction that goes along with its adoption is bigger. There is also a larger probability that parts of the society are not interested in the diffusion of a technology or even have an interest in prohibiting its diffusion. Barriers to the adoption of new technologies can also lie in socio-cultural conditions.

IV. *The friction that goes along with the adoption of a technology creates a feedback loop within which the degree of adoption is determined, but during which major changes in the society itself can also be engendered.*

    If the above skeptical decision-makers have a possibility to control access, the likelihood that a technology will spread in this society is significantly reduced or at least the speed with which a technology diffuses is slower. This may lead us to some cases where diffusion is completely inhibited, while in other cases diffusion goes along with much more friction. In an extreme case where a technology is not compatible with significant parts or aspects of a society, this can lead to a radical and discontinuous change in the system itself.

---

[1] See for instance WOLFGANG, W. (2000), Socio-dynamics: a systematic approach to mathematical modeling in the social sciences, Harwood Acad. Publ., Amsterdam.

The lecture of William Dutton's paper will almost inevitably lead the interested reader to ponder about the many experiences we all have concerning the impact of new technologies on our life. There are still many possibilities to get lost in this labyrinth of different and sometimes contradicting observations. Efforts like Dutton's that aim at conceptualizing the relevant relationships are needed and highly appreciated.

U. Knowledge, Work Organisation and Economic Growth*

Elena Arnal, Wooseok Ok and Raymond Torres

1. Introduction

There is an interesting debate over whether OECD countries are on the eve of a New Economy, an era of higher non-inflationary growth. According to some analysts, the adoption of information and communications technology (ICT), combined with increased economic integration among countries, is transforming economic systems, much like the "electricity revolution" in earlier episodes of economic history (see HELPMAN, 1998). This view does not preclude business cycles, but it does imply that GDP growth rates would be higher over the medium to longer-run.

It is still too early to assess whether these sanguine predictions will materialise. There is some evidence that the economic performance of the United States has been exceptional (at least until recently), but the same cannot be asserted in the case many other OECD countries. In addition, the current weakness of the American economy will undoubtedly instil a measure of caution in this debate. More importantly, although new technology may hold the promise of higher economic growth, policies have a key role to play in ensuring that these potential gains will materialise (OECD, 2000*a*). In particular, the labour market should play an important part in this process. Unfortunately, relatively little attention has been devoted to this question. The aim of this paper is precisely to shed some light on the labour market issues at stake.

More generally, an economy grows either through a wider mobilisation of labour supply or through raising its productivity. Without neglecting the importance of the first factor, this paper focuses mainly on productivity. It analyses the importance for technology-use and productivity of work reorganisation, human capital and labour mobility. More specifically, the purpose of this paper is a) to shed light on emerging trends in the structure of labour markets, notably as regards work

* This paper reproduces the OECD Labour Market and Social Policy Occasional Paper with the same title, for which the proper authorisation has been obtained. It was presented by Wooseok Ok at the International Symposium on "Internet, Economic Growth and Globalisation" which was held at Duisburg and Potsdam/Berlin during August 8-10 2001. We would like to thank Thomas Coutrot (DARES, France), Bill Harley (University of Melbourne) and Juha Antila (Finnish Ministry of Labour) for providing some of the data. We would also like to acknowledge the valuable statistical assistances of Sylvie Jannot and Steven Tobin. The views expressed in this paper are our own and do not necessarily reflect those of OECD member countries.

practices and the nature of skill requirements (Section B); b) to analyse the possible links between labour markets and the growth process (Section C); and c) to discuss policy-related challenges (Section D).

2. The Changing Nature of Work

Over the past few years, the labour market situation has improved significantly in the majority of OECD countries. Unemployment has followed a downward trend for the area as a whole, and few countries continue to suffer from double-digit unemployment rates. This improvement reflects a combination of cyclical and structural factors, including changes in the functioning of labour and product markets resulting from policy reforms and the introduction of new technology. However, this improvement does not come alone, but is accompanied by some significant changes in the nature of work. The purpose of this section is to identify, without pretending being exhaustive, some of these changes which are often masked by the job creation process. These developments include a re-organisation of work within firms, a rising demand for certain types of skills and a change in the employer-employee relationship for certain workers.

2.1 The Diffusion of New Work Practices and New Forms of Work

In the face of an increasingly competitive environment, firms may respond in two different ways. On the one hand, they may reorganise production and work to improve flexibility and reduce X-inefficiencies. This strategy encompasses what is termed in this report "new work practices" (See Box 1). On the other hand, firms can have recourse to external or numerical forms of flexibility, for instance by relying on atypical forms of employment. In this respect, tele-work is one emerging phenomenon of particular interest.

Box 1. New Work Practices: A Real Phenomenon or Management Fad?

The literature contains numerous discussions of the so-called "organisational revolution". The argument is usually that new work practices have profoundly changed the way firms operate (LINDBECK and SNOWER, 2000). According to this view, "traditional" organisations require their employees to have specialised skills consistent with standardised production processes. Reflecting this job specialisation, the argument goes, traditional organisations operate a clear-cut distinction between narrow occupations. In this environment, relatively little attention is given to workers' capacity to acquire multiple skills. In the new types of firms emerging nowadays, this clear-cut distinction of occupations would be breaking down. Workers would be given responsibilities in the area of production, administration, training, marketing, customer relations, and even product innovation. The new, smaller, customer-oriented teams require versatility, cognitive and social competence, as well as judgement. In addition, employees would be involved in

---

management issues such as the evaluation and supervision of their peers, the training of new recruits, the organisation of input supplies, and the choice of financial and accounting procedures. In such a context, what matters is not only the competence in a particular activity, but the ability to change jobs, as well as "soft skills".

In practical terms, new work practices encompass three broad directions of change:

- the new approach is often associated with making <u>production processes "lean" and more responsive to market changes</u>. This is the case of strategies that aim at returning to "core business", "re-engineering" and "outsourcing", all of which are supposed to entail a concentration of the activities of the firm on essential parts of the business, where comparative advantage lies. "Just-in-time" production, "total quality control" systems and "benchmarking" are intended to make the firm more responsive to the market while at the same time encouraging the adoption of practices successful in other organisations.

- other practices involve changes in work arrangements, generally with the aim of <u>decentralising decision-making and improving the flow of information between management and workers</u>. Team-work encompasses a delegation of responsibility to a group of workers, who can suggest or decide jointly the way they work and are responsible for the outcomes. In this case, individual workers are asked to be involved more actively in the task of the other members of the team and are required to have a wider range of knowledge than in traditional organisations. Suggestion schemes, quality circles, flatter management structures and "employee involvement" are supposed to bring front-line workers closer to top-management.

- <u>systems of performance-related pay</u>, though by no means new, are often implemented as part of work reorganisation. Accordingly, workers' pay depends in part on either the performance of the firm (e.g. bonuses, profit-sharing schemes, stock options), or individual performance. In principle, these systems offer stronger incentives to employees to raise their performance and they tend to be associated with team-work and the move to a greater autonomy of workers.

These discussions, however, should be treated with caution. To start with, the terminology is not standardised, so that the concepts often mean different things to different authors. Also it is difficult to understand what is really "new" in this area, and, more importantly, the economic significance of the work practices in question is often unclear. The business literature might tend to exaggerate the extent to which the new practices alter the organisation of work in reality. One of the main aims of this study consists to gauge whether "new" work practices reflect real economic change, as opposed to management "fad".

2.1.1 How Prevalent are New Work Practices Among Firms?

It is difficult to measure statistically the incidence of new work practices, due to some measuring problems. In certain surveys, the question is labelled in terms of whether a specific practice is introduced, and not how many employees are in-

volved in the practice. Inter-temporal and cross-country comparisons are complicated by the fact that surveys often change through time and vary across countries.
Only two surveys have been designed for the purpose of cross-country comparison, namely "EPOC" for ten European countries and "Nordflex" for four Nordic
countries. Keeping these limitations in mind, interesting empirical regularities
emerge from existing surveys.[1]

First, a significant number of respondents report that their firm is adopting *new
systems of production* – though these practices do not cover a majority of enterprises as yet. Thus, according to a survey of firms of European Union countries
conducted during the period 1994-1996, some 14% of establishments had decided
to "downsize" production, 23% had taken initiative to "outsource" certain activities and 13% had adopted a "back to core business" strategy. Likewise, in 1998,
the incidence of "just-in-time" production systems was 23% in the United Kingdom and 36% in France. Finally, in 1996, "best-practice" arrangements such as
"benchmarking" were used in 20% of surveyed firms in the United States. Another
approach is to adopt "quality management", as recommended by public agencies
such as the International Standards Organisation (ISO). In 1998, about 29% of
workplaces had an ISO certificate in France and the figure was 24% in the United
Kingdom.[2]

Second, *team work and practices which aim at a greater proximity between
management and labour* have been adopted on a much larger scale than is the case
of new systems of production. Particularly large is the rate of adoption of practices
which can be accommodated with relatively little change in the overall work organisation structure, e.g. suggestion schemes and weakly autonomous teamwork.
The rate of diffusion is somewhat lower in the case of autonomous team-working
and employee involvement in decision making, which imply a sizeable departure
from the traditional work organisation model. Thus, about 90% of large companies in the United States have suggestion systems and survey feedback, whereas
self-managing work teams and mini-business units exist in 78% and 60%, respectively, of these companies. In the United Kingdom, information-sharing schemes
that can be easily articulated into the existing organisational structure (such as
"use of management chain/cascading information" or "regular meetings with entire workforce") are more widely used than is the case of autonomous team-
working. In France, work groups with weak discretion such as quality circles and
project groups exist in, respectively, 49% and 57% of firms, compared with 37%
in the case of autonomous production teams. In Finland, individual autonomy
exists in 26 to 46% of surveyed firms, while team autonomy exists in 10 to 16% of
these firms.[3]

Third, there is some evidence that *the proportion of firms adopting new work
practices is on the rise*. In the four countries where comparisons through time can

---

[1] See Annex for the description of the surveys used for this study.
[2] In the case of the United Kingdom, the figure concerns BS5750 (standard laid by British
Standard Institute) as well as ISO 9000.
[3] As mentioned above, one should be cautious when making international comparisons on
the basis of existing national surveys.

be made (Australia, France, the United Kingdom and the United States), the rate of adoption of these practices is on the rise in average. It is interesting to note that, despite their still low incidence, practices aiming at encouraging workers' participation in managerial matters (such as self-managed or autonomous team, mini-business units and information sharing about investment plans) are on the rise. In other words, a significant transformation in decision-making may be taking place in some OECD countries.

2.1.2 Telework: An Emerging Form of Work

A number of labour market analysts believe that, increasingly, employers will have recourse to atypical work arrangements, such as contingent labour. This is illustrated by the trend-rise in temporary employment observed in a majority of OECD countries – a well-documented phenomenon. Other forms of atypical work, such as telework, have received considerable attention since it is related with new technology (see Box 2).

Official statistics provide little information on telework and unofficial studies use definitions and methodologies that vary widely.[4] Comparisons between countries are therefore problematic. Despite these difficulties, some patterns can be observed in the OECD area (Figure 1):

- According to a European Commission survey (the EcaTT project), there were in 1999 almost 9 million teleworkers in the European Union, accounting from 6 per cent of the total workforce (EcaTT 2000). This survey includes not only those regularly working at least one day a week away from the office, but also those performing telework occasionally.[5] In two thirds of the cases, telework is performed regularly and in the remaining third as an occasional activity – except in Ireland, the Netherlands and Sweden where the proportions of regular and occasional teleworkers are practically identical. The incidence of telework is considerably higher in Nordic countries than in Southern Europe. These cross-country patterns are associated with differences in ICT penetration. But the quality of telecommunications and attitudes towards this kind of work also fplay a role in explaining cross-country differences in the incidence of telework.

- In the United States, in 1998, there were almost 16 million teleworkers (or telecommuters as defined in the relevant survey), that is 13% of the workforce. The American survey defines teleworkers as those working at home for an outside employer during normal business hours, at least one day a month. Three categories are distinguished, namely full-time employees, contract workers and

---

[4]   Some surveys take into account employees only, in others all forms of employment are considered; some analyse only telework based at home, while others include telework in any location; some specify a minimum number of hours and others take into account only full-time telework.

[5]   The EcaTT survey uses a broad definition of telework which seems to include the five categories defined above.

part-time employees who telecommute informally. The first group represents almost half of the total and the other two groups one quarter each.
- In Japan, there are about 2 million teleworkers, or 8 per cent of the workforce.[6]

Figure U1:   Teleworkers and ICT Penetration in some OECD Countries, 1999-2000

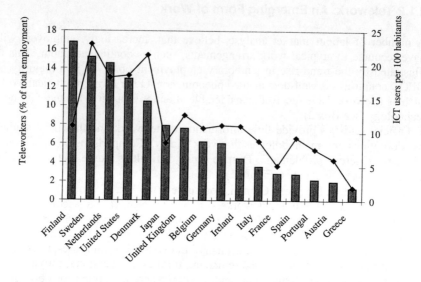

▨ Teleworkers as a percentage of total employment in 1999
◆ ICT users per 100 inhabitants in January 2000

Source: Authors' estimates, for ICT users per 100 inhabitants; and EcaTT Final Report, "Benchmarking progress on new ways of working and new forms of business across Europe", August 2000, for teleworkers.

Box 2. What is Telework?

There is no agreed definition of telework. According to the European Foundation for the Improvement of Living and Working Conditions, telework covers work performed under the following conditions: a) the place of work must be other than the normal workplace of the employer; and b) work necessitates the use of tele-communications (computer, fax, telephone, Internet, etc...). Telework is thus defined functionally and not in legal terms.

Based on this broad definition, some authors (HUWS, 1997; GILLESPIE *et al.*, 1995) have distinguished five main categories of telework: (i) Multi-site telework,

---

[6] Data for Japan are also reported in the EcaTT project, based on Wendy Spinks' sources. Teleworkers are here estimated on the basis of a 1996 survey, which covers only full-time, white-collar employees. So, the definition considered for Japan is much more re-stricted than is the case for European Union countries.

i.e. work partly based in the office and partly at home; (ii) telehome work, *i.e.* work from home and carried out for a single employer; (iii) freelance telework, *i.e.* work from home and carried out, on a freelance basis, for different employers; (iv) mobile telework, *i.e.* work done in different sites using portable equipment to keep in touch with the employer; and (v) relocated back-officers which perform work at distance on the employer's premises.

Telework can facilitate higher labour force participation by creating more room for combining work and family responsibilities. It also gives labour market opportunities for disadvantaged groups such as those with physical disabilities or living in communities in remote or depressed areas. On the other hand, however, telework entails a risk of a deterioration of working conditions, social isolation, exclusion from career opportunities, and downgraded contractual arrangements. There are also risks in terms of privacy (see Box 3).

One key question is whether telework is likely to encourage the labour market participation of under-employed individuals. Partial evidence suggests that, in the European Union, telework has not had much impact on labour supply, at least until recently. According to the European survey, teleworkers are mainly men (75 per cent), of middle age (63 per cent of teleworkers are aged between 30 and 49), highly educated (almost 60 per cent have a high level of educational attainment), and two thirds of them are either professionals or managers. The majority of regular teleworkers work less than 20 hours a week and indeed most teleworkers alternate telework with working on the site firm. By contrast, permanent home-based telework is a marginal phenomenon – representing 2 per cent of total EU workforce only. Telework is concentrated among large firms – telework is possible in three quarters of all establishments with over 500 employees, compared with only 15 per cent in the case of establishments with less than 10 employees.

By contrast, in the United States, telework may have facilitated the labour market integration of disadvantaged groups. Slightly over half of American teleworkers are women (even though among full-time employees the majority of telecommuters are men, relatively young, and are better paid than average). American part-time teleworkers tend to work from home to supplement their regular income, a phenomenon which concerns not only the high-skilled but also other categories like pensioners. Half of the American full-time teleworkers work in small and medium-size firms (of less than 100 employees). Among contract-based teleworkers, 90 per cent are employed in firms with less than 100 employees.

Box 3. Pro's and con's of telework

Benefits/Opportunities	Risks/Uncertainties
1. For employers and work organisation	*1. For employers and work organisation*
• Lower costs (in terms of office space etc). • May increase productivity.	• Polarisation of the work force between protected and unprotected workers.

- Improved motivation derived from a more independent style of work.
- Flexibility.
- Skills retention: the firm can retain people who might not stay in the firm (*e.g.* the other family member has to move; employees taking a career break can continue part-time and remain updated; employees on maternity leave can continue to undertake some tasks).

- Not all the tasks are better done in a self-managing environment. Many tasks gain considerably from close interaction with team members. Hence, telework could hurt productivity or closeness to consumers.

2. For individuals

- Telework may help combine work and family life.
- Reduction of travel time and costs.

2. For individuals

- Erosion of workers' social protection.
- New stresses and damages to family life caused by the difficulty of differentiating work and private life.
- Loss of on-the-job training opportunities.
- Not necessarily good for everybody (people needing external discipline provided by set hours and a managed environment).

3. Other socio-economic dimensions

- Wider employment opportunities: by reinvigorating remote, rural or economically depressed areas.
- Access to work for people with specific difficulties (disabled people; single parents who need to be at home for childcare; people with responsibility for an elderly or sick relative).
- Reduction of traffic congestion and pollution.

3. Other socio-economic dimensions

- Some argue that there could be "social dumping" resulting from the "export" of jobs to low-wage locations.

2.2 A Higher Demand for Knowledge-Intensive Employment

From the outset, it is important to stress that the current growth process is accompanied by high labour demand for all categories of skills. Labour shortages have emerged across the entire occupational spectrum, illustrating a lifting-all-boats effect. In this sense, claims that only highly-qualified labour can participate in today's labour market are unjustified. However, the issue arises whether the diffusion of new technologies and changes in work practices will somehow impact on the relative demand for skilled versus unskilled labour. This is a major policy concern, not only because it raises issues of income inequality but also because certain skills may be regarded as complementary to new technology and work organisation changes – thereby raising efficiency concerns.

2.2.1 Emerging Labour and Skill Shortages

Labour shortages in different sectors and occupations (from ICT workers to agriculture and retail) have been identified as the main factor hampering economic growth in the most recent National Action Plan for Belgium, Denmark, Ireland, Northern Italy, the Netherlands, Finland and Sweden (EUROPEAN COMMISSION, 2000). Labour shortages are especially acute at both ends of the labour market, i.e. among the unskilled and the highly skilled. Thus, the so-called New Economy has raised the demand for many types of labour, not just computer specialists. For example, according to the French Ministry of Labour (2000), during the first six months of 2000 labour shortages have been particularly serious in occupations related to hotels and restaurants, computers, electricity and electronic production as well as agricultural activities and construction. In Australia, skill shortages have emerged in many sectors, particularly in construction, engineering, transport and storage, health occupations and ICT (DEWRSB, 1999).

Regarding the ICT sector, in 2000, there was a shortage of more thant 800,000 new technology specialists in the United States.[7] Other sources also stress the problems associated with the shortage of ICT specialists, without however quantifying the job requirements (US DEPARTMENT OF LABOR, 1999a). The Bureau of Labor Statistics forecasts that, starting in 2006, about 138,000 new highly skilled ICT workers will be needed every year (MEARES and SEARGENT, 1999). The European Commission has estimated that the shortage of ICT specialists in Western Europe could reach the equivalent of 1.7 million jobs in 2003.

Going beyond the occupations where labour shortages occur, it seems that "soft skills", understood as communication and inter-personal skills, are in high demand. In the United Kingdom, the National Training Organisation for ICT has identified the following six skills as critical to the ICT industry: oral communication, problem solving, team working, business awareness and creativity and innovation (DfEE, 1999). Likewise, in the United States, the Information and Technology Association of America estimates that in more than one third of the businesses surveyed, non technical, generic skills -such as communication, problem solving, analytical capacity and the ability to learn quickly- form the core skills needed by ICT managers (ITAA, 2000). More generally, the work practices discussed earlier, notably team work, are likely to raise the demand for soft skills.

Valuable as they are, however, "soft skills" remain complementary to the traditional skills associated with substantive areas of knowledge. Among the latter, ICT literacy is becoming as important as general literacy and numeracy (OECD, 2000b).

---

[7] These estimates come from the business association of the sector. Therefore they have to be taken with care because, as stated by MATLOFF (2000), the business association is prone to present a pessimistic picture, with the aim of raising the number of H-1B visas for foreign workers.

2.2.2 A Shift Towards Knowledge-Intensive Employment

Though the current expansionary phase is accompanied by higher labour demand for both unskilled and skilled labour, there seems to be evidence of a bias in favour of "knowledge-intensive" employment. It is indeed sometimes argued that developed countries have experienced in the past few decades a transformation in which knowledge has become a central element for the organisation and development of economic and social activities.

To the extent that knowledge plays a more important role in economic systems, the demand for workers that generate ideas and knowledge will rise. Therefore, in order to grasp the statistical importance of knowledge for economic growth, it is useful to examine recent changes in occupational patterns based on WOLFF and BAUMOL (1989) and LAVOIE and ROY (1998).[8] According to this approach, occupations can then be categorised into two main groups: non-information and information occupations (or workers), the latter being divided into two sub-categories, namely those manipulating information (data workers) and those generating ideas (knowledge workers). This distinction is supposed to reflect the different aspects of human activity, namely producing goods, providing personal services (non-information occupations) and generating information (See Table 9 for a detailed classification of occupations).

Preliminary findings suggest that the number of knowledge workers, as defined above, has increased markedly over the past few years (Figure 2). Between 1992 and 1999, in the OECD countries for which data are available, the number of knowledge workers rose by almost 5.5 million, that is almost 30 per cent of the net employment gains recorded during this period. Moreover, the incidence of knowledge employment is on the rise.

---

[8] There exist other measures of knowledge-intensive employment, *e.g.* mesures based on literacy data (OECD, 2001a). The results are, however, similar to the ones presented here which are founded on a well-known conceptual framework and have the added advantage of offering a wide scope for empirical analysis vis-à-vis other measures of knowledge-intensive employment. For instance, it is possible to calculate the earnings of knowledge workers and thus to test whether the rise in this type of employment reflects demand or supply factors.

Figure U2:   **The Rising Importance of Knowledge-Intensive Employment**
               (Employment growth by group of occupations in selected OECD countri-
               es[a], average annual percentage change, 1992-1999)

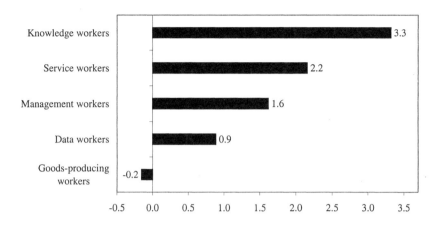

Note: a) The countries considered include European Union member countries and the United States.
Sources: Authors' estimates based on European Labour Force Survey for European countries and BLS, Current Population Survey for the United States.

Figure U3:   **Real Hourly Earnings by Group of Occupations in the United States[a]**
               (Average annual growth - both sexes, 1985-1998)

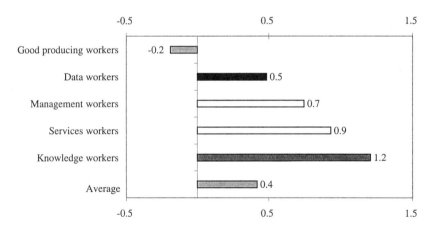

Note: a) Real hourly earnings are calculated as nominal hourly earnings deflated by the private consumption deflator.
Source: Authors' estimates based on BLS, Current Population Survey.

In the United States alone, the number of knowledge workers rose by almost two million between 1992 and 1998, representing over 14 per cent of the net employment created during the period. In European countries a similar pattern can be observed, though in the context of a less intensive job creation process than in the United States. There is considerable variation across countries, however: between 1992 and 1999, Italy, the Netherlands, Spain and the United Kingdom created over 400 thousands jobs in the knowledge occupations, while the number of such jobs fell in France and Portugal.[9] Notwithstanding these this cross-country variation, the contribution of knowledge workers to employment growth is significant among European countries, being responsible for over one in five jobs during the second part of the 1990s. In most OECD countries, knowledge and management workers combined accounted for over half of total jobs created during the 1990s.

Indeed, in the United States (the only country for which such data are available), the wage of knowledge workers has risen much faster than is the case for other occupations, illustrating the shift in demand patterns (possibly related to the adoption of ICT and skill-biased technological change). Between 1985 and 1998, nominal hourly earnings of knowledge workers grew at an average annual rate of 4.1 per cent, higher than the growth observed for the other categories of occupations and almost one point above the overall average. In addition, the level of earnings is also higher: in 1998, knowledge workers earned, on average, 20 to 50 per cent more than other workers – including managers (see Table 10). In real terms, as shown in Figure 3, wage differentials are even more pronounced. While goods-producing workers have recorded a loss in the purchasing power of their earnings over the period 1985-98, the real wages of the other categories of occupations have increased. Since 1985, real hourly earnings have increased at an average annual rate of 1.2 per cent for the U.S. knowledge workers, three times the rate of increase observed for the overall economy. Women have seen an increase of their real earnings relative to their male counterparts in all groups of occupations, even if, on average, they still earned in 1998 between 12 and 25 per cent less than men.

Among the knowledge-intensive occupations, computer specialists have recorded since 1995 the best employment opportunities in Sweden, the United Kingdom and the United States. Nevertheless, the share of computer specialists in total employment remains low (Figure 4). Computer workers have enjoyed an increase of their nominal average hourly earnings of 5 per cent during the period considered, with a clear acceleration in the past three years.[10]

---

[9] It must be noted, however, that methodological differences make cross-country comparisons problematic in this area. In particular, it is sometimes difficult to separate knowledge occupations from managerial ones. In addition, occupational classifications change over time, as has happened in France – which might explain the drop in the registered number of knowledge workers during the 1990s in this country. There is a break in Portuguese data which makes time comparisons during the period under analysis problematic. It seems, in fact, that knowledge-intensive employment is on the rise in Portugal.

[10] However, it will be necessary to check this trend with more recent data. The latest stock market trends of information technology industries may have a large negative impact on the earnings of computer workers.

Figure U4: Share of Computer Workers in Total Employment, 1999^{a} (Percentages)

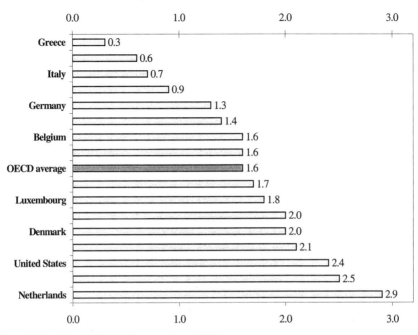

Note: a) Data for the United States refer to 1998.
Sources: Authors' estimates based on European Labour Force Survey for European countries, ABS, Labour Force Survey for Australia and BLS, Current Population Survey for the United States.

Some analysts have suggested that with the expansion of ICT and the Internet, the demand for individuals with special talents or skills will rise considerably. This "winner-takes-all" principle would thus apply to a range of knowledge-intensive occupations. Accordingly, a premium to talent would be paid in the form of higher basic wages and performance-based remuneration, *e.g.* stock options. There seems to be partial evidence in support of this view: the standard deviation of nominal earnings has increased for all categories of workers between 1985 and 1998 but the highest increase has been observed among the knowledge workers, suggesting the presence of a premium-to-talent principle within these occupations (Table 10). This phenomenon, however, has not been extended to other occupations.

It could be argued that the dynamism of knowledge-intensive employment simply reflects higher educational requirements. In fact, the educational attainment of the workforce has improved in the five groups of occupations considered, as shown by the increase in the shares of those having high education as well as by the decrease of the shares of those having low education – a trend which is especially pronounced for female workers in most OECD countries. The ratio of high-educated versus low-educated - defined as the ratio between the number of people employed having tertiary and/or university studies to those having up to secondary studies - has increased in the past years in most countries for all the groups of occupations (Figure 5).

Knowledge workers have on average a higher educational attainment than the other groups of occupations. Almost half of the highly educated workers are among the knowledge occupations. On the other hand, between 50 and 65 per cent of the knowledge workers in European countries have a high educational attainment, defined as tertiary and/or university education, a share that is even higher in the case of the United States (77 per cent). Nevertheless, what is important is that between half and one third of these workers have not reached a university degree, which underlines the importance of on-the-job experience.

Figure U5:   Employment Shares by Educational Attainment and Groups of Occupations, OECD Average (Percentage of high-educated workers within each occupational group)

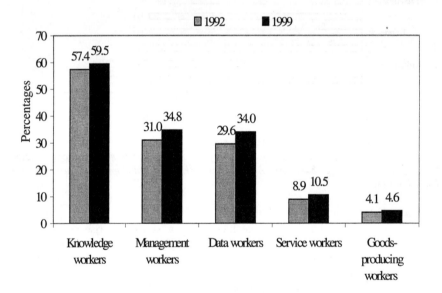

Sources: Authors' estimates based on the European Labour Force Survey for the European countries and on BLS, Current Population Survey for the United States.

2.3 Employee Tenure: Overall Stability Which Masks Important Underlying Changes

In traditional firms, the links between employers and employees have been characterised by relatively long employment attachments. How have these patterns changed in the new economic context? This is an important question not only because employment stability is a crucial dimension of job security and well-being but also because it may be related with economic growth. The length of the employment relationship may indeed be linked with productivity, therefore growth, though the links may go in both directions. On the one hand, a relatively short employee tenure may reflect a greater degree of labour mobility between firms and occupations, thereby facilitating adjustments. This would enhance the extent to which economies will seize the new business opportunities, which would be good for growth. On the other hand, a short employee tenure may deter long-term commitments between workers and employers, reducing firms' incentive to provide training.

As is well known, in English-speaking countries such as Australia, Canada, the United Kingdom and the United States, employee tenure (a measure for job stability) is generally lower than is the case of continental Europe and Japan. Moreover, tenure has generally been stable and has not changed in a common direction for all of the OECD countries during the 1990s.

However, this overall stability hides important underlying changes. First, it appears that tenure for skilled workers has tended to increase, while tenure for unskilled workers has tended to decrease. In many OECD countries, the tenure for unskilled occupations has been reduced whereas tenure for skilled occupations has increased in almost all the countries for which data are available (Figure 6). Even in countries where the tenure for low-skilled workers increased, it has done so much less than in the case of skilled occupations.

Second, tenure has followed diverging patterns by gender. Tenure of female workers tends to increase while the opposite goes true for male workers in many OECD countries. This may reflect a "catch-up" effect and indeed the employee tenure of female workers remains far below that of male workers.

Third, a sectoral analysis of tenure patterns shows that overall stability masks two conflicting phenomena. On the one hand, there is a change in the industrial structure towards low-tenure industries (Figure 7).[11] On the other hand, tenure tends to increase "within" sectors.

Finally, the age profile of the workforce needs to be taken into account. Older workers typically have longer tenure than young workers who just entered the labour market. Hence, population ageing automatically translates into higher tenure – even though the underlying trend may be different. In the case of the United States, employee tenure would have been reduced by 0.2 year during 1996-2000, if the share of each generation had been constant over the period. But what is important is that between 1983 and 2000, median tenure for American male workers aged 55-64 shortened by more than 5 years (RAJNES, 2001).

---

[11] See Box 4 for detailed explanations about the method and interpretation of these results.

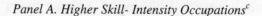

Figure U6:   Changes in Employee Tenure for Selected Occupations[a], 1992-98[b]

Panel A. Higher Skill- Intensity Occupations[c]

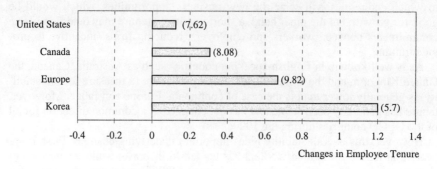

Panel B. Lower Skill- Intensity Occupations[d]

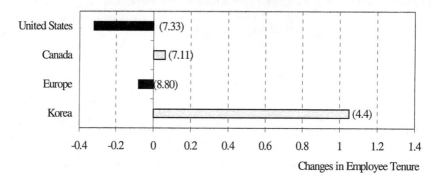

Note: *a*) Numbers between parentheses are the level of employee tenure in the initial year. Employee tenures for the "Europe" are calculated as a simple average over the European countries for which data are available. These countries are Denmark, France, Germany, Netherlands, Portugal, Spain, Switzerland, and United Kingdom. For detailed numbers for individual countries, see Annexe.

b) 1993-1998 and 1996-2000 for Korea and the United States, respectively, in the place of 1992-1998. For the United States, "Professional Speciality Occupations (43-199)" and "Technicians and Related Support Occupations (203-235)" according to the Current Population Survey Code are used.

c) "Professionals (ISOC 2)" and "Technicians and associate professionals (ISOC 3)" except the United States. For the United States, "precision productions, craft, and repair occupations" (SIC 503-699) and "operators, fabricators, and labourers" (SIC703-889) are used.

d) "Plant and machine operators and assemblers (ISOC 8)" and "Elementary occupation (ISOC 9)". For the United States, "precision productions, craft, and repair occupations" (503-699) and "operators, fabricators, and labourers" (703-889) according to the Current Population Survey Code are used.

Sources: National Submissions for Canada, Korea and Switzerland; Current Population Survey for the United States; and for other countries, data were provided by Eurostat.

Figure U7:   Decomposition of Tenure Changes, 1992-98ᵃ

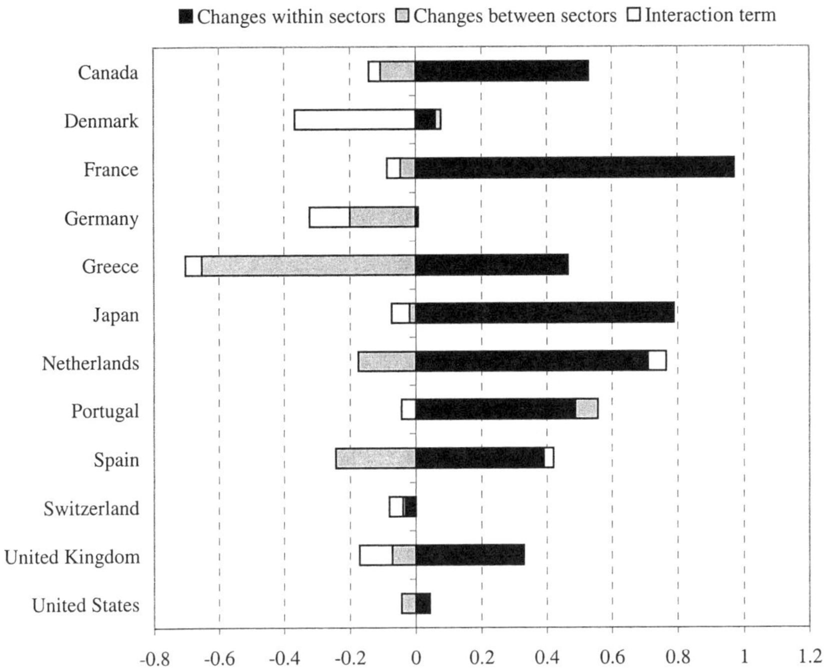

■ Changes within sectors ▨ Changes between sectors □ Interaction term

Note: a) 1996-2000 for United States. Figures for Japan and the United States cannot be compared with those of the other countries due to the different industrial classification.
Sources: National Submissions for Canada and Switzerland; Year Book of Labour Statistics, various issues for Japan; Current Population Survey for the United States; and for other countries, data were provided by Eurostat.

In sum, although at the aggregate level employee tenure is stable, evidence suggests that tenure at low-skilled workers has declined. This, combined with a structural employment shift towards low-tenure sectors, suggests that the perception of weaker employee-employer attachments is not entirely unjustified. Further analysis is clearly needed to better understand these trends.

Whatever the stylised facts, is tenure important for growth? As mentioned earlier, the possible links between tenure and productivity can go in both directions, and the matter should be explored empirically. It seems that low tenure countries have enjoyed faster productivity growth in the recent years (Figure 8). In addition, it seems that low tenure is associated with higher job creation. These relationships may reflect the fact that, hand-in-hand with new technology, new business opportunities have emerged, and countries where labour is more mobile (and tenure correspondingly lower) are better placed to exploit these opportunities at least in the short-run. Over the long-run, however, even high-tenure countries can considerably take advantage of the new economic environment.

**Box 4. Changes in Employee Tenure Between Sectors and within Them:
a Methodology**

Changes in employee tenure may be attributable to either shifts in employment patterns between sectors or structural factors within sectors. The latter reflect a modification in the employer-employee relationship, whereas the former are related to the structure of the economy. It is therefore useful to assess the relative importance of each factor, which is the purpose of this Box.

Employee tenure varies considerably across sectors. For instance, manufacturing workers and civil servants usually have longer tenure than is the case in private services. Changes in sectoral employment shares may therefore have an impact on aggregate tenure, even in the absence of any evolution within sectors. To disentangle the different effects, aggregate tenure is decomposed as follows:

$$(1) \quad \Delta \sum_i P_i T_i = \sum_i \Delta P_i \overline{T_i} + \sum_i \overline{P_i} \Delta T_i + \sum_i \Delta P_i \Delta T_i$$

where P_i and T_i represent, respectively, the share and average tenure of workers employed in sector i; Δ means a change during 1992-1998 (except for the United States where the period 1996-2000 is used) ; and the bar over a variable refers to the value of the variable at the start of the period under analysis.

The first term of the right-hand-side of (1) represents changes in tenure "between" sectors, and the second term represents changes "within" sectors. The third term is a residual, which reflects the "interaction" between the other terms.

As discussed in the text, evidence based on this decomposition suggests that tenure tends to rise within sectors, which may be due to the expansion of several OECD economies – although it could also be attributable to a underlying lengthening in employer-employee relationships.

The evidence also shows that the economic structure is moving towards low-tenure sectors (i.e. the change "between" sectors is negative). This is an important policy-relevant finding. It means that, over the longer-run, workers may have to change jobs more often than is apparent when looking at the aggregate data – and adjustment costs will therefore rise.

Finally, despite the improved economic environment, workers continue to regard job security as an important dimension of their job. Table 1 presents selected indicators of job insecurity. Given the qualitative nature of the surveys on which they are based, the indicators capture individual perceptions. The picture that emerges is one of persistently high job insecurity, despite the new economic context. For the OECD countries as a whole, it is estimated that over half of all workers are worried about the future of their company, and 29 per cent are unsure of their job even if they perform well. True, the situation has improved compared with 1996 – both indicators have declined by 6 percentage points between 1996 and 2000. However, the fact that perceptions of significant job insecurity persist is suggestive. One interpretation of this finding is that job insecurity may be related with firm reorganisation and changes in job requirements – rather than lower employment tenure, for which there is no general evidence.

Figure U8:   Employee Tenure and Multi-Factor Productivity Acceleration

Panel A. Tenure Level and MFP Acceleration

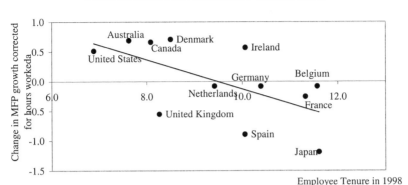

Panel B. Changes in Tenure and MFP Acceleration

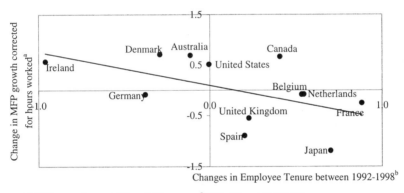

Note: a) MFP growth rate differntial between 1980-95 and 1995-99.
b) Data on employee tenure for the United States refer to 1996 and 2000 in the place of 1992 and 1998.
Sources: Labour Mobility, Catalogue No. 6209.0, February 2000 for Australia; National Submissions for Canada; Year Book of Labour Statistics, various issues for Japan; Current Population Survey for the United States; and for other countries, data were provided by Eurostats. MFP growth rates are estimated by the OECD Secretariat.

The indicators also suggest considerable variation in job insecurity across coun-tries. It is relatively low in Denmark, Finland, Ireland, the Netherlands and Nor-way and high in Greece, Japan, Korea, Poland, Spain and the United States. Inter-estingly, job insecurity is not necessarily low in low-unemployment countries.

Table U1:   Recent Developments in Job Insecurity in OECD Countries

	Percentage worried about the future of their company		Percentage unsure of a job with their company even if they perform well	
	1996	2000	1996	2000
Australia	42	50	33	37
Austria	50	52	23	23
Belgium	62	48	32	26
Canada	55	49	39	27
Czech Republic[a]	55	47	34	35
Denmark	48	43	32	20
Finland	63	42	47	31
France	72	49	42	37
Germany	54	50	36	34
Greece	59	62	25	29
Hungary	67	55	36	26
Ireland	53	40	40	23
Italy	63	47	32	32
Japan	63	65	36	38
Korea	71	62	44	46
Mexico	75	58	18	13
Netherlands	40	43	34	22
New Zealand	36	40	27	34
Norway	40	42	27	17
Poland	63	56	37	31
Portugal	73	75	25	21
Spain	79	70	32	27
Sweden	56	49	40	36
Switzerland	49	45	38	26
United Kingdom	61	48	53	41
United States	62	54	48	37
Unweighted average	58	52	35	30

Note: a) For the Czech Republic, figures in 1996 columns refer to 1997.

Source: Data supplied by International Survey Research.

3. New Work Practices, Skills and Economic Growth

Human capital is an important engine of economic growth. The skills and competencies of the workforce have an impact not only on the level of productivity (thus
per capita income) but also on its growth rate. In particular, technological innovations are likely to be diffused all the more effectively and rapidly when human
capital is high. A recent study based on a new database finds a significant effect of
educational attainment on economic growth (OECD, 2000c). Going beyond these

general findings, labour market institutions are likely to shape the extent to which human capital is effectively utilised in the economy, and thus its impact on economic growth. Unfortunately, this is an under-researched issue, and the purpose of this section is to contribute modestly to fill in the gap by analysing a) how new work practices can help increase productivity, and b) the kind of skills that are likely to be complementary with new technology.

3.1   New Work Practices and Growth

It is sometimes argued that new work practices may contribute to raise productivity at the firm level, and this development, in turn, would translate into economic growth at the macro level (BLACK and LYNCH, 2000). There would be two main reasons for this positive relationship:

- organisational change can be regarded as part of technological change, which contributes directly to the growth process. Organisational change may indeed enhance the efficiency of human and physical capital, thereby paving the way for productivity gains. As the work organisation system founded by Taylor and Ford contributed to boost the productivity of mass-production of homogeneous products, new work practices are considered to play a similar role in the present economic environment characterised by a high degree of product differentiation and stiff product market competition.

- organisational change may contribute to economic growth indirectly, through its mutually-reinforcing relationship with new technologies, notably ICT. Some authors even argue that the so-called "Solow-Paradox" (*i.e.* the observation that, until recently, new technology had not translated into productivity gains) can be attributed to an insufficient response of work organisation systems to the new economic environment (ASKENAZY, 1999). Introducing new work practices may prove necessary to ensure that ICT is implemented effectively. This point is essential for understanding the role of ICT-use (as opposed to ICT-production) as a factor of economic growth.

However, there are also reasons to be sceptical about the possible economic impact of new work practices. Firstly, new practices are not necessarily more efficient than existing ones. There are advantages to traditional systems of job specialisation and management-employee relations. For instance, the delegation of responsibility entails a weaker monitoring on the part of managers, possibly posing a risk in terms of product quality and overall coherence of the tasks of the different employees. Moreover, one should not neglect the costs involved in organisational restructuring (i.e. organisational change is not a free good). An enterprise operates on the basis of norms and arrangements established through time and any major change in these norms and arrangements will inevitably entail some adjustment costs. Secondly, what is efficient for an individual firm is not necessarily efficient for the economy as a whole. Even if new work practices may raise productivity of the firms that implement them, this improvement can well be accompanied with lower productivity in other firms (with little overall effect). This is possible, for example, in the case of outsourcing and when firms lay off "low-productivity" workers and reorganise production with remaining, "high-productivity" ones.

In order to examine the validity of these conflicting arguments, this section presents a brief review of the literature and then carries out a range of empirical tests of the relationship between new work practices and economic growth.

3.1.1 Findings form the Existing Literature

The existing studies suggests that there is a positive relationship between new work practices and firm-level performance[12]. Most studies for the United States find a positive relationship between the incidence of new work practices and labour productivity, Tobin's q, or rates of return.[13] Studies for Australia and the United Kingdom, based on managers' self-evaluation of performance, find that new work practices tend to be associated with higher-than-average labour productivity, better financial performance and improved product quality (ADDISON *et al.*, 2000; CROCKETT, 2000; RAMSEY *et al.*, 2000). Likewise, in a comparative project for Nordic countries, "flexible" work practices are positively correlated with labour productivity. In France, evidence is mixed. Earlier studies found a weak association (COUTROT, 1996; GREENAN, 1996*a*; 1996*b*), whereas more recent ones point to the existence of a positive correlation (CAROLI and VAN REENEN, 1999; COUTROT, 2000*a*).[14]

Interestingly, the existing studies give some guidance on how new work practices matter:

- Like many other types of innovation, changes in work practices do not bring about their results immediately. Both employers and employees need to learn how the new practices can be used effectively. As a consequence, it is perfectly possible that their introduction will reduce the level of productivity in the short run. The weak evidence of the relationship between new work practices and firm performance found by some studies could be interpreted in this light (ASKENAZY, 2000).
- The most consistent finding is that new work practices are associated with improved firm-performance only when the practices are implemented as a bundle – and not separately. In other words, it is the entire system of new practices that brings about efficiency gains, and not each individual component of this system implemented in isolation. This is probably due to the complementarity existing between different practices.
- There is some evidence that the adoption of new work practices goes together with that of ICT. According to some studies, employers rarely regard ICT as

---

[12] For a more exhaustive survey, see ARNAL, OK and TORESS (2001).

[13] CAPPELLI and NEUMARK (1999) find weak support for this relationship, based on a data set covering the period 1977-1996. However, BLACK and LYNCH (2000) find a positive and significant relationship for 1993-1996, based on a similar data set.

[14] One major problem with many of these studies is that they are usually based on the employers' subjective evaluation of the performance of their firm – some studies for the United States, however, use objective performance indicators.

an important motivation for organisational change (NUTEK, 1996). However, these studies also show that the adoption of new technology (including computer hardware and software) affects a larger proportion of the staff in firms that implement new work practices.

True, it could be argued that those firms which adopt new work practices will get a larger share of the market, to the detriment of other firms – *i.e.* the size of the cake would in fact be constant. This is particularly the case when organisational changes improve the extent to which production matches demand requirements – *e.g.* by bringing the nature of products closer to consumer preoccupations.[15] Though there is probably an element of truth in this assertion, few researchers believe that organisational innovations do not bring any real gains at all. In addition, evidence carried out for this study shows that new work practices do have a macroeconomic impact, an issue addressed now.

3.1.2 Empirical Evidence

New work practices are associated with a greater use of ICT

There is considerable evidence that new work practices are introduced hand-in-hand with new technologies, notably ICT. To the extent that ICT is an engine of economic growth, this evidence would suggest that organisational change is also a major factor at work behind the recent growth performance. First, in all countries for which data are available, the incidence of ICT-use in the firms that implement new work practices is much larger than is the case in the firms that do not implement these practices. Thus, in the United States, 58 percent of non-supervisory workers of firms that implement new work practices use computers, that is 9 percentage point higher than in the case of firms that do not implement new work practices (Table 2). Similarly, the average difference in ICT-use among firms that use and do not use new work practices is 15 percentage points according to a survey conducted for the European Union and 10 percent points in both Australia and Finland.

---

[15] Even in this case, however, it could be argued that the quality of output increases, thus raising welfare.

Table U2:   Implementation of New Work Practices and Use of ICT[a]
               (Percentage of firms which use ICT[b]**)**

	Among firms that implement new practices	Among firms that do *not* implement new practices
Australia (1995)	24	14
European Union (EPOC survey, 1994-96)	49	34
Denmark	*50*	*45*
France	*42*	*27*
Germany	*41*	*26*
Ireland	*59*	*46*
Italy	*54*	*43*
Netherlands	*25*	*16*
Portugal	*42*	*30*
Spain	*45*	*33*
Sweden	*55*	*41*
United Kingdom	*63*	*46*
Finland (1996)	62	52
France (REPONSE survey 1998)	46	29
United States (1996)	58	49

Note: a) Figures correspond to averages of estimates carried out for each individual work practice (see Annex for details). Data are not comparable between surveys.
b) Figures for the United States refer to the percentage of non-supervisory workers using computers.
Source: Authors' estimates based on various surveys.

Second, looking at individual practices, it appears that most of them are associated with a high incidence of ICT-use[16]:

- in all countries for which data are available, *employee involvement* schemes are strongly associated with ICT-use. This relationship reflects the fact that ICT facilitates information flows among staff (notably between management and front-line workers), and employee involvement schemes are one way of exploiting this possibility;
- *team-working* is also associated with a relatively intensive use of ICT. This result suggests that team-working and ICT complement each other. ICT facilitates the creation of networks, both formal and informal, while conversely the presence of well-functioning teams provides a justification for introducing ICT;
- similarly, the incidence of ICT-use is higher in firms that implement *new production systems* than is the case of firms that do not implement such systems. The rationale behind this result is that changes in production systems are often associated with the introduction of team-working and employee involvement schemes –which, as just discussed, are strongly related with ICT. There is evi-

---

[16] See ARNAL, OK and TORRES (2001) for the detailed tables.

dence that firms which have modified their production system, without at the same time introducing team-working or employee involvement schemes, tend to be relatively weak users of ICT;[17] and

* the link between job rotation schemes and ICT-use is somewhat weaker than is the case of the other practices reported (especially in the case of the United States).

Figure U9:   New Work Practices and ICT Investment

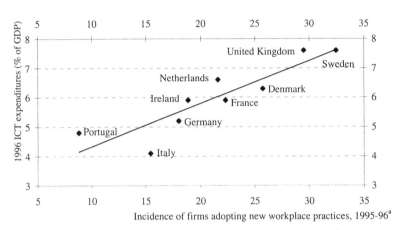

Incidence of firms adopting new workplace practices, 1995-96[a]

Note: a) This is calculated as a simple average of the five new work practice indicators for 9 European countries (see Annex for details). Spain is excluded because of the absence of information about one of the indicators (flattening of managerial levels). ICT expenditures include expenditures on hardware, information technology services and software and telecommunications for the year 1996.
Sources: Authors' estimates based on the EPOC survey; OECD, Science, Technology and Industry Scoreboard 1999 - Benchmarking Knowledge-based economies, 1999.

Finally, a cross-country link between new work practices and ICT can be established by examining evidence for European countries for which comparable data on organisational change exist (Figure 9). The incidence of new work practices is proxied by the average rate of diffusion of a range of indicators, and appears to be strongly correlated with ICT expenditure as a share of GDP. This proxy is subject to a degree of arbitrariness. However, the correlation is suggestive and consistent with earlier evidence.

---

[17] This finding is based on the EPOC survey. For example, when there is no group delegation of responsibility, ICT adoption among firms that flatten managerial structures is no higher than is the case among firms that do not flatten managerial structures. But, in the presence of group delegation of responsibility, 43% of firms that flatten managerial structures have adopted new ICT against 36% for firms that do not flatten managerial structures. A similar pattern is found in the case of "back to the core business".

Direct evidence on the productivity impact

Besides the association which has just been established between new work practices and ICT, a more direct impact on productivity growth can be discerned. As
shown in Figure 10, the diffusion of new work practices is correlated with labour
productivity growth, even though the case of Ireland departs from this relationship.

Productivity gains are particularly large when new work practices are implemented together with ICT. As shown in Table 3, labour productivity growth during 1992-1998 was much faster than average in US manufacturing industries that
combined a high incidence of new work practices with a high incidence of ICT-
use. However, the productivity performance of firms which use ICT and do not
adopt new work practices is rather poor. Studies based on subjective evaluations
of productivity lead to a similar finding. Employers in firms characterised by an
intensive use of both new work practices and ICT tend to report that their productivity is higher than that of competitors. In other firms, employers are not particularly optimistic about their firm's productivity. Likewise, among the Fortune 1000
firms, productivity is expected to rise only in those which use intensively both ICT
and new work practices. Otherwise, the individual productivity effect of either
new work practices or ICT seems to be very small (BRESNAHAN *et al.*, 1999).

Figure U10: New Work Practices and Labour Productivity

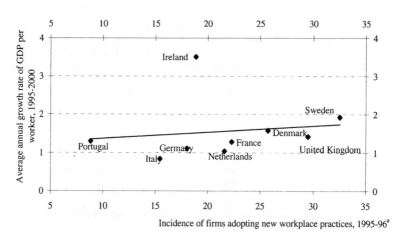

Incidence of firms adopting new workplace practices, 1995-96[a]

Note: a) This is calculated as a simple average of the five new work practice indicators for 9 European countries (see Annex for details). Spain is excluded because
of the absence of information about one of the indicators (flattening of managerial
levels).
*Sources: Authors' estimates based on the EPOC survey and OECD Economic Outlook,
No.68, December 2000.*

Table U3: **The Mutually-Reinforcing Relationship Between New Workplace Practices and ICT, United States (Average annual growth rate of labour productivity, US manufacturing 1992-98 (%))**

	Industries with *high* ICT intensity	Industries with *low* ICT intensity
Industries with *high* incidence of new workplace practices	7.8	1.4
Industries with *low* incidence of new workplace practices	0.5	2.2

Sources: Authors' estimates from NES-EQW 1997 and Gross Product by Industry (BEA).

An association with performance-pay systems, non-standard forms of employment and stress at work

Though there is evidence that new work practices are positively associated with productivity performance, concern has been expressed about the possible impact of these practices on wage inequalities and job precariousness – whose impact on growth over the medium-to-longer run is ambiguous.

Firms adopting new work practices are prone to use performance-pay schemes such as profit-sharing and stock options, with potential productivity (and growth) effects (Table 4). For example, in the United States, 49 percent of firms that implement new work practices provide stock options or profit-sharing schemes to their staff – the figure is 37 percent in the case of firms that do not implement the new work practices. In the case of the European Union, performance-pay systems such as "pay on the basis of team output", profit-sharing and ownership schemes are systematically more prevalent among firms that implement the new work practices than among other firms. Similar results are obtained according to the special surveys conducted for Australia, Finland and the United Kingdom.

Performance-pay systems can be expected to raise productivity. These systems can be regarded as an important organisational arrangement enabling firms to attract skilled labour, motivate workers, and hence achieve a better economic performance (LAWLER, 2000). In particular, when responsibilities in decision-making are delegated to workers or teams, performance-pay systems are likely to enhance team motivation, outweighing the potential risks entailed by weaker management monitoring. However, on the other hand, the increased recourse to performance-pay systems is likely to widen wage inequality between workers. At a macroeconomic level, wider wage inequalities can affect income distribution, thus possibly reducing social support for growth-enhancing policies (see OECD, 2001*b*).

Table U4:   New Work Practices and Selected Performance-Pay Systems[a] **(Percentage of firms which use performance-pay systems)**

	Among firms that implement new practices	Among firms that do *not* implement new practices
Australia (1995)		
Any performance-based payment	37	31
Profit sharing	7	4
Stock options	18	15
European Union (EPOC survey 1994-96)		
Pay on the basis of team output	22	17
Profit sharing	25	18
Ownership schemes	10	6
Finland (1996)		
Pay for the result of team or unit	53	43
France (REPONSE survey 1998)		
Individualisation of wage increase	76	66
Individual bonus	54	51
United Kingdom (WERS survey 1998)		
Any incentive payment scheme	47	41
United States (1996)		
Profit-sharing or stock options	49	37

Note: a) Figures correspond to averages of estimates carried out for each individual work practice (see Annex for details). Data are not comparable between surveys.
Source: Authors' estimates based on various surveys.

It is sometimes claimed that new work practices tend to be associated with a relatively intensive use of outsourcing and non-standard forms of employment. Table 5 provides some support for this assertion: in firms which use new work practices, the incidence of outsourcing arrangements, part-time work and fixed-term contracts tends to be somewhat higher than in firms that do not implement the new practices. While job turnover of skilled workers may be an enriching experience, this is usually not the case when unskilled workers change jobs – these workers tend to lose skills (since their human capital is often firm- or industry-specific), thereby depressing their actual productivity. Also, there is ample evidence that employees with short-term contracts and other non-standard forms of employment are less likely to receive training than their permanent-contract counterparts.

Finally, there is some evidence that new practices are associated with greater stress at work. Employees are more autonomous, and in this sense they may be more satisfied at work, but they are made directly responsible for their performance which in many circumstances will intensify stress. This is why some argue that new production models boil down to "management by stress" (Parker and Slaughter, 1988). Worryingly, in recent years, the incidence of stress and accidents at work has reportedly increased in many OECD countries.[18] According to some studies, this trend is in part attributable to firm re-organisation (ASKENAZY, 1999; FAIRRIS and BRENNER, 2001).

Table U5: New Work Practices and Selected Atypical Forms of Employment[a] (Percentage of firms which have recourse to atypical forms of employment)

	Among firms that implement new practices	Among firms that do *not* implement new practices
Australia (1995)		
Contractors, outworkers and agency employees	72	65
Fixed-term contracts	40	31
European Union (EPOC survey 1994-96)		
Part-time workers	27	23
Denmark	*15*	*15*
France	*42*	*29*
Germany	*22*	*23*
Ireland	*35*	*26*
Italy	*6*	*9*
Netherlands	*34*	*28*
Portugal	*3*	*9*
Spain	*12*	*13*
Sweden	*59*	*59*
United Kingdom	*39*	*33*
United Kingdom (WERS survey 1998)		
Temporary agency employees	25	17
United States (1996)		
Workers from outside the firm	56	36

Note: a) Figures correspond to averages of estimates carried out for each individual work practice (see Annex for details). Data are not comparable between surveys.

Source: Authors' estimates based on various surveys.

3.2 Links Between Skills and Economic Growth

As mentioned earlier, over the past few years, the issue of the links between human capital and economic growth has received considerable attention among researchers. Human capital plays a central role in "new growth" theories, which

---

[18] In the United States, illness due to work pressure has jumped from 18 per cent of all occupational illnesses in 1980 to 65 per cent in 1998 (U.S. Department of Labor, 1999*b*). Similarly, the International Labour Office recently reported that the incidence of mental health problems and the costs related to them have risen during the past decade in the five countries under study, namely Finland, Germany, Poland, the United Kingdom and the United States (Gabriel and Liimatainen, 2000).

make economic growth dependent on the rate of accumulation of physical and human capital. Another strand of the literature examines the issue of knowledge spill-over. Such theories treat knowledge as a public good: once knowledge has been generated by one individual, it becomes accessible to other individuals.

However, an issue which is often ignored in the literature is *how* human capital affects economic growth. In the present context, it can be argued that certain skills are of particular importance for the effective implementation of new technologies. Indeed, certain skills are indispensable complements to new technology.

An econometric analysis of recent growth patterns of the United States confirms that physical capital and skilled labour emerge as complements, while both these factors and unskilled labour are substitutes.[19] It follows that an insufficient supply of skilled labour will constrain economic growth. Analysis of factor proportions in the United States illustrates this result: as shown in Figure 11, physical capital and knowledge-intensive employment have followed similar patterns, even though the relative return to knowledge-intensive employment has increased substantially.[20] By contrast, unskilled employment has fallen relative to the other two factors, despite the reduction in the relative wage of this type of employment. These findings confirm evidence from other studies which show that the cross-country difference in the diffusion of computers crucially depends on differences in human capital (CASELLI and COLEMAN, 2001).

There are several reasons why knowledge may exert a greater influence on economic growth today. First, facilitated by the increased use of ICT, knowledge is diffused more rapidly and widely than ever. The result is that the economic externalities associated with knowledge may have increased. Second, today's economy is dominated by services where intangibles play an important role, knowledge being one of these key intangibles. More generally, the production of goods and services embodies an increasing element of knowledge (e.g. design and consumer services). Ideas and knowledge are the pillars of the so-called "knowledge-based" economy.

While human capital investment is so critical in today's "knowledge-based" economy, the social returns from these investments tend to be higher than their private returns. The problem may have been compounded by the fact that a rising number of unskilled workers face relatively unstable employment conditions, so that firms employing them have little incentive in investment in their human capital. The issue of how policies can address this thorny public good question is treated below.

---

[19] See ARNAL; OK and TORRES (2001) for the detailed results.

[20] Unfortunately, reflecting data constraints, it is not possible to replicate this chart for other OECD countries.

Figure U11: Complementarity Between Physical Capital and Knowledge-Intensive Employment,[a] United States

Indexes, 1984 = 100

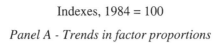

Panel A - Trends in factor proportions

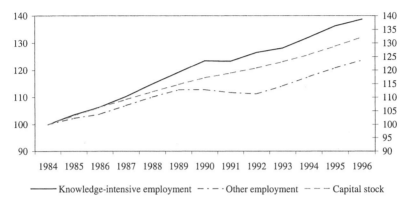

——— Knowledge-intensive employment — · — Other employment — — — Capital stock

Panel B - Trends in factor remuneration[b]

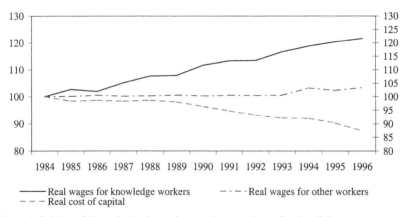

——— Real wages for knowledge workers   — · — Real wages for other workers
— — — Real cost of capital

a) For a definition of "knowledge-intensive employment", see Section 2.2.
b) Real factor remuneration is measured as the ratio of nominal factor remuneration to the value-added deflator.
Sources: Authors' estimates based on BLS, Current Population Survey; and OECD, International Sectorial Database.

4. Policy Issues

It could be argued that decisions regarding work organisation are typically a firm prerogative, one in which policy makers have no direct role to play. Moreover, given that work practices apparently help improve firm performance, it is legitimate to ask why these practices are not embraced more widely (and therefore why there is a need for discussing policies at all). One possible explanation is that introducing these practices involves a reorganisation of the enterprise, which is time-consuming, costly and necessitates an investment effort (notably in the area of training). In addition, certain categories of workers and managers may feel insecure about the new practices — this is especially the case when they lead to downsizing, or when layers of management are suppressed. Even though these perceptions are not always justified, insecure workers and certain managers will tend to oppose change. Governments may thus have an indirect role to play here, mainly by making sure that firms and workers are provided with the appropriate skills and that regulatory frameworks do not overly distort decisions.

More generally, policies are needed to exploit the growth and job opportunities associated with the new economic environment characterised by the rapid diffusion of new technology. First, to seize these opportunities, there is a need for ensuring that workers participate in the labour market actively. Second, governments have to create an environment conducive to the acquisition of skills and competencies that are needed. Third, the issue of whether (and how) labour-management institutions will adapt to the changing economic situation needs to be addressed.

4.1 Mobilising Labour Supply

Discussions about the new economic context should not divert attention from the fact that many OECD countries continue to suffer low rates of labour utilisation. While the employment/population ratio exceeds 70% in the United States and most Nordic economies, the figure is less than 60% in many other OECD countries. Especially low are the employment/population ratios of women (notably in Southern Europe).

Achieving a greater mobilisation of labour supply would also go hand-in-hand with higher productivity gains (thereby economic growth). Indeed, there is evidence that in many of the countries most successful in creating employment, multi-factor productivity has grown fast, thereby confirming that there is no trade-off between productivity gains and job creation, but a mutually-reinforcing relationship (OECD 2000*b*). It can even be hypothesised that multi-factor productivity will tend to accelerate all the faster when spare capacity has been fully utilised – recent developments would lend support to this hypothesis.

Policies that encourage the labour market participation of would-be workers, such as making work pay systems and effective active labour market programmes, should therefore continue to rank high in the policy agenda. In countries where labour shortages have emerged, it is particularly urgent to reinforce the activation elements of labour market programmes – in this regard, the coexistence in certain countries of labour shortages with relatively high unemployment rates is a matter of considerable policy concern. Also, evidence shown in Section B that employee tenure is somewhat lower in countries where multi-factor productivity has accelerated suggests that labour needs to be mobile to exploit the growth potential of new technology. Features of employment regulations that unduly inhibit labour mobility need to be reconsidered. More generally, the labour market policy framework continues to be relevant in the "New Economy", even though certain elements of the framework can be posed in different terms and priorities may have to be rethought.

4.2 Equipping Workers with the Appropriate Skills

The success of technological and organisational innovation depends to a large extent on the ability of individuals to absorb change. It goes without saying that education and a well-functioning training system are of paramount importance in this respect. There is some evidence from a small sample of European Union countries that the rate of adoption of new work practices is positively associated with the level of educational attainment (Figure 12).

In addition, a number of studies have found that enterprises that are prone to train their workers have a relatively high incidence of new work practices (PIL and MACDUFFIE, 1996; GITTLEMAN et al,. 1998; OECD, 1999). Table 6 illustrates this relationship. A consistent finding is that the incidence of training is higher in firms that adopt new work practices than is the case in other firms.[21] This can be interpreted as evidence that training facilitates the adoption of new work practices. More generally, education and training are important not only for economic growth, but also for equity and social cohesion purposes.[22]

In the present circumstances, policies need to tackle the emerging shortage for certain occupations and skills. In the short term, migration policies can help (see below), but more emphasis on policies that enhance human capital is clearly indispensable. Thus, some authors have stressed the need for enhanced coherence between technology policies (which tend to raise the demand for occupations such as scientists) and education policies (which shape the supply-side) – otherwise skill shortages will intensify (ROMER, 2000).

---

[21] Remarkably, there is only one exception to this general pattern, namely the case of "delegation of responsibility to the individual workers" in Finland – though the link does exist in the case of "team delegation of responsibility".

[22] As stated in OECD (2001c), adults with a high level of educational attainment have better-than-average employment and wage prospects, while they also enjoy a relatively good health and life expectancy and a lower-than-average probability of being involved in crime than low-educated individuals.

4.2.1 Education in New Technology

The fact that new technology tends to be skill-biased implies that efforts to up-grade the basic skills and competencies of the youth should be intensified. In addition, there is a need for improving ICT literacy.

Figure U12: New Work Practices and Education

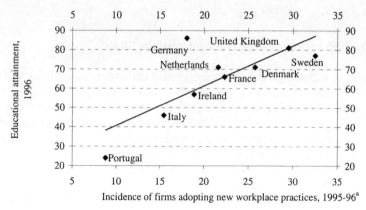

Incidence of firms adopting new workplace practices, 1995-96[a]

Note: a) This is calculated as a simple average of the five new work practice indicators for 9 European countries. Spain is excluded because of the absence of information about one of the indicators (flattening managerial levels). "Educational attainment" is the number of workers aged 25-64 who attained at least upper-secondary education, as a percentage of the total labour force (aged 25-64).
Sources: Authors' estimates based on the EPOC survey; and OECD, Education at a glance – OECD Indicators 1998, 1998.

Societies cannot afford to exclude a large part of their population from access to high-quality education and learning. This is why governments recognise the need for bridging the digital divide caused by an unequal access to new technologies. The problem of access, which is often presented as the main solution to bridge the digital divide, is not the only one which education polices have to solve. Measures to improve the ability of teachers to use ICT effectively in the classroom are also needed. More fundamentally, between one tenth and one third of each youth cohort, depending on the country, does not complete secondary education, which is worrisome in view of the fact that our societies are increasingly knowledge-based. Policies should intensify the efforts to reduce secondary school drop-out rates.

Going forward that premise, the content of education policies needs to reflect the changing requirements of the economy. People with insufficient general skills and low ICT literacy will become socially excluded not only from the labour market but also from services and leisure activities. This is why, within recent efforts undertaken by OECD governments to upgrade educational attainment, many

OECD countries have launched programmes to create a new culture giving priority to new technologies and making the Internet accessible to all since primary schools. The issue arises whether these efforts will match the requirements of the information society in a short period of time.

Table U6.   New Work Practices and Training[a] (Percentage of firms which provide training)

	Among firms that implement new practices	Among firms that do *not* implement new practices
Australia (1995)	**76**	**61**
European Union (EPOC survey 1994-96)	**39**	**27**
Denmark	*44*	*37*
France	*29*	*18*
Germany	*39*	*28*
Ireland	*47*	*27*
Italy	*30*	*28*
Netherlands	*42*	*27*
Portugal	*27*	*24*
Spain	*30*	*27*
Sweden	*33*	*24*
United Kingdom	*53*	*37*
Finland (1996)	**77**	**66**
France (REPONSE survey 1998)	**29**	**20**
United Kingdom (WERS survey 1998)	**15**	**10**
United States (1996)	**82**	**68**

Note: a) Figures correspond to averages of estimates carried out for each individual work practice (see Annex for details). Data are not comparable between surveys.
Source: Authors' estimates based on various surveys.

4.2.2 Vocational and on the-Job Training

Vocational and on-the-job training are especially important for economic growth in the current context. Indeed, much of the productivity gains will occur within firms through re-organisation, a process which is facilitated by training. Also, as shown previously, the demand for certain high-skilled jobs is growing. Many knowledge workers have acquired their competencies through training. And the need for greater labour mobility requires an ability to adapt to different jobs, often in different sectors, and training can play a role in this respect.

Despite the importance of training, it is unclear whether the incentives to engage in further learning are strong enough, from the point of view of both firms and workers (OECD, 1998). Reflecting the well-known "poaching-externality problem", firms have a weak incentive to invest in vocational training because once trained, the employee can leave the firm and get a better wage (HOCQUET, 2000). The result is that firms tend to under-invest in the training of their employees. Instead of upgrading the skills of the existing workforce they will tend to pursue a "buying strategy".

If firms are reluctant to train their workers because of the risk associated to the "poaching problem", much will then depend on the motivation and the capacity of individuals to invest in their human capital. When deciding to improve their employability, individuals face problems of time and resource availability. In addition, qualifications obtained from formal and informal learning are not always recognised, which reduces workers' incentive to engage in training. It is therefore increasingly important that public authorities develop a coherent strategy to co-ordinate the different phases of primary and secondary education with on-the-job training, both in terms of curricula and recognition or certification of formal and non-formal learning. The development of the Computer Driving Licence introduced by Finland as a way to certify ICT computer knowledge provides an interesting case in point.[23]

Evidence also shows that some categories of workers have less opportunities to be trained than others (OECD, 1999). In general, the less-educated, employees of small firms and older and atypical workers are less motivated to invest in their own training and are also likely to be offered relatively few training opportunities. These categories of workers are also those that are most likely to suffer from the organisational changes. It is therefore essential to develop policy measures to improve the distribution of vocational training opportunities.

Box 5. An Innovative Initiative: Individual Learning Accounts (ILAs)

The aim of Individual Learning Accounts (ILAs) is to make training more accessible to all by improving learning opportunities and increasing the amount of learning funded directly by individuals themselves, at a reduced cost. The system is intended to provide greater choice regarding the content of training. Individuals should benefit in the form of higher productivity and earnings, reducing also the risk of unemployment whereas the firm benefits from a reduction of the training costs, increasing at the same time workers' productivity and acquiring a reputation for being a "good" employer. For the government, the cost depends on the level of the subsidy.

In the United Kingdom, ILAs were introduced in April 2000 as a key part of the government strategy on lifelong learning. They consist of a special account with government to help individuals plan and pay for their learning. In the first year of operation of the system, the individual must provide a small contribution to the account (25 GBP) and the government adds 150 GBP.[24] Employers can also

---

[23] The Computer Driving Licence was introduced by Finland in 1995 and has since then been generalised to other European countries through the European Computer Driving Licence Foundation. This system permits to certify that the holder of the licence has acquired the basic concepts of ICT and is able to use a personal computer at a basic level of competence. To get the licence, an examination has to be passed in one of the accredited test centres.

[24] The government has committed itself to support in that way the first million accounts.

make contributions, which can be tax-deductible if used for agreed learning and if contributions go to low-paid workers. To be eligible for the scheme, individuals have to be over 19 years old, and they must be in the labour force and not in full education or on training schemes already publicly supported. After the initial 150 GBP has been spent, ILA holders can be entitled to a series of discounts on courses such as computer literacy.

In Sweden, ILAs are currently being piloted and refined and will probably be in place in January 2002. The last proposal of the government is that approximately one million individuals will receive a basic contribution of 2500 SEK to be supplemented with at least equal contributions by individuals and/or employers. The amount of the account is subject to tax relief on earned income and employers wishing to participate will receive a reduction in payroll tax of 10% of the amount contributed. To be eligible, individuals must be between 30-55 years old and must have an annual income in 2000 ranging from 50000 SEK to 216000 SEK.

A similar system of ILAs has been in place in the United States for some time now, the so-called Individual Development Accounts. These are saving accounts, mainly offered to low and medium-income households, which can be used, among other purposes, to fund education and training (they can also be used for starting a small business). Other countries like the Netherlands and Australia are considering similar systems of ILAs.

To improve the incentives of both firms and workers in the area of training, it is important to review financing arrangements. One possible approach to encourage human capital investment is to place individuals at the core of the decision to learn, while at the same time reducing the risks associated with the "poaching problem". This can be achieved by sharing the costs of training between the different actors (government, the firm, the individual and educational institutions). Thus, during the 1990s, different demand-side financing mechanisms for education and/or lifelong learning, such as voucher schemes, generated great interest and were implemented in some OECD countries. Even though few systematic evaluations of the effects of vouchers have been conducted (apart from the mixed results in terms of student achievement shown by experiments done in the United States (PATRINOS, 1999)), this system still attracts much interest. Other innovative funding strategies, such as Individual Learning Accounts (ILAs), have been developed and recently implemented in some OECD countries. The aim of the ILAs is to encourage learning by adults and increase the effectiveness of the system. Like voucher schemes, ILAs are based on the principle that (a) individuals are best placed to choose what they need to learn and how they want to improve their skills; and (b) costs should be shared by all the actors concerned. As stated in OECD (2000*d*), ILAs can provide training opportunities to groups which do not generally participate in such activities. The idea of ILAs is to raise the overall commitment to training among the less well-trained workers and among those firms which train less – mainly smaller companies (see Box 5).

In addition to funding issues, institutional aspects of training should be reviewed. The involvement of the social partners in vocational training and life-long learning is essential. Public authorities must target less-favoured groups (older workers, the less-educated, atypical workers, ethnic minorities, immigrants etc.) to minimise the risks of unemployment and social exclusion. It is necessary to adapt adequately the methods of learning to take into account the capacities and motivations of each group, as well as their specific needs.

These innovative systems to promote learning are part of a new approach to welfare policies which, instead of supporting income, try to promote human capital and improve individuals' employability. Nevertheless, it must be said that ILAs are only one example of a range of innovative schemes. In addition, since no evaluations exist as yet, it is not possible to assess the extent to which ILAs have contributed to solve problem of under-investment in training, especially of low-skilled workers.

4.2.3 Looking at Migration in a New Light

In some OECD countries, shortages of knowledge workers are being partly addressed by having recourse to foreign labour. For example in the United States, the Federal Government raised in 1998 its visa programme (H-1B) to admit 115,000 foreign skilled workers each year.[25] This ceiling was already reached in March 2000 and employers have asked for 50,000 additional H-1B visas. The ceiling has been raised to 195,000 for the next three years. Similarly, the German government launched in August 2000 a programme allowing 20.000 permanent visas to be issued to computer specialists, whereas Ireland is proposing to allow in 32,000 foreign ICT workers up to 2005. In 1997-1998, Australia granted 3,200 temporary visas to foreign ICT professionals and Japan hopes to attract about 30,000 foreign ICT high skilled technicians and researchers until 2005.

More generally, in the majority of OECD countries, the educational attainment of foreign workers has increased over the last few years (Table 7). This is mainly attributable to a reduction in the incidence of foreign workers with lower secondary education or less. Indeed, the proportion of foreign workers with tertiary education has not increased in most OECD countries, and remains relatively low for the OECD area as a whole.

Different opinions have been expressed regarding these new migration practices. Some consider that migration of highly skilled personnel provides an important channel to fill in specific skill shortages related to ICT and knowledge-intensive occupations. This may ease constraints on economic growth, but at the same time there is also a risk of "brain drain" to the detriment of developing countries. Also some claim that recourse to foreign labour entails a risk of "social dumping".[26]

---

[25] It has been estimated that during the period 1996-1998, the H-1B programme has filled over 70.000 ICT jobs, equivalent to 28% of the average annual demand for IT workers having at least a bachelor's degree.

[26] According to a study for the United States, foreign workers under the H-1B programme receive lower wages than their American counterparts (MATLOFF, 2000).

Table U7:   Foreign Adult Population Classified by Level of Education[a]

	Lower secondary		Upper secondary		Third level	
	1992	1998	1992	1998	1992	1998
Austriab	49.5	45.0	39.9	44.4	10.6	10.6
Belgium	67.2	52.9	18.4	27.1	14.4	20.0
Denmarkb	33.2	32.7	34.8	37.9	32.0	29.4
Germanyc	67.2	46.0	7.1	35.2	12.6	13.1
France	79.3	62.9	9.2	22.3	11.4	14.8
Greece	34.2	41.7	39.1	38.2	26.7	20.1
Irelandc	33.2	28.8	25.3	23.8	40.5	47.0
Italy	58.5	35.4	29.0	45.9	12.5	11.4
Luxembourgc	72.8	56.8	9.2	19.0	15.8	24.2
Netherlands	73.2	46.7	10.2	30.2	15.3	22.0
Portugal	51.3	53.7	13.6	24.8	35.1	16.6
Spain	53.4	46.7	20.6	23.2	26.0	30.1
Swedenb	27.1	26.2	39.8	38.6	28.0	27.8
United Kingdom	58.6	65.9	8.7	13.7	21.5	20.4
United Statesb	35.3	34.5	40.0	40.9	24.6	24.6

Note: a) The educational attainment classification is defined as follows: lower secondary refers to pre-primary education or none, primary or lower secondary; upper secondary refers to upper secondary education or post-secondary non tertiary education; third level refers to tertiary education; b) Data for 1992 refers to 1995; c) Data for 1998 refers to 1997. *Sources: European Labour Force Survey (European countries); and US Census Bureau (United States).*

4.3 Enhancing Employment Adjustment: the Role of Collective Bargaining and Government Regulation

For new technology to lead to higher productivity growth, work needs to be reorganised and the right skills must be available. There is a key role for social partners and governments in this area, going beyond the human capital aspects just discussed. First, the presence of well-functioning labour-management institutions is likely to enhance the effectiveness of work reorganisation. Second, however, some of the existing labour-management institutions such as collective bargaining need to take into account the changing nature of work. Third, certain government regulations are challenged by the emergence of new forms of employment and the need for making wages and working conditions more responsive to the changing workplace.

Institutions which allow a closer contact between management and employees (such as works' councils) can help build a high-skill, high-trust enterprise climate (see ILO (2001) for a recent excellent survey on this issue). Though this is not new, the wave of workplace changes has triggered renewed interest on such institutions. In the European Union, firms allowing worker representatives to be involved in the process of consultation, negotiation and/or decision making adopt more intensively new work practices than is the case of firms without institutions of worker participation (Table 8). They are also more likely to provide training to their workers.

Table U8:   Employee Representation, New Work Practices and Training, European Union, 1994-96

Panel A - Average number of new work practices		
	Among firms with employee representation	Among firms *without* employee representation
Type of representation recognised for the purpose of consultation/negotiation/joint decision making:		
Union representation	1.32	0.97
Works council	1.09	1.05
Advisory committee	1.33	1.03
Panel B - Percent of firms providing training to support decision-making activities		
	Among firms with employee representation	Among firms *without* employee representation
Type of representation recognised for the purpose of consultation/negotiation/joint decision making:		
Union representation	35	29
Works council	29	32
Advisory committee	37	30

Note: a) Owing to lack of data, Spain is excluded from the calculations.
Source: Authors' estimates based on the EPOC survey

What is more, the greater the number of institutions of worker representation, the greater the numbers of new work practices adopted by firms (Figure 13).[27] Other studies find that new work practices are likely to be more effective (and successful) when they are implemented through a collective agreement than is the case in the absence of a collective agreement (see, for example, European Commission, 1997). In a way, these results are not surprising. The potential of labour-management institutions for taking advantage of new technology is manifold. Labour-management institutions at the firm-level facilitate the adoption of employee involvement schemes and improve the flow of information among staff, while they enhance employee involvement in training matters either to increase the overall intensity of training or to distribute training opportunities more evenly among different categories of workers. Unions and other forms of worker representation can usefully address a variety of "public good" issues such as access to training, health care, pension rights and the establishment of support mechanisms to workers' mobility. National governments and international organisations can

---

[27] A previous study (OECD, 1999) also finds that new work practices are more prevalent among unionised firms than among non-unionised ones. Similarly, the existence of works' councils is positively correlated with the adoption of new work practices. The study estimates that the existence of a collective agreement raises the probability of firms to adopt team-working by about five percentage points.

help the process by identifying and facilitating the diffusion of successful cases of new forms of work (*e.g.* the current initiative by the European Union on the "pacts on employment and competitiveness").

Figure U13: Greater Workers' Voice Facilitates the Adoption of New Work Practices

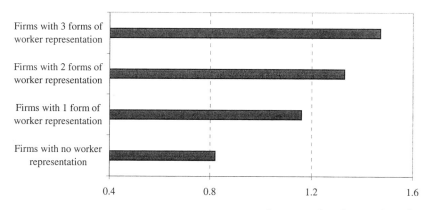

Average number of new work practices

Note: Owing to lack of data, Spain is excluded from the calculation.
Source: Authors' estimates based on the EPOC Survey

Box 6. Some Examples of Collective Bargaining on Telework			
Country	Sector of activity or firm	Beneficiaries	Characteristics of the agreement
Austria	ICT sector IBM and Hewlett-Packard among others.	Employees combining telework with in-the-firm work	• Telework is voluntary and teleworkers' involvement in the firm must be guaranteed. • The agreement specifies the distribution of working time between home and firm. • The firm pays the cost for the equipment (data transmission and telephone). • The home workstation must respect health and safety regulations.
Denmark	Financial sector	60,000 employees on an experimental basis (expired in May 1999)	The agreement specifies the issues that have to be regulated at sectoral and firm levels and individually between the firm and the worker. The sectoral one defines telework as: • Voluntary and reversible at 4 weeks' notice. • Telework must not exceed 50 per cent of the working time over a 13-week period. • The employer is responsible of the equipment and its maintenance. • The teleworker is covered by regulations on health and safety at work.

France	Financial sector Banques Populaires (1996)	Disabled people	• Telework appears as a possibility to work at home on a voluntary basis.
Germany	ICT sector Deutsche Telekom (1995) and IBM (1991)		• Telework is voluntary and reversible. • The employer is responsible for the equipment and its maintenance as well as for additional expenses. • The distribution of working time between home and the firm is agreed on an individual basis.
Italy	Manufacturing Electrolux-Zanussi	Pregnant women or those with small children Two-year programme on an experimental basis	• The aim is to help combining work with family responsibilities. • Even if directed to women on a voluntary basis, men can also participate in line with Italian parental leave legislation.
Norway	ICT sector Vesta		• The workplace (a room at home or rented) must only be used for work. • The worker loses his right to occupy his job in the firm while the agreement lasts. • The employer is responsible for the equipment and its maintenance, and must pay for insurance and domestic expenses. • The worker must take care of the equipment, and must respect professional confidentiality. • The teleworker has the right to receive an unspecified wage bonus. • The conditions for the termination of the telework agreement must be specified.
Spain	DHC International	New recruited staff	The firm must define the jobs appropriate for recruiting staff as teleworkers, considering also disabled people.
Sweden	Trade, commerce and services sector	80,000 employees	• Telework must be voluntary and reversible. • Teleworkers' attendance to meetings should be facilitated. • Teleworkers should have the same rights to information, consultation and professional development as other employees. • The equipment must meet health and safety regulations that can be controlled by employers.
United Kingdom	ICT sector. British Telecom	Managers and professionals	• Telework is voluntary and teleworkers are paid a salary and covered by collective bargaining for all purposes. • The employer pays for equipment and domestic expenses and is responsible for health and safety. • Teleworkers are guaranteed information and communication with the firm and can attend regular meetings.

Source: Secretariat elaboration based on CAPRILE and LLORENS (1998).

However, changes in work practices also raise a number of challenges to traditional labour market institutions and government regulation:

- the growing role of performance-related remuneration reduces the importance of collectively agreed basic wages;
- the tendency to reduce layers of management and to enhance the multi-task nature of jobs (which is an important aspect of team work) calls into question existing systems of job classification;
- the emergence of telework also raises challenges to collective bargaining, since, in most countries, there is no national legislation on telework. In some countries, such as France, Germany, Ireland and the United Kingdom, wages and working conditions of teleworkers are mainly established through collective bargaining, while in others (Belgium, Finland, Greece, Luxembourg, the Netherlands and Portugal) telework is practically not addressed in collective bargaining. Instead, in these countries the individual contract seems to be the norm (Box 6). Some countries have established consultation procedures among social partners to promote a new legislative framework for telework (Portugal and Greece) while others (like Denmark and Ireland) have already issued guidelines on telework after consulting with the social partners. Still others (the Netherlands) have decided that the protection of teleworkers should be identical to that of their regular counterparts. In any case, some principles should be respected and clearly regulated in collective agreements: the voluntary nature of telework; the principle of reversibility; the principle of equality of treatment and of non-discrimination between on-site workers and teleworkers. In addition, telework raises a range of issues regarding safety, data protection and "privacy" of the home;
- on a more general level, working-time regulations should include or enhance hours' flexibility arrangements so as to reduce obstacles to team work and other new work practices; and
- the proliferation of different forms of employment has blurred the traditional distinction between management and employees – which forms the back bone of collective bargaining institutions.

5. Concluding Remarks

The paper shows that, to take advantage of the new economic environment, work needs to be reorganised. In addition, it appears that low-tenure countries have enjoyed faster productivity gains than high-tenure countries – suggesting that an element of "external" flexibility may be important as well. In this respect, providing greater training opportunities and enhancing workers' voice in the process of change stand out as two important policy requirements. But, the study also raises some important analytical and policy-related questions which require further scrutiny.

From the analytical point of view, there is increasing concern that the traditional long-term relationship between employers and employees may be weakening. This study finds no clear trend for aggregate tenure in the OECD area. However, the study identifies some interesting underlying changes. First, relatively low-skilled workers are disadvantaged by the current changes in employee tenure. Second, the industrial structure is moving towards industries with low employee tenure in almost all the countries considered.

Another question arises regarding the traditional distinction between "internal" and "external" flexibility. The diffusion of new work practices suggests that firms are increasingly relying on "internal" flexibility in order to adapt to the changing environment. On the other hand, the study shows that the increasing adoption of these practices does not directly translate into a longer employee tenure in the economy as a whole. Whether new work practices and "external" flexibility are substitutes or complements is not clear, and further work is needed to identify how both types of flexibility interact.

On the policy side, there is consensus that training is of paramount importance for raising the benefits of the new economic environment. In particular, vocational training constitutes an important pillar of human capital. However, most of the available analyses focus exclusively on formal education, while relatively less attention has been paid to firm training. In this respect, it is important to assess to what extent firm training improves workers' employability and productivity, and thus how much it contributes to macroeconomic growth. One of the new approaches to enhance training incentives, namely Individual Learning Accounts, is examined in this study, but the cost-effectiveness of both this and other innovative systems requires further scrutiny.

Finally, the study suggests that greater voice should be given to workers in the process of change. However, the links between institutions of worker representation and firm performance remain controversial and require deeper examination.

Annex I: Survey on New Work Practices Used in the Study

Five surveys for individual countries and one survey among European Union countries are used in the study: *Education Quality of the Workplace – National Employer Survey* (EQW-NES for the United States); *Australian Workplace Industrial Relation Survey* (AWIRS for Australia); *Enquête sur les Relations Professionelles et Négociations d'Entreprise* (REPONSE for France); *Flexible Enterprise* (for Finland); *Workplace Employee Relations Survey* (WERS for the United Kingdom); *and Survey of Employee Direct Participation in Organisational Change* (EPOC) for the European Union. The numbers in the text are calculated as an average of estimates carried out for each individual work practices included in the surveys. The practices taken into consideration in each survey are listed in the following table. ARNAL, OK and TORRES (2001) provide the detailed result for each practice.

	Included new work practices (total number of included practices)
EQW-NES	benchmarking, re-engineering, autonomous teams, regular meetings about work-related issues (5)
AWIRS	semi-autonomous work groups, quality circles, team building, Total Quality Management, just-in-time, job redesign programs, suggestion schemes, management/employees regular formal meetings (8)
REPONSE	quality circles, direct expression group, project group, autonomous production teams, just-in-time, ISO, flattening hierarchical levels (7)
Flexible Enterprise	job rotation, quality circles, work group with individual responsibility, work teams with joint responsibility, daily planning of work by individuals, weekly planning of work by individuals, quality control by individuals, daily planning of work by teams, weekly planning of work by teams, quality control by teams (10)
WERS	autonomous teams, use of management chain / cascading information, regular meetings with entire workforce present, suggestion schemes, problem-solving circles, joint consultative committees, just-in-time, quality control, quality monitoring by employee himself, benchmarking (10)
EPOC	Flattening managerial levels, back to core business, employee involvement, team-based organisation, job rotation (5)

Annex II: Tables

Table U9:   **Classification of Occupations**

Type of workers	US classification	ISCO-88(COM) classification (3-digit level)
1. Knowledge workers		
a) Engineers and applied and social scientists	Engineer, architects and surveyors (43-63), Natural scientists (69-83), Health diagnosing occupations (84-89), Health assessment and testing occupations (95-106), Technicians and related support occupations(203-235, not 213, 229, 233), Social scientists and urban planners (166-173), Lawyers and judges (178-179), Teachers post-secondary (113-154)	Physical, mathematical and engineering science professionals (211, 212, 214), Life science and health professionals (221, 222, 223), Teaching professionals (231), Other professionals (241, 242, 244, 247), Physical and engineering science associate professionals (311, 313, 314, 315), Life science and health associate professionals (321, 322, 323), Other associate professionals (341, 342)
b) Computers specialists	Mathematical and computer specialists (64-68), Computer technicians (213, 229 and 233), Computer equipment operator (308-309)	Computing professionals (213)
2. Management workers	Executive, administrative and managerial occupations (3-37)	Legislators and senior officials (111, 114), Corporate managers (121, 122, 123), Managers of small enterprises (131)
3. Data workers	Teachers except post-secondary (155-159), Counsellors, educational and vocational (163), Librarians, archivists and curators (164-165), Administrative support occupations, including clerical (303-389), except Computer equipment operators (308-309)	Teaching professionals (232, 233, 234, 235), Other professionals (243), Teaching associate professionals (331, 332, 333, 334), Other associate professionals (343, 344), Office clerks (411, 412, 413, 414, 419), Customer service clerks (421, 422)
4. Services workers	Sales occupations (243-285), Service occupations (403-469), Social recreation and religious workers (174-177), Writers and artists (183-199)	Other professionals (245, 246), Other associate professionals (345, 346, 347, 348), Personal and protective services workers (511, 512, 513, 514, 515, 516), Models, sales persons and demonstrators (521, 522), Sales and services elementary occupations (911, 912, 913, 914, 915, 916)
5. Goods-producing workers	Farming, forestry and fishing occupations (473-499), Precision production, craft and repair occupations (503-699), Operators, fabricators and laborers (703-889)	Skilled agricultural and fishery workers (611, 612, 613, 614, 615), Extraction and building trade workers (711, 712, 713, 714), Metal machinery and related trades workers (721, 722, 723, 724), Precision, handicraft, printing and related trades workers (731, 732, 733, 734), Other craft and related trades workers (741, 742, 743, 744), Stationary-plant and related operators (811, 812, 813, 814, 815, 816, 817), Machine operators and assemblers (821, 822, 823, 824, 825, 826, 827, 828, 829), Drivers and mobile plant operators (831, 832, 833, 834), Agricultural, fishery and related labourers (921), Labourers in mining, construction, manufacturing and transport (931, 932, 933)

Source: Secretariat elaboration based on Lavoie M. and Roy R. (1998).

**Table U10:   Nominal and Real Earnings by Occupation in the United States
(US dollars per hour)**

	Nominal earnings			Real earnings[a]		
	1985	1995	1998	1985	1995	1998
Knowledge workers	10.0	15.6	16.9	14.1	15.9	16.4
Engineers and applied and social scientists	*10.2*	*15.7*	*16.9*	*14.4*	*16.0*	*16.5*
Computers	*9.0*	*14.9*	*16.9*	*12.7*	*15.2*	*16.4*
Management workers	8.7	12.5	13.8	12.2	12.7	13.4
Data workers	6.7	9.6	10.4	9.5	9.7	10.1
Services workers	5.0	7.2	8.1	7.0	7.3	7.9
Goods-producing workers	8.0	10.3	11.3	11.3	10.5	11.0
	Standard deviations within each group of occupations					
Knowledge workers	2.7	4.4	4.8	3.8	4.5	4.6
Data workers	1.1	2.0	2.0	1.6	2.0	2.0
Services workers	1.7	2.9	3.0	2.5	3.0	3.0
Goods-producing workers	2.3	2.8	3.1	3.3	2.9	3.0

a) Real hourly earnings are calculated as nominal hourly earnings deflated by the private consumption defator.
Source: Secretariat estimates based on BLS, Current Population Survey.

References

ADDISON, J., SIEBERT, W., WAGNER, J., WEI, X. (2000), Worker Participation and Firm Performance: Evidence from Germany and Britain, British Journal of Industrial Relations, Vol. 83, No. 1, pp. 7-48.

ARNAL, E., OK, W., TORRES, R. (2001), Knowledge, Work Organisation and Economic Growth, Labour Market and Social Policy Occasional Papers No.50, OECD.

ASKENAZY, P. (1999), Technological and Organizational Innovations, Internationalization and Inequalities, PhD dissertation, EHESS, Paris, January.

ASKENAZY, P. (2000), Le développement des pratiques 'flexibles' de travail, in COHEN, D., DEBONNEUIL, M. (eds.), Nouvelle Economie, Conseil d'Analyse Economique, La Documentation Française, Paris, pp. 127-148.

BLACK, S.E., LYNCH, L.M. (2000), What's Driving the New Economy: The Benefits of Workplace Innovation, National Bureau of Economic Research, Working Paper No. 7479.

BRESNAHAN, T.F., BRYNJOLFSSON, E., HITT, L.M. (1999), Information Technology, Workplace Organization, and the Demand for Skilled Labor: Firm-Level Evidence, National Bureau of Economic Research, Working Paper No. 7136.

CAPPELLI, P., NEUMARK, D. (1999), Do 'High Performance' Work Practices Improve Establishment-Level Outcome?, National Bureau of Economic Research, Working Paper No. w7374.

CAPRILE, M., LLORENS, C. (1998), Teleworking and industrial relations in Europe, European Foundation for the Improvement of Living and Working Conditions, November.

CAROLI, E., VAN REENEN, J. (1999), Skill Biased Organizational Change? Evidence from a Panel of British and French Establishments, Couverture d'Orange CEPREMAP No. 9917.

CASELLI, F., COLEMAN II, J. (2001), Cross-Country Technology Diffusion: The Case of Computers, American Economic Review, forthcoming.

COUTROT, T. (1996), Relations sociales et performances économiques, une première analyse empirique du cas français, Travail et Emploi, Vol. 66, No. 1.

COUTROT, T. (2000), Innovations dans le travail: la pression de la concurrence internationale, l'atout des qualifications, Premières Synthèses, MES-DARES, 2000-03, No. 09.2.

CROCKETT, G. (2000), Can We Explain Australian Productivity Growth? Some Evidence form the AWIRS, University of Tasmania School of Economics Discussion Paper 2000/04 (http://www.comlaw.utas.edu.au).

DEPARTMENT FOR EDUCATION AND EMPLOYMENT (DfEE) (1999), Skills for the Information Age.

DEPARTMENT OF EMPLOYMENT, WORKPLACE RELATIONS AND SMALL BUSINESS (DEWRSB) (1999), Skill Shortages in the Trades: an Employment Perspective, September.

ELECTRONIC COMMERCE AND TELEWORK TRENDS (2000), Benchmarking Progress on New Ways of Working and New Forms of Business Across Europe, Final Report, August.

EUROPEAN COMMISSION (Commission of the European Communities) (1997), Green Paper, Partnership for a New Organisation of Work. Brussels.

EUROPEAN COMMISSION (Commission of the European Communities) (2000), Joint Employment Report 2000, COM(2000)551final, Brussels.

FAIRRIS, D., BRENNER, M. (2001), Workplace Transformation and the Rise in Cumulative Trauma Disorders: Is There a Connection?, Journal of Labor Research, winter, forthcoming.

GILLESPIE, A., RICHARDSON, R., CORNFORD, J. (1995), Review of Telework in Britain: Implications for Public Policy, Report prepared for the Parliamentary Office of Science and Technology, University of Newcastle upon Tyne, Centre for Urban and Regional Development Studies, Newcastle, February.

GITTLEMAN, M., GORRIGAN, M., JOYCE, M. (1998), 'Flexible' Workplace Practices: Evidence from a Nationally Representative Survey, Industrial and Labor Relations Review, pp. 99-115.

GREENAN, N. (1996a), Progrès technique et changements organisationnels: leur impact sur emploi et les qualifications, Économie et statistique, No. 298, pp. 35-44.

GREENAN, N. (1996b), Innovation technologique, changements organisationnels et évolution des compétences, Économie et statistique, No. 298, pp. 15-33.

HELPMAN, E., ed. (1998), General Purpose Technologies and Economic Growth, The MIT Press, Cambridge, Massachusetts.

HUWS, U. (1997), Teleworking: Guidelines for Good practice, The Institute for Employment Studies, Report 329, April.

INFORMATION TECHNOLOGY ASSOCIATION OF AMERICA (ITAA) (2000), Bridging the Gap: Information Technology Skills for a New Millenium, April (www.itaa.org).

INTERNATIONAL LABOUR OFFICE (2001), World Employment Report 2001, Geneva.

LAVOIE, M., ROY, R. (1998), Employment in the Knowledge-Based Economy: A Growth Accounting Exercise for Canada, Applied Research Branch, Human Resources Development Canada, R-98-8E, June.

LAWLER, E.E. (2000), Rewarding Excellence: Pay Strategies for the New Economy, Jossey-Bass, San Francisco.

LINDBECK, A., SNOWER, D.J. (2000), Multitask Learning and the Reorganization of Work: From: Tayloristic to Holistic Organization, Journal of Labor Economics, Vol. 18, No. 3, pp. 353-376.

MATLOFF, N. (2000), Debunking the Myth of a Desperate Software Labour Shortage, University of California at Davis, Testimony to the US Judiciary Committee, presented 21 April 1998 (updated frequently on website ftp://heather.cs.ucdavis.edu/itaa.real.pdf).

MEARES, C.A., SARGENT, J.F. (1999), The Digital Workforce: Building Infotech Skills at the Speed of Innovation, US Department of Commerce, June.

MINISTÈRE DE L'EMPLOI ET DE LA SOLIDARITÉ (2000), Premières informations et premières synthèses, DARES, No. 39.1, September.

NUTEK (1996), Towards Flexible Organisations, Swedish National Board for Industrial and Technical Development, B 1996:6, Stockholm.

NUTEK (1999), Flexibility Matters – Flexible Enterprises in the Nordic Countries, Swedish National Board for Industrial and Technical Development, B 1999:7, Stockholm.

OECD (1998), Technology, Productivity and Job Creation: Best Policy Practices, Paris.

OECD (1999), Employment Outlook, Paris.

OECD (2000a), A New Economy? The Changing Role of Innovation and Information Technology in Growth, Paris..

OECD (2000b), ICT Skills and Employment, DSTI/ICCP/IE(2000)7, Paris, mimeo.

OECD (2000c), Links Between Policy and Growth: Cross-country Evidence, ECO/CPE/WP1(2000)12, Paris, mimeo.

OECD (2000d), Financial Resources for Life-Long Learning:Evidence and Issues. Alternative Approaches to Financing Lifelong Learning, DEELSA/ED (2000)50, Paris, mimeo.

OECD (2001a), Education Policy Analysis: 2001 Edition, Paris.

OECD (2001b), Growth, Inequality and Social Protection, DEELSA/ELSA (2001)1, Paris, mimeo.

OECD (2001c), The Well-Being of Nations: The Role of Human and Social Capital, Paris.

PARKER, M., SLAUGHTER, J. (1988), Choosing Sides: Unions and the Team Concept, South End Press, Boston.

PATRINOS, H.A. (1999), Market Forces in Education, The World Bank, Draft paper, July, Washington.

PIL, F.K., MACDUFFIE, J.P. (1996), The Adoption of High-Involvement Work Practices, Industrial Relations, Vol. 35, No. 3, pp. 423-455.

RAMSEY, H., SCHOLARIOS, D., HARLEY, B. (2000), Employees and High Performance Work Systems: Testing Inside the Black Box, British Journal of Industrial Relations, Vol. 38, No. 4, pp.501-31.

RAJNES, D. (2001), A 21st Century Update on Employee Tenure, EBRI Notes, Vol. 22, No. 3, pp. 1-8.

ROMER, P. (2000), Should the Government Subsidise Supply or Demand in the Market for Scientists and Engineers?, National Bureau of Economic Research, Working Paper 7723, June.

U.S. DEPARTMENT OF LABOR (1999a), Report on the American Workforce.

U.S. DEPARTMENT OF LABOR (1999b), Occupational Injuries and Illnesses 1998 (http://stats.bls.gov/).

WOLFF, E.N., BAUMOL, W.J. (1989), Sources of Post-war Growth of Information Activity in the United States, in: OSBERG, L. et al. (eds.), The Information Economy: The Implications of Unbalanced Growth, Institute for Research on Public Policy, Halifax, pp. 17-46.

V. The Quest for Global Leadership in the Internet Age: A European Perspective
(Luncheon Speech)

Sigmar Mosdorf

Professor Heiduk, Professor Welfens, Ladies and Gentlemen:
Thank you very much for the invitation to this conference. It's a great honor and pleasure to speak to this distinguished group of international experts.

***

The subject of my presentation is "The Quest for Global Leadership in the Internet Age: A European Perspective". From my point of view, there are three questions hidden in that wording:

- Firstly: In the global information society, is there something like leadership?
- Secondly: If the answer to that is yes, is it possible and feasible for companies or countries to achieve and/or defend this leadership?
- Thirdly: What are the resulting opportunities for Europe?

I would like to answer these questions in light of three specific issues:

- Internet Governance
- Software Development
- The Digital Divide

***

Let me begin with Internet Governance.
Over the last few years, the Internet has become the driving force of the information age, e.g. when it comes to electronic commerce. Much different from the political and scientific discussions not too long ago, the terms Information Society and Internet Society are used synonymously.

However, most people nowadays only think about how to use the Internet. Only a few spend some time thinking about how this electronic workhorse is surviving. This ignorance is somewhat surprising because without a workable Internet there will be no e-business, e-health, etc.

One of the jobs to be done is the maintenance of the Root Server System and the Domain Name System. For historic reasons, for many years the responsibility for this was exclusively in the hands of the U.S. Department of Commerce. This had been a remarkable source of power for the U.S. Government, namely the global leadership in Internet Governance.

However, when the limitations of this arrangement became visible due to the rapidly growing numbers of Internet users, the international Internet community started to think about a new structure led by the spirit of self-governance. As many of you might know, these efforts led to the creation of the Internet Corporation for Assigned Names and Numbers in October 1998.

For the first time in history, a private not-for-profit organization is taking care of an important segment of technical infrastructure.

With ICANN the global Internet community has established a forum for which regional diversity is one of the guidelines – if not the most important guideline. Although some problems with ICANN still remain, a global leadership position has been replaced by a shared global responsibility. Europe has become one of the key players in the ICANN framework. This is visible, for example, in the work of the Governmental Advisory Committee of ICANN.

Moreover, the introduction of a new top level domain ".eu" is of great importance for European ICT policy because Europe finally is getting its own identity on the net. One of the anticipated side effects of DOT EU will be the growing number of non-English websites. Braking up the language barrier will open the Internet for new regional and social user groups.

***

Ladies and Gentlemen:

In the early years of ICT, computer software was linked to specific hardware systems and therefore was not compatible. Many of you will recall the times when it was impossible to exchange data or programs with friends and colleagues. The resulting user discontent and the worldwide demand for standarized and compatible software might have been one of the reasons for the fact that single companies had been able to gain an outstanding market power.

This global leadership, however, has of course been the seed of the search for alternatives. Without the electronic collaboration of software developers all over the world, something like LINUX could never have happened. Today, Open Source software is widely accepted as an alternative even for large commercial users.

As Europeans we can proudly point out that the roots of LINUX are located in Finland. European software engineers and users are still the driving force behind this movement.

From the Government side, we most welcome the trend towards open source software products because this is one of the steps to achieve more data security in Europe.

***

Ladies and Gentlemen:

It's an open secret that there is no fair contribution when it comes to the use of ICT within and between geographical regions. The more media like the Internet are becoming part of our everyday lives, the less it is acceptable that large parts of civil society have no access to these media.

Especially the issue of the Digital Divide between developed and developing countries is now on the agenda of all the important international fora. There is a growing concern that the gap between North and South is widening due to the fact that the industrialized countries are increasing their productivity by the widespread use of ICT.

The action plan of a high level G8 working group, the so-called DOT Force, has been adopted by the heads of State and Government at the Genoa Summit this summer. Moreover, the United Nations will kick off a dedicated working group in September of this year.

It is common sense that ICT could help the developing countries in two different ways:

- Firstly, ICT could be used as a means to meet the "classic" challenges of development aid, like education and health care.
- Secondly, and this is the even more fascinating aspect, ICT might be a chance for the poor countries of the south to "leapfrog" from rural societies to information societies.

Already today there are many examples of how small and medium-sized companies from developing countries are entering the world market leaving aside the traditional market barriers. In addition, many third world companies today deliver online office or research services for companies in the North. Some Asian countries have become major exporters of ICT expertise.

The long lasting economic leadership of the industrialized countries might be replaced by a situation in which at least parts of the developing world will be able to catch up – online.

However, what is the best way to help these countries now? Just delivering hardware and software wouldn't do it. From the European point of view, many of the developing countries must learn to open their ICT markets in the same way as European countries had to do so some years ago. If we share our European knowledge about "smart regulation", we can lay the neccessary foundation for long lasting success. And success of our partners in the developing world might help us to meet the challanges of globalization.

By the way, please let me just mention that Europe is also a forerunner when it comes to bridging the national Digital Divide.

Moreover, improved access to ICT for senior citizens and disabled persons is high on the agenda of the action plan "e-Europa" that has been adopted by the European Council in Summer 2000.

***

Ladies and Gentlemen:

Let me conclude: Yes, even in the Information Society there is something like global leadership. And, like in the industrial age, this leadership often is visible through market shares. However, rapid flow of information as well as cross-border competition seem to change these structures in the medium and long run.

Global leadership is more and more replaced by global competition with new opportunities for all players. Dominating market power will often be replaced by market power in smaller, specialized markets only.

Europe has a real chance to strengthen its role in the Internet age. However, to achieve this it is neccessary not to copy the former success of others but to develop a unique profile of one's own. Within this context, the cultural diversity of Europe might become our greatest treasure.

With its national activities, Germany will continue to deliver important contributions to Europes' way into the information society.

The "Action Plan for Innovation and Jobs in the Information Society" of 1999 is undergoing a major update right now. Within the framework of the National Alliance for Jobs, the effective use of the job potential of ICT is at the top of the agenda.

Although the New Economy is facing a process of settlement right now, we continue to believe that the effective use of ICT will remain as one of the key factors for economic growth and more jobs.

Thank you very much.

List of Figures

List of Tables

List of Contributors

Prof. Dr. Koichiro Agata
Waseda University, Tokyo, Japan

Dr. Elena Arnal
Organization for Economic Cooperation and Development, Paris, France

Prof. Dr. Matthias Bank
University of Innsbruck, Austria;
AICGS/Johns Hopkins University,
Washington D.C., USA

Dr. Claude E. Barfield
The American Enterprise Institute for
Public Policy Research, Washington
D.C., USA

Prof. Dr. William H. Dutton
Annenberg School for Communication, University of Southern California, Los Angeles, USA

Friedhelm Dommermuth
Regulatory Authority for Telecommunications and Posts, Bonn, Germany

Dr. Caroline L. Freund
Federal Reserve Board, London, UK

Prof. Dr. Mariko Fujii
Research Center for Advanced Eco-
nomic Engineering, University of
Tokyo, Tokyo, Japan

Prof. Dr. Thomas P. Gehrig
Universität Freiburg, Germany and
CEPR, London, UK

Prof. Dr. Torsten J. Gerpott
Gerhard Mercator Universität Duisburg, Germany

Prof. Dr. Thomas Gries
University of Paderborn, Germany

Prof. Dr. Günter Heiduk
Gerhard Mercator University Duisburg, Germany; Institute of International Economics, Gerhard Mercator
University Duisburg, Germany

Christiane Jäcker
BHF-BANK, Düsseldorf, Germany

Dr. Andre Jungmittag
European Institute for International
Economic Relations (EIIW), Pots-
dam University, Germany

Prof. Dr. Günter Knieps
Albert-Ludwigs-Universität Freiburg,
Germany

Christoph Mertens
Regulatory Authority for Telecommunications and Posts, Bonn, Germany

Dr. Marieke de Mooij
Tilburg University, Netherlands

Siegmar Mosdorf
State Secretary, Federal Ministry of
Economics and Technology, Berlin,
Germany

Prof. Dr. Yukio Noguchi
Aoyama-Gakuin University, Tokyo,
Japan

Wooseok Ok
Organization for Economic Cooperation and Development, Paris, France

Dr. Nicole Pohl
Asia/Pacific Research Center, Stanford University, USA; Institute of International Economics, Gerhard Mercator University Duisburg, Germany

Prof. Dr. Harald Sander
University of Applied Sciences, Cologne, Germany

Dr. Donald K. Stockdale
Office of Plans and Policy, Federal Communications Commission, Washington D.C., USA

Dr. Raymond Torres
Organisation for Economic Cooperation and Development, Paris, France

Dr. Christian Thygesen
European Central Bank, Frankfurt/M, Germany

Dr. Diana Weinhold
Development Studies Institute, London School of Economics, London, UK

Prof. Dr. Paul J.J. Welfens
Jean Monnet Chair, European Institute for International Economic Relations (EIIW), Potsdam University, Germany

Further Publications by *Paul J. J. Welfens*

P. J. J. Welfens
Market-oriented Systemic
Transformations in Eastern Europe
Problems, Theoretical Issues, and Policy
Options
1992. XII, 261 Pages. 20 Figs., 29 Tab.,
Hardcover, ISBN 3-540-55793-8

M. W. Klein, P. J. J. Welfens (Eds.)
Multinationals in the New Europe and
Global Trade
1992. XV, 281 Pages. 24 Figs., 75 Tab.,
Hardcover, ISBN 3-540-54634-0

P. J. J. Welfens (Ed.)
Economic Aspects of German Unification
Expectations, Transition Dynamics and
International Perspectives
1992. XV, 527 Pages. 34 Figs., 110 Tab.,
Hardcover, ISBN 3-540-60261-5

R. Tilly, P. J. J. Welfens (Eds.)
European Economic Integration as a
Challenge to Industry and Government
Contemporary and Historical Perspectives
on International Economic Dynamics
1996. X, 558 Pages. 43 Figs.,
Hardcover, ISBN 3-540-60431-6

P. J. J. Welfens (Ed.)
Economic Aspects of German Unification
Expectations, Transition Dynamics and
International Perspectives
2nd revised and enlarged edition
1996. XV, 527 Pages. 34 Figs., 110 Tab.,
Hardcover, ISBN 3-540-60261-5

P. J. J. Welfens
European Monetary Integration
EMS Developments and International Post-
Maastricht Perspectives
3rd revised and enlarged edition
1996. XVIII, 384 Pages. 14 Figs., 26 Tab.,
Hardcover, ISBN 3-540-60260-7

P. J. J. Welfens (Ed.)
European Monetary Union
Transition, International Impact
and Policy Options
1997. X, 467 Pages. 50 Figs., 31 Tab.,
Hardcover, ISBN 3-540-63305-7

P. J. J. Welfens, G. Yarrow (Eds.)
Telecommunications and Energy
in Systemic Transformation
International Dynamics, Deregulation and
Adjustment in Network Industries
1997. XII, 501 Pages. 39 Figs.,
Hardcover, ISBN 3-540-61586-5

P. J. J. Welfens, H. C. Wolf (Eds.)
Banking, International Capital Flows
and Growth in Europe
Financial Markets, Savings and Monetary
Integration in a World with Uncertain
Convergence
1997. XIV, 458 Pages. 22 Figs., 63 Tab.,
Hardcover, ISBN 3-540-63192-5

P. J. J. Welfens, D. Audretsch, J. T. Addison,
H. Grupp
Technological Competition, Employment
and Innovation Policies in OECD
Countries
1998. VI, 231 Pages. 16 Figs., 20 Tab.,
Hardcover, ISBN 3-540-63439-8

P. J. J. Welfens, G. Yarrow, R. Grinberg,
C. Graack (Eds.)
Towards Competition in Network
Industries
Telecommunications, Energy and
Transportation in Europe and Russia
1999. XXII, 570 Pages, 63 Figs., 63 Tab.,
Hardcover, ISBN 3-540-65859-9

P. J. J. Welfens
EU Eastern Enlargement and the Russian
Transformation Crisis
1999. X, 151 Pages. 12 Figs., 25 Tab.,
Hardcover, ISBN 3-540-65862-9

P. J. J. Welfens
Globalization of the Economy,
Unemployment and Innovation
1999. VI, 255 Pages. 11 Figs., 31 Tab.,
Hardcover, ISBN 3-540-65250-7

P. J. J. Welfens, J. T. Addison,
D. B. Audretsch, T. Gries, H. Grupp
Globalization, Economic Growth and
Innovation Dynamics
1999. X, 160 Pages. 15 Figs., 15 Tab.,
Hardcover, ISBN 3-540-65858-0

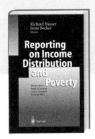
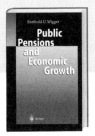

Druck: Strauss Offsetdruck, Mörlenbach
Verarbeitung: Schäffer, Grünstadt